BILINGUALISM
AND THE BILINGUAL CHILD

This is a volume in the
Arno Press collection

BILINGUAL-BICULTURAL EDUCATION
IN THE UNITED STATES

Advisory Editor
Francesco Cordasco

Editorial Board
George M. Blanco
William W. Brickman
Joanna F. Chambers
Joshua A. Fishman
Angelo Gimondo
Hernan La Fontaine

See last pages of this volume
for a complete list of titles.

BILINGUALISM
AND THE BILINGUAL CHILD

Challenges and Problems

**Edited with an Introduction
by
Francesco Cordasco**

ARNO PRESS
A New York Times Company
New York ● 1978

Editorial Supervision: LUCILLE MAIORCA

———◆———

Reprint Edition 1978 by Arno Press Inc.

Arrangement and Compilation Copyright © 1978
by Arno Press Inc.

BILINGUAL-BICULTURAL EDUCATION IN THE UNITED STATES
ISBN for complete set: 0-405-11071-5
See last pages of this volume for titles.

Manufactured in the United States of America

———◆———

Library of Congress Cataloging in Publication Data

Main entry under title:

Bilingualism and the bilingual child.

    (Bilingual-bicultural education in the United
States)
    Includes bibliographical references.
    1. Bilingualism--United States--Addresses,
essays, lectures. 2. Children--Language--
Addresses, essays, lectures. 3. Education,
Bilingual--United States--Addresses, essays,
lectures. I. Cordasco, Francesco, 1920-
II. Series.
P115.5.U5B49   401   77-90569
ISBN 0-405-11108-8

ACKNOWLEDGMENTS

"The Challenge of Bilingualism" was reprinted by permission of the Northeast Conference on the Teaching of Foreign Languages.

Articles from *The Modern Language Journal* have been reprinted by permission of *The Modern Language Journal* published by the National Federation of Modern Language Teachers Association, Inc.

Articles from *The Journal of Social Issues* have been reprinted by permission of *The Journal of Social Issues*, a publication of the Society for the Psychological Study of Social Issues.

INTRODUCTION

The history of American education has been attended by an evolving pattern of innovation and controversy which extends back to very origins of the Republic. Until the very recent past, the genius of American civilization was attributed to its schools, to the opportunities they furnished, and to education's role in an inexorable progress toward an American ideal. Much of this optimism has been shattered in the social currents of equalitarianism which have overtaken our institutions and which now dominate our schools.

Of all of the new developments in American schools, none has been more challenging, and controversial, than bilingual education. What is bilingual education? And how are the controversies which surround it (translated into the adversary constituencies of support and resistance) to be explained? The questions are very real: in 1977 the United States Department of Health, Education, and Welfare sponsored over 600 bilingual projects in teacher training, curriculum-development, and classroom programs, in some 60 languages, at a cost (with state moneys) in excess of $200 million. These efforts have been enthusiastically praised, and at the same time bitterly condemned.

Some 5 million youngsters in the United States come from homes in which generally spoken language is other than English; estimates based on samplings in several states suggest that between 1.8 and 2.5 million American children need bilingual education.

Although a number of typologies of bilingual education have been described (*e.g.*, transitional, monoliterate, partial bilingualism, full bilingualism), bilingual education is best defined as instruction in tw languages: the child's native language and English. A bilingual educational program is one in which a pupil receives instruction in academic subjects in *both* his native language and English. Concomitantly, the student learns about the history and culture associated with both languages, *i.e.*, bicultural education.

There is no doubt that non-English speaking children encounter serious learning problems in American schools. A recent study conducted by the New York State Education Department concluded that "the most distressing incidence of academic failure occurs among a group of children who are handicapped by a language barrier in the classroom—those 160,000 children [in New York] whose native language is not English and whose difficulty comprehending English significantly impedes school performance." A multitude of other studies from all regions of the United States confirm the New York findings.

Widespread efforts in the early 1960's to incorporate bilingual components into American school curricula resulted in the enactment by Congress in 1967 of the Bilingual Education Act as Title VII of the Elementary and Secondary Education Act, the far-reaching, massively funded federal educational statute for disadvantaged children enacted earlier in 1965. With limited resources of their own, states and school districts have relied principally upon the federal statutes to support programs to meet the needs of the bilingual child. The critical educational challenges posed by growing numbers of non-English speaking children have resulted in a number of state legislatures (*e.g.*, Colorado, Illinois, Massachusetts, New Jersey, and Texas) mandating bilingual education; and the 1974 U.S. Supreme Court ruling in *Lau v. Nichols*, which required San Francisco schools to provide bilingual education to non-English speaking pupils (largely Chinese) will undoubtedly accelerate this trend.

Actually, bilingual education is not new in the United States: in a nation as diverse in its origins as ours, this should not be surprising. English has not always been the only language used in American schools. German immigrants (whose progeny make up the largest ethnic group in America) established German-English bilingual schools in Cincinnati, Indianapolis, Hoboken, N.J., Cleveland, and many other cities: these were public schools, and German was not only taught as a subject, it was used as a medium of instruction. Between 1880 and 1917, these schools flourished; they were eagerly supported by a powerful and socially-stratified German community, and only the political tensions of World War I ended their history. In Louisiana, French was used as the medium of instruction, and in New Mexico, Spanish was so used: of course, these were limited efforts and largely early and mid-19th century phenomena, but they confirm a bilingual tradition in America. In New York City, at different times and with differing commitments, the public schools taught children in Chinese, Italian, Greek, Yiddish, and French. In a real sense, present-day efforts in bilingual education are a rediscovery of a respected and traditional American educational practice. Why, then, the resistance by some groups to bilingual education? The answer is complex.

It is not altogether untrue, as a national weekly recently affirmed, that "current bilingual policy is a curious hybrid of pedagogy and politics." Bilingual education is a product of what I have called the social currents of the equalitarianism which engulfed our institutions in the 1960's. It could not have been otherwise, since bilingual education, in its *bicultural* orientations, is a necessary concomitant of the new ethnic consciousness which has recently gripped the American imagination: flowing directly from the Black civil rights movement and new affirmations of identity, came the bristling ethnicity which unleashed proclamations of ethnic pride in Mexican Americans, Puerto Ricans, and in the progeny of earlier European immigrants—Italians, Greeks, Jews, Poles, Slavs, and others. The preservation of languages is an important part of the ideology of the new ethnicity; and thus, bilingual education (in itself, an unassailable pedagogical technique) became embroiled in the controversy surrounding the new ethnicity, its ideologies and interventionist politics. And in these contexts, the resistance to bilingual/bicultural education is not unrelated to dominant themes in American society which have entertained and continue to entertain credence, *e.g.*, inter-ethnic rivalry, the Americanization movement, psychological testing and race typologies, eugenics and hereditarian persuasions, and the "melting pot" theory of assimilation. All of these issues are, and have been, highly controversial and emotionally disturbing episodes in our long history as a people; and each of these themes (and a combination of any and all of them) have served to obscure the very real pedagogic needs to which bilingual education addresses itself.

There is a clear consensus among American educators that the purpose of bilingual education is to help children who have little or no command of English to succeed in school. In the landmark decision in *Lau v. Nichols*, Associate Justice William O. Douglas (who delivered the opinion of the U.S. Supreme Court) said: "There is no equality of treatment merely by providing students with the same facilities, textbooks, teachers, and curriculum; for students who do not understand English are effectively foreclosed from any meaningful education. . . . Basic English skills are at the very core of what the schools teach. Imposition of a requirement that, before a child can effectively participate in the educational program, he must already have acquired those basic skills is to make a mockery of public education."

The contemporary contexts of bilingual schooling in the United States directly impinge on the ideologies that herald the energetic emergence of peoples who find in their cultures and languages the instrumentalities f an evolving enfranchisement; and it would be hazardous to suggest otherwise. In many ways, the ideologies of race, culture, and language (if not new phenomena in American history) have a special importance at this point in time. For bilingual education, they have a crucial significance. How successful bilingual education proves in the United States will depend on how congruent its programs become with the aspirations of the ethnic communities to which the programs are addressed; on the awareness by American educators of the new American ethnicity; on the very participation of ethnic communities in program formulation and evaluation; and on the cogency of those bilingual typologies that (in carefully constructed bicultural frames) can best achieve desired objectives.

Against this background, the appearance of *Bilingualism and the Bilingual Child: Challenges and Problems* is singularly appropriate. It furnishes rich resources which help clarify many of the central issues which surround bilingual education in American schools. Brought together in this volume are the complete texts of the papers assembled in *The Modern Language Journal* symposium on "Bilingualism and the Bilingual Child" (1965); the text of "The Challenge of Bilingualism" presented at Northeast Conference on the Teaching of Foreign Languages (1965); the texts of the papers assembled in the *Journal of Social Issues* on "Problems of Bilingualism" (1967); selections from the huge corpus "Bilingualism in the Barrio" gathered together in *The Modern Language Journal*, in which bilingualism is explored as a *societal* manifestation (1969); and the complete text of the special issue of *The Center Forum* which the Center for Urban Education devoted to bilingualism (1969), an issue which includes materials on Mexican-Americans, excerpts from the Senate *Hearings* on the Bilingual Education Act, notices of German public schools in the United States, evaluative notes on ongoing programs, and a valuable bibliography on teaching bilingual students.

Francesco Cordasco

BIBLIOGRAPHY OF SELECTED REFERENCES

Abrahams, Roger D., and Rudolph C. Troike, eds. *Language and Cultural Diversity in American Education.* Englewood Cliffs, New Jersey; Prentice-Hall, 1972.

Alatis, James E., ed. *Bilingualism and Language Contact: Anthropological, Linguistic, Psychological, and Sociological Aspects.* Monograph Series on Languages and Linguistics, [oa] Washington: Georgetown University Press, 1970.

Allen, Harold B. *Teaching English as a Second Language.* New York: New York: McGraw-Hill, 1972.

Alloway, David N., and Francesco Cordasco. *Minorities and the American City: A Sociological Primer for Educators.* New York: David McKay, 1970.

Andersson, Theodore, and Mildred Boyer. *Bilingual Schooling in the United States*. 2 vols. Austin, Texas: Southwest Educational Development Laboratory, 1970.

Barik. H.C., and M. Swain. *Bilingual Education Project: Interim Report on the Spring 1972 Testing Programme*. Toronto: Ontario Institute for Studies in Education, 1972.

Bilingualism and the Bilingual Child—A Symposium." *Modern Language Journal*, vol. 49 (March, April 1965).

Bilingualism in Education. Department of Education and Science. London: H. M. Stationery Office, 1965.

Bright, William, ed. *Sociolinguistics: Proceedings of the UCLA Sociolinguistics Conference, 1964*. The Hague: Mouton, 1966.

Broman, Betty. "The Spanish-Speaking Five Year Old." *Childhood Education*, vol. 41 (1972) pp. 362-64.

Brown, Roger. *A First Language: The Early Stages*. Cambridge, Mass.: Harvard University Press, 1973.

Bureau of Indian Affairs. *Bilingual Education for American Indians*. Washington: Bureau of Indian Affairs, 1971.

Burma, John., ed. *Mexican-Americans in the United States*. Cambridge, Mass.: Schenkman, 1970.

Burma, John H. *Spanish-Speaking Groups in the United States*. Detroit: Blaine Ethridge, 1974. (originally, Duke University Press, 1954)

Cannon, Garland. "Bilingual Problems and Developments in the United States." PMLA, vol. 86 (1971), pp. 452-58.

Cazden, Courtney B., ed. *Language in Early Childhood Education*. Washington: National Association for the Education of Young Children, 1972.

Cazden, Courtney B., Vera John, and Dell Hymes, eds. *Functions of Language in the Classroom*. New York: Teachers College Press, 1972.

Chomsky, Carol. *The Acquisition of Syntax in Children from Five to Ten*. Cambridge, Mass.: The M.I.T. Press, 1969.

Cohen, Andrew D. *A Sociolinguistic Approach to Bilingual Education*. Rowley, Mass.: Newbury House, 1975.

Cordasco, Francesco. "Another View of Poverty: Oscar Lewis' *La Vida*." *Phylon: The Atlanta Review of Race & Culture*, vol. 29 (Spring 1968), pp. 88-92.

Cordasco, Francesco. "The Challenge of the Non-English Speaking Child in the American School." *School & Society*, vol. 96 (March 30, 1968), pp. 198-201.

Cordasco, Francesco. "The Children of Immigrants in Schools: Historical Analogues of Educational Deprivation." *Journal of Negro Education*, vol. 42 (Winter 1973), pp. 44-53.

Cordasco, Francesco. "Educational Enlightenment out of Texas: Toward Bilingualism." *Teachers College Record*, vol. 72 (May 1970), pp. 608-612. See also, F. Cordasco, "The Bilingual Education Act," *Phi Delta Kappan* (October 1969).

Cordasco, Francesco, advisory editor. *The Puerto Rican Experience*. 33 vols. New York: Arno Press/New York Times, 1975.

Cordasco, Francesco. "Puerto Rican Pupils and American Education." *School & Society*, vol. 95 (February 18, 1967), pp. 116-119.

Cordasco, Francesco. "Teaching the Puerto Rican Experience," in James A. Banks, ed., *Teaching Ethnic Studies: Concepts and Strategies* (Washington: Council for the Social Studies, 1973), pp. 226-253.

Cordasco, Francesco, **et al. Puerto Ricans on the United States Mainland**: *A Biography of Reports, Texts, Critiial Studies and Related Materials*. Totowa, N.J.: Rowman and Littlefield, 1972.

Cordasco, Francesco, and Eugene Bucchioni. *The Puerto Rican Community and Its Children on the Mainland: A Sourcebook for Teachers, Social Workers and Other Professionals*. Metuchen, N.J.: Scarecrow Press, 1972.

Cordasco, Francesco, and Eugene Bucchioni. *The Puerto Rican Experience: A Sociological Sourcebook*. Totowa, N.J.: Littlefield, Adams, 1973.

Cordasco, Francesco, and Eugene Bucchioni. "A Staff Institute for Teachers of Puerto Rican Students." *School & Society*, vol. 99 (Summer 1972).

Cordasco, Francesco, and Leonard Covello. *Studies of Puerto Rican Children in American Schools: A Preliminary Bibliogaraphy*. New York: Department of Labor, Migration Division, Commonwealth of Puerto Rico, 1967. Also in *Education Libraries Bulletin*, Institute of Education, University of London, No. 31 (Spring 1968), pp. 7-33; and in *Journal of Human Relations*, vol. 16 (1968), pp. 264-285.

Cordasco, Francesco, *Bilingual Schooling in the United States: A Sourcebook for Educational Personnel.* New York: McGraw-Hill, 1976.

Cortes, Carlos E., advisory editor. *The Mexican American.* 21 vols. New York: Arno Press/New York Times, 1974.

Covello, Leonard. *The Social Background of the Italo-American School Child: A Study of the Southern Italian Family Mores and Their Effect on the School Situation in Italy and America.* Edited and with an Introduction by F. Cordasco. Leiden, The Netherlands: E.J. Brill, 1967; Totowa, N.J.: Rowman and Littlefield, 1972.

Edelman, Martin. "The Contextualization of School Children's Bilinlgualism." *Modern Language Journal*, vol. 53 (1969), pp. 179-82.

Engle, Patricia L. *The Use of Vernacular Languages in Education. Language Medium in Early School Years for Minority Language Groups.* Washington: Center for Applied Linguistics, 1975. (Bilingual Education Series, No. 3)

Finocchiaro, Mary. *Teaching English as a Second Language.* Rev. ed. New York: Harper & Row, 1969.

Fisher, John C. "Bilingualism in Puerto Rico: A History of Frustration." *The English Record*, vol. 21 (April 1971), pp. 19-24.

Fishman, Joshua A. *Bilingual Education: An International Sociological Perspective.* Rowley, Mass.: Newbury House, 1976.

Fishman, Joshua, et al. "Bilingualism in the Barrio." *Modern Language Journal*, vol. 53 (March, April 1969).

Fishman, Joshua A. *Language Loyalty in the United States.* The Hague: Mouton, 1966.

Fishman, Joshua A. *Language and Nationalism.* Rowley, Mass.: Newbury House, 1973.

Fishman, Joshua A. "The Measurement and Description of Widespread and Relatively Stable Bilingualism." *Modern Language Journal*, vol. 53 (1969), pp. 153-56.

Fishman, Joshua A. "The Politics of Bilingual Education." In James E. Alatis, ed., *Bilingualism and Language Contact* (Georgetown University Round Table on Languages and Linguistics, 1970). Washington: Georgetown University Press, 1970, pp. 47-58.

Fishman, Joshua A., ed. *Readings in the Sociology of Language.* The Hague: Mouton, 1968.

Fishman, Joshua A. "A Sociolinguistic Census of a Bilingual Neighborhood." *American Journal of Sociology,* vol. 75 (1969), pp. 323-39.

Fishman, Joshua A. *Sociolinguistic: A Brief Introduction.* Rowley, Mass.: Newbury House, 1971.

Fishman, Joshua A., and Heriberto Casiano. "Puerto Ricans in Our Press." *Modern Language Journal,* vol. 53 (1969), pp. 157-62.

Fishman, Joshua A., Robert L. Cooper, and Roxana Ma, eds. *Bilingualism in the Barrio.* Language Science Monographs 7, Indiana University. The Hague: Mouton, 1971.

Fishman, Joshua A., and John Lovas. "Bilingual Education in a Sociolinguistic Perspective." *TESOL Quarterly,* vol. 4 (September 1970).

Fitzpatric, Joseph. *Puerto Rican Americans: The Meaning of Migration to the Mainland.* Englewood Cliffs: Prentice-Hall, 1971

Gaarder, A. Bruce. "Bilingual Education: Central Questions and Concerns." *New York University Quarterly,* vol. 6 (Summer 1975), pp. 2-6.

Gaarder, A. Bruce. "The First Seventy-Six Bilingual Education Projects." In James E. Alatis, ed., *Bilingualism and Language Contact* (Georgetown University Round Table on Languages and Linguistics, 1970). Washington: Georgetown University Press, 1970, pp. 163-178.

Gaarder, A. Bruce. "Organization of the Bilingual School." *Journal of Social Issues,* vol. 23 (1967), pp. 110-20.

Gaarder, A. Bruce. *Bilingual Schooling and the Survival of Spanish in the United States.* Rowley, Mass.: Newbury House, 1977.

Geffert, Hannah N., et al. The Current Status of U. S. Bilingual Education Legislation. Washington: Center for Applied Linlguistics, 1975. (Bilingual Education Series, No. 4)

Goldstein, Wallace L. *Teaching English as a Second Language: An Annotated Bibliography.* New York: Garland Publishing, 1975

Gumperz, John J., and Dell Hymes, eds. *Directions in Sociolinguistics: The Ethnogaraphy of Communication.* New York: Holt, Rinehart & Winston, 1972.

Havinghurst, Robert J. *The National Study of American Indian Education.* Chicago: University of Chicago Press, 1970.

Hickey, T. "Bilingualism and the Measurement of Intelligence and Verbal Learning Abilities." *Exceptional Children*, vol. 39 (1972), pp. 24-28.

Hymes, Dell. *Foundations in Sociolinguistics: An Ethnographic Approach.* Philadelphia: University of Pennsylvania Press, 1974.

Hymes, Dell, ed. *Studies in the History of Linguistics: Traditions and Paradigms.* Bloomington: Indiana University Press, 1974.

John, Vera P., and Vivian M. Horner. *Early Childhood Bilingual Education.* New York: The Modern Language Association of America, 1971.

Kessler, Carolyn. *The Acquisition of Syntax in Bilingual Children.* Washington: Georgetown University Press, 1971.

Kloss, Heinz. *The American Bilingual Tradition.* Rowley, Mass.: Newbury House, 1977.

Lambert, Wallace E., J. Havelka, and C. Crosby. "The Influence of Language Acquisition Contexts on Bilingualism." *Journal of Abnormal and Social Psychology,* vol. 56 (1958), pp. 239-244.

Lambert, Wallace E., and Richard C. Tucker. *Bilingual Education of Children: The St. Lambert Experiment.* Rowley, Mass.: Newbury House, 1972.

Levine, H. "Bilingualism, Its Effect on Emotional and Social Development." *Journal of Secondary Education,* vol. 44 (1969), pp. 69-73.

Mackey, William F. *Bilingual Education in a Binational School: A Study of Equal Language Maintenance Through Free Alteration.* Rowley, Mass.: Newbury House, 1972.

Mackey, William F. *Bilingualism as a World Problem.* Montreal: Harvest House, 1967.

Mackey, William F. and Von Niede Beebe. *Bilingual Schools for a Bicultural Community.* Rowley, Mass.: Newbury House, 1977 (Cubans in Miami, Fla.)

Mackey, William F. and Theodore Andersson, eds. *Bilingualism in Early Childhood.* Rowley, Mass.: Newbury House, 1977.

Malkoc, Anna M., and A.H. Roberts. "Bilingual Education: A Special Report from CAL-ERIC." *Elementary English* (May 1970), pp. 713-725.

Paulston, Christina B. *Implications of Language Learning Theory for Language Planning: Concerns in Bilingual Education.* Washington: Center for Applied Linguistics, 1974. Bilingual Education Series, No. 1)

Pedeira, Antonio S. *Bibliografia Puertorriquena, 1493-1930.* Madrid: Imprenta de Hernando, 1932; reissued with a foreword by F. Cordasco, New York: Burt Franklin, 1974.

Sanches, Mary, and Ben Blount, eds. *Sociocultural Dimensions of Lanlguage Use.* New York: Academic Press, 1975.

Saville-Troike, Muriel. *Bilingual Children: A Resource Document.* Washington: Center for Applied Linguistics, 1973. (Bilingual Education Series, No. 2)

Saville, Muriel R., and Rudolph C. Troike. *A Handbook of Bilingual Education.* Washington: Center for Applied Linguistics, 1971.

Spolsky, Bernard, ed. *The Language Education of Minority Children: Selected Readings.* Rowley, Mass.: Newbury House, 1973.

Spolsky, Bernard and Robert L. Cooper, eds. *Frontiers of Bilingual Education.* Rowley, Mass.: Newbury House, 1977.

Trueba, Henry T. *Bilingual Bicultural Education for the Spanish Speaking in the United States.* Champaign, Illinois: Stipes Publishing Co., 1977.

Ulibarri, Horacio. *Interpretive Studies on Bilingual Education.* Washington: U.S. Office of Education, 1969.

United States. Cabinet Committee on Opportunity for the Spanish Speaking. *The Spanish Speaking in the United States: A Guide to Materials.* With a Foreword by F. Cordasco. Detroit: Blaine Ethridge, 1975. (Originally, G.P.O., 1971)

Vildomec, V. *Multilinlgualism.* Leiden, The Netherlands: Sythoff, 1963.

Von Maltitz, Frances Willard. *Living and Learning in Two Languages: Bilingual-Bicultural Education in the UnitSd States.* New York: McGraw-Hill, 1975.

Walsh, Marie A. *The Development of a Rationale for a Program to Prepare Teachers for Spanish-Speaking Children in the Bilingual-Bicultural Elementary School.* San Francisco: R & E Research Associates, 1976.

Woodford, Protase. "Bilingual-Bicultural Education: A Need for Understanding," in Gilbert A. Jarvis, ed., *The ACTFL Review of Foreign Languages Education*, vol. 6 (Skokie, Illinois: National Textbook Co., 1974), pp. 397-433.

CONTENTS

Fishman, Joshua A., THE STATUS AND PROSPECTS OF BILINGUALISM IN THE UNITED STATES (Reprinted from *The Modern Language Journal*, Vol. XLIX, No. 3) Menasha, Wis., March, 1965

Andersson, Theodore, A NEW FOCUS ON THE BILINGUAL CHILD (Reprinted from *The Modern Language Journal*, Vol. XLIX, No. 3) Menasha, Wis., March, 1965

Christian, Chester C., Jr., THE ACCULTURATION OF THE BILINGUAL CHILD (Reprinted from *The Modern Language Journal*, Vol. XLIX, No. 3) Menasha, Wis., March, 1965

Gaarder, A. Bruce, TEACHING THE BILINGUAL CHILD: Research, Development, and Policy (Reprinted from *The Modern Language Journal*, Vol. XLIX, No. 3) Menasha, Wis., March, 1965

Hakes, David T., PSYCHOLOGICAL ASPECTS OF BILINGUALISM (Reprinted from *The Modern Language Journal*, Vol. XLIX, No. 4) Menasha, Wis., April, 1965

Fishman, Joshua A., BILINGUALISM, INTELLIGENCE AND LANGUAGE LEARNING (Reprinted from *The Modern Language Journal*, Vol. XLIX, No. 4) Menasha, Wis., April, 1965

Rojas, Pauline M., INSTRUCTIONAL MATERIALS AND AIDS TO FACILITATE TEACHING THE BILINGUAL CHILD (Reprinted from *The Modern Language Journal*, Vol. XLIX, No. 4) Menasha, Wis., April, 1965

THE CHALLENGE OF BILINGUALISM (Reprinted from *Foreign Language Teaching: Challenges to the Profession*, Reports of the Working Committees, Northeast Conference on the Teaching of Foreign Languages) Princeton, New Jersey, 1965

Macnamara, John, BILINGUALISM IN THE MODERN WORLD (Reprinted from *The Journal of Social Issues*, Vol. XXIII, No. 2) April, 1967

Hymes, Dell, MODELS OF THE INTERACTION OF LANGUAGE AND SOCIAL SETTING (Reprinted from *The Journal of Social Issues*, Vol. XXIII, No. 2) April, 1967

Fishman, Joshua, BILINGUALISM WITH AND WITHOUT DIGLOSSIA; DIGLOSSIA WITH AND WITHOUT BILINGUALISM (Reprinted from *The Journal of Social Issues,* Vol. XXIII, No. 2) April, 1967

Kloss, Heinz, BILINGUALISM AND NATIONALISM (Reprinted from *The Journal of Social Issues*, Vol. XXIII, No. 2) April, 1967

Gumperz, John J., ON THE LINGUISTIC MARKERS OF BILINGUAL COMMUNICATION (Reprinted from *The Journal of Social Issues*, Vol. XXIII, No. 2) April, 1967

Macnamara, John, THE BILINGUAL'S LINGUISTIC PERFORMANCE—A PSYCHOLOGICAL OVERVIEW (Reprinted from *The Journal of Social Issues*, Vol. XXIII, No. 2) April, 1967

Ervin-Tripp, Susan, AN ISSEI LEARNS ENGLISH (Reprinted from *The Journal of Social Issues*, Vol. XXIII, No. 2) April, 1967

Lambert, Wallace E., A SOCIAL PSYCHOLOGY OF BILINGUALISM (Reprinted from *The Journal of Social Issues*, Vol. XXIII, No. 2) April, 1967

Gaarder, A. Bruce, ORGANIZATION OF THE BILINGUAL SCHOOL (Reprinted from *The Journal of Social Issues*, Vol. XXIII, No. 2) April, 1967

Macnamara, John, THE EFFECTS OF INSTRUCTION IN A WEAKER LANGUAGE (Reprinted from *The Journal of Social Issues*, Vol. XXIII, No. 2) April, 1967

Fishman, Joshua A., BILINGUALISM IN THE BARRIO (Reprinted from *The Modern Language Journal*, Vol. LIII, No. 3) Menasha, Wis., March, 1969

Fishman, Joshua A. and Heriberto Casiano, PUERTO RICANS IN OUR PRESS (Reprinted from *The Modern Language Journal*, Vol. LIII, No. 3) Menasha, Wis., March, 1969

Cooper, Robert L. and Lawrence Greenfield, WORD FREQUENCY ESTIMATION AS A MEASURE OF DEGREE OF BILINGUALISM (Reprinted from *The Modern Language Journal*, Vol. LIII, No. 3) Menasha, Wis., March, 1969

Cooper, Robert L. and Lawrence Greenfield, LANGUAGE USE IN A BILINGUAL COMMUNITY (Reprinted from *The Modern Language Journal*, Vol. LIII, No. 3) Menasha, Wis., March, 1969

Cooper, Robert L., TWO CONTEXTUALIZED MEASURES OF DEGREE OF BILINGUALISM (Reprinted from *The Modern Language Journal*, Vol. LIII, No. 3) Menasha, Wis., March, 1969

Edelman Martin, THE CONTEXTUALIZATION OF SCHOOLCHILDREN'S BILINGUALISM (Reprinted from *The Modern Language Journal*, Vol. LIII, No. 3) Menasha, Wis., March, 1969

Berney, Tomi D. and Robert L. Cooper, SEMANTIC INDEPENDENCE AND DEGREE OF BILINGUALISM IN TWO COMMUNITIES (Reprinted from *The Modern Language Journal*, Vol. LIII, No. 3) Menasha, Wis., March, 1969

Findling, Joav, BILINGUAL NEED AFFILIATION AND FUTURE ORIENTATION IN EXTRAGROUP AND INTRAGROUP DOMAINS (Reprinted from *The Modern Language Journal*, Vol. LIII, No. 4) Menasha, Wis., April, 1969

Ronch, Judah, Robert L. Cooper and Joshua A. Fishman, WORD NAMING AND USAGE SCORES FOR A SAMPLE OF YIDDISH-ENGLISH BILINGUALS (Reprinted from *The Modern Language Journal*, Vol. LIII, No. 4) Menasha, Wis., April, 1969

Cooper, Robert L., Barbara R. Fowles and Abraham Givner, LISTENING COMPREHENSION IN A BILINGUAL COMMUNITY (Reprinted from *The Modern Language Journal*, Vol. LIII, No. 4) Menasha, Wis., April, 1969

Silverman, Stuart H., THE EVALUATION OF LANGUAGE VARIETIES (Reprinted from *The Modern Language Journal*, Vol. LIII, No. 4) Menasha, Wis., April, 1969

Fertig, Sheldon and Joshua A. Fishman, SOME MEASURES OF THE INTERACTION BETWEEN LANGUAGE, DOMAIN AND SEMANTIC DIMENSION IN BILINGUALS (Reprinted from *The Modern Language Journal*, Vol. LIII, No. 4) Menasha, Wis., April, 1969

Silverman, Stuart H., A METHOD FOR RECORDING AND ANALYZING THE PROSODIC FEATURES OF LANGUAGE (Reprinted from *The Modern Language Journal*, Vol. LIII, No. 4(Menasha, Wis., April, 1969

Terry, Charles E. and Robert L. Cooper, A NOTE ON THE PERCEPTION AND PRODUCTION OF PHONOLOGICAL VARIATION (Reprinted from *The Modern Language Journal*, Vol. LIII, No. 4) Menasha, Wis., April, 1969

Fishman, Joshua A., SOME THINGS LEARNED; SOME THINGS YET TO LEARN (Reprinted from *The Modern Language Journal*, Vol. LIII, No. 4) Menasha, Wis., April, 1969

BILINGUALISM (Reprinted from *The Center Forum*, Vol. 4, No. 1) New York, September, 1969

THE STATUS AND PROSPECTS
OF BILINGUALISM IN THE UNITED STATES

Joshua A. Fishman

The Status and Prospects of Bilingualism in the United States*

JOSHUA A. FISHMAN, *Yeshiva University*

I. The Current Status of Non-English Language Resources in the United States

1. In 1960 the non-English language resources of the United States were undoubtedly smaller than they had been a decade or two previously. Nevertheless, they were still huge, both in absolute terms and relation to their twentieth century high-water marks in the two decades, 1920 to 1940.[1]

Approximately nineteen million individuals or eleven percent of the entire American population possessed a non-English mother tongue in 1960. The mother tongues involved represent a very high proportion of those extant throughout the world that have evolved to the point of becoming standard literary languages as well as not a few that have not yet reached

this stage of development. Relative to 1940, the quantitative position of the "colonial languages"—Spanish, French, and German—has remained far better than that of all but the most recently reinforced immigrant languages. However, even in the case of most of those

* Presented at the Conference for the Teacher of the Bilingual Child, University of Texas, June 8–10, 1964, and prepared while the author was a Fellow (1963–1964) at the Center for Advanced Study in the Behavioral Sciences, Stanford University.

[1] Joshua A. Fishman et al., *Language Loyalty in the United States*, New York: Yeshiva University, 1964. A mimeographed report, in three volumes, to the Language Research Section of the United States Office of Education, Department of Health, Education, and Welfare. A one volume summary, published by Mouton, will appear in 1965.

immigrant languages that did *not* benefit from post-war immigration and that have suffered most from internal attrition and external apathy, there were still subgroups with sufficient cultural-linguistic intactness to maintain functional bilingualism and to provide good prospects of marked gain in either functional or cultural bilingualism from well designed and vigorous reinforcement efforts.

2. The non-English press boasted over 500 periodic publications in 1960 and continued to have a circulation of approximately five and one-half millions, as well as a "pass-along" readership estimated to be equally large. Although non-English dailies and weeklies have regularly lost circulation since 1930, monthlies have experienced circulation gains in recent decades. Non-English broadcasting also seems to be in a far better state of health in 1960 than was usually thought to be the case—with over 1600 "stations" broadcasting more than 6,000 hours of non-English language programs every week in the continental United States. However, this latter picture largely reflects the continued strength of Spanish broadcasting, which alone accounts for two thirds of all non-English broadcasting in the United States. Furthermore, both the non-English press and non-English broadcasting, with the exception of Spanish broadcasting, are largely dependent upon and oriented toward a first generation clientele. The latter, in turn, represents slightly less than half of the claimants of almost all non-English mother tongues in the United States. Thus, although immigrant status itself is not predictive of either language maintenance or language loyalty, both of these phenomena are heavily dependent upon immigrant status; the colonial languages constituting the only noteworthy exceptions to this generalization.

3. In 1960 there were clearly 1800 (and probably a good many more) ethnic "cultural" organizations in the United States. Many of these, including the largest among them, serve first, second, and third generation members. Nearly three-quarters of all ethnic cultural organizations favor maintenance of the particular non-English mother tongue appropriate to their respective origins. However, the very fact that ethnic organizations have been more successful than either the non-English press or non-English broadcasting in attracting second and third generation interest has also led most of them to exceedingly marginal and passive approaches to ethnicity and to language maintenance. The organizations represent bulwarks of structural more than of behavioral-cultural pluralism.

4. The most active language maintenance institution in most ethnic communities in the United States is the ethnic group school. Over 2,000, and perhaps as many as 3,000, such schools currently function in the United States. More than half offer mother tongue instruction even when there are many "non-ethnics" and "other-ethnics" among their pupils. On the whole, they succeed in reinforcing or developing moderate comprehension, reading, writing, and speaking facility in their pupils. However, they are far less successful in implanting retentivist language attitudes which might serve to maintain language facility after their students' programs of study have been completed, approximately at age fourteen. Although the languages learned by pupils in ethnic group schools are normally "ethnic mother tongues," rather than true mother tongues, the levels of facility attained usually are sufficient to provide a foundation for cultural bilingualism. However, this foundation is rarely reinforced after the completion of study in the ethnic group school.

5. Mother tongue teachers in ethnic group schools rarely view themselves as powerful factors in determining language-maintenance outcomes. They do not believe that their pupils accomplish overly much, particularly with respect to the more active aspects of language maintenance. They typically report that their pupils become decreasingly interested in mother tongue instruction as they advance through the grades and they typically attribute this and other instructional difficulties to parental apathy or opposition to the mother tongue. They most frequently view the mother tongues that they teach as not being among the most prestigeful in the United States, an honor reserved for French and Spanish almost exclusively. However, the determinants of language prestige, unlike the determinants of instructional difficulties, are attributed to "Ameri-

can" rather than to ethnic factors. When group maintenance is seen as being in conflict with language maintenance, the former is frequently preferred, except in the case of mother tongue teachers associated with very recent immigrant groups, most of whom reject the possibility of any such conflict.

6. The relationship between ethnicity, religion and language remains strong, although the middle term, religion, tends to withdraw ever more rapidly from the tri-partite association. Religion is organizationally "successful" in the United States; and therefore, its less successful companions, ethnicity and language, lean upon it heavily for support. However, the more "successful" religion becomes, the more de-ethnicized it becomes, the more amenable to mergers with other de-ethnicized churches, and the more disinterested in language maintenance. Language maintenance in historically ethnic churches is continued on a habitual rather than on an ideological-purposive basis, on ethnic rather than on religious grounds, and in conjunction with adult rather than youth activities. The triple melting pot leading toward de-ethnicized Catholicism, Protestantism and Judaism and the mere passage of time represent the two most prevalent religious solutions to the "embarrassment" of language maintenance. Traditional *ritual protection* of non-English vernaculars, such as exists in the Greek Catholic and Eastern Orthodox Churches, functions more as a significant delaying factor than as a crucial outcome factor in this connection.

7. Ethnic cultural-organizational *leaders* and *rank-and-file* ethnics display essentially similar patterns in conjunction with language-maintenance efforts and processes. In both instances, immigrants are more retentive, within the family and outside of it, than are second generation individuals. In both instances, organization membership and organizational activity have become more important means of insulating ethnicity than language. In both instances, older children are more linguistically retentive than younger children, first children more so than last children, children more so than grandchildren, organizationally-affiliated children more so than unaffiliated children. Whereas first generation leaders consist of both cultural and organizational activists, second generation leaders are almost exclusively organization activists. Although they favor language maintenance, they do so with essentially non-ethnic rationales and their support for language maintenance is more frequently attitudinal rather than overt. Philosophies or rationales of biculturalism and bilingualism are weak or non-existent.

8. There are two large worlds of non-English languages in the United States. One is the officially recognized and supported world of "foreign language" instruction in non-ethnic public and private high schools and colleges. The other is the largely unrecognized and unsupported world of ethnic language-maintenance efforts. These two worlds meet in the persons of foreign language teachers, over half of whom are of an immediate ethnic background appropriate to one of the languages they teach. Teachers of ethnically more infused, less prestigious languages, e.g., German and Italian, as contrasted with French and Spanish, particularly those at the college and university level, are most likely to have been ethnically exposed and to favor, attitudinally, language maintenance efforts. However, these same teachers are also under the greatest strain toward professionalization and are, therefore, least inclined to utilize for instructional purposes the resources of minority cultural-linguistic groups such as native speakers, publications, broadcasts, choral-dramatic presentations.

9. Detailed integrative case studies of six separate cultural-linguistic groups have tended to provide independent support for the above generalizations. In general language maintenance and language shift have proceeded along quite similar lines in the three high-prestige colonial languages, French, Spanish, German, and in the three low-prestige immigrant languages, Yiddish, Hungarian, Ukrainian that were studied in great detail. Although differing widely with respect to period of settlement, numerical size, balance between low-culture and high-culture language retentivism, religious protection of the vernacular, and social mobility of their speakers, the drift has been consistently toward anglification and has become accelerated in recent years. Differences between the six language groups seem to be

great only in connection with the *rate of change* toward anglification. Only in the case of Spanish and Ukrainian speakers are relatively sizeable contingents of young and youthful bilinguals still available. In the Ukrainian case this is primarily due to recent large immigration. In the Spanish case it is due to the absence of economic mobility. Symbolically elaborated ethnicity, language loyalty, and religious protection of the vernacular are *absent* in the Spanish case and *present* in the case of Ukrainian. All in all, certain pervasive characteristics of American nationalism (social mobility on a non-ethnic, ideological, mass-culture base) and certain pervasive characteristics of most immigrant heritages (non-ideological ethnicity, "backwardness") seem to have been much more effective in jointly producing essentially similar outcomes than have the various uniquenesses of ethnic heritages or of immigrational-settlement patterns in safeguarding cultural and linguistic differences.

10. The modal characteristics of language-maintenance efforts among southern and eastern European immigrants arriving during the period of mass immigration can be roughly summarized as follows:

a. Language was rarely a consciously identified or valued component of daily, traditional ethnicity. Ethnicity itself was minimally-ideologized or organized in terms of conscious nationalistic or symbolic considerations.

b. Rapid immersion in the American metropolis and in American national values resulted in the fragmentation of traditional ways. These fragments of ethnicity that were retained in a disjointed and altered fashion were usually insufficient for the maintenance of functional bilingualism beyond the first generation.

c. Ethnicity and language maintenance became increasingly and overly dependent on the major organizational institution previously available in the "old country" setting and most successfully transplanted to the United States: the church. However, the church increasingly withdrew from ethnicity and from language maintenance in order to pursue its own organizational goals.

d. Attempts to utilize the formal organizational mechanisms of high culture and of industrialized metropolitan and modern national life on behalf of language and culture maintenance proceeded without the benefit of a popular ideological base that could either complete with or be joined to that of American nationalism.

e. As a result, neither traditional intactness nor ideological mobilization was available to the second generation. "Revolts" were common when maximal retentivist claims were advanced by the first generation and become uncommon when such claims were no longer pressed.

f. The second generation "outgrew" the fragmented ethnicity of the first but frequently retained an attachment to even more marginal expressions of ethnicity via the church, other organizations, and familial remnants of traditional ethnicity. While these have been insufficient for functional language maintenance, they have often preserved a positive attitudinal substratum toward the ethnic language and culture. This positiveness becomes more evident as the second generation advances through adulthood.

g. The third generation approached ethnicity with even greater selectivity, frequently viewing the ethnic mother tongue as a cultural or instrumental desideratum and viewing ethnicity as an area of appreciation or a field of study. De-ethnicized language maintenance elicits interest in the third generation although facility is rare.

11. Of all the foregoing, what can be considered new or striking in the light of previous studies or common knowledge? Certainly, the availability of systematic empirical data, rather than anecdotal impressions, is new for many of the topics under discussion. The vastness of language-maintenance efforts, even after generations of attrition, is certainly striking, but so is the fact that these efforts are so largely habitual and unfocused even within the very operation of organizations, schools, churches, and the mass media. The conscious, ideologically based and rationally directed efforts of language loyalists normally reach and influence only a small fraction of even the first generation of speakers of non-English languages. The uniformally changed role of religion with respect to language maintenance, from initially wholeheated support to implacable opposition or unmovable apathy, is also striking

and, hitherto, largely unappreciated. Similarly striking is the fact that opposition to language maintenance in the second and third generations of immigrant stock is now most commonly in a low key and un-ideologized. The days of bitter language disputes seem to be over, even between the age groups involved in such disputes in former decades. The continuation of favorable language maintenance sentiments much beyond the time of language maintenance behavior is also striking, particularly in that it goes hand in hand with a continued acceptance of ethnicity and even a search for ethnicity of an appropriately selective and marginal nature. Whereas language maintenance becomes a progressively weaker and smaller component of such ethnicity, organizational and religious involvement, cultural interests, and modified-disjointed festive acts become relatively stronger and are maintained much longer. Thus it is that the most striking fact of all comes into focus, namely, that a vast amount of language maintenance can exist side by side with the gradual disappearance of language maintenance, with the two *interacting* and *contributing* to each other.

12. *Summary and interpretation of findings.* Today, language maintenance in the United States is strongest among those immigrants who have maintained greatest psychological, social and cultural distance from the institutions, processes and values of American core society.[2] Ideological protection of non-English mother tongues without concomitant withdrawal from interaction with American society, the pattern adopted by urban religionists and by secular-cultural nationalists in the United States, has been a somewhat less effective bulwark of language maintenance than has ethnic-religious *separatism* based upon intact, rural Little Traditions. Where neither ideological nor ethno-religious protection has obtained language shift has proceeded in proportion to mobility within the larger sphere of American society, as reflected by indices of education, occupation, or income. Either type of protection was exceedingly rare. As a result, between-group differences in language maintenance came to reflect immigrational recency, settlement concentration, numerical size and social mobility much more than they reflect between-group

differences in post-immigrational maintenance efforts. Within group differences in language maintenance also came to depend primarily on the same set of factors, together with rurality, and to a smaller but nevertheless noticeable degree, upon conscious maintenance efforts *per se*.

Our current information concerning behaviors directed toward ethnic mother tongues on the part of their erstwhile and sometime speakers must be viewed in the perspective of the transitions that these tongues have most commonly experienced in the United States. From their original positions as vernaculars of entire religio-ethnic communities they are now the vernaculars only of very recent or atypical sub-populations. From their earlier position of use in all of the domains of life related to the particular socio-cultural patterns of their speakers they are now predominantly employed in fewer and in particularly symbolic or restricted domains.

a. Attitudinal-affective behaviors.

Concomitant with the accelerated de-ethnization and social mobility of erstwhile or sometime speakers and their offspring, and concomitant with their relegation to fewer and narrower domains, non-English mother tongues have frequently experienced increases in general esteem during the past 15–20 years. They are more frequently viewed positively and nostalgically by older first and second generation individuals who characterized them as ugly, corrupted and grammarless in pre-World War II days. The third generations view them, almost always via translations, with less emotion but with even greater respect. Thus, instead of a "third generation return" there has been an "attitudinal halo-ization" within large segments of all generations, albeit unaccompanied by increased use. This development, a negative relationship between use rates and attitudinal positiveness over time, was not foreseen by most earlier studies of language maintenance or language shift in immigrant contact settings. In the United States this development

[2] Joshua A. Fishman, *Language maintenance and language shift: The American immigrant case within a general theoretical perspective* (Mimeographed and submitted for publication).

is an aspect of the continued and growing affective functioning of increasingly marginal ethnicity. In the absence of basic economic, geographic, cultural or psychological separation between most ethnics and American core society, ethnic mother tongues survive longest at two extremes: the highly formal (the ritual-symbolic) and the highly intimate (the expressive-emotive). At these extremes they remain available to successive generations as reminders of ethnicity, and, when needed, as reaffirmers of ethnicity.

b. *Overt behavioral implementation of maintenance or shift.*

Most language reinforcement efforts, though much weakened by ideological and numerical attrition, continue along the traditional lines of information programs, religio-ethnic schools, periodic publications, broadcasts, cultural activities, etc. However, even in connection with language reinforcement efforts the transition to more marginal ethnicity and to more restricted language maintenance is evident. Thus, taking the field of ethnic periodic publications as an example, we note concomitant and continued shifts from more frequent to less frequent publications as well as shifts from all mother tongue, to mixed, to all English publications. However, the process of de-ethnization has also brought with it a few novel avenues of reinforcement. As even the more "exotic" ethnic mother tongues, those not usually considered among the major carriers of European civilization, and therefore, heretofore most frequently associated with foreign ethnicity in the minds of average Americans, have ceased to be primarily associated with immigrant disadvantages or with full blown religio-ethnic distinctiveness, and have been increasingly introduced as languages of study and research at the university, college, and public high school levels. Although bilingual public schools such as those that existed before the First World War have not been reintroduced (except on a very halting, belated and experimental basis), the bilingual college, or monolingual non-English college, which passed from the American scene at about the same time, has been reintroduced of late.[3] Seemingly, massive displacement has greater inhibitory

impact on language planning efforts than i does on language reinforcement efforts. Th latter are essentially conservative and seem t require less in the way of highly specialize leadership. The former are essentially modifica tory and dependent upon expert linguistic ac vice in concert with compliance producing c persuasive authority. Thus archaic or rusti orthographic, lexical and structural feature continue to characterize most non-Englis mother tongues spoken in the United State and interference proceeds apace, both becaus planning and enforcing authorities are lackin and because the old find it more difficult t adopt innovations.

Vocal advocates of language shift have pra tically disappeared, although institutional sup port for shift still exists along quiet but pe vasive lines. Religious bodies have been pa ticularly persistent in de-ethnicizing parish and anglifying church activities as they hav gained in institutional autonomy and centra ization. The Roman Catholic Church has bee most active along these lines whereas church in which non-English languages are rituall protected, like the Byzantine Rite Cathol or Eastern Orthodox churches, have, by con parison, remained relatively conservative i this respect. In general, religion has mo quickly and more successfully disassociate itself from ethnicity and arrived at indepen ent legitimization in the United States tha has the use of non-English mother tongue *per se.*

c. *Debilitating factors.*

Lest the immediately foregoing remarks b misinterpreted as an attack on religion in gen eral, or as an implication that religious organ tions have been particularly responsible (mos "causative") in conjunction with the enfeeble ment of language maintenance in the Unite States, let me hasten to indicate that such not the case. Elsewhere, I have spelled out i

---

[3] Experimental bilingual elementary grades were r cently attempted in Texas (1958–60) and are now bein conducted in Florida (1963–66). At the college level th University of the Pacific (Stockton, California) has esta lished Covell College in which Spanish is the language instruction in all classes. "The Ford Foundation Projects Bilingual Education," *The Modern Language Journal*, Vo XLVIII, No. 4 (April, 1964), pp. 239–241.

reat detail the major forces that seem to me to have been operative in this connection.[4] I will only mention them very briefly here:

Pre-contact factors. In general, very few pre-World War I immigrants to the United States brought with them an explicit valuation of their mother tongue. The majority came from pre-industrial, largely rural, peasant settings in which language, folkways, religion and husbandry were intertwined into a wholistic Little Tradition which provided little conscious or traditional preparation for language maintenance in American industrial metropoli. However, only a very few rural immigrants came with a conscious and separatist's commitment to their tradition. Of those who came from urban backgrounds, only a minority were deeply influenced by symbolically elaborated ethnicity (national-ism) which created Great Traditions and, in certain instances, converted languages into causes." In a majority of cases, city life had merely detradionalized and de-ethnicized those who later became immigrants, rather than having provided them with an ideological substitute for primordial ethnicity. Finally, the few that came with serious intellectual and emotional commitments to their language, culture and people rarely possessed a rationale which made such commitments pertinent to permanent interactive settlement in the United States. Interwar and post-World War II immigrants more frequently possessed urban backgrounds, familiarity with the standard version of their mother tongue, its literature and their national history. Nevertheless, they were even more de-traditionalized and de-ideologized from the point of view of commitment to diaspora maintenance of language, culture and people than earlier immigrants.

Host-society factors. The rapidly developing, manpower-hungry, industrial-commercial metropoli in which the majority of immigrants settled further weakened the traditional social relationships and pre-established role structures in which the use of their mother tongues was customarily involved.[5] In addition, American nationalism was primarily non-ethnic or supra-ethnic in comparison with the nationalisms of most of Europe. Consisting primarily of commitment to the ideals of American democracy, rationality in human affairs, political and social equality, unlimited individual and collective progress, it did not obviously clash with or demand the betrayal of immigrant *ethnic* values or patterns. In the absence of significant traditional, ideological or occupational separatism or exclusionism among either immigrants or hosts there were few reinforcers of language maintenance and few barriers to language shift.

The above thumb-nail sketches must not be hastily accepted as constituting a paradigm for the progress of language maintenance or language shift in all possible immigrant-based contact settings. It may be applicable only to those settings characterized by sharply unequal power configurations between immigrants and hosts, by incorporation as the type of control, by marked plurality and recent immigration as the plurality pattern, by intermediate stratification and substantial mobility within the social structure, and by widespread mutual legitimization of acculturation and de-ethnization as accompaniments of urbanization, industrialization, mass culture and ever-widening social participation. In general, we know (or suspect) much more about the dynamics of language maintenance and language shift in the American immigrant contact situation than we do about these processes in settings involving two indigenous populations utilizing more equally "official" languages; e.g., Riksmaal-Landsmaal in Norway, Spanish-Guarani in Paraguay, Schwyzertütsch-Romansh in Switzerland, Dutch-French in Belgium, Welsh and English in Wales, etc. This imbalance has resulted in a skewing of conclusions and concepts among students of language maintenance and language shift.[6] If the above-mentioned parameters have any general value this is due to the fact that they have revealed that language shift may be accompanied by a heightening of certain attitudinal, cognitive, and implementa-

---

[4] Joshua A. Fishman, "Language maintenance in a supra-ethnic age," in Fishman et al., *Language Loyalty in the United States*, Chapter 22.

[5] As of 1960 the national rate of urban residence was 70% whereas the rate among the foreign born was 84%. The discrepancy was even greater in former years.

[6] Joshua A. Fishman, "Language maintenance and language shift as a field of inquiry; a definition of the field and suggestions for its further development," *Linguistics*, No. 9 (November, 1964), pp. 32–70.

tional responses to languages that are being displaced. In general, ethnicity appears to be a much more stable phenomenon than language maintenance. On the one hand, most immigrants became bilingual (i.e., English displaced hitherto exclusive use of their mother tongue in connection with certain sources and domains of variance in language use) much before they embarked on de-ethnization or seriously contemplated the possibility of bi-culturism. On the other hand, marginal but yet functional ethnicity lingers on, and is transmitted via English, much after the ethnic mother tongue is completely lost or left untouched. Curiously enough, the lingering of marginal ethnicity supports respect, interest and nostaliga for the ethnic mother tongue. This development prompts language loyalists to entertain renewed hopes for revitalization even though displacement is far advanced. Thus, the very resultants of deep-reaching socio-cultural change also carry with them the seeds of further change and of counter-change.

II. *Implications for the Preservation of Bilingualism in the United States*

1. After many generations of neglect and apathy, American speakers of non-English languages have, of late, become objects of more positive attention than has previously been their common lot in most American communities. They have not been proclaimed national heroes, nor have they been the recipients of public or private largess. Indeed, for the general public, they continue to be objects of curiosity in that their atypicality is obvious even if it is no longer considered shameful. Nevertheless, the attitude toward them *has* changed. They are now more frequently viewed as commanding a gift, a rare commodity, a skill which has "suddenly" become a valuable asset for the country, and therefore, for themselves as individuals. As a result, there have been a number of recent efforts to study the distribution of this commodity and to consider ways of safeguarding it. The Language Resources Project itself may be viewed as one such effort; there have been a few others and there could be many more if it were fully and finally decided to pursue a consistent and effective policy of language maintenance, reinforcement

and development. We urgently need high level concern with the formulation of such a policy in full awareness of its purpose, its costs and its risks.

In view of our growing concern today for the protection and cultivation of bilingualism, let me say very frankly that we must guard against sentimentalizing bilingualism as much as against deprecating it. If bilingualism has its assets and if its protection and facilitation are related to our democratic values and our national needs, then let me add that bilingualism also has its costs and its debits. A brief review of the manifold differences between the 52 linguistically homogeneous and the 62 linguistically heterogeneous independent nations of today will quickly reveal that linguistics heterogeneity can be decidedly a mixed blessing.[7]

Linguistically homogeneous polities are economically more developed, educationally more advanced, politically more modernized, and ideologically-politically more tranquil and stable. They reveal more orderly, more libertarian and more secular forms of interest, articulation and aggregation, greater division of governmental powers, and less attraction toward personalismo and leadership charisma. All in all, linguistic homogeneity characterizes the nation-state in which primordial ties and passions are more frequently under control; cultural-religious homogeneity and enlightenment are more advanced, more modern forms of heterogeneity via associational, institutional and political groups are fostered, and the good life is economically within the reach of a greater proportion of the populace. If there is any fly in this ointment it is that some homogeneous polities have been in such a hurry to approach these desirable end-points that they have felt a need for more "decisive" authoritarian guidance in the political and economic areas in order to do so.

In general we find here the well-known relationships between industrialization, urbanization, modernization, westernization, Christianization and homogenization that has been explicated by modern political philosophy, history and sociology during the past century. In

[7] Joshua A. Fishman, *Some contrasts between linguistically homogeneous and linguistically heterogeneous polities* (Mimeographed and submitted for publication).

most instances linguistic and, more generally, cultural homogeneity has been interpreted as a consequence of the other processes and characteristics enumerated above. Linguistic and cultural parochialism and particularism have usually been interpreted as giving ground as man becomes ever more at home in the complexities of society on a larger and presumably higher scale. However, the cohesiveness of so many of the distinctions between linguistically homogeneous and heterogeneous polities prompts the question as to whether causal forces may not have been at work *in the opposite direction as well*. Is it possible that an appreciable level of linguistic and cultural homogeneity may have facilitated the "Westernization" of the West? This question (or more probably, this suspicion) must be in the minds of many planners in currently underdeveloped nations. It may require an exceptional concern, by force or by choice, for linguistic heterogeneity in order to preserve or reinforce such heterogeneity in the face of the obviously greater economic efficiency of linguistic homogeneity. It remains to be seen whether linguistically and culturally heterogeneous Africa and Asia can move forward significantly into the "modern world" without either bringing about or being helped along by the greater degrees of homogeneity recorded in Western experience.[8]

2. The problems of language maintenance in the United States are being considered at the very time that our country is convulsed as never before by the need to liberate millions of citizens from primordial restrictions of a particularly debilitating and shameful kind. This co-occurrence heaps additional difficulty upon any attempt to distinguish between various primoridal attachments and to strengthen some while weakening others. Since native linguistic competence cannot be preserved without preserving some form of strong paralinguistic difference, my discussion of language maintenance at this time runs the risk of eliciting charges of parochialism and ghettoization or worse. Actually, two different kinds of ghettos must be overcome. One is the parochialism of ethnic superiority which rejects change and egalitarian participation in the modern culture and in modern society at large. This type of

ghetto is far weaker in the United States than it has ever been, and it is becoming increasingly enfeebled. The other parochialism is that which considers everything ethnic to be foreign or worthless. This type of ghetto, regrettably, is still all too evident around us. The co-existence of these *two* kinds of parochialism implies that there is no easy route to language maintenance in the United States. Language maintenance in the United States is faced by the task of consciously strengthening certain carefully selected cultural *differences* at the same time that we strain to attain other carefully selected cultural similarities or equalities. Language maintenance must pursue both unity and diversity, both proximity and distance, both particularism and cosmopolitanism. However, in all of these respects, language maintenance is merely a reflection at the national-cultural level of a problem that every mature individual must solve within himself even when ethnic considerations are entirely absent.

The cultural and political unity of the United States seems to be sufficiently assured that there need be no fear of the spectre of "Balkanization" as a result of non-English language maintenance and "non-core" ethnic cultural diversity within sub-groups of the American population. There is no longer any reasonable basis upon which to fear an entrenchment on our shores of the political and economic cleavages which primordial cultural and linguistic diversity have forced upon Belgium or Canada in the West, or upon India and Ceylon in the East. A common pattern of commitment to and participation in American political processes and socio-cultural values has developed and has become increasingly established among almost all sub-groups within American society. Common patterns of food preference, of entertainment, of occupational aspiration, of dress, of education, and of language have become

[8] Let me add, parenthetically, that economic development is a much stronger "cause" of all the foregoing characteristics than is linguistic heterogeneity. Wealthy, linguistically heterogeneous nations are much more similar to wealthy linguistically homogeneous nations than they are to poor nations, whether linguistically homogeneous or heterogeneous. When level of economic development is controlled the only remaining correlates of linguistic heterogeneity *per se* are sectionalism and political enculturation.

ever more widely and deeply engrained. However, the process of strengthening these unities and communalities has proceeded so far as to endanger the cultural and linguistic diversity that many sub-groups desire and that may well benefit our national welfare and our cultural enrichment. Our political and cultural foundations are weakened when large population groupings do not feel encouraged to express, to safeguard and to develop behavioral patterns that are traditionally meaningful to them. Our national creativity and personal purposefulness are rendered more shallow when constructive channels of self-expression are blocked and when alienation from ethnic-cultural roots becomes the *necessary* price of self-respect and social advancement regardless of the merits of the cultural components under consideration. For those groups that desire it, there must be *openly sanctioned* and *publicly encouraged* avenues of linguistic and cultural distinctiveness which will provide both a general atmosphere as well as specific facilitation for diversity within the general framework of American unity. Mutual acceptance, permissiveness and support at an official policy level must be at the base of this diversity, rather than either functional exploitation in times of need or the mere absence of restriction alone. Certainly, now that the basic patterns of American nationhood are safely established and have momentum of their own, cultural and linguistic diversity deserves to be protected for its own sake, as a "good" of American reality and as a "given" of democratic sensitivity. Both a general atmosphere or climate and particular organizations or structures are required to bring such a state of affairs into being.

Elsewhere, I have made a number of detailed recommendations for the reinforcement of language maintenance in the United States.[9] These necessarily derive from my values and biases concerning the general worthwhileness of safeguarding linguistic and cultural diversity in American life. They also derive quite directly and necessarily from my values and biases concerning the spheres in which such diversity is desirable and the intensiveness with which language maintenance is to be pursued. Far different recommendations would flow from a model of American society which aimed at

securing cultural autonomy within an officially protected multi-language and multi-culture political framework. Far different recommendations would be offered on the basis of a desire to maintain major population groups on a fully intact, separate, monolingual, non-English speaking basis. No such *verzuiling* is desired;[10] nor is it a *sine qua non* for the successful pursuit of language maintenance. Every nation, new or old, that engages in language maintenance efforts must define the domains in which cultural and linguistic unity must receive precedence over cultural and linguistic diversity. Every nation, developing or developed, that pursues planned reinforcement of language maintenance must decide on the appropriateness of extensive vs. intensive efforts toward that goal.

My recommendations, which I will merely enumerate rather than discuss, neither envision nor seek the disestablishment of English as the common language of American unity and as the basic language of American culture, government and education for all Americans. Rather, they have in mind the planned reinforcement of non-English languages and their underlying non-core cultures for those who desire them, for those who are willing and able to expend considerable efforts and sums of their own to maintain institutions and organizations of their own on behalf of their languages and cultures, and for those who are willing to do so within a framework of mutual interaction with American core society and its democratically maintained and developed institutions and processes. Thus, not only is cultural pluralism espoused but cultural bilingualism, rather than merely functional bilingualism *per se*, is focused upon. Non-English languages and non-core cultures are considered to be maintainable and reinforceable primarily within the spheres of American-ethnic family life, within the spheres of the self-defined American-ethnic community, self-defined American ethnic-school and cul-

---

[9] Joshua A. Fishman, "Planned reinforcement of language maintenance in the United States; suggestions for the conservation of a neglected national resource," in Fishman et al., *Language Loyalty in the United States*, Chapter 21.

[10] D. O. Moberg, "Social differentiation in the Netherlands," *Social Forces*, Vol. 39, No. 4 (May, 1961), pp. 333–337.

tural organization, under the direction of the self-defined American-ethnic teacher, writer, artist and cultural or communal leader. Both language maintenance and ethnicity have become and must remain entirely voluntaristic behaviors in the United States. Their ideological mainsprings must derive from an interpretation of Americanism, American culture and American national well being. However, such behaviors and interpretations are particularly dependent on an encouraging and facilitating environment. It is to recommendations for such encouragement and facilitation, leading to language maintenance for such populations and in such spheres, that we will turn our attention.

3. *Ingredients of a policy of planned reinforcement of language maintenance in the United States.*

a. *Establishing a climate for language maintenance.*

(i) Statements by high public officials to the *general public* that cultural differences, here and now, on an every day as well as on a "high culture" and festive level, are meaningful, desirable and worth strengthening.

(ii) The establishment of a "Commission on Biculturism (or Bilingualism) in American Life" with national, regional, and local subdivisions to publicize bilingualism and mobilize opinion and action in favor of it.

(iii) The establishment of ethnic neighborhoods and settlements as national monuments.

b. *Specific support of language maintenance*

(i) Encouragement of "country of origin-contacts" on the part of naturalized citizens and their families: visits, clubs, courses, publications, language maintenance prizes.

(ii) Encouragement of immigration to the United States by language loyalists, cultural leaders, language teachers, etc., more intelligent immigration policy oriented toward skills rather than toward national origins.

(iv) Financial and other aid to language maintenance organizations and efforts of American ethnic groups: schools, press, radio, theatres, camps, etc.

(v) Public school effort: (a) attraction of native speakers to language teaching, and greater diversification of languages taught; (b) preparation of special teaching materials

for the bilingual child; (c) granting of credit for out-of-school language mastery; (d) establishment of bilingual public schools, etc.

(vi) The establishment of a "Department of Language Maintenance" in the United States Office of Education.

4. *Conclusions:* It is odd indeed that a nation that prides itself on "know how," resourcefulness and ingenuity should be so helpless with respect to deepening and strengthening its own inner life. We laugh at the taboos of "backward" peoples and pride ourselves on our own rational procedures. Yet, in the entire area of ethnicity and language maintenance we are constrained by a taboo stronger than those which govern our sexual or racial mores. Sex problems and race issues are discussed in the press, debated in Congress, studied in schools and accorded consideration by foundations. In the area of ethnicity, however, wise men react as children: with denial, with rejection, with repression. If language loyalty and ethnicity had truly ceased to function in major segments of American intellectual and cultural life, if they really evoked no pained or puzzled feelings of responsibilities unmet and sensitivities undeveloped, these topics would receive far more open, more dispassionate, and more imaginative consideration. Fortunately and unfortunately this is not yet the case.

Many American intellectuals reveal particular ambivalence or hostility in connection with discussions, whether at a theoretical or applied level, concerning ethnic or ethno-religious participation in the United States. Many American intellectuals are themselves of second and third generation background. More than most of their countrymen they are likely to have been "liberated," intellectually and overtly, if not emotionally, from the claims and constraints of many primordial ties and biases. As a result, they are more unlikely than most Americans to take kindly to serious consideration of the *values* of ethnic-religious participation, not to mention consideration of ways and means of reinforcing such participation. To the extent that they acknowledge pervasive value commitments beyond those directly related to their own academic specialties these commitments usually take the form of assisting various population groups to gain liberation from constraints that impede their full participation in higher levels of social-cultural life. However, the particular ethnocentric ingredients of this value commitment usually remain unexamined. Such commitments may well assume the complete relevance of the intellectuals' own experiences and convictions as a goal for their own countrymen and for all of mankind. The very completeness of their own divestment from ethnicity and religion may prompt all-or-none distinctions between primordiality and modernity, between particularism and cosmopolitanism, to the end that reality is severely misconstrued. For most of mankind these distinct guiding forces are in constant and complementary interaction. Indeed, these forces are in a world-wide process of mutual accommodation, each providing benefits and exacting tolls unknown to the other. The problem of ethnically based language maintenance in the United States, or in various other developed or developing nations, is precisely the problem of readjusting an unbalance between these two forces so as to permit all men to benefit more freely, more creatively, and more maturely from each, rather than from only one or the other.

On the basis of data obtained by the Language Resources Project and on the basis of impressions gained in the pursuit and analysis of these data it would seem that there are still good prospects of maintaining or attaining cultural bilingualism among many different carefully selected sub-groups of ethnic background in the United States. It would also seem that these groups can be so selected, over and above their self-selection, and so instructed that the advantages, vis-à-vis bilingual facility, of having an ethnic mother tongue would be considerable in comparison with otherwise matched groups of monolingual English speakers. Thus, the problem is rather less whether or not this *can* be done than it is one of whether or not it *should* be done. In many ways human talents are like other resources: they must be discovered and preserved if they are to be available. However, in other ways, human talents are quite unique; they can be prompted, augmented and *created* by appropriate recognition, training and reward. Within every language group studied there are sub-groups consciously ready, willing and able to benefit from a more favorable "language policy" in the United States. The adoption of such a policy would itself create additional sub-groups of similar capacity, above and beyond those currently discernible.

In her fascinating volume *New Lives for Old*,[11] Margaret Mead points out that Western interest in preserving the "quaint" customs and cultures of primitive peoples has often been no more than a thinly disguised means of excluding these people from independent regulation of their own affairs and from reaping the fruits of their own personal and natural resources. Certainly, every people must have the right to reject its past, to break sharply with its heritage and to adopt a new way of life. However, just as "guided traditionalism" may be a subterfuge for exploitation and the prolongation of backwardness, so "guided acculturation" may be a subterfuge serving exactly the same ulterior purposes. Either approach can be used for the self-aggrandizement of the "powers that be." Neither approach is calculated to develop freedom of choice or creative cultural evolution.

Language maintenance in America does not require, nor would it benefit from, the forced ghettoization of linguistic groups. However, neither will it benefit from the non-productive sentimentality of ethnicity for one day a year, from the instrumentalism of "anti-communist letters to the homeland" to influence elections, or from the pollyanna-like pageantry in which little children sing and dance bedecked in partly mythical and wholly archaic folk costumes. Language maintenance will benefit only from explicit and substantial public recognition of its value and its legitimacy, and from public support for those willing and able to engage in it. The same must be said for ethnicity, with the additional emphasis that without greater recognition for meaningful, evolving ethnicity, there can be no enduring or widespread language maintenance in the United States.

Ethnicity in America is not an all-or-none affair. Nor is it a logical affair. Nor is it at all understandable or describable in Old World terms alone. For some it is composed of half forgotten memories, unexplored longings, and intermittent preferences. For others, it is active, structured, elaborated and constant. For

[11] Margaret Mead, *New Lives for Old* (New York: William Morrow and Company, 1956).

me it is exclusionary and isolating. For others is an avenue toward more secure and more thentic participation in general American fairs. For some it is hidden and has negative conflicted overtones. For others it is open, sitive and stimulating. For some it is archaic, changing and unalterable. For others it is olving and creative. For some it is a badge of ame to ignore, forget and eradicate. For hers it is a source of pride, a focus of initial valties and integrations from which broader yalties and wider integrations can proceed. ot all modes of ethnicity contribute to lan- age maintenance, but many do. All in all, the riation and variability of ethnicity in Amer- a today are largely unknown. This represents stumbling block to the American sociologist applied linguist whose approaches to ethnic- y are usually far too simple and far too con- scending. It represents a major gap in our ility to understand or facilitate language aintenance. Above all else, however, the ab- nce of such knowledge represents an area of lf-ignorance for all Americans— philosophers, holars, and laymen alike. It is certainly high me that we begin to know ourselves, accept rselves, and shape ourselves in this area just realistically and just as determinedly as we ve tried to do in many other areas in recent ars.

"The point about the melting pot is that it did not happen. . . . The fact is that in every generation, throughout the history of the American Republic, the merging of the varying streams of population differentiated from one another by origin, religion, outlook has seemed to lie just ahead—a generation, perhaps, in the future. This continual deferral of the final smelting of the different ingredients . . . suggests that we must search for some systematic and general cause for this American pattern of sub-nationalities . . . which structures people, whether those coming in afresh or the descendants of those who have been here for generations, into groups of different status and character.[12]

The above observations require only minor extension from the point of view of this presentation, namely, that precisely because they are true, after two centuries of pretence to the contrary, it is high time that the diversity of American existence were recognized and channeled more conscientiously into a creative force, rather than be left as something shameful and to be denied, at worst, or something mysterious and to be patronized, at best. Rethinking our unwritten language policy and our unproclaimed ethnic philosophy in this light may yet bring forth fresh and magnificent fruits.

[12] N. Glazer and P. D. Magnahan, *Beyond the Melting Pot*, Cambridge; Massachusetts Institute of Technology and Harvard University Press, 1963, pp. 290–91.

A NEW FOCUS ON THE BILINGUAL CHILD

Theodore Andersson

A New Focus on the Bilingual Child*

Theodore Andersson, *University of Texas*

EVERY professional group needs periodically to pause to take stock, to focus anew, and to make a fresh start. I believe that this is an opportune moment for modern-foreign-language teachers to do just this.

To many it will appear that with the passage of the National Defense Education Act in 1958 the teaching of modern languages has just taken such a new direction. This is true. We *have* plotted a new course to follow, but we are still far from having persuaded all—or perhaps even a majority—of our colleagues that the new objectives are better than the old. There are still many language teachers who believe that in stressing understanding and speaking in the early stages of a second-language learning we will inevitably neglect reading and writing and especially the study of literature. Nothing could be farther from the truth. On the contrary, we believe that a sound basis in hearing, understanding, and speaking will assure better achievement in reading and writing, and will permit a more intimate understanding of literature and indeed of other aspects of a foreign culture.

But while our profession still needs to work hard to consolidate the theoretical gains envisaged by the Foreign Language Program of the Modern Language Association of America and by the Congress of the United States in its National Defense Education Act and succeeding legislation, we need to foresee and plan our next advance.

The language laboratory, television, and teaching machine enthusiasts will perhaps envision our next step as a harnessing of these technological devices for the greater efficiency of teaching. I am completely in favor of continuing to study and experiment with these and other devices, which should be made to serve language teachers and learners more efficiently. Programed instruction appeals to me particularly, for two reasons. In order to program material successfully, a teacher needs to observe and test the learners' reaction to the materials which will have the inevitable effect of improving his teaching. And secondly, self-instruction with the aid of a machine puts the chief responsibility for learning on the student, which is where it belongs.

Important as is the progress represented by the audio-lingual emphasis in language teaching and by the proper ancillary use of the language laboratory, television, and of programed self-instruction, it is rather in another area that we can hope for a more important new advance in language learning. In giving our attention to the bilingual child, we have perceived the importance of solving serious educational problems for those of our children whose first language is not English. It is precisely in this area I believe, that we have our best chance to score a real educational breakthrough.

Dr. Joshua A. Fishman has estimated in his recently concluded report on *Language Loyalty in the United States*[1] that there were in 1960 some nineteen million native speakers of European languages other than English in the United States, or eleven per cent of our entire population. The figure would be considerably increased if it included speakers of all other languages. We have at a guess speakers of more than fifty different languages, not only the well known European languages such as Italian spoken, according to the conservative 1960 census figures, by more than three and a half million; Spanish, spoken by nearly three and a half million; German, spoken by over three million; Polish, spoken by over two million; and French, spoken by over one million, but also such languages as Eskimo, in Alaska; Chinese,

* Presented at the Conference for the Teacher of the Bilingual Child, University of Texas, June 9, 1964.

[1] A mimeographed report, in three volumes, to the Language Research Section of the United States Office Education.

156

apanese, Hawaiian, Visayan, Tagolog, and ortuguese, in Hawaii, and more than a dozen merican Indian and Asian languages in addition to all the European languages, spoken in e continental United States. It is a matter of ational as well as professional interest for us to eserve these languages and to provide their eakers with an education which takes them operly into account. In this vital and complex adertaking modern language teachers have a antral role to play; but they need the help of lleagues in the social sciences—linguists, sychologists, anthropologists, and sociologists and in professional education and politics. or, as Joshua Fishman has written, "the preservation and revitalization of America's nonanglish language resources (even for the purse of cultural bilingualism) requires, first and remost, several planned modifications in the als and processes of American society." (Vol. I, last chapter, p. 12.)

Without dwelling too long on our past and esent sins in foreign-language education let rather select seven "deadly" sins which most gently need correction and which bilingual lucation, if well conceived and executed, can lp us eliminate.

Let us first try to put behind us the almost eless two-year sequence of foreign-language udy in our high schools. Our need of language mpetence in this shrunken world is surely as eat as that of European nations, where reign languages—and usually more than one are studied from four to ten years. And in eading for a six-year high-school sequence of idy for a modern foreign language I should e also to plead for a four-year sequence for eek and/or Latin. The present two-year sequence serves only to guarantee a slow death for e classics, for it fails to provide a reservoir of udents from which must be recruited future assics teachers. The classics today are as badly as were the modern languages in 1930 after e notorious Coleman Report had "settled" a two-year sequence of study in high school. The late start made in learning modern languages in school is the second sin which needs be eliminated. Most pupils begin at the age fourteen or fifteen, when the human mind is ast receptive to this kind of learning. If Euro-

pean children can continue foreign-language study for as much as ten years, it is because they begin at the age of ten to twelve, or even earlier now. Justification for an early start, resting on psychological, neurological, social, political, and economic grounds, is to be found in a report published by the UNESCO Institute for Education in Hamburg in 1963 entitled *Foreign Languages in Primary Education: the Teaching of Foreign or Second Languages to Younger Children.*

The non-existence in many communities of public kindergartens and nursery schools is sin number three. Educational psychologists are so well aware of the sensitivity of three-, four-, and five-year-old children and therefore of the educational importance of these early years that one is surprised not to hear more frequent protests against this educational waste. These years would be particularly valuable for language learning, for we know that children of this age can, under ideal conditions, absorb as many languages as are spoken in a given environment. The exploratory language class, which was doomed to fail in our junior high schools, belongs here if it belongs anywhere.

Our traditional misconception of language almost exclusively in terms of grammar, reading, writing, and *belles lettres* is the fourth sin crying for elimination. Without for a moment underestimating the value of literacy and literature, teachers who understand the nature of language and the process of language learning believe that the learning of speech should precede that of writing, especially for the young learner; that the learning of usage by direct imitation of authentic models should precede the formal study of grammar; and that literature should be studied not less intensively but in relation to other aspects of a culture.

Our sin number five is our preference to hire John Smith over Juan Suárez for a Spanish-teaching vacancy for which both are otherwise equally well qualified but for which Juan Suárez offers an additional qualification: his authentic Spanish. Just as a student needs an authentic speaker as a model, so he needs as a teacher an authentic, well educated representative of another culture if he is to be imbued by direct experience with some intimate understanding of this culture. We should therefore reserve on our teaching staffs a larger place for well qualified native-speaking teachers of foreign languages. In Texas, where Spanish is widely taught in the schools—though not extensively enough—and where at least one Texan out of seven speaks Spanish natively, only about one out of four teachers of Spanish is a native speaker of Spanish. One out of two would be a better ratio to aim at immediately. I know of one high school in a non-Spanish-speaking area which has reached the ratio of two out of three to the satisfaction of all concerned.

Our inflexible, credit-counting education of teachers constitutes a sixth sin. Certification should be no substitute for qualification, especially now that we have the Modern Language Association Foreign Language Proficiency Tests for Teachers and Advanced Students to help us measure proficiency as objectively as possible.

Coming a little closer to home, we must confess to our seventh education sin: our failure to encourage our Spanish-speaking children to speak Spanish, as we commonly do in school and on the playground, and our failure to respect the great Hispanic culture of which our Spanish speakers are modest representatives. This is part of an unthinking, inconsiderate, and self-defeating national policy to destroy non-English languages and cultures in the United States—whether French, German, and Spanish or Eskimo, Navaho, and Hawaiian. While paying generous lip service to respect for individual differences, we have to the present made little effort even to understand the special needs of our non-English-speaking citizens. In this connection let me call to your attention an unpublished paper by my colleague, Dr. Mildred Boyer, on the subject of "Individual Differences and the War on Poverty,"[1] which is calculated to deepen our understanding of this problem. We show our disregard for other languages by not learning them. We tend to equate Hispanic culture, for example, with the under developed, disadvantaged standard of living of Spanish speakers among us without taking thought as to what is responsible for this depressed living standard. It is the culmination of irony that where Spanish-speaking children are at an age that would make it easy and rela-

tively inexpensive to help them to maintain and improve their language we do all we can to destroy it. And when we do find that we need adult citizens in great numbers who can understand and speak Spanish or other languages, we must through legislation repair at great cost the damage we have thoughtlessly done.

To rehearse our principal shortcomings in language education, especially as it relates to Spanish-speaking children, is already to point the way to needed reform. Fortunately we have the benefit of the knowledge and experience of many individuals: psychologists, sociologists, language educators, professional educators, educational administrators, and others. It is easy for a college professor while standing comfortably aloof from the fray to discourse on what should be done. The practical educators must restore a balance and bring us back to a sense of reality as needed.

At the risk of occasionally offending this sense of reality, let me in conclusion sketch a course of action which theory suggests would be appropriate at least in Texas and perhaps in other parts of the Southwest, and also to any other educational system which enrolls in substantial numbers children whose first language is not English. Later discussion and experimentation will reveal whether the theory of my rough plan is sound and whether it can stand the test of experimentation in a variety of real situations.

Since both theory and previous experiments, described, for example, in the UNESCO publication, *The Use of the Vernacular Languages in Education*, suggest the rightness and the effectiveness of using a child's mother tongue to begin his formal schooling, I suggest that it is most logical that Spanish-speaking children and their parents be oriented for school and be greeted in school by teachers who speak Spanish natively. Instruction should be done in Spanish and in English in such proportion as to build the child's sense of security. For the child whose experience has been exclusively or nearly exclusively in Spanish and who therefore understands and speaks Spanish within the limits of his experience, the teacher's first educational objectives should be to expand the pupil's ex-

[1] Forthcoming in *Educational Forum* under a modified title.

erience in order to increase his mastery of poken Spanish and to begin, when he is ready, o teach the elements of reading and writing in panish. A reasonable period of time every day hroughout the whole period of schooling hould be reserved for Spanish so that the child ay steadily increase his control of oral comrehension, speaking, reading, writing, and rammar, as well as an understanding of the terature and culture of his heritage. The ultiate objective would be thorough literacy in panish, as well as in English, the development f a sense of pride in identifying with Hispanic ulture, and an active desire to maintain and ultivate the Spanish language and culture, hile at the same time cultivating skill and ride in American speech and culture.

Since at the outset the average Spanisheaking child will know little or no English, he ould be introduced very gradually into Engsh with great care not to destroy his security d confidence.

Those who have seen adult college students espair because they cannot with their deient knowledge of English penetrate the rriers of intellectual and even physical isolaon can well realize the terror which must eset a small child entering upon his first hooling without even the warming comfort of understanding and affectionate word in a nguage which previously served him thus.

There need be no apprehension concerning s ultimate capacity to speak English. The ain medium of instruction in most schools will English, so that the Spanish-speaking child ll normally have ample opportunity to hear d, when ready, to speak English. How long will require to develop a readiness for readg and writing in English will have to be demined experimentally. However, as soon as is ready, perhaps in the second grade, he ould begin and thereafter receive steadily ineased instruction and opportunity to practice. The development in each language should be quential and properly paced and should proed in such a way that each reinforces the her. Theoretically the best results may be excted in schools having approximately equal mbers of English and Spanish speakers. glish-speaking pupils can learn to under-

stand and speak Spanish while the Spanish speakers learn to understand and speak English. In this situation the children will teach each other informally but perhaps even more effectively than can the teachers.

Since such a language program should have for its goal not only to teach English as a second language to Spanish speakers and Spanish as a second—hopefully no longer a foreign—language to English speakers, but also to safeguard our children's mental health and to correct popular misconceptions concerning the nature of language, the process of language learning, and the nature and content of culture, the parents and indeed the whole community would need to be brought into the program. In this somewhat new extension of the usual educational process language teachers and educational administrators will need the help or social scientists and even public relations specialists. Educators cannot afford in an operation of this kind to leave the community in ignorance of what is happening lest the old misconceptions, prejudices, or lethargy destroy our efforts.

Clearly, in all this the language teacher plays a central though only a partial role. For this reason it is urgent that teacher education institutions undertake at the earliest to recruit and prepare teachers with the necessary wisdom, personality, knowledge, and skill to carry out such a program. Such teacher candidates, who may already understand and speak Spanish competently, should not be delayed by being forced into a lock-step program of teacher preparation. Following the *Standards for Teacher-Education Programs in Modern Foreign Languages* recently issued by the Modern Language Association as the result of a conference at its administrative offices in New York on December 13, 1963, the most promising teachers or teacher candidates should be sought out and prepared in a flexible, almost individual, program and licensed to teach at the earliest possible moment on the basis of demonstrated proficiency, however acquired. Such a pilot program is in its initial stage at The University of Texas under the direction of Dr. Joseph Michel.

These then, in conclusion, are the possibilities facing educators in bilingual areas. We have really been discussing two subjects. First we need to correct our present miseducation of Spanish speakers in the South and Southwest; and secondly, once we have learned how to manage the language education of bilinguals, we need to apply the same principles to la guage education in general. A new focus on t bilingual child could well serve to trigger an ir portant revolution in American education.

THE ACCULTURATION
OF THE BILINGUAL CHILD

Chester C. Christian, Jr.

The Acculturation of the Bilingual Child*

CHESTER C. CHRISTIAN, JR., *Texas Western College*

IN CONSIDERING the acculturation of the bilingual child, we should bear in mind that he almost invariably begins by being a monolingual child, and as such offers us no more special problems than any so-called "normal" child. He learns the language of his parents and becomes a member of their culture just as all children do. The special problems to be considered are those created when this first language and culture are supplemented or even replaced by a second language and culture which are imposed upon him by the larger society. His parents require him to go through the first process, and the school system requires him to go through the second. He is not at liberty to refuse to do either. When he's one year old, he doesn't tell his parents, "No, I won't speak your language. It's better for me to begin learning English immediately." And when he's six years old, he doesn't tell his teacher, "No, I'm not going to speak English. I already get along quite well in my own language, thank you." By birth, he must speak the language of his parents, because he has to communicate with them. By law, he must speak English, for he has to spend at least ten years of his life in a school system in which English is the only medium of instruction. To the extent that he suffers as a result of the concomitant pressures put on him, he is a victim of this social situation into which he has been born. He himself has done nothing to create it, he doesn't understand it, and we should have no cause for surprise when he reacts against his parents or his teachers or both. Since he is not able to function effectively within either culture so long as he feels that it is imposed upon him, it seems desirable to attempt to work out a solution of his problems not only for his benefit, but to enable him to contribute to the maintenance of our society and the development of our culture.

In attempting to do this, the fact has often been ignored that to human beings born into any language and culture, that language and culture represent their own existence as human beings—their own particular way of being human—and that taking this away from them is in a very real sense an attempt to take away their lives—an attempt to destroy what they are and to make of them a different kind of being. This is true even when they are willing to assist in this process of destruction.

In the first six years of his life, the child undergoes a process of acculturation which imprints its effects much more indelibly than any other process he will go through in the remainder of his life. Through the learning and use of the language of his parents, he learns not only to obtain certain fundamental satisfactions, such as those of sustenance and human response, but he learns to organize and give meaning to all that he perceives through his senses. He may even say without exaggeration that it is through this process that the child becomes a human being. He does not become a person except by becoming a certain kind of person, and the kind of person he becomes—even the nature of what he perceives—is dependent upon the words he uses and the meanings which have been given to them by the culture of which he is a part. In the words of a contemporary Spanish writer, the child comes to "think the world by means of the word." And that world which comes to exist in his mind is a reflection of the language he speaks and of the culture it repre-

* Presented at the Conference for the Teacher of the Bilingual Child, University of Texas, June 8-10, 1964.

sents; it is a world bequeathed to him by a particular historical process of which he is the most recent product, it is the most meaningful heritage that his parents can give him. It will come to represent to him not only the essential nature of human life, but his own existence as an individual. One might easily predict that it will not be easy to do away with it. He may be made ashamed of it and may even learn to despise it, but it will remain with him for the rest of his life.

The meanings which have been given to him in one culture do not exist in other cultures, and therefore cannot be replaced. It is a fallacy, for example, to assume that there is an English equivalent for the Spanish word *mamá*—or that there is a Spanish equivalent for the English word *mama*. These and hundreds of other words which give to the child his existence in terms of his relation to others and to the world occur in cultural contexts which do not coincide. And teachers who do not know these meanings usually find the response of the pupil who knows no others baffling, annoying, and exasperating. Then, when the child begins to discover that the teacher does not understand, he develops negative reactions not only to the teacher but to the educational process, and finally to the entire culture and language which the teacher represents. Or conversely, he may decide that his parents have provided him with an inferior world, and subsequently attempt to reject entirely what they have provided for him as a cultural base upon which to build a meaningful life. This may mean that the life he chooses will lack the essential meanings which have their roots in infancy, roots which are nourished by the words his parents have taught him.

It is a personal tragedy, and there is much evidence to indicate that it is a social tragedy, when an adult resents and even despises the language and culture of his childhood. Bossard and Boll, in their study of the sociology of child development, tell of cases in which children avoid meeting their parents in public because they were unable to speak English with them. "The child who rejects the parental language rejects, as it were, the parent who speaks it."[1]

When the social scientist speaks of acculturation, he usually refers to a process of mutual influence of two cultures which are in contact.

Practically speaking, however, we generally imply a process of changing emphasis and changing loyalties from one language and culture to another, and more specifically, the change in language and culture of a conquered group to that of the conqueror. This is often said to be necessary to promote uniformity. But, as the anthropologist Kroeber has remarked, "Much modern acculturation of minorities is directed by the majority culture, and their assimilation is consciously furthered as something desirable. Uniformity has a way of commending itself to majorities."[2]

In view of what we can learn from human history, this is not at all surprising. The conquered have always had to learn the language of the conqueror in order to gain advantage from him. The conqueror has never been able to afford to pass through the somewhat ridiculous stage of floundering in the language—and culture—of those he has conquered. It might not only damage his prestige, but once peaceful and stable relations were established it might allow those he has conquered to compete quite successfully with him.

We in the United States have had what looks on the surface like quite another philosophy of acculturation. The popular idea of the "melting pot" is that all cultures in the United States should fuse to become our one great common culture. But this does not seem to be what has happened. What seems to have happened is that people from many cultures have come here looking for what their own countries have not offered them, and they have been willing to give up much of their culture for the sake of expedience in getting what they want. Many of them have not realized what they have given up until they have seen how far the children are willing to carry the process the parents have begun. Expediency has begotten expediency, until we have developed a culture which has been one of great practical success, which has made possible the dehumanization which urban industrial life requires to operate at its greatest efficiency, one in which the person identifies

[1] James Herbert Siward Bossard and Eleanor Stoker Boll, *Sociology of Child Development*, New York: Harper and Brothers, 1960, 3rd edition, p. 272.

[2] Alfred L. Kroeber, *Anthropology*, New York: Harcourt, Brace and Co., Inc., 1947, p. 434.

himself with the function he is performing in society—with the job at hand—rather than with his historical, cultural, and linguistic antecedents. The negation of traditional cultural forms has allowed their replacement by cultural forms adapted to the immediate technological situation. This has undoubtedly been an important factor contributing to our unequalled material success, but it has left us with few roots. It has left us with an existence which, from the point of view of other cultures, often seems shallow, crass, and provincial.

Paradoxically enough, however, our material success has been so great that we seem to be turning toward non-material goals in our culture as a luxury we can now afford. We are living the abundant life as no other nation in the history of mankind has ever lived it, but many of us are unable to enjoy this wealth fully as long as we feel that some are not sharing it. We are taking a broader view of the nature of the abundant life. We are even coming to the conclusion that other cultures than that which dominates here may have an intrinsic and irreplaceable value.

Not long ago our government was so insistent that the Indians become acculturated that whenever possible they separated the children from the influence of their parents by putting them into boarding schools and not allowing them to speak the language they had learned at home. This experiment was not successful, but if we had been able to take the children from their parents as soon as they were born, it probably would have been. However, this type of acculturation is no longer felt to be desirable; and at present some Indian groups are now encouraged to retain their language and learn through it about their own culture—that is, the culture of their parents. In some federally sponsored schools, they are even taught in their native language, and in terms of their own background learn English and are introduced to Anglo-American culture. Dr. James Officer, Associate Commissioner of Indian Affairs, in a report to the Tucson Conference on Teaching English as a Foreign Language (May, 1964), indicated that this appears to be a much more satisfactory solution of the problem of acculturation than any previously tried. The pupil seems more secure, the parents less resentful,

and the result is a greater benefit to society.

Some of the conclusions which were derived from a conference called in November, 1963, by the then Vice President of the United States Lyndon B. Johnson, as Chairman of the President's Committee on Equal Employment Opportunity, also show the new direction the government is taking with respect to the acculturation of minorities in the United States. It was decided at this meeting that the schools should capitalize on the bi-cultural situation in the Southwest rather than ignore it or even attempt to stamp it out. It was felt desirable to erase the "reigning Anglo" stereotype, to recognize the value of the Mexican cultural heritage, and to show the Mexican-American why he should be proud of his cultural background and recognize himself as capable of offering something extra to the culture at large. At that conference Anthony J. Celebrezze, Secretary of Health, Education, and Welfare, was moderator of a discussion group in which it was decided that "schools must provide acculturation for Mexican-American children through bilingual instruction in Spanish and English, and must make use of the curriculum to reflect Spanish as well as American traditions, and should hire teachers trained in both cultures. Only through such a modified educational program can the Mexican-American child be given the sense of personal identification which is necessary to his educational maturation."[3] It was also suggested that schools employ bilingual counselors who would go into the homes of bilingual children to discuss the educational and personal problems of the children in terms which the parents can understand.

Heretofore, the problem of the acculturation of the bilingual child has been considered largely a local problem. It has recently become a problem of national concern largely because of its intimate relationship to other national programs—with the civil rights program, the war on poverty, the attempt to establish equal economic opportunity for everyone, to adjust to automation and to the disappearance of jobs except for the educated, and to the betterment of our image abroad. New methods of dealing

[3] Quoted from the oral summary of the conference proceedings read by John W. Macy, Jr., Chairman, United States Civil Service Commission.

h the problem have not come about as a re-
: of a sudden impulse or sudden illumination
the part of our social and political leaders.
ey have been suggested as a result of the
sideration of present-day necessities in the
t of past trial and error. It has been found
t neither ignoring cultural differences nor at-
pting to do away forcibly with minority
guages and cultures has been successful in
eloping the personal and social potential-
s of the bilingual child.

'here is also a new attitude in a nation which
in the past few years become more secure in
lf, more expansive, and more understanding
ther peoples. This new attitude is well ex-
ssed by Morris Raphael Cohen in his
obiography: "I have never been able to
re the views of my fellow citizens who look
n the very existence of a foreign press as a
: of treason, who would make the speaking or
ting of a foreign language a crime. These
ple are doubtlessly influenced by patriotic
tives, but their conception of Americanism is
narrow and unworthy of the great tradition
American liberalism. The patriotism of these
ple is a narrow nationalism copied from, or
imitation of, European nationalism. The
erican tradition is federalism, which allows
diversity instead of dull uniformity. The
y name 'United States' and our motto,
Pluribus Unum' express this."[4]

'his paragraph is particularly important in
t it was quoted by the Hearing Examiner for
Federal Communications Commission as a
t of a decision made last year to give a per-
to an English language rather than a Span-
language radio station to broadcast from a
' in Texas.[5] The decision clearly shows the
iod of transition through which we are
ng. The technical basis of its being in favor
the English language station was the
tence of a public policy in Texas expressed
he laws stating that all teaching in public
ools in Texas must be in English, and that
children between the ages of 7 and 16 must
nd public schools unless they attend a
ate or parochial school in which classes
st be taught in English. The Hearing Ex-
ner stated that this law is itself based upon
fact that it seems desirable to promote what
termed "mutual understanding" in the

United States, and he thought that such understanding requires the greatest possible use of
English.

The Hearing Examiner, however, qualified
this decision by a statement which points in a
direction our government as a whole seems to
be taking. He stated that he might have
lessened the emphasis on this public school law
of Texas if those who requested the Spanish
language station had focused more on the
Spanish-speaking community as a culture
group, giving evidence that it is a vigorous cultural unit, and "indicating that an all-Spanish
radio station would have contributed substantially to its growth as an admirable factor
in a nation which appreciates cultural diversity." He said, however, that the testimony in
favor of the Spanish language station "scarcely
mentioned, if at all (as one possibility) any
artistic stirrings within the group which would
leaven the picture, inevitable on the basis of
this record, of a deprived, submerged people."

The fact that such communities in our Southwest are so often composed of "deprived, submerged people" may well be due to the fact that
our educational system does not allow their
children to build upon the linguistic and cultural system which has been provided for them
by their parents. This condition might be recti-
fied by the introduction of a process of acculturation which would conform to the definition
given by social scientists: the mutual influence
of cultures in contact. We would modify the
educational system so that the pupil may develop as far as possible in each of the two cultures represented by the languages he speaks.
This might become a process in which knowledge and sensitivity obtained in one culture
could develop even further than it otherwise
would as a result of insights obtained through
the other culture. This would seem much pref-
erable to the blocking of development in each
culture because of the limitations one has in the

[4] Morris Rafael Cohen, *A Dreamer's Journey*, Boston:
Beacon Press, 1949, p. 220.

[5] Initial Decision, FCC 63D-46, by Hearing Examiner
Herbert Sharfman, April 19, 1963, re: Applications of J. R.
Earnest and John A. Flache, c/b as *La Fiesta Broadcasting
Company* (Docket No. 14411, File No. BP-14116) and
Mid-Cities Broadcasting Corporation (Docket No. 14412,
File No. BP-15073), both of Lubbock, Texas.

other—which is the situation of several million United States citizens at the present time.

We often fail to realize that those who speak a language other than English are thereby psychologically and culturally prepared to enter a realm of thought, feeling, imagination which is different from that available to them in English, but which is not therefore less important to their development. Among the Spanish-speaking, for example, this preparation might enable them to enter this world through the works of Cervantes in a much more real and intimate sense than they will ever be able to do through the works of Shakespeare. Since it is this world which releases the creative potentialities of our men and women of genius, it may be that by cutting off their development toward entry into it by any door other than English, we are destroying whatever significant contributions to it that a bilingual child might potentially make.

It is sometimes said that physicians have an advantage over members of other professions in that they can bury their mistakes. We might say that we teachers, however, have an even greater advantage in that our mistakes will usually bury themselves. Our successes flower into visibility, becoming those we take into account as individuals; our failures, on the other hand, simply dissolve into that great mass of human society whose members are recognized on a statistical rather than an individual basis. Too often throughout the Southwest our successes have been John and Mary; and our failures have been Juan and María.

The triumph of the individual in any culture is always the triumph of education; and when a significant part of that education is acquired in school, we in the teaching profession can justifiably be proud. The failure of the individual may be due to his own weakness, the weakness of the educational system, or to the inappropriateness of the culture which might offer him success, and therefore its educational system, to the fulfillment of potentialities which he might offer.

We should not forget that one of the major aspects of our role as educators is the transmission of the culture of which we are a part. Often our limitations are due to the fact that we think of this role in terms of the transmission of certain specialized aspects of this culture which

we have acquired through great effort and p tience, and regard these aspects as unquestio ably universal. We fail to realize that these s cialized aspects of a culture have no mean apart from the value system, social system, a communications system which makes th transmissible.

That these systems are different in differe cultures means that there are complications the educational process where there is an tempt to superimpose meanings from one c ture onto another. They may even occur wit a culture. For example, when I was a pupil in East Texas school, I once asked my algeb teacher, "What is algebra good for?" S answered, "I think that engineers use it." I years the image stayed with me of the opera of a locomotive working algebra problems as whistled down the track. The answer we g our bilingual pupils is often as meaningless them as that one was to me.

The pressure to do something about the culturation of our bilingual children has co as a result of their failure to take what we gard as their place in our society because of incredibly increasing demands for educat which our civilization makes, and because many of them lack this education. To provid for them will not be a simple matter. In present world, education can no longer be garded as simply a technique by which pupil is prepared for one of a known set of ro which he is to play in our culture. Automat is developing so rapidly that if this is our c cept of education, we teachers will soon be placed by machines, joining our bilingual pu among the technologically unemployed.

The best teachers are not technicians; th are artists. They understand the subject in deepest sense. They know the possibilities a the limitations of the media which will b present this subject to the world, and th create works of art which are appropriate to a place or time. Before it is completed, the teac does not know what the product of his labor be like, just as the artist does not know wh his painting will be like until it is done. painting may be worthless or it may be pri less; we do know that if he has a numbe canvas and puts the correct colors in the cor sponding numbers, the result will be worthl

The possibilities of bilingualism in our country have not yet been explored. In order to educate the bilingual child successfully, we need know more than we know at present. Yet this moment of our history demands that we educate him successfully while in the process of learning how to do so. We need to educate him for a world with which we are not acquainted— the intellectually and emotionally expanding world of the future. We tend to try to educate people for the world in which we have lived; this is why education always lags behind art, literature, science, and even technology. Our most creative geniuses in the arts and the sciences have usually been a generation or more ahead of our societies as a whole; our educational systems are usually a generation or more behind. We can no longer afford this situation. We need more creative genius in education, and I do not believe that there is any area in which such genius could more likely create miracles than in the field of the education of the bilingual child. With imagination, ideas, and a willingness to act upon our best hunches, we may be able to deepen and strengthen our entire cultural heritage.

TEACHING THE BILINGUAL CHILD

A. Bruce Gaarder

Teaching the Bilingual Child: Research, Development, and Policy*

A. BRUCE GAARDER, *United States Office of Education*

1.0 Classroom-based research
1.1 Basic plan for bilingual students
1.2 Basic plans for bilingual schools
1.21 Bilingual school for both EMT and N-EMT pupils
1.22 Variant plan
1.3 Variables affecting language learning
1.4 Analogy and inference vs. analysis
1.5 Foreign language, literary studies, and other academic fields
2.0 Cooperation with organized ethnic groups
3.0 Community- and region-based research
3.1 Studies of dialect variation
3.2 Languages in contact
3.3 Sociological studies of peoples in contact
3.4 Attitude formation
3.5 Bilingual dominance configuration
4.0 Research based on the bilingual individual
4.1 Interviews-in-depth of "balanced" bilinguals
4.2 Studies of second-language acquisition
4.3 Bilingualism and a third language
5.0 Teaching materials
5.1 Contrastive analyses and teaching materials
5.2 Teaching materials on all levels of style

WE DO not need to observe the careers of such brilliant men as Julian Green, Salvador de Madariaga, and Joseph Conrad to know that bilingualism can be an invaluable intellectual and social asset. Innumerable cases attest to this truism. Nor do we need to observe many bi-illiterate speakers of two languages to know that in some cases bilingualism correlates negatively with a full measure of personal development. This paper assumes that whether the bilingualism of a child is to be a strong asset or a negative factor in his life depends on the education he receives in both languages.[1] The child in this case is the native-born American youngster whose mother tongue is not English. The concern is for both that mother tongue and English. Since it has been our public school tradition either to ignore that mother tongue or to discourage its use, this paper is concerned chiefly with research efforts designed to strengthen and maintain it, on the further assumption that strengthening and maintaining the mother tongue will contribute powerfully

---

* A workpaper presented at the Conference for the Teacher of the Bilingual Child, University of Texas, June 10, 1964.
[1] A. Anastasi, and F. Cordova, "Some Effects of Bilingualism upon Intelligence Test Performance of Puerto Rican Children in New York City." *Journal of Educational Psychology*, Vol. 44, No. 1 (January, 1953). These researchers reached the typical conclusion: "Whether or not bilingualism constitutes a handicap, as well as the extent of such a handicap, depends upon the way in which the two languages have been learned. . . . " p. 3.

and directly to the development of the personality and intellect and in turn increase the student's ability to learn English and through English.

On these assumptions the most important issue is unmistakable: At what age, by what means, to what degree, and in what relationship to his studies in English, should the child achieve literacy in his mother tongue?

An international "Committee of Experts" convened by UNESCO in 1951 to discuss the use of vernacular languages in education declared that "It is axiomatic that the best medium for teaching a child is his mother tongue."[2] The committee included in its report a world-wide survey showing that it is indeed generally conceded that every child should begin his formal education in his mother tongue. Nevertheless, educational practice in the United States supports the "ethnocentric illusion" that for a child born in this country English is not a foreign language, and virtually all instruction in schools is through the medium of English. It would seem, therefore, that among the research projects most needed is a series of classroom-based studies to test as a hypothesis that statement which the rest of the world considers axiomatic.

1.0 Classroom-based research

This research would be undertaken simultaneously in a number of situations, described typically below, and with the conditions approaching those noted in each case.

1.1 Basic plan for bilinguals

In actual practice, there are anomalies in the foreign language development policies in American education which approach the fraudulent. One of these is the situation in the American high school which results, for example, in the bilingual French-English speaking child's making the lowest grade in the French class. This anomaly, a commonplace whether in French or Spanish or German, is easy to explain if not to justify: the teacher has only a smattering competence in the foreign language and her attempts to communicate in it embarrass both herself and the native speakers in her class. I have heard teachers explain

this inability to communicate with Mexican-American pupils in New Mexico by saying that the Spanish they taught and spoke was "Castilian." In addition the teacher is using a book and methods geared exclusively to the supposed needs of the monolingual majority of the class. Consequently, the bilingual students, who in most cases have more "knowledge" and mastery of the tongue than the teacher or the classmates will ever have, sit confused, neglected, and too often conclude that there is something wrong with the language they speak and with themselves for speaking it.

The same anomaly pervades the thing called FLES and every other level of language teaching: the Federal Government encourages a multi-million-dollar expenditure annually for language development (in both the "common" and the "neglected" languages)[3] but no part of the effort is directed specifically to the further development of those same languages in the more than one in ten Americans who already have a measure of native competence in them. Rather our generally unformulated, national policy is at best to ignore, at worst to stamp out, the native competence while at the same

[2] *The Use of Vernacular Languages in Education* (Monographs on Fundamental Education—VIII) UNESCO, Paris, 1953, p. 11.

Other studies of particular interest in this regard and basic to the topic of this paper are:

Pedro A. Cebollero, *A School Language Policy for Puerto Rico*. Superior Educational Council of Puerto Rico. Educational Publications Series II, No. 1, 1945.

Einar Haugen, *Bilingualism in the Americas: A Bibliography and Research Guide*. American Dialect Society Publication, No. 26. University of Alabama Press, 1956.

H. H. Stern, (ed.) *Foreign Languages in Primary Education: The Teaching of Foreign or Second Languages to Younger Children*. (Report on an International Meeting of Experts, 9–14 April, 1962, International Studies in Education, UNESCO Institute for Education, Hamburg, 1963.) Contains a chapter "Research problems concerning the teaching of foreign or second languages to younger children" by John B. Carroll.

Uriel Weinreich, *Languages in contact, findings and problems*. New York: Publication of the Linguistic Circle of New York, No. 1, 1953; also The Hague: Moulton and Co., 1963.

[3] Report on the National Defense Education Act—Fiscal Years 1961 and 1962, U.S. Department of Health, Education, and Welfare, Office of Education publication OE-10004-62, U.S. Government Printing Office, Washington, 1963.

time undertaking the miracle of creating something like it in our monolinguals.[4]

Development, rather than research, is called for here: application of long-known methods in many and varied experimental settings at every level, K to 16, to make each student's bilingualism all that it can be. Specifically, the experimentation here recommended focuses exclusively on the development of a high level of literacy in the non-English mother tongue (N-EMT). This is not "foreign language" or "second language" study as these are traditionally conceived and organized and does not involve monolingual speakers of English except as noted in item 5 below. In brief, each "experiment" is simply the provision of at least one class daily in mother tongue study and study through the mother tongue for all N-EMT students.

Some specific suggestions are in order, to help avoid the worst of the mistakes that mar experimentation of this kind.

1. The teacher should be a vigorous literate native speaker of the standard variant and, if possible, of the student's variant of the language. For work at the upper elementary school level and above, the teacher should have learned *through the medium of the N-EMT* the subject matter to be taught. His competence could be determined and his certification based on the results of proficiency tests such as those the Modern Language Association has prepared for the five common languages. Pennsylvania and New York have already used these tests for this purpose. For languages lacking such standardized tests, examination of teacher candidates could be by examining committees.

2. The N-EMT pupils would for the most part follow the normal curriculum in English. Their schedules would be adjusted, however, to provide at least one period daily in the N-EMT.

3. The N-EMT would be the exclusive medium of instruction in all N-EMT classes. From the beginning, instruction would be focused on the language per se only a minimum part of the time. The major emphasis would always be on the regular subjects of the curriculum, mathematics, science, the social studies, etc., learned through the medium of the non-English language.

4. Only native "speakers" of the non-English language would be admitted to these classes, with the single exception noted in item 6 below. The minimum requirement for classification as a native "speaker" would be sufficient proficiency in listening comprehension to understand normal conversation and simple explanations.

5. Given the widely varying background of such native speakers, there might be need for a pre-test for placement purposes. Such a test for speakers of Spanish has been developed by the public schools of Albuquerque, New Mexico.

6. At the high school level monolingual students who are learning the same second language could be admitted to these classes of native speakers as a special honor if they demonstrate unusual aptitude for such learning.

7. When administratively possible, double academic credit should be granted: for the foreign language study per se, and for the work in the subject field taught through the foreign language. For example, a class in geography studied in Polish could earn credit in Polish and in geography.

8. One class period daily would suffice for this instruction. Experimentation could be directed to the question of whether three weekly periods would be enough to develop a high enough level of literacy.

9. Experimentation of this kind could begin without loss at any academic level, with any number of students from 2 to 35 in a class. If the number of non-English mother tongue speakers in a school is quite small, the children may well be grouped on levels of competence without too much regard for grade level. Thus, pupils in grades 1, 2, and 3 could be together, or those in 3, 4, and 5, or those in 4, 5, and 6.

10. The section in this paper on *Contrastive analyses—teaching materials* is pertinent here.

---

[4] See the introductory statement, Title I, Sec. 101 of the NDEA "Findings and Declaration of Policy": "The Congress hereby finds and declares that the security of the Nation requires the fullest development of the mental resources and technical skills of its young men and women. . . . This requires programs that will . . . correct . . . the existing imbalances in our educational programs which have led to an insufficient proportion of our population educated in . . . modern foreign languages. . . . "

Particularly important is the emphasis on learning through the language rather than concentrating solely on the language itself.

1.1 Basic to the two-language development program under discussion is the need to reinforce the non-English ethnic group's self-image as speakers of their native language. Irrespective of the extent to which their speech deviates from "cultivated standard"—and in some cases there may be virtually no deviation—they are likely to regard their language as somehow inferior, unsuited for use in one or more domains strongly dominated by the official language, and themselves as weakly representative speakers of the tongue. Here the concept of linguistic relativity, sometimes exaggeratedly espoused by descriptive linguistics, should be strongly emphasized. Whatever the speaker's dialect and idiolect it should not be suggested that he is to give it up and thereafter speak and write in another, different, "better" way. (Common observation shows that he will never forget it and will be able to return to it at will throughout his life.) Rather he is to learn *another*, a third language or language style which will be more appropriate and effective in other situations in which he might aspire to take part.

1.2 *Basic plans for bilingual schools*

The program set forth on the accompanying chart is most applicable in schools where at least half of the pupils at all elementary grade levels are N-EMT speakers. It is meant to develop bilingualism in both English mother tongue (EMT) and N-EMT pupils. It is modeled closely on the Coral Way elementary School bilingual program established in 1963 with Ford Foundation support in Dade County, Florida. The director of the Ford Foundation Project is Dr. Pauline M. Rojas.

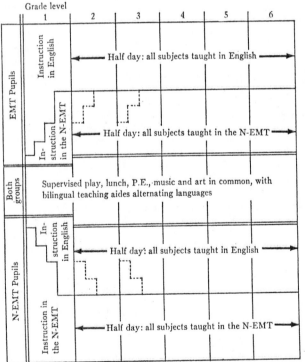

1.21 *Bilingual school for both EMT and N-EMT pupils*

Solid lines show program in full operation after the first year. Dotted lines show staging in grades 2 and 3 during first year of program.

Except for the bilingual aide work the EMT and N-EMT groups are not combined until each group has developed sufficient competence in its second language. This point should be reached by the 4th grade in the second year of the program. Those pupils who enter the program in grade 1 are expected to reach sufficient competence in the second language to be mixed to some extent in grade 2 and for almost all work in grade 3 and thereafter.

Note: The stepped lines which represent the staging in grades 1, 2, and 3 are merely suggestive of the time allotments rather than exactly proportionate to them.

1.22 Variant plan

First grade	Second grade	Third grade
Oral English—English reading, with grouping by ability—English writing	Oral English—English reading—English writing	Oral social studies in English—English reading—English writing
Oral Spanish—Spanish reading with grouping by ability—Spanish writing	Oral Spanish—Spanish reading—Spanish writing	Oral social studies in Spanish—Spanish reading—Spanish writing
Mathematics in English Art in English	Mathematics in English Art in English	Mathematics in English Science (oral) in English (demonstrations)

Fourth grade	Fifth grade	Sixth grade
Social studies in English with readings—English reading—English writing	Social studies in English with reading and writing—English reading—English writing	Same as for Fifth grade
Social studies in Spanish, with readings—Spanish reading—Spanish writing	Social studies in Spanish with reading & writing—Spanish reading	
Mathematics in English—Science in English with reading & writing	Mathematics in English—Science in English with reading & writing	

Each language group should be at least one-third of the total group at each elementary grade level. All pupils are together at all times except for ability grouping in grade 1. Teaching in Spanish approximately one-third of the day by highly literate, trained native speaking teacher; in English two-thirds of the day by a *different* person of same qualifications. Playground supervision alternating every other day in the two languages.

Points to be borne in mind:

1. All teachers responsible for a second language *as a subject* should be trained as second language teachers.
2. All other teaching is done by normal elementary school teaching methods.
3. Is the N-EMT group as proficient in the use of English and in other learnings as a comparable group which received no instruction in the mother tongue?
4. Is the EMT group as proficient in the use of English and in other learnings as a comparable group which received no instruction in a second language?[5]
5. The non-English language instructors should be highly literate in that language and should have studied in that language the subjects they are to teach through it.
6. It seems reasonable to suppose that the best reading (or listening or discussion) material for any child is that "which touches his own life experience so that he can see his experience in symbol form and identify himself in and with it. That is the reason many teachers or beginners prefer

to begin the teaching of reading with simple experience stories composed by the children."[6]

1.3 Variables affecting language learning

In Montevideo, Uruguay, there have long been K-6 second-language schools. Crandon Institute is a specific example. The case is cited from personal observation by Miss Elizabeth Keesee, Specialist for Foreign Languages, United States Office of Education. These schools have the following characteristics:

a) All instruction is (for example) in English at all levels.

[5] Walter B. Leino, and Louis A. Haak. *The Teaching of Spanish in the Elementary Schools and the Effects on Achievement in Other Selected Subject Areas.* St. Paul Public Schools, St. Paul, 1963. The researchers found that taking time from the arithmetic, language, and social studies periods in order to introduce 15 minutes daily instruction in Spanish had no detrimental effect upon pupil achievement in those three subject areas. The study was conducted for three years in the elementary schools of St. Paul.

[6] Ruth G. Strickland, "The interrelationship between language and reading." *The Volta Review*, Vol. 60, No. 7 (September 1958), pp. 334–336.

b) Classes of about 30 students under the charge of a single teacher.

c) All playground and out-of-class speech in Spanish. (Virtually all students are native speakers of Spanish or prefer that tongue.)

d) Parents and students highly disposed to foreign language learning.

e) Most students from upper or upper-middle socio-economic class.

f) All teachers natively competent in the school language and well trained for their work.

g) Production of highly literate, native-like use of English in all students.

There are similar schools in Texas where all or virtually all of the pupils are native speakers of Spanish and where English is the sole medium of instruction. The analogy with the Montevideo situation weakens at items d, e, and f, which, it may be reasonably hypothesized, contributed much to the achievement of item g. These three variables should be investigated, with the object of modifying the school situation so as to offset or overcome pupil deficiencies attributable to them.[7]

1.4 Analogy and inference vs. analysis

A major question besetting foreign language teachers is the shifting inter-relation between learning by analogy and learning by analysis at each stage or maturity level from infancy to adulthood. "Traditional" language teaching methods have relied heavily on analysis; "audio-lingual" methodology purports to depend heavily on analogy. If all pupils began language learning in grade one there would be no problem. Since there are in fact beginning groups at ages 6 to 25 and older, one pattern cannot fit them all. An approach to this problem could be made by a study of the age of onset and relative strength at each age level of the components of language learning aptitude isolated by Carroll,[8] the motivational and attitudinal factors described by Lambert and his associates,[9] plus ability to reason by analogy and inference basic to all first language learning. Armed with the results of such study the language teacher could better adjust his dosage of analogy (pattern drill, overlearning) and analysis (rules, explanations) to suit his learners.

Since analogical reasoning (I walked, I talked, ergo, I runned) and inferential determination of meaning (for example each of us knows thousands of "words" but only a few score or hundreds were learned consciously by dictionary or other word study) are basic to first language learning and in lesser degree to second language mastery, there is need for a study of these two processes and for the development of teaching procedures which will 1) make students aware of their function, 2) give step-by-step practice in the conscious application of both processes, and 3) exploit both processes at every point in the language course.[10]

1.5 Foreign language, literary studies, and other academic fields

The traditional curricular pattern in American colleges and universities—and in secondary schools offering more than two years of foreign language study—has produced a mutually supporting relationship between language study and only one other academic field: literary

[7] On parent and student aptitudes see Wallace Lambert, Robert C. Gardner, R. Olton, and K. Tunstall, A study of the roles of attitudes and motivation in second-language learning. Mimeographed. McGill University, 1961. For an overview of the relation between intelligence and socio-economic status see Kenneth Eells, Allison Davis, Robert J. Havighurst, Virgil E. Herrick, and Ralph W. Tyler, Intelligence and Cultural Differences. Chicago: The Uuniversity of Chicago Press, 1951.

[8] John B. Carroll, and Stanley M. Sapon. Modern Language Aptitude Test (MLAT). New York: Psychological Corporation, 1958.

John B. Carroll, "A factor analysis of two foreign language aptitude batteries," The Journal of General Psychology, Vol. 59, (1958), pp. 3–19.

[9] R. C. Gardner, and Wallace F. Lambert. "Motivational variables in second-language acquisition" in Canadian Journal of Psychology, Vol. 13, (1959), pp. 266–272.

Wallace E. Lambert, R. C. Gardner, R. Olton, and K. Tunstall. A study of the roles of attitudes and motivation in second-language learning. Mimeographed. McGill University, 1962.

[10] A beginning in this direction has been made in the secondary school Spanish series by Lagrone, McHenry, O'Connor, et al. See "Developing Reading Skills" in Teacher's Manual for Español: Hablar y Leer, New York: Holt, Rinehart and Winston, 1962, pp. ix–xiv.

A research project entitled "The Method of Inference in Foreign Language Comprehension, Learning and Retention" is underway at New York University under the direction of Dr. Aaron Carton. The project is supported by the Language Development Program of the United States Office of Education.

udies. This has meant that following the "introductory" and "intermediate" courses (and sometimes a bit of "advanced composition," or conversation"), the only further formal courses involving foreign language have been courses in the corresponding literature. This practice leaves out of account the possibility that some students might wish to do advanced study in a foreign language applied to specialization in an academic field other than literature.

Notable deviations from the language-to-literature tradition are found in those institutions which offer work in the "neglected" languages. It is not unusual for the courses in such languages as Chinese, Arabic, or Persian to have been introduced at the insistence of "area" specialists as a means of strengthening advanced offerings in their fields.[11] This is not the case with the more commonly taught languages.

It seems particularly important to provide for bilinguals at the college level the opportunity to capitalize on their non-English language professional specialization, in, for example, political science, international law or relations, anthropology, or economics, related specifically to foreign regions where that language is spoken. This would require developing the same strong, mutually-reinforcing relationship between foreign language study and other fields now exists only for literary studies. A good deal of preliminary work along this line has been done at Goucher College in Baltimore for majors in International Relations and Political science, including the expansion of library holdings, indices of periodicals, preparation of a tape library of speeches, etc., presentation of portions of courses through the foreign language, requirement of oral and written reporting in the language, and portions of tests and final examinations to be written in the language.[12]

Cooperation with organized ethnic groups[13]

Nationwide there are ethnic groups, societies, churches, and parochial schools with a strong commitment to the maintenance and development of competence in a language other than English. Judged in the light of a policy which considers competence in modern foreign languages as a national asset, the efforts of these groups should be strongly encouraged, supported, and coordinated where feasible with those of the public schools. Within the limited context of this paper the salient needs are two:

1. Language materials and instruction-through-language materials for such teaching.

2. Standardized tests suitable for use in grades 4, 6, 8, 10 and 12 to measure achievement in the four language skills.

3.0 Community- and region-based research

3.1 Studies of dialect variation

Any effort to develop the full potential of the bilingualism of native American speakers of a language other than English could profit from answers to two questions:

1) What is the range of dialect variation within the entire community of American speakers of that language?

2) How does the dialect variant of the particular group of speakers under consideration differ from the standard variant which you want them to learn? This information is essential to the production of teaching materials, particularly for use in secondary schools and above. The most casual observation will show marked differences, for example, between the Spanish spoken in the northern Rio Grande Valley and that of San Antonio. Are these regional differences marked enough to warrant different teaching materials for students in the two areas?

3.2 Languages in contact

Much needs to be done to clarify the changing status of the two languages in contact in the bilingual at every level. Of particular interest

---

[11] For an overview of this practice, see Joseph Axelrod, and Donald N. Bigelow, *Resources for Language and Area Studies* (A Report on an Inventory of the Language and Area Centers Supported by the National Defense Education Act of 1958), Washington, D.C.: American Council on Education, 1962.

[12] Brownlee Sands Corrin, *Research on Values and Uses of Foreign Languages for Instruction and Study in the Social Sciences* (Political Science and International Relations), Baltimore: Goucher College, 1962.

[13] This entire matter is discussed masterfully in Joshua A. Fishman, and associates, *Language Loyalty in the United States*. Dittoed. New York: Yeshiva University, 1964, passim and chapter 21.

in the context of this paper—apart from basic linguistic surveys of each bilingual speech community—are linguistic *interference, borrowings,* and *switching*. These matters are treated in great detail by Haugen[14] and Weinreich,[15] and both authors suggest many approaches to research. Pertinent to these issues is Fishman's observation that " . . . if a strict domain separation becomes institutionalized such that each language is associated with a number of important but distinct domains, bilingualism can become both universal and stabilized even though an entire population consists of bilinguals interacting with other bilinguals.[16]

3.3 *Sociological studies of peoples in contact*

Because it is constantly changing, the dynamics of a two-language community—whether a neighborhood, an entire town or a region—can never be sufficiently studied. Research of the kind done by Oscar Lewis and his associates in Tepoztlan (Mexico) if performed in the typical American setting where two peoples, each with its own mother tongue, come in contact exclusively through only one of those languages, the socially dominant one, would help the teacher, the school administrator, and the policy makers to act more wisely. To be most useful this research should show both the anthropologist's concern for the dynamics of belief and behavior systems under stress and in contact, and the scientific linguist's awareness of language as a factor in interpersonal and inter-group relationships.[17]

Research on the conflict of two languages within the individual personality requires first that the investigator realize that for a child whose mother tongue is not English, English is a foreign language. The difficulty of grasping this point is typified in the Kohut-Lerea research reported here in footnote No. 20. These highly sophisticated researchers, referring to the 25 Polish-, three Norwegian-, and two Greek-speaking children they worked with, said, "The bilingual subjects in this study acquired a dual language system because of exposure to a second language in the home."

3.4 *Attitude formation*

The work of Wallace Lambert and his associates indicates strongly that the mastery of a

second language depends on two independent sets of factors, intelligence and aptitude on the one hand, and on the other hand a complex of motivation and attitudes vis-à-vis the people and culture represented by the second language. Lambert's social-psychological theory of language learning affirms that ". . . the learner's ethnocentric tendencies and his attitude toward the other group are believed to determine his success in learning the new language." Here Lambert refers particularly to "success" in the degree that identifies the learner with the second language community, i.e., including native-like mastery of phonology. In the light of this theory there is in the American Southwest, Louisiana, and Canadian-French New England marked ethnocentrism, an authoritarian orientation and unfavorable attitudes in both the English and non-English groups of speakers. There is more than a suggestion of a cruel dilemma if Lambert's "integrative" attitude (studying as if one desired to become a member of the other group) is required in order to produce the highest degree of second language mastery. In this case the research need prompted by the fact that psychologists are currently working on the problem of changing attitudes. It therefore suggests itself that studies and experiments directed toward the formation of more favorable attitudes and motivations in the Lambertian sense might be fruitful.

[14] Haugen, op. cit., passim

[15] Weinreich, op. cit., passim

[16] Fishman cites in support of this Joan Rubin, "Stability and change in a bilingual Paraguayan community." Paper presented at the meeting of the American Anthropological Association, San Francisco, November 21, 1963. See also Rubin's article "Bilingualism in Paraguay," in *Anthropological Linguistics*, Vol. 4, No. 1 (January, 1962), pp. 52–.

[17] Oscar Lewis, *Life in a Mexican Village: Tepoztlan Restudied*. Urbana, Illinois: University of Illinois Press, 1963. Oddly enough, although Tepoztlan is a bilingual community, Lewis gives virtually no attention to the language problem. For the linguist's orientation to these matters see John J. Gumperz, "Types of linguistic communities," and Joan Rubin, "Bilingualism in Paraguay," both in *Anthropological Linguistics*, Vol. 4, No. 1 (January, 1962), Indiana University.

[18] Wallace E. Lambert, "Psychological Approaches to the Study of Language," *The Modern Language Journal*, Vol. XLVII, No. 3 (March, 1963), p. 114.

Bilingual dominance configuration

ithout denying the likelihood that most
kers of a given age and socio-economic level
n area of stable population will speak alike,
ust be recognized too that members of a
ority group, speakers of a subordinate lan-
ge, in a period of linguistic transition where
ngsters sometimes cannot communicate
their grandparents, in areas of marked
an vs. rural differences (some of them
ersed annually by uneven waves of illiter-
or semi-literate foreign national migrant
kers of the same tongue) subjected on every
to forces of acculturation, all attending
ools of greatly varying excellence and where
nstruction is given in a dominant language,
part of an increasingly mobile society—the
nbers of such a minority group may also
er widely among themselves in their use of
h their native language and the dominant
. That is to say, their bilingualism will
w wide variations in pattern, quite apart
n the relative excellence of their use of the
guage. They will differ with respect to their
ve or passive control of the language (Does
"bilingual" think in the language? Does he
h understand and speak it? Can he write?
only read?); with respect to the *situation*
re the language is used (Home? Church?
b? Work? With his children? Or only with
parents? With his boss as well as his sub-
inates? In public?); and with respect to
cs and styles of usage (Can he discuss reli-
n, the malfunctioning of his automobile, his
fession, in both languages? Can he send and
eive at each stylistic level as well in one lan-
ge as in the other?) Are there technical or
listic gaps in his vocabulary? All of the above
o say that there is immediate need for the
struction of a survey instrument which will
ermine the *bilingual dominance configuration*
given group or individual.[19]

t is important to know the "dominance con-
ration" of any bilingual group that becomes
ubject of study, for at least three reasons:
) With such knowledge those charged with
education of the bilingual child or adult are
ter equipped to appraise him and prepare a
rse of study for him.
) The dominance configuration, determined
iodically and combined with tests of lan-

guage proficiency, would be the surest means of
determining changes in the status of language
maintenance and language shift in bilingual
speech communities.

3) It seems likely that an accurate index of
bilingual dominance would be a powerful
weapon in support of the position that "balanced" bilinguals will not score below monolinguals in tests of both verbal and non-verbal
intelligence. Armed with an adequate instrument for determining the bilingual diminance
configuration, it would be possible to replicate,
in effect, in any of our bilingual areas, the Peal-
Lambert study of bilingual ten-year-olds in
Montreal which gave strong evidence that *if
the children are equally well educated in both
languages*, i.e., "balanced" bilinguals, they are
superior in both verbal and non-verbal intelligence to monolinguals, and also appear to
have greater mental flexibility, a superiority in
concept formation, and a more diversified set of
mental abilities.[20]

4.0 Research based on the bilingual individual

4.1 Interviews-in-depth of "balanced" bilinguals

Despite conditions of learning which do not
favor the development of highly literate "balanced bilingualism" in Americans who enter
school with a mother tongue other than English,
some individuals do achieve this goal. It is
hypothesized that a study of a representative
sample of such persons would produce information of value to educators concerned with the

[19] The problem of devising such an instrument has been
studied most recently by Dr. Joshua Fishman of Yeshiva
University. The whole matter is carefully analyzed in his
unpublished paper "Domains of Language Behavior in
Multilingual Settings," 1964. Uriel Weinreich has proposed
a dominance configuration on a different basis: op. cit. pp.
74–80. Wallace Lambert judged bilingual "balance" by
combining an association fluency test, a picture vocabulary
test and other measures. See footnote No. 20. Also see
Lambert's article "Measurement of the linguistic dominance of bilinguals," *Journal of Abnormal and Social
Psychology*, Vol. 50 (1955), pp. 197–200.

[20] Wallace Lambert and Elizabeth Peal, "The Relation
of Bilingualism to Intelligence" *Psychological Monographs:
General and Applied*, No. 546, Vol. 76, No. 27, 1962 (Ameri-
can Psychological Assoc., 1333 16th St., NW, Washington,
D.C.). Cf. also Louis Lerea and Suzanne M. Kohut, "A
Comparative Study of Monolinguals and Bilinguals in a
verbal Task Performance, *Journal of Clinical Psychology*,
Vol. XVII, No. 1 January, 1961 , pp. 49-52.

bilingual child. The need here is for a survey instrument with which to conduct interviews-in-depth of adults identified as "highly literate balanced bilinguals." "Balance" in this case cannot be expected to mean absolute parity, since this is always impossible. Rather it would mean a relatively equal number of important domains associated with each language, and relatively equal literacy in each. The difficulty of identifying such persons except by personal observation suggests that this research might follow the development of the index of bilingual dominance configuration noted elsewhere in this paper.

4.2 Studies of second-language acquisition

There is urgent need for a study of second-language acquisition under "natural" (co-ordinate) conditions at at least three age levels, infancy, six years, and 15 years to determine the sequence of learnings in the three language systems: phonology, morphology and syntax. Each such study should be conducted with the assistance of a person competent in descriptive linguistics in order to note the complete process of developing phonemic discrimination.[21] By "natural" conditions is meant total immersion in the second language environment in a school and play situation, e.g., a monolingual American child placed in a French-language boarding school in France. Such a study could provide invaluable insights into the sequencing of second language learning materials.

Along with this day-by-day study of the acquisition of a second language to the point where the basic structures of the language have been mastered, there is need for longitudinal studies of the development of the bilingual children through the twelfth grade.

4.3 Bilingualism and a third language

There is much informal, usually subjective, evidence to support the belief that bilingualism acquired by natural means facilitates the learning of a third language. It is also quite common to be told that the second language should be taught in such a manner as to facilitate the later acquisition of a third. This latter is especially so because although most Americans have little opportunity in school to study any language other than French, German, or Spanish, many

might find in later years a greater need Chinese, Polish, or Twi. The research indica in this connection is on two levels:

1) Development of objective evidence (possibly through case studies of individu of the relationship of bilingualism to t language learning and the conditions mechanisms by which the relations manifests itself.[22]

2) Application of those conditions mechanisms to the formal school learn of a second language in order to facili maximally the learning of a third one.

5.0 Teaching materials

5.1 Contrastive analyses and teaching materi

The immediate need is for a study of range of dialect variation. Thereafter, w should begin on an analysis of the stand form contrasted with each dialectical vari to facilitate the production of teaching terials. The third step would be the teach materials themselves,[23] designed for preser tion through that language and with at le the following features:

1) intensive oral drill from recorded patte

2) extensive reading and listening to corded literature,

3) extensive use of sound films on techn and other subjects to broaden the

---

[21] For a suitable methodology and much pertinent see Ruth Hirsch Weir, *Language in the Crib*. The Ha Mouton and Co., 1962. See also Werner F. Leopold's cl study *Speech Development of a Bilingual Child*. 4 Evanston, Ill.: Northwestern University Press, 1939

[22] Uriel Weinreich (op. cit.) says that Gali (Alexan Gali, "Comment mésurer l'influence du bilinguis *Bureau International d'Education*, No. 86, pp. 123-136), posed an appropriate line of experimental investigatio determine whether or how bilingualism helps in the acq tion of a third language.

[23] For a first effort in this direction see the work of Gerard J. Brault and associates to produce such mate for use with Franco-Americans in New England: *Cou langue française destiné aux jeunes Franco-Americ* Philadelphia: University of Pennsylvania, 1963. Also tinent is the research of Ruth I. Golden reported in *fectiveness of instructional Tapes for Changing Regi Speech Patterns* (final report on U. S. Office of Educa Title VII project No. 559), Detroit (Michigan) Pt Schools, 1962.

dents' horizon and sense of his own possibilities,

4) controlled composition

5) increasing emphasis on learning through the language rather than learning the language as an end in itself.

5.2 Teaching materials on all levels of style

A body of materials (in both printed and recorded form) consisting of short selections— usually paragraphs—of exposition, narration, dialogue, etc., graded by difficulty and each presented in variant forms corresponding to the levels of style distinguished in Joos' *The Five Clocks*.[24] It is not suggested that such materials would fill the stylistic gaps in the vocabulary of "unbalanced" bilinguals but they could be used to develop an awareness of those levels.

[24] Martin Joos, *The Five Clocks. International Journal of American Linguistics*, Vol. 28, No. 2, Part V (1962).

Contributors

JOSHUA A. FISHMAN teaches psychology of language and sociology of language in alternate semesters at Yeshiva University's Graduate School of Education where he is Professor of Psychology and Sociology as well as Dean. In recent years he has investigated bilingualism, language maintenance and language shift in the United States, from which the study published in this issue is derived. Currently he is concentrating on these same topics in the newly developing nations. His *Readings in the Sociology of Language* is scheduled for publication later this year as is his *Language Loyalty in the United States*.

THEODORE ANDERSSON, Professor of Romance Languages at the University of Texas, is currently on leave in Santiago as Educational Advisor to the Government of Chile. His previously published article in these pages in October, 1963, "Do We Want Certified Teachers or Qualified Ones," has been receiving wide attention.

CHESTER C. CHRISTIAN, JR., is a candidate for a Ph.D.

degree in Latin American Studies at the University of Texas, specializing in Latin American literature and sociology. He has M.A. degrees in sociology and in Spanish, and teaches Spanish at Texas Western College in El Paso. In 1963, he and his wife, Jane M. Christian did research for the Language Resources Project of the United States Office of Education on "Spanish Language and Culture in the Southwest," in a project which was directed by Dr. Joshua A. Fishman.

A. BRUCE GAARDER, at present Specialist in Foreign Languages for the United States Office of Education, was for five years (1959–64) chief of the Language Research Section of that office. His most recent academic post was at Louisiana State University (1947–59) as Associate Professor of Spanish. Dr. Gaarder is interested especially in the development of programs of bilingual education for American children who have a mother tongue other than English.

The Executive Committee of the Central States Modern Language Teachers Association, at its meeting in Chicago in May, 1964, has appointed Mr. Frank Naccarato as director of the newly created Teacher Placement Service for this association. Member teachers seeking employment or change of position and schools in need of foreign language teachers may write to Mr. Frank Naccarato, Dean of Men, Morton Junior College, 2423 South Austin Boulevard, Cicero 50, Illinois.

PSYCHOLOGICAL ASPECTS OF BILINGUALISM

David T. Hakes

Psychological Aspects of Bilingualism*

DAVID T. HAKES, *University of Texas*

IN 1956, Einar Haugen wrote, in his book *Bilingualism in the Americas*, "The locus of bilingualism is in the individual mind. The psychological study of the bilingual is therefore of central importance in the analysis of bilingualism. . . . While little has been done so far beyond the elaboration of a terminology, the psychological approach promises experimentation which could bring with it new linguistic insights as well."[1]

While the promise of psychological contributions to the understanding of bilingualism still exists, there still is little more than a promise. Almost the only aspect of bilingualism which has received much psychological attention is its effects on intelligence test performance. Aside from this, there has been very little psychological study which is directly relevant to the problems of bilingualism and the bilingual individual since Haugen pointed to the promise of this line of endeavor.

Haugen and numerous other linguists have suggested that before an adequate *linguistic* account of bilingualism can be presented, it is first necessary for the linguist to present adequate descriptions of the languages involved. For an adequate *psycholinguistic* account, still more is needed.

The area of psycholinguistics is primarily concerned with the learning and use of language by the individual. Needless to say, before any sort of an account of the processes and problems involved in the learning of a second language can even be approached, some sort of account must be made of the various processes involved in the individual's learning of his first, or native, language. Going beyond this, some account should also be made of the functions which language serves for this individual. Only when considerable progress had been made in these direc-

tions can we hope to have anything very intelligent to say about the added complications arising in second language learning. A consideration of what has been learned about some of the processes and problems of language learning may suggest some of the psychological implications of bilingualism.

Language behavior starts with the babbling of the infant.[2] Many authorities (e.g., Carroll 1960) have questioned whether babbling can be considered the "true" beginning of language or whether there is some sort of break between this stage of development and true language. But one thing appears certain: it is during the babbling stage, early in life, that the infant begins to gain control over his vocal apparatus.

It is interesting to note that while babbling the infant emits sounds which occur in languages other than his native language (Tischler 1957). But later on, these sounds disappear. The child raised in an English-speaking community will emit umlauted vowel sounds, rolled "r's", and even sounds produced with the intake of breath rather than its expulsion—sounds which later in life he finds it difficult to master or even to approximate.

This raises a first problem. What causes the child to lose the ability to emit sounds which do not occur in his native language? And, more im-

* Presented at the Conference for the Teacher of the Bilingual Child, University of Texas, June 9, 1964.

[1] Publication #26 of the American Dialect Society, University, Alabama: University of Alabama Press, 1956, page 69.

[2] For a recent, comprehensive review of the literature on language development, see S. M. Ervin, and W. R. Miller, "Language development"; in H. W. Stevenson (Ed.), *Child Psychology, The Sixty-second Yearbook of the National Society for the Study of Education, Part I* (Chicago: University of Chicago Press, 1963).

portantly, how does his random babbling become transformed into the highly organized and intelligible sounds which the child later emits? Tentatively, we may suggest that the answer to both questions is the same and that it is the child's parents, eager to hear the child "talk to them" who are responsible. The mechanism seems to be that the parents and other adults reward those sounds in the child's babbling which most closely resemble sounds in the native language.

For the child to learn to speak early is considered a good thing in most societies. Besides, parents are generally very flattered when their child first recognizes them. So when the child first emits something which sounds vaguely like "ma" or "da" the parents are likely to shower rewards on him. These rewards may be no more than a smile, speaking to the child, or simply paying attention to him.

The result of this selective attention, or reward, by the parents is that those sounds which approximate the native language, and are rewarded, tend to increase in frequency while those which do not approximate the native language, and are not rewarded, occur less frequently, eventually disappearing. They die from lack of nourishment.

It is, then, through selective reward by the parents and other members of the language community that the sounds which the child uses are gradually shaped into the sounds of the language. But this is, of course, only the first step in the process. For while the child may begin to develop speech in this way, it is speech which is still meaningless. It is still semi-random sound and not speech in response to objects or events in the child's environment.

This poses a second problem. How does the child learn to emit a particular pattern of sounds only when it is appropriate? This, of course, is the problem of the learning of meanings, of references, or of semantic relationships between stimuli in the child's environment and responses in his speech behavior. While the first problem, that of acquiring the speech sounds of the language, appears to be fairly simple (even though it is not), this second problem does not even appear simple.

Brown (1958) has suggested that the learning of semantic reference might be dubbed the "original word game." Basically the game involves two people—the child (or learner) and the parent (or teacher). According to Brown, the game proceeds something like this. The child, who by now has some sounds approaching words, emits these sounds as he wanders around his environment. At first, of course, the parents do not really care whether he is talking "about anything" or not. They are too pleased that he is talking at all. But the parents soon grow weary of all this noise which the child makes. And as the child grows older, the parents' expectations increase. The child is expected to start talking "about something."

The result is that the parents begin to be more selective in what they will reward. Now, the child must not only emit sounds which sound like words, but he must also do so only when they are appropriate. In short, the parents begin to pay attention to whether the thing which the child "names" (and at this point it can hardly be called "naming") is actually present. And the child is rewarded only when the thing named is present.

For example, when the child first acquires a response which sounds something like "doggie," he tends to emit this in a great variety of situations—when a dog is present, or a cat, or a horse or perhaps even when there is nothing present which is even vaguely animal. But if the parents reward the child selectively, that is, only when a dog is actually present, we can observe the same sort of process we observed in the learning of speech sounds. The frequency with which "doggie" occurs in the presence of a dog increases. And conversely, the frequency with which "doggie" occurs when a dog is not present decreases. The child has begun to *discriminate* between those situations where "doggie" is likely to be rewarded and those in which it is not.

Here we have the essentials of the original word game. The child emits a word, and the parents, in effect, tell him whether or not he is correct. It goes without saying, of course, that if the parents are too strict at first, that is, if from the beginning they reward "doggie" only when it is appropriate, the child will not be rewarded very often and will probably stop talking altogether. It is necessary first for the parents to build up the strength of the response and then to teach its appropriate use.

It never ceases to amaze me that parents, who probably know nothing about learning theory and who certainly do not consciously use it in teaching their children to talk, do as well as they do. While it appears to be only by accident that parents, in fact, do just about what the learning theorist would tell them to do, it is certainly a fortunate accident.

But to return to the original word game. It appears that the process is considerably more complicated than I have suggested so far. For example, when the child is learning to use "doggie," he is probably also learning to use "kitty." And, somehow, he has to learn when each of these is an appropriate response. In other words, he has to learn the difference between a dog and a cat. This is a problem of differentiation which we, as adult speakers, have mastered so well that it does not seem to be very difficult. But stop and think for a moment. What are the characteristics of a dog which are different from those of a cat? They are both four-legged animals and probably fairly small. Both have fur, two eyes, two ears and so forth.

To be sure, there are some differences. Dogs are likely to be larger, but not necessarily so. The two do tend to make different noises. But the chances are that neither one is making any noise when the child sees them, and especially not if he sees pictures of them. This really then is not much help.

Obviously, there are differences between them. But the differences are fairly subtle. And consequently, it is difficult for the child to learn what they are. But this is only a part of the problem, for the child must learn to discriminate a dog not only from a cat but also from everything else in his environment. And the characteristics of a dog which discriminate it from a cat are not going to be the same ones which discriminate if from, say, a wolf.

So the process of learning to "name" a dog correctly consists of forming a set of complex and difficult discriminations as well as learning to emit the sequence of sounds "doggie." And if the problems are great in learning what a dog is, imagine the difficulty the child is going to have with "truth" or "justice" or "God."

But while the problems of learning appropriate references for his vocabulary are great, they are not insurmountable, as is evidenced by the fact that the problems are solved by every individual who learns a language.

One thing which seems to help in this process of acquiring references or meanings, and this is something about which we know very little, is that somewhere during the learning process the child learns not only the necessary discriminations but also learns that he is playing the original word game. Although he is probably unable to tell you what the game is or what its rules are, he seems to become aware that there is a game to be played and that playing the game correctly leads to rewards. When he reaches this point, he is no longer simply emitting words and being rewarded, he is now actively playing the game, searching out places in which to try out his new vocabulary. Once he has arrived at this stage, the nature of the game is different. And the rate at which he learns new references increases greatly.

This is also a period in which vocabulary increases rapidly. For when the child learns that some four-legged animals are dogs and some are not, it is very useful for him to have names for those which are not. In short, learning the appropriate referent for "doggie" signals that there are other referents which are not named "doggie" but which have other names. And the task now is to learn what these other names are as well as to what they refer.

As I just stated, very little is known about how the child learns to play the original word game. In fact, we have not as yet even developed a very adequate language for talking about the process. But it is apparent that somewhere in his language development the child learns that things in his environment have names and that learning these names is rewarding. You might say that he learns how to go about learning what these are (cf., Miller, Galanter, and Pribram, 1960; James and Hakes, in press).

We have talked so far about the learning of speech or, if you wish, the vocabulary of the language. We have also talked about the learning of meanings or references. But we have left out of our account the role of grammar. Though this is very uncertain ground, grammar appears to be sufficiently important that we should not pass by without considering it.

First, let us note that whatever a person says

comes out in a sequence. Beyond a very young age, even the child does not go around emitting single words. Rather, he emits sequences of words, and the order of the sequence makes a difference (at least in English), as in the two sequences: "John hit Mary" and "Mary hit John."

It would be tempting to think that the orderliness of these sequences is a simple matter—that as a sequence is being emitted, one word determines what the next word will be. But unfortunately, such a simple left-to-right creation of sentences is inadequate on both linguistic and psychological grounds (cf., Chomsky, 1957). The most obvious reason is that what is emitted is influenced both by what precedes and by what follows as when, in English, the adjective precedes the noun which it modifies.

A more likely answer is that the individual generates or composes what is said before he emits it. But the nature of this composition process appears to be extremely complex, and the working out of the process is a task which is far from complete (Chomsky, 1957; Osgood, 1963).

But what is more important here are the answers to two questions. First, how does the child go about learning the structure, or grammar, of his native language? And secondly, how does the learning of grammar affect the other learning processes which we have already mentioned?

To the first question, no very definite answer can be given. It would appear that the grammar which the child learns is learned from the verbal behavior of others around him. We have pointed out that the child is likely to be rewarded for emitting a word only when it is appropriate in terms of the situation. But once he has passed the stage of one-word utterances, there are other restrictions placed on what he can say which will be rewarded. A word is appropriate only in certain situations, but it is also appropriate only in certain positions in an utterance or sentence.

What is being emphasized is that words occur in verbal contexts, and different words are appropriate only in different contexts. "Dog" cannot be used in the same verbal contexts as "eats," at least if the child is going to be rewarded.

In much the same way in which the child learns the appropriate stimulus situations for the use of a word, he also learns the appropriate verbal contexts for the word's use. The processes involved are the observing of how other people use the word, using it himself in sentences which he has composed, and either being rewarded or not rewarded. Again, while the processes sound simple, their application is not. Likewise, the grammar which the child learns through their application is also not simple.

There are several observations about the learning of grammar which may be relevant here. The first is that the child appears to have learned most of the grammatical rules of his language by the time he begins school (cf., Brown and Fraser, 1963), that is, before anyone has ever told him what the rules are. So, for example, before he learns the traditional definition of a noun—that it is the name of a person, place or thing (a totally inadequate definition in the first place)—he has already learned that those things which are later called nouns are words which fit into certain positions in sentences and not into others. In other words, any word which fits the "noun positions" belongs to the class of nouns (cf., Fries, 1952).

What is important here is that the rules are not learned explicitly, that is, by definition. Rather, they are learned by observing and attempting to create sentences. What this means, of course, is that the child's grammar is going to be no better than that of his tutors, and these are going to be mainly his parents, other adults in his immediate environment and his peers. By the time the schoolteacher gets a chance, the child may have some considerable unlearning and relearning to do.

A second interesting point is that the young child's grammar is likely to be much better than it appears at first glance. When the child is using two and three word utterances, these often appear not to be very grammatical. But these sentences, like "Where kitty?" and "Daddy gone" have a definite structure. More importantly, this structure is very closely related to that of the adult's language.

It has been suggested (Brown and Fraser, 1963) that the child takes the adult's grammar as a model and then leaves parts of it out. The parts which are omitted are quite consistent—

the child omits those parts which contribute little to the meaning of the sentence—the articles, conjunctions, auxiliary verbs and so forth —and leaves in only those parts which are essential for being understood. As he grows older, more and more of the omitted parts are inserted until his sentences are like those of the adult.

We can think of the child's grammar as being an abbreviated or telegraphic form of the adult's more complete grammar rather than as something only remotely related. This implies, of course, that the rules of the child's grammar are the same; there are just fewer of them. Consequently, the child is not going to have to discard his rules and learn others as he matures. He simply has to learn to use the rest of the rules.

But we have considered so far only the processes involved in the learning of grammar, processes which seem to be similar to those involved in the learning of reference. There is more.

The linguist is generally inclined to consider the semantic and grammatical aspects of language as being independent (e.g., Chomsky, 1957). And perhaps for purposes of describing the adult's language this is appropriate. But it appears that in terms of language learning grammar and reference are not independent. The structure of the language is used in learning word meanings; and conversely, word meanings are used in learning the language's structure.

We have pointed out that the child learns both what the appropriate situations and the appropriate verbal contexts for the use of a word are. Going one step further, we can suggest that each of these is used to assist the learning of the other. Take, for example, the sentences:

"Here Daddy."
"Here Mommy."
"There Daddy."
"There Mommy."

There are several things which are consistent in these sentences. "Daddy" and "Mommy" both occur in the same (second) position. And they are, of course, words that belong to the same grammatical class and also have a good deal of similarity of meaning. The same is the case with "Here" and "There." Both occur in the same position—but a different position from

"Daddy" or "Mommy"—they both belong to the same grammatical class, and they are similar in meaning.

Now when we hear the child emit a new sentence, such as "Here kitty." we should not be at all surprised to hear him also emit "There kitty." Similarly, once he has emitted "Where Daddy?", we should also expect to hear "Where Mommy?" and "Where kitty?". In short, the grammatical framework into which a particular word fits indicates that that word belongs to a grammatical class and that it can be substituted in other sentence frames for other members of the same class. The child is extending his repertory of sentences by substituting new words in old sentence frames and using old words in new sentence frames.

In addition, he is also learning that words which fit into common grammatical frames have some similarity in meaning. To be sure, "Daddy," "Mommy" and "kitty" are far from meaning the same thing. But they are considerably more similar in meaning than "Daddy" and "here." Thus the child has a clue to a part of the meaning of words by simply noting the positions in which they occur in sentences; the grammatical position indicates some of the semantic characteristics.

The relationship probably works in the reverse direction as well. If the child learns that "kitty" and "doggie" refer to similar things, we may expect him to use them in the same positions in sentences: the case in which the meanings of the words indicate their grammatical status. (See Brown and Fraser, 1963; Jenkins, 1962, for a more extended treatment of this relationship.)

We have here a very rough outline of some of the processes which appear to be involved in the learning of language. There are, of course, a great many others. We have placed the emphasis on the child as speaker rather than listener, and no mention has been made of the processes involved in learning to read or write. But even from this limited discussion, I think it is apparent that the learning of a language is an extremely complex and time-consuming process. When, in addition, the individual acquires a second language as well, the problems are multiplied.

There are, of course, many variables which

are going to affect second language learning: the degree to which the first language has been mastered, the similarity of the situations in which the two are learned and used, the age of the learner, his socio-economic background, and others too numerous to mention. All of these, at least to some extent, are going to influence the nature and extent of the bilingual's problems.

Of course, there are not just problems; there are some advantages for the second language learner as well. For example, to the extent that the individual has learned to play the original word game—has learned how to learn language—he will be benefited.

But the problems are legion, and some of these are worth suggesting.

First of all, we noted earlier that sounds which do not occur in the person's native language occur during the babbling stage and then tend to disappear. To the extent that these will be used in the second language, they must be recovered. In both speaking and hearing, the individual must learn to make additional discriminations in order to hear and produce sound differences which signal differences in meaning in the second language. In other words, sounds which are treated as the same in the native language may be treated as different in the second language, and having learned not to discriminate between them, the individual must now learn to discriminate between them—but only in the second language.

But a far greater problem arises in connection with the original word game. Consider, for example, the problem faced by a Spanish speaking child when he's placed in an English speaking situation. He is confronted with a referent, say, a dog, about which he wishes to speak. He has already learned what a dog is—that it is different from a cat, a horse, and so forth. And he has already learned the Spanish name for dog. He is now faced with the problem of learning the English name "dog."

This is a situation which the learning theorist recognizes as a particularly difficult one. In learning theory terms, the individual has acquired one response to the stimulus, dog. Attempting now to acquire a second response to the same stimulus provides what is referred to as a negative transfer situation (Postman, 1961). The previously learned response will interfere with learning the new response in the sense that *the new learning will be more difficult than if there had been no previous learning*. In addition, when the new response, the English word "dog," begins to gain some strength, it, in turn, will interfere with the old response, the Spanish word for dog. It will, in short, be very difficult for the individual to retain both responses to the same stimulus. And this interference will occur for every word which the individual attempts to add to his second-language vocabulary except for the few cases where there was no word in the native language vocabulary.

Complicating the problem further is the fact that words in the two languages are rarely synonymous. Situations are frequent in which what is referred to with a single word in one language may be referred to by a number of words in the other. Thus, objects or events which are "lumped together" in the native language may be "split apart" and named separately in the second language. And, of course, the converse holds as well. The individual must acquire new discriminations not only at the sound, or phonemic, level, he must also do so at the semantic level.

The learning situation of the bilingual is, then, a situation in which interference and confusion between the verbal responses of the two languages are inevitable.

But this is only the beginning of the problem. Interference operates not only in the learning and selection of the appropriate response in the appropriate language, it operates at the grammatical level as well. To the extent that the grammars of the two languages are similar but not identical, there will be interference. Differences in word order must be learned, such as whether the adjective precedes or follows the noun it modifies, whether the object precedes or follows the verb, and so on. Here, as at the phonemic and semantic levels, the differences are likely to be subtle and difficult to learn, and confusion the result.

It would appear that one of the causes of this great interference is the difficulty of discriminating the situations in which one language is appropriate and those in which the other is appropriate. We have pointed to the fact that the child must learn to discriminate between objects and events in his environment in order to attach the correct label or name to each. And the same learning-to-discriminate problem exists when the labels are words in different languages for the same or similar objects or events.

One point which we have not stressed is that language is social behavior. For it to develop, it must be rewarded. And unlike much other behavior, language can be rewarded only by another person—the environment provides few rewards for talking. In spite of having just re-read *Tarzan of the Apes* (Burroughs, 1912), I find it extremely difficult to believe that anyone ever learned language without an audience to reward him.

But the audience serves other functions as well as that of providing reward. It is also a stimulus in the sense that in the presence of some people one response is appropriate and in the presence of others another is appropriate. Thus the bilingual is faced with the problem of discriminating audiences, learning to respond in English to some people and in Spanish to others.

This general sort of discrimination has to be learned by all children, whether bilingual or not. For the child has to learn that verbal behavior which is appropriate for his peers may not be rewarded by his parents. But the problem is compounded for the bilingual. He has to learn to discriminate a greater number of different audiences, and some of those which he must learn to discriminate are not very different. For example, the Latin child in Texas has to learn to discriminate between his peers when he is in school (or at least within earshot of a teacher)—an audience for English—and the same peers when he is playing with them outside of school—an audience for Spanish. The audience is composed of the same people in both cases and differs mainly in terms of where these prople are.

Causing still further problems is another aspect of the audience. We have talked about the audience as either presenting or withholding rewards. But members of the audience may serve an additional function. They may punish if the behavior is inappropriate. In the case we spoke of a moment ago, if the child speaks Spanish in school, he is likely to be punished. And, if he speaks English at home or among his peers outside of school, he may also be punished.

Now punishment is a curious thing. Its effects are quite different from what they appear. The normal use of punishment is, of course, to eliminate the punished behavior. And, in the short run, it appears to have this effect. If the Latin child is punished for speaking Spanish in school, he may well be less likely to do so in the future. But the effect of punishment is *not* to weaken behavior but rather only to suppress it. The behavior hasn't really disappeared; it's being held down by the fear of further punishment—by anxiety. The emotional behavior of anxiety has become stronger than the punished behavior. But the effect is not that of getting the child to speak English rather than Spanish. The effect is, more likely, that the child will stop talking in school altogether.

There is a further consequence. The child learns a new audience discrimination—between punishing and non-punishing people. Having learned this discrimination, the punished behavior (and perhaps all behavior) is less likely to occur in the presence of a punishing audience (emotional behavior occurs instead), but *it is just as likely to occur when the punishing audience is not present.*

It is remarkable how finely this discrimination between punishing and non-punishing audiences can be made. Most children learn that their parents are punishing audiences for four-letter Anglo-Saxon words. But they also learn that their parents are less likely to be punishing when other people are present. As a result, the four-letter words are likely to come out when company comes to call, in public places, and other situations where they are particularly embarrassing to the parents. Since this is exactly the sort of behavior the punishment was intended to eliminate in the first place, it is rather apparent that punishment not only does not have the desired effect but is, in fact, having exactly the opposite effect. And the child's anxiety level is raised in the process.

That language learning is an extremely complex and difficult process is the inescapable conclusion. The difficulties are multiplied when, even under the best of circumstances, the individual is faced with learning not one, but two languages. And, unfortunately, the circumstances are seldom as good as they ought to be.

An individual who attempts to learn a second

language, regardless of the circumstances, is going to have a difficult time of it. There is simply too much evidence that interference and negative transfer are inevitable for the bilingual to a far greater extent than for the monolingual. In addition, of course, there is the obvious point that the bilingual has more to learn, phonemically, semantically and grammatically than the monolingual.

The point, then, is that it will never be possible to make the learning task as easy for the bilingual as it is for the monolingual. But this does not imply that the task for both cannot be made considerably easier than it usually is.

I have attempted to suggest some of the processes and problems which are involved in learning a language and some of the special problems which may arise for the individual trying to learn not one but two languages.

It would be risky to suggest solutions to the problems raised. As was noted earlier, we know far too little about language learning in general and still less about bilingualism. I think there is hope that in the future we will know enough about these problems to feel confident in making some suggestions about ways in which they might be alleviated. The promise which Haugen (1956) saw in the psychological approach to language and bilingualism is still there. But it will still have to be fulfilled in the future.

REFERENCES

Brown, R. *Words and things.* Glencoe, Illinois: The Free Press, 1958.

Brown, R., and Fraser, C. "The acquisition of syntax." In Cofer, C. N., and Musgrave, B. S. (Eds.), *Verbal behavior and learning: Problems and processes.* New York: McGraw-Hill, 1963.

Burroughs, E. R. *Tarzan of the Apes.* New York: Frank A. Munsey Co., 1912.

Carroll, J. B. "Language development." *Encyclopedia of educational research.*, New York: The Macmillan Company, 1960, 744–752.

Chomsky, N. *Syntactic structures.* 's-Gravenhage: Mouton and Co., 1957.

Fries, C. C. *The Structure of English.* New York: Harcourt, Brace & Co., 1952.

Haugen, E. *Bilingualism in the Americas: A bibliography and research guide.* University, Alabama: University of Alabama Press, 1956.

James, C. T., and Hakes, D. T. "Mediated transfer in a four-stage, stimulus-equivalence paradigm." *Journal of Verbal Learning and Verbal Behavior* (in press).

Jenkins, J. J. "A mediational account of grammatical phenomena." Paper read at a "Symposium on sequential verbal behavior," Midwestern Psychological Association Convention, Chicago, May 4, 1962.

Miller, G. A., Galanter, E., and Pribram, K. H. *Plans and the structure of behavior.* New York: Holt, 1960.

Osgood, C. E. "On understanding and creating sentences." *American Psychologist*, 1963, 18, 735–751.

Postman, L. "The present status of interference theory." In Cofer, C. N. (Ed.). *Verbal learning and verbal behavior.* New York: McGraw-Hill, 1961.

Tischler, H. "Schreien, Lallen und Erstes sprechen in der Entwicklung des Säuglings." *Zeitschrift für Psychologie,* 1957, Vol. 160, pp. 210–263.

BILINGUALISM, INTELLIGENCE
AND LANGUAGE LEARNING

Joshua A. Fishman

Bilingualism, Intelligence and Language Learning*

Joshua A. Fishman, *Yeshiva University*

FEW behavioral science fields have been plowed as frequently, and fewer yet have produced more contradictory findings, than the relationship between bilingualism, intelligence and language learning. Nevertheless, it is precisely such a topic which fascinates the layman, the teacher and the researcher alike for it has in it many of the ingredients that distinguish between the trivial and the vital topics of scholarship; namely, social relevance and theoretical centrality to basic processes of human interaction. Well over half the world is bilingual today, even by a fairly strict definition of this term.

Certainly, we must try to find out what this implies for personality, for intelligence, for society, and for culture.

While I do *not* claim to have single-handedly sundered the Gordian knot of "bilingual problems" I do believe that much of this knot has arisen as a result of our too quickly pulling at

* A paper prepared for the "Conference on the Teaching of the Bilingual Child," University of Texas, Austin, Texas, June 8–10, 1964. Dr. Fishman was a Fellow, 1963–64, Center for Advanced Study in the Behavioral Sciences, Stanford, California.

one or another thread protruding from it. My own approach has been to view bilingualism in two separate perspectives. One perspective is that of *cross-cultural comparisons*. The other is that of the *diversity of concomitants, antecedents and consequences*. It seems to me that we cannot hope to really understand bilingualism in the United States unless we fully recognize the *diversity of bilingual settings* within our own country and throughout the world. A cross-cultural view enables us to see that *there are many different kinds of bilingualisms* and that it is unwise to make or to seek pat statements that apply equally well to all of them. It also seems to me that we cannot hope to really grasp the relationships between bilingualisms and intelligences, or between bilingualisms and language learning, unless we know what *political, social, cultural, or economic variables to control* or partial out of our analyses. I here emphasize the former perspective, which emphasizes the differential description of bilingualism, and refer my readers to other sources[1] for a more detailed discussion of the latter, the manifold antecedents, concomitants and consequences of bilingualism.

The description of bilingualism

The description of bilingualism has been tackled by a great number of investigators from different disciplines, each being concerned with a somewhat different nuance. Linguists have been most concerned with the analysis of bilingualism primarily from the point of view of *switching or interference*. The measures that they have proposed from their particular disciplinary point of departure distinguish between phonetic, lexical and grammatical proficiency and intactness.[2] At the other extreme stand educators who are concerned with bilingualism in terms of *total performance contrasts* in very complex contexts (the school, even the society).[3] Psychologists have usually studied degrees of bilingualism in terms of speed, automaticity, or habit strength.[4] Sociologists have relied upon relative frequencies of use in different settings. Thus, since a great number of different bilingualism scores or quotients are already available, the social-psychologist interested in bilingualism must decide which, if any, are appropriate to his own concerns. If particular sensitivities to language behavior or if particular *organized* approaches to the data of habitual

language use characterize the social psychology of bilingualism, these must be brought into play in evaluating the methods suggested by scholars from other disciplines who have approached the quantification of bilingualism with other sensitivities or points of view.

The need for a combination of interrelated measures

It would seem, therefore, that the linguist's concern with interference and switching is a necessary ingredient of the social-psychological study of bilingualism, if only to give a more refined answer to the question, "*Which* language is being used?" This question may be easier to answer in some cases than in others (e.g., it may be easier to answer in connection with encoding than in connection with inner speech; it may be easier to answer in connection with writing than in connection with speaking; it may be easier to answer in connection with formal and technical communication than in connection with intimate communication) for the "density" of interference and switching varies for the same individual from occasion to occasion and from

---

[1] Joshua A. Fishman, "Language maintenance and language shift as a field of inquiry." *Linguistics*, 1964, no. 9, 32–70.

[2] Thus, Haugen suggests, "distinct tests . . . on each of the levels of phonemics, grammar, and basic lexicon" (Einar Haugen, "Bilingualism in the Americas: A Bibliography and Research Guide," Publication No. 26 of the American Dialect Society, University, Alabama: University of Alabama Press, 1956, p. 76), with several further differentiations within these levels, some of which are indicated below. Mackey goes even further and suggests that separate measures are also required at the semantic and stylistic levels (Wm. F. Mackey, "The Description of Bilingualism," *Canadian Journal of Linguistics*, 1962, 7, 51–85.)

[3] Among the most recent measures are those of Herschel T. Manuel which seek to enable "educators to compare the achievement of a student in one language with his achievement in another (H. T. Manuel, "The Preparation and Evaluation of Inter-Language Testing Materials," Austin: University of Texas, 1963. A mimeographed report of Cooperative Research Project Number 681.) It is typical of educational concerns to be more interested in determining the overall extent of bilingualism than in describing it in terms of quantified componential analysis.

[4] A convenient review of modern psychological approaches to the measurement of bilingualism is contained in Wallace E. Lambert, "Psychological approaches to the study of language"; Part II: "On second-language learning and bilingualism." *The Modern Language Journal*, 1963, 47, 114–121., in which Lambert discusses his own studies as well as those of others.

situation to situation. Although interference and switching are lawful behaviors, there are types of bilingualism in which even linguists will be hard pressed to determine the answer to "Which language is being used?" particularly if a single supra-level answer is required.

Similarly, the educator's concern with relative proficiency, the psychologist's concern with relative ease or automaticity, and the sociologist's concern with relative frequency of language use in a contact situation are also necessarily of concern to the student of the social-psychology of bilingualism, for these all provide important indications of whether, when and to what degree conservation or change are operative. Thus, in conclusion, the contribution that the social-psychologist can make to the description of bilingualism is precisely his awareness that (a) *various* measures are needed if the social realities of multilingual settings are to be reflected and that (b) these measures *can* be *organized* in terms of relatively *general* variance considerations. Of the many approaches to variance in language use that are possible the following have greatest appeal to me:

a. *Media variance: written, read and spoken language.*[5] Degree of bilingualism may be quite different in these very different media.

b. *Role variance:* Degree of bilingualism may be quite different in connection with *inner speech* (in which ego is both source and target), *comprehension* (decoding, in which ego is the target), and *production* (encoding, in which ego is the source). Where bilingualism is resisted, inner speech may be most resistant to interference, switching and disuse of the mother tongue (i.e., it may be least bilingual). Where bilingualism is conscious and desired, the reverse may be true.[6]

c. *Situational variance: formal, semi-formal, informal, intimate, et cetera.*[7] Situational styles pertain for example to consideration of intimacy, distance, formality-informality, solidarity-non-solidarity, status or power equality-inequality. Thus certain styles within every language, and in multilingual settings, certain languages in contrast to others, are considered by particular interlocutors to be indicators of greater

intimacy, informality, equality, and the like. Not only do multilinguals frequently consider one of their languages more dialectal, more regional, more sub-standard, more vernacular-like, more argot-like than the others, but, in addition, they more frequently associate one of their languages with informality, equality, or solidarity than they do the other. As a result, one is more likely to be reserved for certain situations than the other. Thus, where bilingualism is resisted more intimate situations may be most resistive to mother tongue interference, switching or disuse.

[5] Writing and reading are differentiated as separate media not only because they may be pursued in different languages, but because each is capable of independent productive and receptive use. In general, the formal dimensions presented here make use of more distinctions than may be necessary in all multilingual settings. Both empirical and theoretical considerations must ultimately by involved in selecting the dimensions appropriate for the analysis of particular settings.

[6] Unfortunately, the term *role* is currently employed in several somewhat different ways, eg. "role in society" (major, untouchable, bank-president), "role relation" vis-à-vis particularly others (husband-wife, father-child, teacher-pupil), "occasional role" (chairman, host, spokesman), and "momentary role" (initiator of a communication, respondent, listener). It is in this last sense that the term "role" will be used in connection with "role variance" above, while it is in the sense of "role-relation" that the term "role" will be used subsequently in our discussion of differentiations within the domains of language behavior.

[7] I am indebted to the work of many others for this tripartite division into media, role and situational sources of variance. Floyd Lounsbury suggested this particular *nomenclature* when I presented him with my dissatisfaction at referring to these distinctions in terms of "levels," "aspects," "modes," or other commonly used and insufficiently denotative designations. The distinctions themselves have a long history. They are obviously related to the distinction between "receiving and sending bilinguals," "oral and visual bilinguals," and "close and distant bilinguals" suggested by Mary Haas (Claude Levi-Strauss, Roman Jakobson, C. F. Vorgelin, and Thomas Sebeok. Results of the conference of anthropologists and linguists. Memoirs, Supplément to *International Journal of American Linguistics*, 1953, 19, no. 42); to the distinctions within "mode of use" (speaking vs. writing and reading) suggested by Weinreich (Uriel Weinreich, "Languages in Contact," New York: Linguistic Circle of New York, 1953, p. 75); to the discussion of comprehension, production, frequency distortions and levels of style provided by Haugen (*op. cit.*, p. 85), and to the distinction between "internal functions" and "external functions" made by Mackey (*op. cit.*, pp. 55 and 63). Similar or related distinctions have certainly also been made by others.

The reverse may be true when bilingualism is fully desired.

The relevance of situational variance to the description of bilingualism is equally great, whether we are concerned with stabilized bilingual settings or with the more fleeting settings which characterize the American immigrant case. Consider for example the case of two government functionaries in Brussells who usually speak French at the office except when they bump into each other. The two of them grew up together in the same Flemish speaking town and went to school together. Their respective sets of parents strike them as being similarly "kind-but-old-fashioned." These two functionaries share many common experiences and points of view, or think they do, or pretend they do, and therefore they tend to speak to each other in the language which represents for them the intimacy that they share. The two do not cease being government functionaries when they speak Flemish rather than French to each other; they merely prefer to *treat* each other as intimates rather than as functionaries.

However, the careful observer will also note that the two do not speak Flemish to each other invariably. When they speak about world affairs, or the worlds of art and literature, not to mention the world of government, they tend to switch into French or to reveal far greater interference in their Flemish, even though, for the sake of our didactic argument, the mood of intimacy and familiarity remains clearly evident throughout. Thus, neither reference group membership nor situational style, alone or in concert, fully explain the variations that can be noted in habitual language choice in multilingual settings. It must also be observed that situational styles, however carefully delineated, may still not provide us with much substantive or procedural insight into the socio-cultural organization of any particular multilingual setting.

The fact that two individuals who obviously prefer to speak to each other in X nevertheless switch to Y, or vacillate more noticeably between X and Y, when discussing certain topics leads us to consider topic per se as a regulator of language use in multilingual settings and as a parameter in the description of bilingualism. It is obviously possible to talk (medium and role) about the national economy (topic) in a thoroughly informal way (situational style) while relating oneself to one's family (reference group). Under such circumstances—even when reference group and situation agree in requiring a particular language—it is not uncommon to find that topic succeeds in bringing another language to the fore.

The implication of topical regulation of language choice is that certain topics are somehow handled better in one language than in another in particular multilingual contexts. This congruence may be arrived at by several different but mutually reinforcing routes. Thus, some multilingual speakers may "acquire the habit" of speaking about topic x in language X partially because that is the language in which they were *trained* to deal with this topic (e.g., they received their university training in economics in French), partially because they and their interlocutors may *lack the specialized terms* for a satisfying discussion of x in language Y, partially because *language Y itself may currently lack as exact or as many terms* for handling topic x as those currently possessed by language X, and partially because it is considered *strange* or *inappropriate* to discuss x in language Y. The very multiplicity of sources of topical regulation implies that *topic* may not be a convenient analytic variable when language choice is considered from the point of view of the *socio-cultural organization* of a multilingual setting. It tells us little about the patterns of societally relevant spheres of activity. We may arrive at these latter patterns if we enquire *what it means* when a significant number of people in a particular multilingual setting at a particular time have received certain kinds of training in one language rather than in another; or *what it reveals* about a particular miltilingual setting if language X *is* actually less capable of coping with topic x than is language Y. Does it not reveal more than merely a topic-language relationship at the level of face-to-face encounters? Does it not reveal that certain socio-culturally *recognized spheres of activity* are, at least temporarily, under the sway of one language, and, therefore, perhaps of one sub-population, rather than another? Thus, while topic is doubtlessly a crucial consideration in understanding language choice variance in our two hypothetical government functionaries, we must seek a means of examining and relating their individual and momentary choices to relatively stable patterns of choice that exist in their multilingual setting as a whole. It is in this connection that we have recourse to the concept of *domains of language* behavior.

Domains of Language Behavior

a. The concept of domains of language behavior seems to have received its first partial elaboration from students of language maintenance and language shift among *Auslandsdeutsche* in pre-World War II multilingual settings. Germany settlers were in contact with many different non-German speaking populations in various types of contact settings and were exposed to various kinds of socio-cultural change processes. In attempting to chart and compare the fortunes of the German language under such varying circumstances Schmidt-Rohr seems to have been the first to suggest that *dominance configurations* needed to be established to reveal the overall-status of language choice in various domains of behavior.[8] The domains recommended by Schmidt-Rohr were the following nine: the family, the playground and street, the school (subdivided into language of instruction, subject of instruction, and language of recess and entertainment), the church, literature, the press, the military, the courts, and the governmental administration. Subsequently, other investigators either added additional domains (e.g., Mak,[9] who nevertheless followed Schmidt-Rohr in overlooking the work-sphere as a domain), or found that fewer domains were sufficient in particular multilingual settings (e.g., Frey,[10] who required only home, school and church in his analysis of Amish "triple talk"). However, what is more interesting is that Schmidt-Rohr's domains bear a striking similarity to those spheres of activity which have more recently been independently advanced by some anthropologists, sociologists, social psychologists and linguists for the study of acculturation, intergroup relations, and bilingualism. Domains, such as these, regardless of their number, are oriented toward *institutional contexts* or toward *socio-ecological co-occurrences*.[11] They attempt to designate the *major clusters of interaction situations that occur in particular multilingual settings*. Domains such as these help us understand that *language choice* and *topic*, appropriate though they may be for analyses of individual bilingual behavior at the level of face-to-face verbal encounters, are themselves related to widespread socio-cultural regularities. Language choices, cumulated over many individuals and many choice instances, become transformed into the processes of *language maintenance* or *language shift*. Furthermore, if many individuals (or subgroups) tend to handle topic x in language X, this may well be because this topic pertains to a *domain* in which that language is dominant for their society or for their sub-group. Certainly it is a far different social interaction when topic x is discussed in language Y *although it pertains to a domain in which language X is dominant*, than when the same topic is discussed by the same interlocutors in the language most commonly employed in that domain. By recognizing the existence of domains it becomes possible to contrast the language of topics for particular subpopulations with the language domains for larger populations.

b. The appropriate designation and definition of domains of language behavior obviously calls for considerable insight into the socio-cultural dynamics of particular multilingual setting at particular periods in their history. Schmidt-Rohr's domains reflect multilingual settings in which a large number of socio-ecological co-occurrences, even those that pertain to governmental functions, are theoretically

---

[8] Georg Schmidt-Rohr, *Mutter Sprache*, Jena: Eugen Diederichs Verlag, 1936. (Title of first edition: *Die Sprache als Bildnerin der Völker*. Munich, 1932.)

[9] Wilhelm, Mak "Zweisprachigkeit und Mischmundart in Oberschlesien," *Schlesisches Jahrbuch für deutsche Kulturabeit*, 1935, 7, 41–52.

[10] J. William Frey, "Amish 'triple talk.'" *American Speech*, 1945, 20, 85–98.

[11] We can safely reject the implication encountered in certain discussions of domains that there must be an invariant set of domains applicable to all multilingual settings. If language behavior is related to socio-cultural organization, as is now widely accepted, then different kinds of multilingual settings show benefit from analyses in terms of different domains of language use, whether defined intuitively, theoretically, or empirically.

permissible to all of the languages present, or, at least, to multilingual settings in which such permissiveness is sought by a sizable number of interested parties. Quite different domains might be appropriate if one were to study habitual language use among children in these very same settings. Certainly, immigrant-host contexts, in which only the language of the host society is recognized for governmental functions, would require other and perhaps fewer domains, particularly if younger generations constantly leave the immigrant society and enter the host society. Finally, the domains of language behavior may differ from setting to setting not only in terms of number and designation but also in terms of level. Thus, in studying acculturating populations in Arizona, Barker,[12] who studied bilingual Spanish Americans, and Barber,[13] who studied trilingual Yaqui Indians, formulated *domains at the level of socio-psychological analysis:* intimate, informal, formal and intergroup. Interestingly enough, the domains defined in this fashion were further specified at the *societal-institutional level.* The "formal" domain, e.g., was found to coincide with religious-ceremonial activities; the "intergroup" domain consisted of economic and recreational activities as well as of interactions with governmental-legal authority, etc. The interrelationship between domains of language behavior defined at societal-institutional level and domains defined at sociopsychological level (the latter being somewhat similar to situational analyses discussed earlier) may enable us to study language choice in multilingual settings in newer and more stimulating ways. One approach to the study of just such interrelationships will be presented below in the discussion of the *dominance configuration.*

c. The "governmental administration" domain is a social nexus which brings people together *primarily* for a certain *cluster of purposes.* Furthermore, it brings them together primarily within a certain set of role-relation and environment co-occurrences. Although it is possible for them to communicate about many things, given these purposes and contexts, the topical variety is actually quite small in certain media (e.g., written communication) and in certain situations (e.g., formal communication), and is noticeably skewed in the direction of

domain purpose in most domains. Thus, domain is a socio-cultural construct abstracted from topics of communication, relationships between communicators, and locales of communication, in accord with the institutions of a society and the spheres of activity of a culture, in such a way that *individual behavior and social patterns can be distinguished from each other and yet related to each other.*[14] The domain is a higher order of abstraction or summarization which arrives out of a consideration of the socio-cultural patterning which surrounds language choices that transpire at the intra-psychic and socio-psychological levels. Of the many factors contributing to and subsumed under the domain concept some are more important and more accessible to careful measurement than others. One of these, topic, has already been discussed. Another, role-relations, remains to be discussed. Role-relations may be of value to us in accounting for the fact that our two hypothetical governmental functionaries, who usually speak an informal variant of Flemish to each other at the office, except when they talk about professional or sophisticated "cultural" matters, are themselves not entirely alike in this respect. One of the two tends to slip into French more frequently than the other, even when reference group, medium, role, situational style, topic and several other aspects of communication are controlled. It so happens that he is the supervisor of the other.

Domains and Role-Relations

In many studies of multilingual behavior the family domain has proved to be a very crucial one. Multilingualism often begins in the family and depends upon it for encouragement if not for protection. In other cases, multilingualism

[12] George C. Barker, "Social functions of language in a Mexican-American Community," *Acta Americana*, 1946, 5, 185–202.

[13] Carroll Barber, "Trilingualism in Pascua: Social functions of language in an Arizona Yaqui Village," M.A. Thesis, University of Arizona, 1952.

[14] For a discussion of the differences and similarities between "functions of language behavior" and "domains of language behavior" see Fishman, *op. cit.* "Functions" stand closer to socio-psychological analysis, for they abstract their constituents in terms of individual purposive-motivational factors rather than in terms of socio-cultural organization.

.hdraws into the family domain after it has
:n displaced from other domains in which it
s previously encountered. Little wonder then
it many investigators, beginning with
aunshausen[15] several years ago, have differ-
;iated *within* the family domain in terms of
)eakers." However, two different approaches
ve been followed in connection with such
ferentiation. Braunshausen, and more re-
itly Mackey,[16] merely specified family "mem-
-s": father, mother, child, domestic, govern-
and tutor, etc. Gross,[17] on the other hand,
; specified *dyads* within the family: grand-
her to grandmother, grandmother to grand-
her, grandfather to father, grandfather to
ther, grandmother to mother, grandfather to
id, grandmother to child, father to mother,
ther to father, etc. The difference between
se two approaches is quite considerable. Not
y does the second approach recognize that
eracting members of a family (as well as the
ticipants in most other domains of language
avior) are *hearers* as well as *speakers* (i.e.,
t there may be a distinction between multi-
;ual *comprehension* and multilingual *produc-
*), but it also recognizes that their language
avior may be more than merely a matter of
ividual preference or facility but also a mat-
of *role-relations*. In certain societies particu-
behaviors (including language behaviors)
expected (if not required) of *particular indi-
uals vis-à-vis each other*. Whether role-rela-
is are fully reducible to situational styles for
purpose of describing habitual language
ice in particular multilingual settings is a
tter for future empirical determination.
[he family domain is hardly unique with
pect to its differentiability into role-rela-
ns. Each domain can be differentiated into
e-relations that are specifically crucial or
ical of it in particular societies at particular
es. The religious domain (in those societies
ere religion can be differentiated from folk-
ys more generally) may reveal such role-rela-
ns as cleric-cleric, cleric-parishioner, parish-
er-cleric, and parishioner-parishioner. Simi-
ly, pupil-teacher, buyer-seller, employer-em-
yee, judge-petitioner, all refer to specific
e-relations in other domains. It would cer-
nly seem desirable to describe and analyze
guage-use or language choice in a particular

multilingual setting in terms of the crucial role-
relations within the specific domains considered
to be most revealing for that setting. The distinction between own-group-interlocutor and
other-group-interlocutor may also be provided
for in this way.[18]

In summary, it seems that degree of bilingualism may be quite different in each of
several discriminable domains of language behavior. Such differentials may reflect differences
between interacting populations and their
socio-cultural systems with respect to autonomy, power, influence, domain centrality, etc.

*Some Empirical and Conceptual Contributions of
Domain and Dominance Analysis*

A description and analysis of the *simultaneous, interacting impact* of all of the above-mentioned sources of variance in language use
(media, role, situational and domain variance,
with the latter being further divisible into topical and role-relations components) provide a
bilingualism dominance configuration. Dominance configurations may be used to summarize
data on the bilingual behavior of many individuals who constitute a defined sub-population. Repeated dominance configurations for the
same population, studied over time, may be
used to represent the direction (or flow) of language maintenance and language shift in a particular multilingual setting. Contrasted dominance configurations may be used to study the
differential impact of *various* socio-cultural processes (urbanization, secularization, revitalization, etc.) on the *same* mother tongue group in
different contact settings, or the differential impact of a *single* socio-cultural process on *differ-

[15] Nicholas Braunshausen, "Le bilinguisme et la
famille," in *Le Bilinguisme et l'Education*, Geneva-Luxem-
burg: Bureau International d'Education, 1928.

[16] Wm. F. Mackey, "The description of bilingualism,"
Canadian Journal of Linguistics, 1962, 7, 51–85.

[17] Feliks Gross, "Language and value changes among the
Arapaho," *International Journal of American Linguistics*,
1951, 17, 10–17.

[18] These remarks are not intended to imply that *all* role-
relation differences are necessarily related to language-
choice differences. This almost certainly is *not* the case.
Just which role-relation differences *are* related to language-
choice differences (and under what circumstances) is a
matter for empirical determination within each multilingual
setting as well as at different points in time within the same
setting.

TABLE I. YIDDISH-ENGLISH MAINTENANCE AND SHIFT IN THE UNITED STATES: 1940–1960
Comparisons for Immigrant Generation "Secularists" Arriving Prior to World War I (First language shown is most frequently used; second language shown is increasing in use)

Sources of Variance			Domains of Language Behavior					
			Neighborhood					
Media	Role	Situational	Family	Friends	Acquaints.	Mass Med.	Jew. Orgs.	Occup.
Speaking	Inner*	Formal	X	X	X	X	X	X
		Informal	Y, E	Y, E	Y, E	E, E	Y, E	E, E
		Intimate	Y, E	Y, E	Y, E	E, E	Y, E	E, E
	Comp.	Formal	X	X	E, E	E, E	Y, E	E, E
		Informal	E, E	E, E	E, E	E, E	Y, E	E, E
		Intimate	Y, E	Y, E	X	X	X	X
	Prod.	Formal	X	X	E, E	X	Y, E	E, E
		Informal	E, E	E, E	E, E	X	Y, E	E, E
		Intimate	Y, E	Y, E	E, E	X	X	X
Reading	Comp.	Formal	Y, E	X	X	X	Y, E	X
		Informal	Y, E	X	X	X	Y, E	X
		Intimate	E, E	X	X	X	X	X
	Prod.**	Formal	Y, E	X	X	Y, E	Y, E	X
		Informal	Y, E	X	X	Y, E	Y, E	X
		Intimate	E, E	X	X	E, E	X	X
Writing	Prod.	Formal	X	X	X	X	Y, E	X
		Informal	E, E	E, E	X	X	Y, E	X
		Intimate	E, E	E, E	X	X	X	X

* For "speaking—inner—" combinations the domains imply topics as well as contexts. In all other instances they im contexts alone.
** For "reading—production—" combinations the distinction between "family" and "mass media" domains is also a tinction between reading to others and reading to oneself.

ent mother tongue groups in similar contact settings.

The domain concept has facilitated a number of hopefully worthwhile contributions to the understanding of bilingualism and language choice. It has helped organize and clarify the previously unstructured awareness that language maintenance and language shift proceed quite unevenly across the several sources and domains of variance in habitual language choice. Certain domains appear to be more maintenance-prone than others (e.g., the family domain in comparison to the occupational domain) across all multilingual settings characterized by urbanization and economic development, regardless of whether immigrant-host or indigenous populations are involved. Under the impact of these same socio-cultural processes other domains (e.g., religion) seem to be ve strongly maintenance oriented during earl stages of interaction and strongly shift orient once an authoritative decision is reached th their organizational base can be better secur via shift. Certain interactions between doma and other sources of variance seem to rema protective of contextually "disadvantage languages, even when language shift has a vanced so far that a given domain as such h been engulfed. On the other hand, if a str domain separation becomes institutionaliz such that each language is associated with number of important but distinct domai bilingualism can become both universal a stabilized even though an entire populati consists of bilinguals interacting with other linguals.

FIGURE I

Type of Bilingual Functioning and Domain Overlap During Successive Stages of Immigrant Acculturation

Bilingual Functioning Type	Domain Overlap Type	
	Overlapping Domains	Non-Overlapping Domains
mpound nterdependent or fused)	2. *Second Stage:* More immigrants know more English and therefore can speak to each other either in mother tongue or in English (still mediated by the mother tongue) in several domains of behavior. Increased interference.	1. *Initial Stage:* The immigrant learns English via his mother tongue. English is used only in those few domains (work sphere, governmental sphere) in which mother tongue cannot be used. Minimal interference. Only a few immigrants knew a little English.
oordinate ndependent)	3. *Third Stage:* The languages function independently of each other. The number of bilinguals is at its maximum. Domain overlap is at its maximum. The second generation during childhood. Stabilized interference.	4. *Final Stage:* English has displaced the mother tongue from all but the most private or restricted domains. Interference declines. In most cases both languages function independently; in others the mother tongue is mediated by English (reverse of Stage 1, but same type.)

The concepts of domain and dominance have also helped refine the distinction between coordinate bilingualism and compound bilingualism[19] by stressing that not only does a continuum rather than a dichotomy obtain, but by indicating how one stage along this continuation may shade into another.[20]

As indicated by Figure I, most late 19th and early 20th century immigrants to America from Eastern and Southern Europe began as compound bilinguals with each language assigned to separate and minimally overlapping domains. The passage of time involved increased interaction with English-speaking Americans, social mobility, and acculturation with respect to other-than-language behaviors as well so that their bilingualism became characterized, first, by far greater domain overlap (and by far greater interference) and then by progressively greater coordinate functioning. Finally, language displacement advanced so far that the mother tongue remained only in a few restricted and non-overlapping domains. Indeed, in some cases, compound bilingualism once more became the rule, except that the ethnic mother tongue came to be utilized via English, rather than vice-versa as was the case in the early immigrant days. Thus, the domain concept helps place the compound-coordinate distinction in greater socio-cultural perspective, in much the same way as it serves the entire area of language choice. More generally, we are helped to realize that the initial pattern of acquisition of bi-

lingualism and subsequent patterns of bilingual functioning need not be in agreement (Figure II). Indeed, a bilingual may vary with respect to the compound versus coordinate nature of this functioning in connection with each of the sources and domains of variance in language choice that are represented in the dominance configuration. If this is the case then several different models of interference may be needed to correspond to various stages of bilingualism and to various co-occurrences of influence on language choice.

Bilingualism, Intelligence and Language Learning

If the foregoing has demonstrated anything at all, it may well be as follows: the adequate

[19] Susan M. Ervin and C. E. Osgood. "Second language learning and bilingualism." *Journal of Abnormal and Social Psychology*, 1954, 49, Supplement, 139–146.

[20] In popular terminology the compound bilingual thinks in one language and translates into the other, while the coordinate bilingual thinks in whichever language he is using at the moment. More precisely, the compound bilingual has two fused language systems, while the coordinate has two discrete ones. The distinction is not absolute; a great many bilinguals actually have a system and a half, partly compound and partly coordinate. But the experience of aphasics shows that the coordinate bilingual may lose one of his languages without having this loss affect the other, while the compound bilinguals are equally affected in both. (Einar Haugen, "Bilingualism as a Goal of Foreign Language Teaching," in Virginia F. Allen, editor, *On Teaching English to Speakers of Other Languages*, Champaign, Illinois: National Council of Teachers of English, 1965, pp. 84–88.

Figure II

Initial Type of Bilingual Acquisition and Subsequent Domain Overlap Type

Bilingual Acquisition Type	Domain Overlap Type	
	Overlapping Domains	Non-Overlapping Domains
Compound (Interdependent or fused)	Transitional bilingualism: the older second generation. The "high-school-French" tourist who remains abroad somewhat longer than he expected to.	"Cultural bilingualism": the bilingualism of the "indirect method" classroom whereby one language is learned through another but retained in separate domains.
Coordinate (Independent)	Widespread bilingualism without social cleavage: the purported goal of "responsible" French-Canadians. The "direct method" classroom.	"One sided bilingualism" or bilingualism with marked and stable social distinctions such that only one group in a contact situation is bilingual or such that only particular domains are open or appropriate to particular languages.

description of bilingualism is a subtle and difficult undertaking. If this demonstration has any relevance it may well be that any simple statement about the relationship between bilingualism and language learning must, of necessity, be in error[21]—not because the researchers who attempt such statements are incapable, and certainly not because they are knaves—but simply because they have unknowingly based their conclusions on data from one cell of the acquisition type—domain overlap configuration.

Bilingualism has been a characteristic of political and cultural elites throughout world history. Skilled and cultured tutors or companions have been and are still being employed to impart a native, coordinate grasp of "other tongues" to the children of the wealthy and the culturally sophisticated. Both of the languages mastered by these children, their mother tongues and their "other tongues," are commonly learned in contexts of respect, literacy, and fluency. Where this is not the case, where the vernacular of an elite suffers in comparison with some superposed language, no implication of low intelligence or of low verbal aptitude is drawn from the fact that the elites and their children are rather limited in the mastery of their vernacular. It is merely recognized that the vernacular is currently of lesser functional or attitudinal value in the particular social context of elitist families and the best reflection of their verbal ability, therefore, is derived from their "other tongue" usage. Certainly, where everyone is of similar class *and* of similar bilinguality *no substantial relationship between*

bilingualism and intelligence is possible.

Similarly, it is only to be expected that individuals who are socialized in verbally unstimulating and non-communicative environments will develop less verbal proficiency, whether they are monolingual or bilingual. They will necessarily score lower on verbal tests of ability and, frequently, will score equally low on conceptual tests of any kind, since their environments are also experientially impoverished and since most non-verbal concepts are frequently facilitated by verbal mediators. If, in addition, such individuals should be tested for verbal ability in an "other tongue" with which they have only limited experience (limited in every way: in domains, in role-relations, in topics, in media, in roles and in situational styles) we are merely adding insult to injury or irrelevance to impertinence.

Finally, given some awareness of the necessary complexity of adequate descriptions of bilingualism and the diversity of bilingual set-

[21] I find particularly objectionable the recent one sentence summary by Benard Berelson and Gary A. Steiner, not only because it is incomplete and, therefore, inacurrate, but because it is most likely to gain widespread acceptance as authoritative: "Children taught two languages from the start are handicapped in both, as compared to the rate of a child learning either language alone. The difference becomes increasingly noticeable with age, to the extent that the child may have serious language difficulties upon entering school." *Human Behavior: An Inventory of Scientific Findings.* New York, Harcourt, Brace and World, 1963, p. 61. This statement demonstrates the frequent confusion between the reliability of findings and their validity. It leads away from, rather than toward an examination of varying contexts of bilingualism.

tings we need not be surprised that there are settings in which the more bilingual actually appear to be superior in verbal intelligence than the less bilingual or the monolingual. This is certainly the case when monolingual masses are compared to bilingual elites. In addition, where good opportunity for fluency in both languages exists for all social classes, where both languages are considered prestigeful, where there is no official allocation of languages to domains and where bilingualism is voluntaristic rather than obligatory, there is every reason to expect the more intelligent to gravitate toward more balanced bilingualism and toward bilingualism at a higher level of competence. This is exactly what we find, although to a lesser degree, even when social class is held constant.[22]

Thus, we can either find *no* relationship, a negative relationship or a positive relationship between bilingualism and intelligence, depending on where in the dominance configuration, where in the acquisition-domain sequence, and where in the social structure we look. Similarly, there are various possible relationships between bilingualism and language learning. Interference can be minimized if coordinate mastery is coupled with nonoverlapping domains. This combination is not always a feasible goal for language instruction where limitations of time, of talent, and of milieu are considerable. Under such circumstances we may have to settle for compound-overlapping bilingualism which is

more replete with interference and which is more obviously instrumental in character. On the other hand, it involves fewer and less serious identity problems.[23]

If by "bilingualism" we mean equal, advanced and non-interfering mastery of two or more codes in conjunction with *all possible interactions* between media, roles, situations, domains, role-relations and topics, we are probably defining a highly theoretical and highly unnatural condition. No natural bilingual population has ever existed that would fit these specifications. Every natural bilingual population makes differential use of its several languages and this differential use both serves to integrate the society as well as to preserve its bilingualism. Both artificiality and anomie are involved in the cases of the rare translators and the equally rare language teachers with perfect, balanced, and advanced bilingualism configurations. The attainment of such configurations need not and cannot be our goal as we labor to advance bilingualism in bilinguals and monolinguals alike.

[22] Elizabeth Peal and Wallace E. Lambert. "The relation of bilingualism to intelligence." *Psychological Monographs*, 1962, 76, no. 27.

[23] Wallace E. Lambert, R. C. Gardner, H. C. Barick, and K. Tunstall. "Attitudinal and cognitive aspects of intensive study of a second language." *Journal of Abnormal and Social Psychology*, 1963, 66, 358–368. Simon N. Herman, "Explorations in the social-psychology of language choice." *Human Relations*, 1961, 14, 149–164.

INSTRUCTIONAL MATERIALS AND AIDS
TO FACILITATE TEACHING
THE BILINGUAL CHILD

Pauline M. Rojas

Instructional Materials and Aids to Facilitate Teaching the Bilingual Child*

PAULINE M. ROJAS, *Dade County Public Schools, Florida*

THE over-all objective in the education of the bilingual child is his integration into the main stream of American life. This does not mean that the bilingual child must give up his own language and culture, but rather that he must be so educated that he will be able to operate in English when the situation demands English and operate in his own language when the situation demands the use of his own lan-guage. It is the obligation of the school to make him literate in both languages. For the bilingual child to be able to operate effectively in the English-speaking world, he must acquire the language to the degree necessary for whatever role his abilities, education and social accepta-bility enable him to play. In addition, the

* Presented at the Conference for the Teacher of the Bi-lingual Child, University of Texas, June 10, 1964.

school must give him a workable knowledge of the behavior patterns and value system of the dominant group.

What does he have to learn when he learns English and what kind of materials are needed to enable him to learn what he needs? The linguists tell us that the learner of English as a second language must learn to understand and produce (1) the basic features of the English sound system and (2) the basic features of the grammatical system of English, as well as vocabulary. In other words, he must be able to communicate in English. The materials he needs in order to learn to use the basic features of English automatically, as does a native speaker, are materials which incorporate them in a context which is appropriate to his age and background of experience.

The classroom teacher cannot analyze the English language and set up her own body of materials. Even if she had sufficient competency in linguistics to do this, the result would be chaotic. With each teacher operating independently, some features of the language would not be taught at all and others presented over and over again.

What the classroom teacher needs for teaching the language is materials in which the basic features of English are embedded in teachable units in such manner that they meet the communication needs of non-English-speaking pupils.

Unfortunately, such materials for beginning children are extremely scarce. The teachers' guides to The Fries American English Series,[1] which were originally intended for use with non-English speaking pupils who already knew how to read and write Spanish, contain the basic patterns of English sequentially arranged and are to that extent valuable as source material. English for Today,[2] another series intended for pupils of elementary and secondary school age, should also be valuable as source material.

The books of The Fries American English Series contain multiple suggested activities to induce aural-oral practice which are appropriate for beginning bilingual pupils or can be adapted to their needs. These books also contain excellent material on the pronunciation problems of Spanish-speaking pupils in footnotes, appendices and in the units themselves.

In addition to materials for structured oral practice, beginning first grade pupils need special materials for a developmental reading program with accompanying writing experiences. Recently attempts have been made to produce beginning reading materials which implement the advances in linguistic science which have relevance for the teaching of reading. One of these attempts is the Miami Linguistic Readers Series now being produced under a Ford Foundation grant to the Board of Public Instruction, Dade County, Florida. These materials consist of pupil's books, teacher's manuals, seatwork books, "big books" and charts.

The basic assumptions[3] underlying these reading materials and developed by the staff producing them, are essentially as follows:

1. In developing beginning reading materials the focus must be on the skills involved in the process of reading rather than on the uses to which reading is put after the process is mastered.

2. The implementation of the alphabetic principle in beginning reading materials should be in terms of spelling patterns rather than in terms of individual sound-symbol correspondences.

3. The child must learn to read by structures if he is to master the skills involved in the act of reading.

4. Structure as well as vocabulary must be controlled.

5. The materials must reflect the natural language forms of children's speech.

6. The content of beginning reading materials must deal with those things which time has shown are truly interesting to children.

7. The learning load in linguistically oriented materials must be determined in terms of the special nature of the materials.

8. The child must have aural-oral control of the material he is expected to read.

9. Writing experiences reinforce listening, speaking and reading.

[1] Boston: D. C. Heath & Company, 1952.
[2] New York: McGraw-Hill, 1961.
[3] Office of Bilingual Education, Dade County. Public Schools, Miami, Florida.

10. The materials must be so selected and organized that they will enable the learner to achieve success as he moves along.

These assumptions[4] are implemented in the materials of the *Miami Linguistic Readers Series* as follows:

1. Aural-oral practice is provided to precede and accompany each segment of the reading program, with special attention given the pronunciation difficulties of the learner.
2. Grammatical structures as well as lexical items are controlled.
3. The materials are organized in such a way that they tend to induce the habit of reading by structures.
4. The spelling patterns of the English writing system are presented systematically.
5. Language forms are presented within the range of what the learner has acquired or is acquiring in order to meet his daily communication needs.
6. Exercises, themes and formats of high interest level are provided, thus promoting a favorable attitude toward books and learning.
7. Attention is focused on the reading process rather than on the uses of reading.
8. Writing activities for systematic reinforcement of the listening, speaking and reading are included.
9. Materials are so organized and graded that the learner's success constantly reinforces his developing skills.
10. Maximum repetition of spelling patterns in relation to total vocabulary load is provided.

It is hoped that readers like the *Miami Linguistic Readers* will make the learning of the skills involved in the process of reading more easily acquired by bilingual pupils than do the traditional basal readers now commercially available. Unfortunately, linguistically based reading materials are only now beginning to be produced. It will undoubtedly be a long time before they will be available to the majority of teachers of bilingual pupils. In the meantime, teachers will have to continue to use the traditional type materials which they now have.

Whatever the series being used, caution must be taken to make sure that bilingual children have ample opportunity to practice listening to and speaking all of the material that they will be expected to read. In beginning book reading, teachers should model the reading of the material sentence by sentence so that the children will get adequate practice in reading by structures imitating the model provided by the teacher. Individual reading will follow group reading as the pupils' skills develop.

In the writing experience provided in the beginning stages, the children must be given the patters to model rather than be expected to create on their own. They should be helped to avoid writing mistakes.

In summary then, the materials appropriate for meeting the academic and communication needs of beginning bilingual children in English should be those that contain the basic features of English sound and structure arranged in teachable units. The materials in the bilinguals' developmental reading program should be built around the spelling patterns of English. Both kinds of material must be practiced orally until it can be understood and spoken. Systematic practice in listening to, speaking, reading and writing linguistically sound materials will surely enable bilingual children. to acquire English much more efficiently and economically than has been possible heretofore. Inasmuch as we already know a great deal about acceptable language teaching methods, the great lack today is for equally acceptable materials.

[4] Office of Bilingual Education, Dade County Public Schools, Miami, Florida.

The Challenge of Bilingualism

The Challenge of Bilingualism

Outline

Introduction

1. Some Facts About Bilingualism in the United States
1.1 A socio-historical overview
    1.1.1 The question of language loyalty
    1.1.2 Demographic data: prospects for the future
    1.1.3 The non-English and ethnic group press
    1.1.4 Foreign language broadcasting in the United States
    1.1.5 Ethnic group organizations and schools

2. Bilingualism and the Schools
2.1 Is bilingualism a handicap?
    2.1.1 Findings against bilingualism
    2.1.2 The case for bilingualism

3. Bilingual Education for Bilingual Children
3.1 Types and characteristics of bilingual programs
    3.1.1 Guidelines for elementary schools where most pupils have only passive knowledge of the N-EMT and no problems with English (Program A)
    3.1.2 Guidelines for elementary schools where N-EMT children have problems with English as a second language (Program B)
    3.1.3 Guidelines for developing bilingualism in both EMT and N-EMT pupils (Program C)
    3.1.4 Guidelines for N-EMT literacy program for bilingual pupils in junior and senior high schools (Program D)
3.2 Teaching materials for programs of bilingual education
3.3 Qualifications of teachers for programs of bilingual education

4. Recruitment of Educated Bilinguals as Foreign Language Teachers
4.1 Certification based on proficiency examinations
4.2 Certification following intensive training in institutes
4.3 Appraisal and recommendations

Key Propositions

Appendix

ABBREVIATIONS USED

EMT	English mother tongue
ESL	English as a second language
N-EMT	non-English mother tongue
SES	socio-economic status
WISC	Wechsler Intelligence Scale for Children

The Challenge of Bilingualism

INTRODUCTION

There is a multi-million-pupil question at the American educator's door, to which the times at last are demanding an answer. Bluntly put, it is this: in view of our country's need for citizens highly competent in foreign languages, in view of our vast expenditure of energy and funds to teach foreign languages, why does virtually no part of the effort and money go to develop and maintain the competence of those 19,000,000—children and adults—who already speak the languages natively? Why is it our public school policy to ignore or stamp out the native competence while at the same time undertaking the miracle of creating something like it in our monolinguals?

The authors of this report believe that the time is at hand, that national attitudes are favorable, and that funds are available to develop and utilize the non-English language resources of American ethnic groups, and that the opportunity is especially favorable for establishing programs of bilingual education for bilingual children in the public schools. There are over three million such children. The task of making them broadly literate in the non-English mother tongue is a task for the foreign language teaching profession.

The report is not concerned with foreign language teaching in the usual sense: it does not deal with the learning problems of monolinguals. Nor is it concerned primarily—except in its Part Four—with developing bilinguals as a source of foreign language teachers. The concern is three-fold: developing the non-English mother tongue for its powerful integrative effect on the child's personality, developing it as an adjunct to education and a career, and developing it as a national resource.

Each of the four parts of the report is essential to an overview of the problem and potential of bilingualism. Combined, they provide facts, tentative guidelines, and examples necessary for making professional decisions and taking action in this field.

PART ONE reveals the extent of bilingualism in conterminous United States, gives an idea of the dynamics of increase or decrease for all the major languages, and shows the strengths and weaknesses of current efforts to maintain the non-English mother tongues.

PART Two is a review of research concerned with the phenomenon of bilingualism *per se* and its possible effects upon the intellectual development of the bilingual person.

PART THREE builds upon the facts and theories of the previous two parts and offers tentative guidelines for the establishment in the public schools of programs of bilingual education for bilingual children. Consideration is given also to the associated problem of teaching English as a second language.

PART FOUR describes two tested procedures for recruiting educated bilinguals for employment as teachers of foreign language: the use of standardized proficiency examinations and the use of intensive institute training. Data are presented to compare the examination scores of these recruits with the scores of teachers prepared by other means.

This is the foreign language teacher's business. It is new business on an agenda of ever-greater scope and challenge.

1. PART ONE: SOME FACTS ABOUT BILINGUALISM IN THE UNITED STATES

1.1 *A socio-historical overview**

Non-English languages of the continental U.S. are commonly classified into 3 groups: (a) indigenous languages, (b) colonial languages, and (c) immigrant languages.

1. The indigenous population is estimated to be as great as or greater than when European colonization began in earnest. Nevertheless, many of the original tribes have disappeared entirely. The Federal Government has vacillated between policies oriented towards forced de-tribalization and tribal autonomy. This on-again, off-again treatment has greatly weakened the ability of Indians to retain their languages and their interest in doing so.

Of the nearly 300 separate American Indian languages and dialects extant, only roughly 40 percent have more than 100 speakers. In the case of about 55 percent of these languages, the remaining speakers are

---

* Section 1.1 is largely adapted from *Language Loyalty in the United States* by Joshua A. Fishman and associates. Prepublication dittoed edition, New York, Yeshiva University, 1964.

of advanced age. These facts imply that many of the languages are destined to disappear as living tongues. Currently, efforts are under way among American Indian organizations to safeguard Indian tribal lands and to strengthen tribal autonomy. These efforts do not include specific emphasis upon language maintenance.

2. Of the colonial languages spoken by 16th, 17th, and 18th century colonizers, English, Spanish, French, and German continued to be spoken in the 19th and 20th centuries, but Russian, Swedish, and Dutch did not survive. Their use in the U.S. today is a result of their re-introduction with immigrant status. Of these languages Spanish has the greatest number of speakers in this country. The ancestry of most Spanish speakers in the United States is not European but Mexican-Indian. To the large indigenous Spanish-speaking population, there have been added in recent years large contingents from Mexico, Puerto Rico, Cuba, and other quota-free Spanish American countries. Thus Spanish has dual colonial-immigrant status.

The situation of French as a colonial language is only superficially similar to that of Spanish. Most Franco-Americans are of post-colonial immigrant stock. German represents a mixture of colonial and im-migrant statuses. Although a great variety of German dialects were spoken in colonial days, it is only in connection with several non-prestige variants—commonly called "Pennsylvania Dutch"—that linguistic con-tinuity with colonial times has been maintained. The vast majority of German speakers in the U.S. today are of post-colonial origin.

3. Any consideration of language maintenance efforts in the U.S. must stress the immigrant languages, since these are the most numerous and their speakers have been exposed to the assimilative forces of American life for the shortest period of time. Mass immigration from Europe lasted from approximately 1880 to 1920. Subsequently, mass immigration has occurred only in the Latin American Spanish-speak-ing case. Millions of speakers of scores of languages arrived on our shores: peasants and townsmen, illiterates and literati, speakers of prestigious and speakers of officially unrecognized tongues, avowed language loy-alists and others who had no particular awareness of their language. They, their children and grandchildren represent a great and largely untapped resource of language teachers and language learners. It is the purpose of this report to examine the nature and extent of these

human resources and to suggest programs for activating and developing them.

1.1.1 *The question of language loyalty*. The Americanization of immigrants has been explained on the basis of irresistible attractiveness of American mass-culture, the destruction of immigrant folkways under the impact of industrialization and urbanization, the openness and ampleness of the American reward system through public education to social mobility, the geographic mobility of our population, which favored adoption of a lingua franca and other equally recent and common cultural denominators, the emphases on childhood and youth and the outdating of adult values and patterns, and even an "Old World weariness" which immigrants purportedly carried with them at a subconscious level. Although the U.S. was born, grew up, and came of age during two centuries in which nationalism reached unsurpassed heights in western history, the vast majority of the millions of immigrants to the U.S. were innocent of nationalistic sentiments or ideologies in their daily lives. Ethnicity of a traditional, particularistic, and non-ideological character—rather than nationalism in its strident and symbolically elaborated manifestations—guided their behavior in most cases. The languages that they spoke were related to the countless acts of everyday life rather than to "causes" or ideologies. Indeed it was only *after* immigration that group and language maintenance sometimes became conscious goals. American "nationalism" has been non-ethnic from the very first. From the days of the Pilgrim fathers American leaders have ideologized morality, opportunity, progress, and freedom. Ethnicity has been considered irrelevant. There was no apparent logical opposition between the ethnicity or nationalism of incoming immigrants and the ideology of America. Individually and collectively immigrants could accept the latter without consciously denying the former. However, acceptance of the goals and values of America placed them on the road to accepting American life-styles, customs, and the English language. Just as there is hardly any ethnic foundation to American nationalism so there is no language awareness in conjunction with the use of English. The English language does not figure prominently in the scheme of values, loyalties, and traditions by which Americans define themselves as "American." Americans have no particular regard for English as an exquisite instrument, no particular concern for its purity, subtlety, or correctness. The fact that so few Americans command any other language than English is largely a result of educational failure, cultural provincialism, and the absence of pragmatic utility for bilingualism, rather than an outgrowth of any conscious attachment to English. Given the lack of ethnic and linguistic awareness roundabout them, the linguistic facility and interest of immigrants steadily diminished or atrophied once they had painlessly and unconsciously accepted the American dream. Anti-foreigner movements (at times, more narrowly anti-Catholic ones) and the opposition to German language and culture during the two World Wars are clearly historical exceptions related to unusual circumstances on the national and international scenes. More normal by far has been the unplanned attrition of minority cultures. More linguistic and cultural treasures were buried and eroded due to mutual permissiveness and apathy than would ever have been the case had repression and opposition been attempted. Immigrant minorities were virtually never forbidden to organize and maintain their own communities, organizations, schools, or publications.

Language loyalty in the U.S. could not but be related to the tenor of American-European relationships, and was at times fanned by the perpetuation on our shores of Old World rivalries and tensions. However, these animosities rarely had more than a brief or intermittent attraction for most immigrants. American social and economic realities were too novel and too inviting and the immigrant populations were too varied and scattered for this aspect of language loyalty to maintain firm footing.

There have always been some immigrants who viewed themselves explicitly as the preservers and saviors of their old country languages and heritages. These language loyalists founded political groups, schools, choral and dramatic societies, and literary and scholarly associations. They established publications at an intellectual level substantially higher than that of the mass-immigrant press or of the mass-English press. They organized societies, institutes, and congresses for the very purpose of linguistic and cultural self-maintenance. All in all, their long-term impact on most immigrant groups was probably negligible. The tradition of struggling for linguistic and cultural self-maintenance is an old one on American shores—even if not a particularly successful one.

To question the wisdom or the necessity or the naturalness of the de-ethnicization of immigrant populations strikes many as questioning the very legitimacy of America's national and cultural existence. Since "Americans" have no ethnic roots in past millennia, as do many other peoples of the world, the Americanizing process itself, i.e. the de-ethnicization of immigrants, takes on a central role in the formation of the national identity and national self-concept of most Americans. Nevertheless, ethnic groups and ethnicity, language loyalty and language maintenance still exist on the American scene. Even Americans of western European origin continue to recognize their ancestry and to partially define themselves in accord with it.

The future of ethnicity and of language maintenance in America is a function of the kind of America we would like to see. It is a problem for Americans of all backgrounds and on all economic levels. The fact that third and subsequent generations frequently continue to think of themselves in partially ethnic terms and frequently maintain positive attitudes and interests with respect to the heritages of their grandparents is a very significant fact about American life, a far more significant one than the fact that acculturation to general American patterns frequently begins in the very first generation. Theoretically, the American melting pot should have been even more successful than it has been. Perhaps the absence of well-defined or deeply-rooted American cultural patterns—which might have been substituted for immigrant cultures—is behind the ultimate failure of the melting pot as much as it is behind its success.

There has been a constant and growing interplay between public Americanization and private ethnicity throughout our brief national existence. The upshot of this process may be that ethnicity is one of the strongest unrecognized facets of American life—in politics, in religion, in consumer behavior, in life-styles, and in self-concepts.

A lack of attention—indeed a repression from awareness—has characterized our reaction to the efforts of minority cultural groups to maintain and develop their particular heritages as vibrant (rather than as ossified or makeshift) lifeways. Only recently has a change of heart and a change of mind become noticeable. It is an open question whether this change represents an instance of "better late than never" or an instance of "too little and too late."

1.1.2 *Demographic data: prospects for the future.* The only official data on non-English mother tongues in the United States are those collected by the Bureau of the Census in 1910, 1920, 1930, 1940, and 1960. These reports, together with informed estimates of non-English mother tongue figures for the native born as of 1960 ("informed estimates" since the 1960 Census provides no mother tongue data for either the native-of-foreign parentage or the native-of-native parentage) permit overall profiles of intergenerational comparison for the principal non-English languages spoken in the United States today:

a. SHARP LOSSES: Characterized by sharp losses in most generations (or by a sharp loss in at least one generation, and moderate losses in each of the others) are Norwegian, Swedish, Czech, Slovak, Slovenian, Finnish, German, Danish, and Yiddish. These languages would seem to require unusually large immigration and revitalization movements if their further decline is to be stemmed.

b. MODERATE LOSSES: Characterized by moderate losses in most generations (but by sharp losses in none) are French, Lithuanian, Rumanian, Polish, Hungarian, Russian, and Portuguese. These languages would seem to require continued sizable immigration and/or effective language maintenance movements if they are not to slip into the sharp loss category during the next decade.

c. MODERATE GAINS: Four languages have experienced moderate gains in at least two generations (and neither sharp losses nor sharp gains in any): Dutch, Italian, Arabic, and Serbo-Croatian. They might be able to withstand serious erosion without special maintenance efforts during the next decade, but with such efforts their position might be appreciably reinforced.

d. SHARP GAINS: Three languages have experienced sharp gains in at least two generations (and at least moderate gains in the remaining generation): Greek, Ukrainian, and Spanish. These languages would seem to be in no immediate danger of decline in the near future. Their creative maintenance cannot be assured, however, on this basis alone and deserves special attention if it is to be secured.

In 1940 the numerically strongest non-English mother tongues in the United States were German, Italian, Polish, Spanish, Yiddish, and French, in that order, each being claimed by approximately a million and a half or more individuals. In 1960 these same languages remained the "big six" although their order had changed to Italian, Spanish, German, Polish, French, and Yiddish.* All in all, the 23 non-English mother tongues for which a 1940-1960 comparison is possible lost approximately a sixth of their claimants during this interval. Nevertheless, the total non-English resources of the nation are still very substantial, accounting for nearly 11 percent of the total 1960 population (and for an appreciably higher proportion of the white population). See Table 1 of the Appendix, 1940-60 totals and percentage of change for 23 languages.

Of the 19,381,786 claimants of a non-English mother tongue in 1960, it is conservatively estimated that 3,199,604 were persons 6 to 18 years of age. See Table 2 in the Appendix for the calculations leading to this estimate.

It is unwise to arrive at conclusions concerning current language status from even the most reliable mother tongue data. Early childhood exposure is not the same as current language utilization and facility. Most Americans claiming non-English mother tongues have also learned English. In many cases—particularly among the native born claimants of non-English mother tongues—the mother tongue may have become quite dormant and may be utilized rarely, if at all. Thus, mother tongue data, without supplemental information concerning current language facility and use, mask distinctions running a gamut from active and constant non-English monolingualism to active and constant English monolingualism. The only way to remedy our current lack of basic data is to conduct a "current language use and facility census." There is much precedent for this being done by the Bureau of the Census as a special study, but thus far the Bureau has not been impressed with the need for such information.

1.1.3 *The non-English and ethnic group press.* The non-English press (which traces its origins back to Ben Franklin's *Die Philadelphische Zeitung* of 1732) still boasts an overall circulation of approximately 4 million today. If we add to the above figure the circulation of those ethnic publications (as distinguished from scholarly publications for non-ethnic readers) which publish sections of each issue in a non-Eng-

---

* In terms of a single composite index of language maintenance potential, the non-English mother tongues with best numerical prospects for the future as of 1960 were Spanish, German, Italian, French, Polish, and Dutch, in this order.

lish language (while other sections are published in English), the total circulation rises to about five and a half million. A. W. Ayer's *Directory* for 1960 lists 61 non-English *dailies*. This is a 57 percent decline since 1930, with the sharpest losses for Norwegian, Swedish, Danish, French, Arabic, German, and Czech, all of which lost three quarters or more of their number, with Scandinavian dailies disappearing entirely. Since 1950, Ukrainian, Italian, Greek, Portuguese, and Rumanian dailies have not decreased in number.

Ayer reports 188 non-English *weeklies* in 1960, a decline of 63 percent relative to 1930. There was a decrease of 34 percent during the 1950-60 decade alone. Only in the case of Near Eastern languages did the number of weeklies increase during the 1930-60 period (by 300 percent). All others show sharp, regular decrease. The most precipitous decreases occurred with weeklies published in "Other Germanic (Dutch),", Italian, "Other Romance," Spanish, German, Polish, Scandinavian, and Yiddish, in which decreases of 70 percent or more occurred.

The fortune of the 106 *monthlies* reported by Ayer for 1960 was improved by a 34 percent increase relative to 1930. This is the only growing segment of the non-English language press. The largest increases have been registered by Ukrainian, Hungarian, "Other Slavic," Polish, Spanish, and Greek. Ayer reported a total of 107 publications in 1960 which combine English with a non-English tongue.

1.1.4 *Foreign language broadcasting in the United States.* In 1956 the American Council for Nationalities Services reported 1,005 foreign language radio "stations"* in continental United States broadcasting a total of 5,442.08 hours a week for an average of 5.42 weekly per station. In 1960 a total of 6,214.70 hours were broadcast over 1,340 "stations" for an average of 4.64 hours a week. Thus, in terms of average hours of broadcasting a week, foreign language broadcasting experienced a decrease of 14.4 percent from 1956 to 1960, even though the total number of "stations" increased by 33 percent and the total hours increased by 14 percent during the same period. The languages most used in 1960 were Spanish, Italian, Polish, German, French, Yiddish, and Portuguese, in that order. Spanish alone accounts for two-thirds of all the foreign language broadcasting in the United States today.

1.1.5 *Ethnic group organizations and schools.* There is no way of de-

* A station broadcasting in three languages is counted as three stations.

terming accurately the number of ethnic organizations in the United States today. It would seem safe to say that there are at least 15,000 functioning formal organizations founded by and for particular groups of ethnics including over 1,800 with "language-embedded" cultural interests. There are between 2,500 and 3,000 ethnic group schools in the United States (whole-day, weekday-afternoon, and week-end), and between 1,000 and 1,200 of these offer formal instruction in the ethnic mother tongue. Of these, the weekday-afternoon schools, due to the characteristics of their teachers and their curricula, represent the most intensive language maintenance programs still predominantly under ethnic control in the United States. Ethnic group schools which no longer teach the mother tongue tend to explain that discontinuation on the following grounds (grounds which seem to be heavily interspersed with feelings of guilt and with attempted rationalizations as if one had abandoned an old and weak relative and now had to find polite and sensible reasons for doing so): parents and children are indifferent to the mother tongue and have no interest in seeing it taught (30 percent); parents or parishioners are actually opposed to further teaching of the mother tongue (21 percent); over-crowded curriculum (11 percent); mother tongue unimportant in the United States (10 percent); students of different national backgrounds enrolled in the school (9 percent); anti-mother tongue pressures inspired by World War I and World War II (9 percent); lack of competent teachers (6 percent); and discontinuation demanded by church authorities (4 percent).

2. PART TWO: BILINGUALISM AND THE SCHOOLS

2.1 *Is Bilingualism a Handicap?*

Before making decisions regarding the education of children who are bilingual, it would be advisable to consider some of the factors which play a part in determining the effects, if any, of bilingualism on the child's development. It has often been asserted that bilingualism is a handicap, making the child confused mentally, affecting his capacity to move ahead in school, etc. Is there any truth in such assertions? Research findings dealing with the effects of bilingualism on intellectual functioning are contradictory. The majority of investigators conclude that bilingualism has a detrimental effect on intelligence, although others have found little or no relation between bilingualism and intelligence. A few studies have actually found evidence suggesting that bilingualism may have favorable intellectual consequences.

The problem here is to attempt to find some order in the confusion. First, we must determine what has been meant by the term "bilingualism." Most of the studies did not adopt an unambiguous definition of bilingualism. It is equally important to delimit the meaning of "handicap" in this context: emotional, social, academic, and intellectual disturbances or drawbacks. The idea that bilingualism may create an intellectual handicap raises the issue of the nature of intellectual development. Earlier views of intelligence as a predetermined, fixed ability, which merely unfolds autonomously in an adequate environment, would preclude the possibility that the learning of two languages could have a major effect on intelligence. However, as a result of an accumulation of more penetrating studies over the years, current psychological theory suggests that the potential intelligence of an individual can be realized to varying degrees, depending in large part on the nature and extent of the environmental stimulation. If an individual is placed in a restricted or impoverished environment, less of his potential intelligence will develop than if he is placed in an enriching environment. This extremely important notion makes one examine the bilingual case to determine if bilingual and bicultural experiences—those that afford the learner contrasting perspectives of his environment—are restrictive or enriching ones.

The "handicap" question then is too general, but it is a summary of more specific ones that have the advantage of leading to empirical answers. The following questions suggest themselves to the psychologist:

a) Does the learning of two languages from childhood at home have any favorable or unfavorable influence on the child's cognitive and social development? That is, is there any systematic difference between the cognitive development of a child who is speaking two languages during this development and a child who is speaking only one?

b) Does the learning of a second language in school at a given stage have any effect on the child's development?

c) What other factors play a part in determining the effects, if any, of bilingualism on development? Factors that come to mind are: the degree of mastery of the two languages, the age when learning the second language starts, the learner's IQ, his socio-economic background, the community's attitude toward the second language group.

When the problem is analyzed in this manner, it becomes possible to look for and find at least partial answers by means of research. The major point is that it is not instructive to make a general statement concerning the effects of bilingualism on development. One must specify under what conditions, if any, bilingualism exerts a favorable influence on the child's intellectual, social, or academic development and under what conditions it exerts an unfavorable influence.

2.1.1 *Findings against bilingualism.* Most of the empirical studies of bilingualism's effects on development have been concerned primarily with the effects on intellectual or cognitive development. Only a few have also considered the effect on academic achievement and hardly any have dealt with social adjustment.

In general, the studies in this area have been conducted without giving due consideration to many of the crucial factors mentioned above. Bilingualism was often not measured at all and the child's intellectual ability was often measured in his second language, not in the language in which he was most proficient. Nevertheless, most of the researchers concluded on the basis of their studies that the "bilingual" child was at a disadvantage intellectually. A few of the better controlled studies will be mentioned here to show how the problem has been investigated and the difficulties that have arisen with this approach. Following this, we will summarize the results arising from all the studies.

In 1946, Darcy reported* on research carried out with 212 American pre-school children of Italian parentage. Her subjects were divided into two groups—monolingual or bilingual—on the basis of their scores on a rating scale of the amount of contact they had with both English and the second language. The two groups were then matched for age, sex, and social class. A verbal test (the Stanford-Binet) and a nonverbal one (The Atkins Object-fitting test) were administered to both groups and the obtained scores were compared. The results indicated that "In every age and sex division, the mental ages of the monoglots surpassed those of the bilinguists on the *Stanford-Binet Scale*, while on the *Atkins Test*, the performance of the bilinguists was consistently superior to that of the monoglots" (p. 41). The author concluded from this that her

---

* Bibliographical references to the studies cited are found in the Appendix.

bilingual subjects suffered from a language handicap in their performance on the *Stanford-Binet Scale*. However, the subjects were so young (from 2-6 to 4-6 years) that it would not be advisable to draw any general conclusions from this study. Even if the bilinguals suffered from a language handicap at this age, they might overcome it later. Also the intelligence of infants and pre-school children is known to be somewhat difficult to determine accurately. For the pre-school child, the performance items are the more reliable indicators of intelligence, and Darcy found the bilinguals actually did better than the monolinguals on such items.

Levinson (1959) tested American-born Jewish pre-school monolingual and bilingual children of similar socio-economic level and found them to perform alike on the Goodenough Test and most subscales of the Wechsler Intelligence Scale for Children (WISC). However, on the Stanford-Binet and the WISC Arithmetic, Vocabulary, and Picture Arrangement subtests the monolinguals scored higher. It should be noted that the subjects of this study were pre-school children.

Johnson (1953) introduced a technique for objectively measuring the linguistic balance of a bilingual speaker, by dividing the number of words he produced in English in five minutes by the number produced in Spanish. A performance (Goodenough Draw-a-Man) and a verbal (Otis) test were administered to the subjects, 30 Spanish-English bilingual boys in the United States. The Goodenough IQ for these children was about average for the total population, but the Otis IQ was considerably below average. The results indicated that the more bilingual the subjects were the better they did on a performance test and the poorer on a verbal test. The fact that all the subjects in this study were boys may have something to do with this finding, since boys are usually less advanced in the verbal area than girls. There was no mention of the socio-economic status of the subjects used.

Spoerl (1944) tested all the bilingual freshmen enrolled at an American college. These were matched with a group of monolingual freshmen for sex, age, and intelligence. The socio-economic status of the two groups was similar, although the bilinguals were slightly lower. A student was considered bilingual if he had learned two languages before school entrance. No differences were found between monolinguals and bilinguals on the 1937 Stanford-Binet or Purdue Placement Test. A slight inferiority was shown by the bilingual students on five of the verbal items of the Stanford-Binet scale.

Even though most of the studies in themselves cannot be considered conclusive, a general trend does emerge from their results. In the area of verbal intelligence, the majority of the studies examined (including these as well as others) found that bilinguals did not perform as well as monolinguals on standardized tests. On performance or nonverbal intelligence tests, some studies found no difference between the two groups and about an equal number found that the bilinguals performed significantly better than the monolinguals. On the basis of results such as these, most investigators concluded that the bilinguals suffered from a language handicap which interfered with their functioning in the verbal area. They did not state that the bilinguals were intellectually inferior, that is, that they had less intelligence, but just that they gave evidence of a language deficiency.

2.1.2 *The case for bilingualism.* Very few individuals have ever developed equivalent or "balanced" skills in their two languages. Most language-learning environments are biased so that the bilingual has more extensive experience with one or the other of his languages. Parents, for example, may contribute to the bias to the extent that they are sensitive to current notions of bilingual confusion or to the degree they feel comfortable in keeping one language associated with family matters. Thus, although many people consider themselves or are considered by others as bilingual, their speech reveals that one of the two languages is dominant. It is certain that most of those considered bilingual for the purposes of educational and psychological studies of the sort considered here were not equally fluent in the two languages. ("Balanced" bilinguals, however, can be found after a good deal of testing and selection. One study to be mentioned below was conducted with bilinguals who, because of their early bicultural experiences, had developed fairly equivalent skills.) Therefore, it is not at all surprising to find that bilinguals, when called upon to manipulate ideas rapidly or form concepts in their second language, do not fare as well as native speakers of that language. The standard intelligence tests in English draw heavily on verbal skills and assume a native knowledge of English (American) cultural traditions. One could hardly expect many bilinguals to have acquired this degree of knowledge and in any case, an intelligence test which draws heavily on such knowledge would not seem to be a good indicator of intellectual functioning *per se*. An analogous case would be to decide the intellectual fate of second language teachers on the basis of their ability to make inferences or form concepts in a second language under time pressure! The performance or nonverbal intelligence tests which measure such cognitive processes as concept formation, reasoning, analogical thinking, with as little dependence as possible on any one language, would seem to be more suitable instruments for getting at the basic intellectual ability of bilinguals, since the bilingual is free to use whichever language he prefers or, indeed, no language at all. An examination of the performance of the bilinguals on such tests reveals that in some studies they performed the same as the monolinguals, while in an equal number they performed significantly *better* than the monolinguals.

From this discussion it follows that if a bilingual were measured in his native or dominant language and compared to monolinguals in that language, he might be expected to do as well or maybe even better on both the verbal and nonverbal sections of the test.

Peal and Lambert (1962) conducted a study which provides evidence on this point. They administered a test standardized in French Canada to two groups of French-Canadian children, one group clearly monolingual in French and the other group clearly balanced bilinguals, as determined by tests of comparative skill in the two languages. Both groups had French as a main language, but the bilinguals had also learned English. The two groups were equated on other variables considered to be relevant, socio-economic status (SES), age, sex. The results indicated that the bilinguals were significantly *superior* to the monolinguals on *both* verbal and nonverbal tests. This finding suggests that under certain circumstances, bilingualism appears to have a favorable effect on intellectual development: the bilinguals were equally fluent in their two languages; they were tested in their first language; they were tested on a test standardized for their first language group; and they were of the same SES and age as the monolinguals.

Is there any theoretical reason to expect that the learning of two languages from early childhood should have differential effects on intellectual development than the learning of only one language? It was mentioned earlier that the nature and extent of development of the intellectual potential is believed to depend on the environmental experiences of the individual. Within this theoretical framework, one may view bilingualism as an enriching experience. The bilingual child has two ways of perceiving and two ways of responding to things in his environment; he masters two linguistic systems; he is exposed to and must learn to adjust to two different sets of cultural experiences. If these experiences are considered to be enriching in any way, they might be expected to have some effect on the bilingual's developing intelligence. Some of these "extra" experiences that the bilingual child undergoes may be thought to help him in the areas of concept formation, manipulation of symbols, flexibility, etc., all of which are basic aspects of intellectual functioning. Some theoretical grounds do seem to exist for expecting favorable effects of bilingualism. It must be remembered, however, that the extent of these effects will be tempered by other variables, such as the SES of the child, the balance between his two languages, his intellectual potential.

The general finding that bilinguals, when tested in English (their second language), did poorer than monolinguals on verbal items, suggests that they know English less well, at least as it is needed for intelligence tests. But do the bilinguals nevertheless do as well academically as the monolinguals? Do they perform as well as monolinguals on other verbal tasks?

Evidence pertinent to these questions may be found in Spoerl's study (1944). She noted that the bilinguals in her study had done consistently better in school work than the monolinguals even though their IQ's did not differ significantly and their performance on several verbal items was somewhat poorer. Further evidence comes from a reanalysis of the Peal and Lambert data. If monolingual and bilingual subgroups are selected such that the overall mean IQ of the two groups is equal, we note that the bilinguals are significantly ahead in school grade. A similar finding emerges from a recent study by Anisfeld (1964) in which two groups of subjects—one monolingual and the other bilingual— equated on IQ, SES, sex, etc., differed significantly on school marks and school grade, the bilinguals being ahead. A study by Lerea & Kohut (1961) found that a group of bilinguals took significantly fewer trials on a verbal learning task than did a group of monolinguals matched with them for age, IQ, sex, and SES, suggesting that part of the bilingual's precocity in school may be attributed to a superior skill at learning.

There is, then, both empirical evidence and theoretical support for the notion that some forms of bilingualism may not be a handicap, but may be an important asset in some areas of development. Let us now return to our original three questions and see if it is possible to supply at least partial answers to them.

a) Does the learning of two languages from childhood have any influence on the child's cognitive development? Learning two languages in this fashion seems to have no effect or a slightly favorable effect on the child's functioning in the nonverbal areas of intelligence. Under certain circumstances, it seems to have an adverse effect on the child's performance on verbal intelligence tests, though this adverse effect generally does not show up in school work, where the bilingual child has been found to be ahead of his monolingual peers. This suggests that verbal intelligence tests are poor instruments to use alone if one wants a true picture of the level of cognitive functioning of a bilingual child. Under other circumstances, the bilingual has even been found to be more proficient than monolinguals of his age on the verbal tests themselves.

b) Does the learning of a second language in school at a given grade have any effect on the child's development? This question prompts us to distinguish among several different learning situations which lead to bilingualism. Let us take examples from an English-speaking country. A child may be raised in a home where language X *and* English are spoken and then attend a school where only English is spoken. A child may learn language X at home, and English in the community and at school where English is the medium of instruction. A child may learn only English at home and at school until a second language (X) is introduced at a given grade level. Unfortunately, these distinctions have not been made in previous studies of bilingualism. However, it appears that most of the studies were concerned with children who spoke a language other than English in the home or who spoke two languages in the home before school entrance. Several of the studies mentioned were done with pre-school children who were already bilingual. It would be instructive to determine by research if the effects of bilingualism differ depending on the age at which the second language is introduced and the place, either home or school. A research start has been made on this problem in a recent investigation by Anisfeld (1964), who compared the mean IQ of two groups of 14-year-old bilinguals (matched on SES). One group had learned various second languages at home, the other had learned Hebrew at parochial school. Those with school training had the higher IQ's, although the difference was not statistically significant. In any case, no general conclusion can be drawn from this study, since the two groups differed significantly in the degree to which they had mastered the second language, with the group who had learned it at school being more skilled. Further research planned specifically for the study of this problem of optimum age of learning and the most appropriate situation for learning a second language is clearly called for. It would be important to determine whether learning the second language at home or at school affected the child most favorably, and what variables determine this effect. For example, it might be shown that parents who have faulty control over the sound system and syntax of the second language should not attempt to teach it to their pre-school children, since they develop habits which the school finds harder to eradicate than it would have been to start the second language from scratch. Current notions in the psychology of human abilities would lead us to expect that the earlier the exposure to the second language, the more profound the effect. It is generally thought that the child's intellectual abilities continue to develop rapidly and are quite flexible at least until puberty. After that time intelligence tends to become more stable and less responsive to environmental stimulation. Whether the learning of a second language at different periods within this pre-puberty era would have differential effects is still to be determined.

c) What other factors play a part in determining the effects, if any, of bilingualism on the child's total development? One variable which seems to be important is the degree of mastery of the two language systems and the equivalence of skills. Peal and Lambert used only "balanced" bilinguals and found them to be superior to monolinguals in both verbal and nonverbal aspects of intellectual functioning. Other studies, using bilinguals with one language definitely dominant, found different results. This suggests that the quality of mastery the bilingual has in his second language may be related to the effects the bilingualism will have on him.

Socio-economic status is another important variable. Since SES is related to intellectual development in general, it would obviously show its effects in the development of bilinguals. Earlier studies reporting large intellectual deficits for bilinguals as compared to monolinguals were found to be faulty, since the bilinguals were actually from lower class homes and it is known that monolinguals of the same SES would also be intellectually deficient (Jones, 1960). In certain settings, bilingualism may be associated with lower SES and it is important to remember that any intellectual deficit found may be due to the cultural deprivation associated with underprivileged living conditions and not due to the knowledge of two languages, *per se.*

Other factors which may affect the child's social adjustment and consequently his intellectual development are the relative prestige of the two languages he speaks and the comparative attitudes of the community in which he lives toward speakers of the two languages. If his mother tongue and the cultural group it represents are looked down on by the community, the child may find himself caught between the two communities in a culture conflict and this conflict will likely express itself in the comparative skills he develops in his two languages and his ability to express himself on measures of intelligence. Anisfeld and Lambert (1961) found that Montreal Jewish children who identified with the Jewish group and appreciated the values and contributions of Jewish culture generally did better in the study of Hebrew than children who held ambivalent attitudes vis-a-vis their own group and culture. Another factor which may determine the effects of bilingualism on development is the way in which the second language is introduced and learned. Preliminary studies have indicated that if the second language is used as a medium of instruction (after a minimum proficiency is acquired) rather than merely taught as a subject, the students become much more fluent in it and more nearly equivalent in their two language skills.

There are likely to be many other factors, not as yet uncovered, that also affect the bilingual child's development. At the present time it seems fair to state that although a number of investigators have concluded that the bilinguals whom they studied suffered from a language handicap which interfered with their functioning in the verbal area, there is no evidence to show that the supposed "handicap" was *caused* by the subjects' bilingualism *per se*. It would be more fruitful to seek that cause in the inadequacy of the measuring instrument and in other variables such as socio-economic status, attitude toward the two languages, and educational policy and practice regarding the teaching of both languages.

3. PART THREE. BILINGUAL EDUCATION FOR BILINGUAL CHILDREN

Of the 4,934,036 persons of school age (6-18) in the United States who are of appropriate background to claim a non-English mother tongue (N-EMT), we have estimated that 3,199,604 in 1960* did in fact retain some use of that tongue. However, the extent and nature of the bilingual resource varies widely. There are counties where virtually everyone speaks Spanish, hamlets in Louisiana where French is the rule except with "les américains." In some cities a majority of the children in every school building speak Spanish; in others the N-EMT pupils are concentrated in certain residential areas. A second degree of complexity is found in those cities where the N-EMT population represents not one but a number of different languages—Chinese, Italian, Polish—and the children are enrolled together in the same schools. The groups of N-EMT children may be only tiny minorities in their schools. Complexity of a third degree is added when "interference" between English and the mother tongue gives rise to the special problems of learning English as a second language. The fourth degree of complexity stems from wide variation in the extent of the pupils' command of their N-EMT. Some are still monolingual. Some understand the language readily, speak, even read and write it. Some can only understand and speak; still others only understand the spoken language. Some use non-standard dialects. Bilinguals also differ widely with respect to the *situations* where the language is used (Home? Church? Play? With one, or both parents? With grandparents? In the presence of monolingual speakers of English?); and with respect to *topics* and *styles of usage* (What can they talk about? Do they control, for example, both informal "tu" and formal "vous?").

---

* See Section 1.1.2 above and Table 2 in the Appendix. The situation in 1965 does not differ significantly from that in 1960.

3.1 *Types and characteristics of bilingual programs*

Bearing in mind the extremely wide range of differences among bilingual children and the situations where they are found, the following types of program in bilingual education for bilingual children are offered as no more than tentative models which must be adapted in every case to the circumstances prevailing in each separate school which undertakes such a program. The guidelines are based upon the best available pertinent experience with first and second language teaching, but they are innovations in contemporary American education and should be undertaken only after careful planning. This is not "foreign language" or "second language" study as traditionally offered in the schools, and does not involve monolingual speakers of English except in Program C and in Program D.

There are some assumptions basic to all of the programs.

1. The basic desideratum is complete realization of the potential of each individual child.

2. The N-EMT pupil's success in school and integration with the dominant culture requires a thorough command of English. Therefore, priority must always be given to English.

3. English can be mastered with native-speaker competence by N-EMT pupils.

4. The most effective way to teach English to N-EMT pupils is by the use of special second language teaching methods.

5. For the fullest development of N-EMT children they should become literate as soon as possible and to as high a degree as possible in their mother tongue. This is best done by using the mother tongue as a second medium of instruction. (This does not conflict with state laws which require that English be the medium for all except foreign language instruction. The courses here proposed are essentially foreign language instruction, but the course content is modified to make the teaching more effective and at the same time reinforce the work in other subject areas.)

6. N-EMT pupils do not master concepts and academic subject content presented through English if they do not have sufficient mastery of English. To avoid this retardation their concept and content learning

may advantageously be through the N-EMT until they master English sufficiently.

7. The N-EMT used as a medium of instruction in the social sciences, mathematics, science, etc., reinforces the pupils' grasp of these subjects.

8. The minimum requirement for participation in any N-EMT development program is the ability to understand ordinary conversation and simple explanations given in the language by a native speaker.

9. The educational goal for N-EMT pupils should be bilingualism and biculturalism.

10. The strongest allies in N-EMT development are the ethnic organizations which are already committing funds, time, and energy to language maintenance. The efforts of these organizations should be recognized and their language schools strengthened by every means, including cooperative arrangements with the public schools.

Program planning and teacher orientation:

Since the four programs outlined are innovations in contemporary American education great care should be taken to inform and orient all sectors of the community, particularly the school officials, faculty, the parents and the pupils themselves, of the rationale, procedures, and goals of any program before it is undertaken.

The scheduling, assembly of materials and orientation of teachers for these programs is a task of such magnitude as to warrant involving all participating personnel in an inservice workshop during the summer preceding inauguration of the program. N-EMT programs should not be book-centered to the exclusion of firsthand experiences.

An essential aspect of the two-language development programs is the strengthening of the non-English speakers' self-image as representatives of their mother tongue. Regardless of the degree to which their linguistic habits may deviate from the accepted standards of a cultivated speaker— and often there is little or no deviation—the non-English speakers are almost certain to think of their language as inferior and of themselves as poor speakers of it when living in an area dominated by English. It is here that linguistic relativity which the scientific linguists so often over-emphasize, should be stressed. One should never suggest that the non-English speaker give up his dialect in favor of a "better" way of writing or speaking. Instead he should be encouraged to develop skill with *another* though related language which will be better suited to new situations which he may face one day.

3.1.1 *Guidelines for elementary schools where most pupils have only passive knowledge of the N-EMT and no problems with English* (Program A)

a. ENGLISH LANGUAGE ARTS AND OTHER CURRICULA. Follow the normal curricula of the school.

b. NON-ENGLISH MOTHER TONGUE DEVELOPMENT—Grades 1-6.

For full development of the child, for maximum integration of home and school, and to make their bilingualism an asset, all N-EMT pupils in this category should be grouped for 30-45 minutes daily for instruction in and through the mother tongue. The N-EMT instruction will follow the normal first grade progression from reading readiness to reading, and then will include social studies, science, health, and arithmetic, all taught in the N-EMT. Except for the limited time devoted to the N-EMT language art *per se*, the N-EMT period will serve to reinforce learning in the normal areas of the curriculum. Instruction is to be focused on language learning *per se* only a minimum part of the time. The major focus will always be on other things, geography for example: reading about it in books written in the N-EMT, discussing it and writing about it in the N-EMT, and by all normal means development of a high degree of literacy in that tongue.* Much emphasis should go to learning through *experiences* with persons, animals, materials, pictures, activities. Reading should be related to experience. Every encouragement should be given to N-EMT pupils to participate voluntarily in the N-EMT program throughout elementary school. However, pupils whose parents do not wish them to participate should be excused from the program.

3.1.2 *Guidelines for elementary schools where N-EMT pupils have problems with English as a second language* (Program B). If the number of pupils entering the first grade with insufficient competence in English does not exceed about 10 percent of the total of all children in that grade, they can be safely assimilated into the English mother

---

* Experience with Franco-Americans who retain only a passive knowledge of French shows that speaking ability is recovered through the use of active audio-lingual techniques: dialogue, dialogue adaptation, choral responses, pattern drills and patterned interrogation, rather than through unstructured questioning and "spontaneous" replies.

tongue (EMT) group if they are distributed equally among all first grade sections and if their teachers are aware of the problems of teaching English as a second language (ESL). If the number of such pupils exceeds 10 percent and is sufficient to form a separate class, the N-EMT pupils may be separated in one or more N-EMT sections taught in the N-EMT and with ESL taught as a subject. This procedure is advisable for three reasons:

1. A proportion of N-EMT pupils much in excess of 10 percent can be expected to establish group solidarity to the extent that they cannot safely be assimilated into the EMT group without much special attention to their English language problems. This amount of attention cannot be given in a mixed N-EMT and EMT group without loss to the latter.

2. The necessary special attention can be given only by a trained ESL teacher.

3. The N-EMT pupils, if required to learn through English before they are ready to do so, will fall behind in other areas of the curriculum. Therefore, their concept and content learning should proceed in the mother tongue until they have gained sufficient mastery of English.

a. ENGLISH LANGUAGE DEVELOPMENT—GRADE I—KEY POINTS:

1. Classify pupils in accordance with their command of English and group them homogeneously.

2. Give intensive instruction in English as a second language for a major and increasing portion of the day, using the best of present day modern language teaching resources.

3. Reclassify the pupils at least four times a year and regroup them according to each pupil's progress in English.

4. In teaching N-EMT first graders to read and write use only content that they have learned to understand and say.

5. As soon as the N-EMT pupils, or any portion of them, have the oral-aural readiness and sufficient reading ability in English to merge with the regular EMT pupils on their grade level, they should be placed in regular EMT classes. This point of readiness to merge will come earlier for some pupils than for others.

b. NON-ENGLISH MOTHER TONGUE DEVELOPMENT—GRADES I-6

At the beginning of the first grade the portion of the school day not used for introducing ESL is devoted to normal first grade instruction in and through the N-EMT, covering the usual areas: social science, science, mathematics, health, etc. The time devoted to N-EMT work decreases to correspond to the increased time given to the English language development noted in *a* above.

In the second grade the amount of instruction in and through English will be increased gradually, the time being devoted to ESL, social studies, science, arithmetic, health, etc. From the third grade through the sixth, all N-EMT pupils will devote all but 30-45 minutes daily to regular instruction in English and through the medium of English. The 30-45 minutes daily will be N-EMT work designed to reinforce learning in the normal academic areas of the curriculum. Pupils should be encouraged to use the N-EMT freely on the playground, in the corridors, and the cafeteria.

3.1.3 *Guidelines for developing bilingualism in both English mother tongue and non-English mother tongue pupils* (Program C). This program is most applicable in schools where at least half of the pupils at all elementary grade levels are N-EMT speakers.*

1. All pupils, EMT and N-EMT, receive approximately half of their instruction daily in each language.

2. The program can be initiated simultaneously in grades 1-3 provided the time devoted to instruction in the second language during the initial year of the program is staged in each of the three grades so as to increase the proportion to one-half gradually. After the initial year of the program this staging takes place in the first grade only. In all other grades after the initial year half of the instruction is in each of the languages.

3. In the beginning stages (of grades 1-3 the initial year and grade 1 thereafter) the basic skills and concepts are always introduced in the first language of the child. These skills and concepts are then incorporated into the second language program as part of a language learning experience.

4. At each grade level classes are paired: one group of N-EMT pupils and one group of EMT pupils. For each such pair of classes there is one native N-EMT teacher and one native EMT teacher, plus a bilingual teacher aide for each two pairs of classes.

* Modeled closely on the Coral Way Elementary School bilingual program established in 1963 with Ford Foundation support in Miami, Florida, and directed by Dr. Pauline Rojas.

5. The native EMT teacher is responsible for the academic instruction in English of a pair of classes: one of N-EMT pupils and one of EMT pupils. The native N-EMT teacher is responsible for the instruction in the N-EMT of the same pair of classes. The bilingual teacher aides assist in the music, art, physical education and supervised play at all grade levels, using both languages as media of instruction.

6. Except for the inclusion of a strong emphasis on second language learning for all children, the curriculum of the bilingual school is the normal one for elementary schools. Virtually all of the work in the N-EMT reinforces the work done in English.

7. The time allotted to learning the basic skills and concepts compares favorably with the time regularly allotted in monolingual schools, the only difference being that in the bilingual school the time is divided between the two languages.

8. Except for the bilingual aide work (v. 5 above) the EMT and N-EMT groups are not combined until each group has developed sufficient competence in its second language. This point should be reached by the fourth grade in the second year of the program. Those pupils who enter the program in grade one are expected to reach sufficient competence in the second language to be mixed to some extent in grade two and for almost all work in grade three and thereafter.

TIME ALLOTMENTS AND STAGING. As an illustration of staging (in grades 1-3 during the initial year and in grade 1 thereafter) for the purpose of increasing gradually the amount of instruction given through each second language, the time distribution schedule for grade one in the Miami bilingual school is included here.

WEEKS	TOTAL TIME	VERNAC-ULAR	SECOND TONGUE	BOTH TONGUES	SECOND LANGUAGE DISTRIBUTION
1-4	210	190	20	0	Enrichment, songs, games
5-12	330	175	60	95*	Enrichment, systematic drill, arithmetic
13-24	330	140	95	95*	Enrichment, systematic drill, arithmetic, social studies, science, health, art

| 25-36 | 390 | 140 | 155 | 95* | (Same as above, plus reading) |

* Supervised play 20, lunch 30, physical education 30, music 15. Total: 95 minutes.

3.1.4 *Guidelines for N-EMT literacy program for bilingual pupils in junior and senior high schools* (Program D). This program is designed for junior and senior high school pupils with a native tongue other than English. It is designed to develop literacy in that tongue more effectively and more completely than is possible when the N-EMT pupils are placed in classes with monolingual EMT pupils who are beginning the study of that, to them, foreign language. The use of texts, methods, and teachers prepared for teaching monolingual beginners is frustrating, embarrassing, and ineffective with pupils who know the language as a mother tongue.

a. *English language development*

The N-EMT pupils follow the regular curriculum of the school except for the daily class period devoted to "foreign" language study, i.e., the study of their mother tongue.

b. *Mother tongue development for N-EMT pupils*

The N-EMT pupils are placed together at each grade level in language classes separate from EMT pupils. (If the number of N-EMT pupils at a given grade level is insufficient to form a "class" pupils from as many as three grade levels can be placed together if they have a common background in the mother tongue.) The "foreign" language is the exclusive medium of instruction. From the beginning, instruction is focused on language learning only part of the time and incidentally. The major focus at all levels is on learning regular academic subject matter through the N-EMT: social science, science, mathematics, literature. Monolingual students in the school who are sufficiently advanced in the study of the same language may be admitted to these classes *as a special honor*. This will ordinarily not be feasible until the monolingual's fourth year of language study. Academic credit should be granted for the "foreign" language study *per se* and, when administratively possible, for the work in the subject field taught through the medium of the language.

3.2 *Teaching materials for programs of bilingual education*

The need for and supply of materials can be stated thus:

EMT PUPIL	BILINGUAL PROGRAMS
a. learns English and through English*	All programs
b. learns second language**	Program C (2.1.3)
c. learns through the second language***	Programs C, D (2.1.3 and 2.1.4)

NON-ENGLISH MOTHER TONGUE PUPIL

a. learns the N-EMT and through the N-EMT***	All programs
b. learns English as a second language	Programs B, C (2.1.2 and 2.1.3)
c. learns through English*	All programs

* Regular state adoptions for English language.

** There is a dearth of these materials for grades one and two. The Ford Foundation project in Miami under Dr. Rojas is preparing English readers for speakers of Spanish in grades one and two.

*** Regular texts used in countries where the N-EMT is spoken. For Spanish, Puerto Rican or Mexican texts; for French, Canadian French texts, etc.

If the N-EMT students' speech is a non-standard dialect it is likely that they can be led most efficiently to a mastery of the standard variant by the use of specialized materials, including audio-lingual drills, which are based on a contrastive analysis of the two variants.*

* Materials of this kind have been developed to facilitate mastery of "standard" French by Franco-Americans in New England. Produced under an Office of Education contract by Bowdoin College, they have been tried out at three NDEA institutes for Franco-American teachers of French and in numerous secondary and elementary schools in New England. For teachers there are two volumes: *Manual for Franco-Americans* (82 pp. mimeo) and *Workbook for Franco-Americans* (61 pp. mimeo) both with tape recordings. For students the text is *Cours de langue française destiné aux jeunes Franco-Américains*, scheduled for regular publication in 1965. It includes dialogues, pattern drills, graded readings and appropriate tape recordings. The authors are Gerard J. Brault, Alexander Hull, Solange DuBoff, Emmanuel Jacquart and Norman D. Deschênes.

3.3 *Qualifications of teachers for programs of bilingual education*

The teacher should be a literate native speaker of the standard dialect and if possible of the student's variant of the language. For work at the high school level and above, the teacher should have learned through the medium of the second language the subject matter to be taught. This is essential because of the impossibility of improvising or translating extemporaneously the special terminology and phraseology that are inseparable from each academic discipline and professional field. The teacher's competence could be determined and his certification based on the results of proficiency tests such as those prepared by the Modern Language Association for the five common languages and distributed by the Educational Testing Service. For languages lacking such standardized tests, certification could be based on the report of a state examining committee.

Experience with Franco-Americans has shown that while the ideal mother tongue teacher is a member of the same ethnic group as his students, his effectiveness depends as much upon his Americanness and modernity as upon his pedagogy and linguistic competence. Students do not sympathize readily with a teacher who is foreign to American language and culture and too prone to praise "Old Country" values and customs.

The mother tongue teacher must, above all, know how to cope with dialectal variations, without disparagement of the student's idiolect and free of the misconception that the parents' speech is a serious impediment to learning. All teachers of young children should be thoroughly familiar with the processes of child growth and development.

4. PART FOUR: RECRUITMENT OF EDUCATED BILINGUALS AS FOREIGN LANGUAGE TEACHERS

The shortage of qualified foreign language teachers at all levels of instruction in the United States does not require documentation here. It is not alone that enrollments have increased faster than the supply of teachers. There is also an unmet demand for new kinds of specialists: to staff the third, fourth, fifth and sixth levels in secondary schools where formerly only 2 years of instruction were offered; to teach new languages—Russian, Chinese, Japanese, and Arabic; to fill state and city supervisory positions; to man expanded teacher training programs; to teach in the elementary schools; above all to satisfy the increasing insistence that foreign language and literature courses be taught through the medium of the foreign language itself. The implied challenge to help meet the shortage by better use of our bilingual resources is obvious.

Two ways of recruiting are currently in use. They are presented here in comparative terms for two reasons: that they may be the more easily judged by a profession which is increasingly zealous about maintaining professional standards; and that, if found adequate, they may be more widely applied throughout the nation.

4.1. *Certification based on proficiency examinations*

The first way is typified by the New York State college proficiency examination program. One hundred fifty two- and four-year institutions* in New York, in cooperation with the State Education Department, now permit qualified individuals to earn college credit or meet teacher certification requirements in modern foreign languages by examination without attendance at regular college classes.

Recently a woman applied to the New York State Education Department for certification as a language teacher in the schools. She was a native-born German, highly literate in the language, but her college-earned credits were for French. She was certified readily for French, but could not be certified to teach the language she knew best, her native tongue. The New York plan has sought to correct this inequity by stating certification requirements in terms of proficiency demonstrated by examination, as well as in terms of college credit hours.

The examinations used in New York—as elsewhere—are the *Modern Language Association Foreign Language Proficiency Tests for Teachers and Advanced Students*, available for French, German, Italian, Russian, and Spanish, and covering seven competencies: listening comprehension, speaking, reading, writing, applied linguistics, culture and civilization, and professional preparation.

Three levels of need are met by the New York plan: 1) Persons with the American baccalaureate or its foreign equivalent who are otherwise qualified can satisfy by examination all foreign language requirements

---

* The extent of the participation of these institutions varies widely.

for certification. There are also certain requirements in general education and professional preparation. There is an examination in Educational Psychology, and one in History of Education is being prepared. A candidate for certification may teach a year without certification and, if the performance is attested as satisfactory by the local school administration, the student teaching requirement is waived. All other requirements must be met before the candidate may be employed as a teacher. Eventually it will be possible for an individual with a baccalaureate degree to satisfy all New York State certification requirements by a combination of examinations and experience. 2) Certified teachers may extend the coverage of their certificates to include foreign language teaching or additional foreign languages by taking the proficiency examinations. 3) College students may meet foreign language requirements by the same examinations.

The proficiency tests were first given in New York under this plan in May 1963, and were offered again in December 1963 and May 1964.

A total of 425 individuals have taken the foreign language proficiency tests. Of these, 149 have satisfied the language requirements for provisional (24 hrs.) or permanent (39 hrs.) certification, and 29 had been certified by October 1964. See Table 3 in the Appendix for details.

Whether New York teachers who are certified in part on the basis of proficiency tests are, as a group, better or worse than those whose credits were all earned by taking formal courses remains to be seen. Insofar as the test results can be used as indicators, the tested group compares favorably with teachers nation-wide who have taken the *MLA Proficiency Tests*, and with a group of 650 graduating foreign language majors in 40 New York colleges and universities, who took the *Tests* in May 1964.* The bilingual candidates for certification did better than the NDEA Institute group as a whole and the college student majors in all of the tests except the one on Professional Preparation. No special evaluation has been made of the effectiveness of these persons as teachers. See Table 4 in the Appendix for the scores of all the groups.

Other states known to be recruiting educated bilinguals as foreign

---

* The 650 were a pilot group examined as a preliminary to a nation-wide administration of the Tests in 1965 to a very large sample of all foreign language majors in American colleges and universities, part of an investigation of foreign language study being conducted by Harvard University under the direction of Dr. John B. Carroll.

language teachers on the basis of proficiency examinations are Pennsylvania, West Virginia, Delaware, New Hampshire, Connecticut, and California. All depend on administration of the *MLA Proficiency Tests for Teachers and Advanced Students.*

The Pennsylvania plan differs from that of New York by granting provisional 3-year certification to candidates who have the equivalent of the American baccalaureate and make criterion scores on the *MLA Proficiency Tests.* These persons may then complete the requirements in "professional education" by in-service work by the time they have taught 3 years, and receive the permanent certificate. The Pennsylvania plan has made a special effort to recruit foreign born and trained persons.

Pennsylvania was one of the first states to require that any person seeking employment for the first time in the state as a secondary school foreign language teacher give evidence of proficiency by satisfactory performance on the *MLA Proficiency Tests.* As of November 1964 approximately 75 bilinguals had been certified as foreign language teachers in the Pennsylvania schools by credit examination procedures. U.S. citizenship is not a requirement.

In West Virginia there is provision as in New York and Pennsylvania for certification as language teachers of persons who have never taught before and of teachers of other subjects who wish their certification to include foreign language. West Virginia requires the American baccalaureate or its foreign equivalent, and grants a provisional 3-year certificate with no additional "professional education" requirements if satisfactory scores are made on the *MLA Foreign Language Proficiency Tests.* Foreign-born persons who are not college graduates can qualify for emergency permits by making minimal acceptable scores on the tests.

The citizenship requirement for teaching in West Virginia can be waived for foreign language work only. The fact that most West Virginia high schools require the foreign language teacher to double in a second subject area has, in fact, made it difficult to place successful non-citizen candidates. Beginning in the spring of 1965 all foreign language majors in West Virginia colleges are expected to take the *MLA Proficiency Tests* as a requirement for certification in that field.

In California, where approximately 400 candidates had taken the *MLA Foreign Language Proficiency Tests* leading to certification, the citizenship requirement for foreign language teaching has been liberalized to the extent that it can be met by an affidavit that the candidate will undertake to become a citizen when and if applicable law makes it possible. Persons with the American baccalaureate or its foreign equivalent who pass the *MLA Foreign Language Proficiency Tests* must take a three semester hours methods course, after which they receive a renewable conditional certificate for two years. They must make up all educational deficiencies.

The University of Texas has a pilot project to prepare bilinguals for language teaching. Participants must have a B.A. degree or equivalent, and be registered in the University during the semester in which they wish to be recommended for certification. They must take the *Graduate Record Examination* and the *MLA Proficiency Tests*. After their acceptance into the program, a practicum is arranged and the teaching of each candidate is observed by a committee. Deficiencies or weaknesses may be remedied through course work or by a reading program prescribed by the committee. A related activity was a summer institute in 1962 at the University to train Spanish speaking elementary and secondary school teachers as supervisors for foreign language programs.

4.2 *Certification following intensive training in institutes*

The second way currently used to recruit educated bilinguals as teachers of foreign languages is by offering intensive pre-service training as the basis for certification. Thus far this means has been used only with Cuban speakers of Spanish, but it is believed to be applicable to persons proficient in other languages, whether or not foreign born and foreign educated.

The institute training program was begun when a recent international development brought to the United States a new resource of language teachers: approximately 250,000 Cuban refugees, native speakers of Spanish. Among these are many well-educated persons, people of broad cultural background who were on relatively high socio-economic levels in Cuba in occupations or as members of professions which they cannot exercise in the United States. As a result, there are in the Miami area journalists, teachers, lawyers, judges, and other professional persons, now working as busboys, taxi drivers, factory hands. Some of them have found satisfactory employment. In particular, a number of

English-speaking former teachers are serving as teacher's aides in the Miami area until they can meet the requirements for certification as regular teachers in our public schools.

In cooperation with the efforts of the Cuban Refugee Program of the U.S. Office of Education and the Cuban Refugee Center in Miami to rehabilitate and relocate these persons, the State University of Iowa conducted the first such institute for 7 weeks in the summer of 1963 to prepare Cuban refugees for service as Spanish teachers in the secondary schools of the United States. Thirty trainees were enrolled. Nineteen of the group were experienced teachers and eleven had degrees in law. Twenty-eight completed the institute work and have been teaching since September of 1963 in high schools, most of them in the state of Iowa.

In the fall of 1963 Indiana State College opened a twelve-month institute for 50 Cuban enrollees, to prepare them as secondary school or college teachers of Spanish. From among some 200 applicants interviewed, the director of the Indiana State College institute selected fifty strong candidates with professional training and experience not directly transferable to this country: 29 lawyers, 9 doctors of pedagogy, and 12 who had almost completed the doctorate. After the course ended in August of 1964, 33 secured positions in Indiana high schools, 5 in high schools of other states, and 6 had college positions in Indiana and elsewhere. There was one drop-out, one death, and four are now housewives. A second 12-month institute of the same kind opened at Indiana State College in September of 1964.

It has been the policy of Indiana State College to select candidates of such educational attainments that they could be given senior standing and receive a B.A. at the end of the 12 months of training, and could earn some graduate credit toward the master's degree. This was done for all holders of Cuban doctorates in law, pedagogy, or philosophy and letters. Those trainees who had completed 4 out of 5 years of the Cuban program of higher studies were granted first semester senior standing and also received the B.A. The year's institute training qualified the candidates for a provisional secondary school teaching certificate, the same certificate granted to other graduates in education at the college. Indiana does not require citizenship of public school teachers, but many of the trainees have initiated steps to become citizens.

The curriculum at the Indiana State College institutes included work in the history of education, psychology, English taught as a second language, Spanish literature, and teaching methods—a total of 40 semester hours. Teaching practice was provided during an 8-week period away from the campus in regular secondary schools, where the trainees were oriented to classroom work, to the entire program of an American high school, and to life in an American community.

The Indiana institutes have been jointly sponsored by the college, the Indiana Language Program, and the U.S. Office of Education. The trainees paid no tuition. The first 12-month institute cost $101,090, contributed in the following amounts:

	1963-64	*1964-65*
Indiana State College	$30,000	$32,500
Indiana Language Program	25,000	5,000
U.S. Office of Education	46,090	81,000

The institute trainees received monthly allotments as follows from the Indiana State Welfare Office:

Single person	$ 55
Married couple	85
Couple with one dependent	115
Couple with two dependents	145
Couple with three dependents	165

Trainees at the second Indiana institute (1964-65) have met a part of their expenses by borrowing on the pattern of the NDEA Title II student loan program. The cost to the U.S. Office of Education noted above as $81,000 will be reduced by $1,500 per student by this means.

Other programs to recruit bilingual Cubans as teachers of Spanish have been organized. As of October 1964 a total of 182 persons thus prepared and certified were known to be teaching, in fifteen States and Puerto Rico. Nine of these were teaching in colleges. See Table 5 in the Appendix for the extent of this activity in all places to date.

4.3. *Appraisal and recommendations*

No more than subjective opinion is available to assess the effectiveness of these recruited bilinguals as teachers in the classroom. Nor is it easier, be it said, to measure the classroom performance of teachers prepared and certified by the more common procedures. One measure of the success of the Cubans is that of those employed in 1963-64 almost 100 percent have had their contracts renewed. Without recourse to bilinguals recruited in the two special ways here described, approximately 51 percent of our teachers of foreign language at all levels are already drawn from the ethnic group corresponding to the language they teach and can reasonably be classified as teachers of their mother tongue.

Certification on the basis of proficiency examinations is deplored by some critics as a way of down-grading professional preparation, i.e., courses in "education." Others hail the procedure as a way of basing certification on achievement rather than "mere" credit counting. The intensive institute procedure can be viewed as a way of by-passing the normal teacher-training faculties and experiences. What is the place in foreign language teaching for the person who would teach his mother tongue? Opinion has it that such persons are often weak in methodology, often fail to understand the young American learner. Too, there is a current illusion that the N-EMT speaker's deviations from the "standard" dialect are more grievous and less acceptable in the classroom than the "pure" (untainted by ethnicity and social class distinctions) rash of errors which mark the tongue and pen of many teachers to whom the foreign language is still foreign. The authors of this report believe that the potentials of the native speaker and of the non-native speaker are equally high as language teachers, and that facilities are now available to make them equally competent.

RECOMMENDATIONS:

1. All institutes designed to recruit and train bilinguals should administer the *MLA Foreign Language Proficiency Tests* to their trainees if for no other reason than to give objective evidence to the trainee himself, to the profession and to the public that high standards are set and maintained.

2. The two recruiting procedures should be combined and applied vigorously, nation-wide, to bring into the profession a larger number of American-born native speakers of the foreign languages taught in our schools.

3. The use of the intensive training institute should be extended experimentally to recruit educated speakers of languages other than Spanish.

4. The intensive training institute procedure should be applied to recruit as teachers of FLES in the elementary schools young American-born native speakers of Spanish and French who already have the baccalaureate and certification for work in the elementary schools.

5. Both the intensive training institute and the proficiency examination procedures could be used to exceptional advantage to provide teachers for service (part-time or full-time) in the programs of bilingual education for bilingual children outlined in sections 3.1.1, 2, 3, and 4.

6. There is increasing interest in replacing the usual course at the final level of instruction (4th, 5th, or 6th) in secondary schools with a course in another subject area, given through the foreign language medium. For example, French IV might be a course in world geography taught entirely in French. Either of the two procedures could be used to recruit suitable teachers for this specialized work.

7. Candidates for certification on the basis of the *MLA Foreign Language Proficiency Tests* should not be required to take additional work in any of the competencies in which they make satisfactory scores. The student or apprentice teaching requirement must be met by actual classroom teaching experience under close supervision.

8. The citizenship requirement should be waived for teachers of foreign language.

KEY PROPOSITIONS

1. There are still over 3 million school-age individuals in continental United States who retain the use of a non-English mother tongue.

2. Although some of these are encouraged and assisted to retain their non-English mother tongue by ethnic communities, schools, organizations, publications and radio programs, these institutions and media are frequently too weak and too adult-centered to accomplish this goal by themselves. Public encouragement and assistance are sorely needed if this valuable language resource is to be retained and developed.

3. Bilingualism *per se* has not been shown to produce an intellectual handicap. If such a handicap exists in some bilinguals, its cause must be sought in such factors as the measuring instrument used, socio-economic conditions, attitudes toward the two languages, and educational policy regarding the two languages.

4. Every N-EMT child should, for his own sake and in the national interest, have the opportunity to become strongly literate in his mother tongue.

5. The development and administration of programs to produce a high degree of literacy in the school child's non-English mother tongue is a responsibility of the foreign language teaching profession.

6. The most effective literacy training in the mother tongue does not concentrate on that language *per se*, but rather uses it as a medium of experience and instruction in a wide variety of other areas.

7. The shortage of foreign language teachers can be lessened and the profession strengthened by recruitment of educated bilinguals—whether foreign trained or not—and their certification on the basis of proficiency tests or special institute training. This is applicable to all languages taught in the schools.

APPENDIX

TABLE 1

1940-60 totals for 23 languages

Language	1940 Total	1960 Total	Total Change n	%
Norwegian	658,220	321,774	−336,446	−51.1%
Swedish	830,900	415,597	−415,303	−50.0%
Danish	226,740	147,619	−79,121	−34.8%
Dutch/Flemish	289,580	321,613	+32,033	+11.1%
French	1,412,060	1,043,220	−368,840	−26.1%
German	4,949,780	3,145,772	−1,804,008	−36.4%
Polish	2,416,320	2,184,936	−231,384	−9.6%
Czech	520,440	217,771	−302,669	−58.2%
Slovak	484,360	260,000	−224,360	−46.3%
Hungarian	453,000	404,114	−48,886	−10.8%
Serbo-Croatian	153,080	184,094	+31,014	+20.3%
Slovenian	178,640	67,108	−111,532	−62.4%
Russian	585,080	460,834	−124,246	−21.2%
Ukrainian	83,600	252,974	+169,374	+202.6%
Lithuanian	272,680	206,043	−66,637	−24.4%
Finnish	230,420	110,168	−120,252	−52.2%
Rumanian	65,520	58,019	−7,501	−11.4%
Yiddish	1,751,100	964,605	−786,495	−44.9%
Greek	273,520	292,031	+18,511	+6.8%
Italian	3,766,820	3,673,141	−93,679	−2.5%
Spanish	1,861,400	3,335,961	+1,474,561	+79.2%
Portuguese	215,660	181,109	−34,551	−16.0%
Arabic	107,420	103,908	−3,512	−3.3%
Total*	21,786,540	18,352,351	−3,434,189	−15.8%

* Adding the figures for "all other" languages reported by the Census and the generational estimates based upon them, the two totals would become 1940: 22,036,340; 1960: 19,381,786.

TABLE 2

Americans 6-18 years of age with non-English mother tongue
(N-EMT) in 1960

Total claimants of N-EMT in conterminous U.S.[1]		19,381,786
Total claimants of Spanish	3,335,961[1]	
Total foreign born		
claimants except Spanish	7,118,190[2]	
Total American Indians	523,591[3]	
	10,977,742	10,977,742
Total claimants except above 3		
classes	8,404,044	
Children 6-18 in this group		
(23.6%)[2]	1,983,354	
Estimated percentage of these		
children with N-EMT (16%)[2]	317,336	317,336
Total foreign born claimants, except		
for Spanish language	7,118,190	
Children 6-18 in this group		
(15%)[4]	1,067,728	1,067,728
Total claimants of Spanish, native		
and foreign born, including Puerto		
Ricans in continental U.S.[5]	5,108,586	
Children 6-18 in this group		
(34%)[6]	1,736,919	1,736,919
Total American Indians	523,591	
Children 6-18 in this group[7]	146,035	
N-EMT children	77,621	77,621
Estimated total persons 6-18 in conter-		
minous U.S.A. having a N-EMT[8]		3,199,604

[1] Fishman, Joshua, et al. *Language Loyalty in the United States*. Pre-publication dit-toed edition. New York: Yeshiva University, 1964. Chap. 2, pp. 37, 38 and passim.

[2] *U.S. Census of Population 1960—U.S. Summary—General Population Characteristics*. Washington, D.C.: Government Printing Office 1962, Table 46.

Mother tongue teachers report very minimal levels of "typical mother tongue mastery among entering pupils" in their schools. In general "understanding" is reported as being a little more prevalent than "speaking" ability when pupils enter the first grade. Even "understanding" is reported only by 18% to 20% of mother tongue teachers. Unilingual pupils who understand the mother tongue only are not only extremely rare but are reported only by mother tongue teachers in Weekday Afternoon and Weekend Schools. By the end of the first year of instruction some increment in pupil understanding and speaking ability—particularly in the former—is frequently reported by mother tongue teachers in all school types. Thus, either "fair" or "fluent" pupil understanding is claimed by 26% to 38% of mother tongue teachers by the end of the first year of attendance, although only approximately half that number claimed that pupils had any understanding of the tongue on entering the first year of study.

[3] Estimate by Bureau of Indian Affairs, 1964.

[4] Percentage estimate reduced from normal (23.6 percent) for total population because of large number of old persons in this group.

[5] Samora, J. *Spanish-Speaking Peoples* (unpublished staff paper prepared for U.S. Commission on Civil Rights, 1964). Demographic data from *U.S. Census of Population* 1960. PC(1)D Series, PC(2)-1D and PC(2)-1B. There is an obvious inconsistency between the Fishman data for the Spanish speaking peoples and the figure reported by Samora. The decision to use the Samora estimate for Spanish does not imply that the problem of the inconsistency has been in any way resolved, a task beyond the resources of the committee. ABG

[6] Census data show 38.1 percent persons aged 5-19 in Puerto Rico as compared to 27.2 percent for continental U.S. population. Data show 34.7 percent persons ages 5-19 among those of Spanish surname in five Southwestern states.

[7] Bureau of Indian Affairs counts 121,035 in states which have special Indian schools. Of these an estimated 60 percent at least understand the N-EMT. No separate count of Indian children is made in states which place them all in the public schools: Calif., Idaho, Mich., Minn., Neb., Oregon (has one separated group), Texas, Wash., and Wisc. Of the estimated 25,000 in these states at least one-fifth have a N-EMT.

[8] No attempt is made here to include data for the outlying possessions. The number of insular Puerto Ricans was 2,349,544 in 1960 and the proportion of children aged 6-18 approximately 34 percent, i.e., 798,844.

TABLE 3

1963-64	TOTAL	FRENCH	GERMAN	ITALIAN	RUSSIAN	SPANISH
Number Taking	425	126	79	40	26	154
Passed All Parts	149	61	29	12	3	44
Provisional	24	9	2	7	1	5
Permanent	125	52	27	5	2	39
Certificates Issued	29	5	8	5	1	10

TABLE 4

Modern Language Association Foreign Language Proficiency Tests for Teachers

1. Pretest Scores—All Teachers NDEA Summer 1962 Institutes
2. Pretest Scores—New York State Teachers NDEA Summer 1962 Institutes
3. Scores—New York State Candidates for Certification 1963
4. Scores—New York State Candidates for Certification May 1964
5. Scores—Graduating Foreign Language Majors—NYS Colleges

CANDIDATES

	1. ALL NDEA			2. NYS NDEA			3. May 1963			3. Dec. 1963			4. May 1964		5. FL Majors (Carroll Study)	
	No.	Mean	Sigma	No.	Mean	Sigma	No.	Mean	Sigma	No.	Mean	Sigma	No.	Mean	No.	Mean
FRENCH																
Listening	1582	37.8	8.9	221	41.5	8.4	35	51.4	6.3	27	50.1	7.8	57	50.1	345	43.9
Speaking	1517	70.9	18.2	215	77.5	15.0	35	102.2	17.1	25	111.3	15.1	57	98.9	332	73.8
Reading	1582	43.0	10.9	221	49.1	10.2	35	59.3	8.6	27	60.0	7.6	57	57.8	347	49.1
Writing	1581	42.9	12.6	221	50.5	11.3	35	60.7	10.9	27	67.7	11.7	59	59.7	347	47.4
Applied Ling.	1582	44.7	7.8	221	48.9	8.0	35	47.8	6.5	27	48.1	9.8	55	46.8	182	48.8
Civ.-Culture	1580	43.4	8.4	221	48.5	8.8	35	52.3	9.8	28	53.7	11.5	55	52.9	182	48.7
Prof. Prep.	1582	59.6	8.1	450	62.5	8.2	35	54.1	7.1	30	57.6	9.6	60	56.5	166	61.2
GERMAN																
Listening	468	38.5	9.2	42	42.5	9.6	23	51.7	5.2	12	54.8	2.2	41	50.9	71	45.3
Speaking	459	79.1	15.7	42	89.2	13.6	23	120.7	12.2	12	118.6	27.6	42	120.5	66	91.8
Reading	469	44.4	12.1	42	50.8	12.8	23	63.7	5.1	12	65.6	2.8	41	62.2	71	53.6
Writing	469	46.2	16.8	42	55.7	16.0	23	65.0	10.8	12	68.4	8.7	41	65.1	71	55.9
Applied Ling.	468	46.2	8.9	42	51.3	8.8	23	51.8	6.9	12	51.6	5.6	41	45.2	25	47.5
Civ.-Culture	468	46.3	9.8	42	51.9	9.5	23	54.9	8.2	12	53.6	11.1	41	54.7	24	52.2
Prof. Prep.	468	58.6	8.3	450	62.5	8.2	23	53.8	9.7	12	53.1	9.8	43	51.4	22	59.3

RUSSIAN

Listening	227	37.5	7.1	45	39.6	7.3	11	53.4	2.5	None			8	49.0	46	41.4
Speaking	224	72.9	17.4	45	78.0	14.6	11	112.1	8.8				9	99.1	43	77.8
Reading	227	35.4	10.1	45	35.9	10.1	11	63.2	5.8				8	54.8	46	42.1
Writing	227	47.4	16.8	45	51.6	13.1	11	77.7	4.6				8	63.5	44	58.9
Applied Ling.	186	40.8	6.5	34	43.3	5.2	11	43.6	6.4				8	41.9	18	45.6
Civ.-Culture	227	46.2	9.5	45	47.4	10.4	11	48.8	10.6				9	46.4	14	51.8
Prof. Prep.	186	56.7	8.8	450	62.5	8.2	11	44.3	6.7				8	48.9	6	55.0

SPANISH

Listening	1460	40.1	8.1	144	45.6	7.0	48	50.5	4.9	28	49.0	4.2	66	49.4	189	43.5
Speaking	1420	76.5	21.1	135	87.3	19.1	48	110.0	14.0	26	102.9	14.2	66	97.9	182	74.9
Reading	1461	42.6	10.5	145	49.8	10.3	48	59.3	7.5	28	56.7	9.5	67	57.8	191	46.9
Writing	1460	47.6	14.0	145	57.2	11.9	48	67.5	10.0	28	64.6	13.1	68	68.4	191	52.9
Applied Ling.	1460	43.7	7.9	146	46.9	8.7	48	40.0	5.8	30	40.1	6.3	72	39.6	111	44.6
Civ.-Culture	1462	50.3	9.9	144	58.0	10.0	48	56.0	8.3	28	55.1	7.0	65	55.1	111	55.3
Prof. Prep.	1462	59.3	7.9	450	62.5	8.2	48	51.8	8.7	33	52.7	8.2	72	52.6	102	61.1

TABLE 5

College	Year	Term	Number of trainees	Certificates granted
Kutztown State College (Pa.)	Summer '64	9 weeks	27	27
College of Great Falls (Mont.)	1964-65	12 mos.	28	—
U. of Miami*	1962-63	8 mos.	50	50
U. of Miami*	1963-64	12 mos.	70	69
U. of Miami*	1964-65	12 mos.	80	—
Kansas State Teachers College	1964-65	12 mos.	42	11**
State University of Iowa	Summer '63	8 weeks	30	28***
State University of Iowa	Summer '64	8 weeks	22	22***
Indiana State College	1963-64	12 mos.	50	47
	1964-65	12 mos.	50	—
U. of the Pacific (Calif.)	1964-65	12 mos.	30	—

* This was "extension" rather than full-time study.
** Certified and employed after one term, i.e., before the end of the institute, four as college teachers.
*** Certification is "temporary."

REFERENCES

Anisfeld, Elizabeth Peal. A comparison of the cognitive functioning of monolinguals and bilinguals. Ph.D. thesis, McGill University, 1964.

Anisfeld, M., & W. E. Lambert. Social and psychological variables in learning Hebrew. *J. Abnorm. Soc. Psychol.*, 1961, *63*, 524-529.

Darcy, Natalie. The effect of bilingualism upon the measurement of the intelligence of children of pre-school age. *J. Educ. Psychol.*, 1946, *37*, 21-44.

Johnson, G. B. Bilingualism as measured by a reaction-time technique and the relationship between a language and a non-language intelligence quotient. *J. Genet. Psychol.*, 1953, *82*, 3-9.

Jones, W. R. A critical study of bilingualism and nonverbal intelligence. *Brit. J. Educ. Psychol.*, 1960, *30*, 71-76.

Lerea, L., & S. M. Kohut. A comparative study of monolinguals and bilinguals in a verbal task performance. *J. Clin. Psychol.*, 1961, *27*, 49-52.

Levinson, B. M. A comparison of the performance of bilingual and monolingual native-born Jewish pre-school children of traditional parentage on four intelligence tests. *J. Clin. Psychol.*, 1959, *15*, 74-76.

Peal, Elizabeth, & W. E. Lambert. The relation of bilingualism to intelligence. *Psych. Monogr.*, 1962, *76*, No. 27 (Whole No. 546).

Spoerl, Dorothy T. The academic and verbal adjustment of college-age bilingual students. *J. Genet. Psychol.*, 1944, *64*, 139-157.

BILINGUALISM IN THE MODERN WORLD

John Macnamara

JOURNAL OF SOCIAL ISSUES
VOLUME XXIII, NUMBER 2, 1967

BILINGUALISM IN THE MODERN WORLD

Perhaps the first impression which the reader of this issue will receive is that bilingualism is far more widespread than he imagined. This is not the result of any deliberate plan, yet so many contributors refer to so many bilingual settings that the effect is just as forceful as if it had been planned. Americans in general and American academics in particular are so accustomed to a seemingly monolingual environment that they are likely to be surprised by the extent of bilingualism. Indeed few among them suspect that for the majority of those who speak it, English is a second language. Before going on to the more central problems of the issue it might, then, be profitable to elaborate a little on the magnitude of these problems in terms of the number of persons involved.

Most nation's of Europe—whether Western or Eastern, Northern or Southern, or Central—are multiethnic and as a result multilingual. As national ideologies involve ever increasing proportions of their populations in national processes, the proportions of these populations which become bilingual grows accordingly.

The Catalans, Basques and Galicians in Spain; the Bretons and Provencals in France; the Welsh and Scots in the United Kingdom; the Flemings and Waloons in Belgium; the Romansh in Switzerland; the Valoise, Piedmontese, Germans in Italy; the Frisians in Holland; the Laps throughout Scandinavia; the Italians, Hungarians, Slovenes, Croations, Albanians and Macedonians in Yugoslavia; the Germans, Poles and Slovaks in Czechoslovakia; the Germans and Ukrainians in

1

Poland; the Hungarians in Rumania; the Macedonians in Bulgaria; the Turks in Cyprus; the Greeks in Turkey; the Finns, Estonians, Latvians, Lithuanians, White Russians, Ukrainians, Germans, Jews and various peoples of the Caucases in the Soviet Union—these are merely the most obvious bilingual populations in Europe, after generations and even centuries of national unification, transfer of populations, expulsion and genocide. Little wonder then that European scholars, governments and voluntary organizations continue to be highly interested in bilingualism (Vildomec, 1963; UNESCO, 1966; *Europa Ethnica*, 1967).

If bilingualism is still so widespread and so diversified in Europe, how much more so is it in Latin America, Africa and Asia! In these continents, too, there are numerous instances of bilingualism based on ethnic differentiations within the body politic (e.g. Quechua in Peru; the many linguistic groups in India; Guarani in Paraguay, etc.). Bilingualism which is due to the distance (and formerly the social gulf) between the vernacular and the standard varieties is also found (e.g. Classical Arabic on the one hand and Egyptian, Syrian, Iraqui and other varieties of vernacular Arabic on the other—the differences being far greater than between, say, Chaucerian English and contemporary Bostonese). Finally, widespread bilingualism occurs because of the revival and expansion of national languages formerly not spoken for centuries or used only for limited purposes by restricted populations— e.g. Hebrew in Israel, Swahili in Tanzania, Bahasa Indonesia in Indonesia, and Pilipino (Tagalog) in the Philippines.

However, besides these kinds of bilingualism, there is another type which characterizes many of the new and developing nations. Many such nations have frontiers that are no more than arbitrary lines drawn on the map by agreement between formerly contending colonial powers. As a result, many new nations are marked by such extreme ethnic diversification (far beyond any European nation) that no indigenous language can hope to become the instrument of national unification and development. In addition none of the indigenous languages is currently equipped to deal with the modern world of technology and bureaucracy (UNESCO 1953; Bull, 1955). Certainly these languages could be developed as literary, commercial and industrial instruments, as were English, Spanish and French many centuries ago and as were Finnish, Bulgarian and Ukrainian more recently. However, given the context of ethnic diversification, pressing exigencies of modern nationhood, and the heritage of excolonialism and neocolonialism, it appears impossible (or inadvisable) to wait to develop the indigenous languages as instruments of modern commercial, technocratic and literary communication. In order to obviate these difficulties, languages of wider communication, such as English or French, have been adopted as national languages and, as a result, countless new bilinguals have been and are being created.

Diglossia . . . a Recurrent Theme in this Issue

But it is not enough merely to list bilingual situations or to classify them according to their origins. One recurrent theme in this issue is that it is more important to ask what functions are served by each of the languages in a bilingual situation, and what settings and functions are considered appropriate to each by their speakers. Such questions, which for some time have been a major concern of sociolinguists, were given initial prominence by Charles A. Ferguson (1956) who not only described a particular type of bilingual situation, but coined the now popular term *diglossia* to describe it. Diglossia, as Ferguson defines it, "is a relatively stable language situation in which, in addition to the primary dialects of the language (which may include a standard or regional standards), there is a very divergent, highly codified (often grammatically more complex) superposed variety, the vehicle of a large and respected body of written literature, either of an earlier period or of another speech community, which is learned largely by formal education and is used for most written and formal spoken purposes but is not used by any sector of the community for ordinary conversation". An example of diglossia is the coupling of Standard German and Swiss German in the German-speaking cantons of Switzerland. The whole adult population knows both varieties, but employs them for distinct functions. In the decade since the appearance of Ferguson's article the term diglossia has been generalized to all situations in which a *high* or standard variety is employed for the purposes of more formal communication, and a *low* or relatively uncultivated variety is employed for the purposes of more intimate communication. Fishman makes particular use of this more refined contrast in his article, but it also underlies the articles of Hymes and Gumperz and to some extent that of Kloss.

Fishman, Hymes and Gumperz also stress the further point that both bilingualism and diglossia are best not considered in isolation, but rather as salient examples of a capacity for code variation which is also to be found among monolinguals. In order to appreciate this point it is necessary to recall the work of such scholars as Bernstein (1961) and Labov (1966) who showed that the differences between the English spoken by upper and lower class native English speakers can be surprisingly large. In fact such differences in what is generally considered to be a single homogeneous code can in some cases match the linguistic code differences of bilinguals. However, for the present purpose, the point to note is that several contributors advocate the use of a single theoretical model to handle all code variation whether monolingual or bilingual, and Hymes actually proposes such a model in detail. This development is of great value in allowing us to see bilingual functioning in much broader perspective than has hitherto been the case.

Other Themes . . .

Other themes running through the issue relate more specifically to the psychological and educational aspects of bilingualism. Ervin-Tripp and Lambert discuss the effects of attitudes toward race and language on the individual bilingual. Ervin-Tripp's paper deals with the effects of such attitudes, and those of other factors, on the acquisition of English by Japanese women who married English-speaking Americans and came to live in the United States. This study is of particular interest in that it is one of the very few which combines the theoretical frameworks and techniques of both psycholinguistics and sociolinguistics. Lambert studies the effects of social attitudes on the individual bilingual's perception of himself in each of his two language roles and on his perception of others with whom he comes in contact. Taken together these two papers treat of language learning and of norms and attitudes which the learner acquires often quite unconsciously together with language. Thus these studies complement the work of sociolinguists who study language usage from the point of view of society by adding the dimension of the individual within society.

Two other papers, those by Gaarder and Macnamara, study problems relating to the education of bilinguals with special reference to the use of the "weaker" language as medium of instruction. Education is of course the meeting point of those cross winds which others observe in isolation, but which the educator must deal with in combination without the leisure to await the outcome of academic researches. For these reasons studies of the educational problems associated with bilingualism are at once particularly valuable and particularly difficult.

While the issue does throw new light on some aspects of these problems it does not carry articles on two perennial problems of the greatest importance, the effect of bilingualism on the cognitive and linguistic development of children. Critical summaries of relevant research may however be found in Darcy (1953 and 1963), Peel and Lambert (1962) and Macnamara (1966).

Bilingualism and the Developing Nations

For many bilinguals in the new and developing nations the languages of wider communication to which they are exposed (such as English, French, Spanish, Russian, Arabic, Chinese and Swahili) will doubtless remain *weaker* languages. Some will master only the written form of these languages and only rarely use them in face to face communication. Others on the contrary will never learn to read and write these languages and will function in them only at the level of speech.

In either case, the burden of functioning in a weaker language must be added to the already great burdens of the poor nations of the world. Many consider this to be a necessary but passing burden, one which will be lifted within a few generations as the new *foreign* languages become *indigenized* and displace the local vernaculars that now divide the citizens. Obviously, however, some vernacular speakers will resist displacement of their mother tongues and the possibilities of secessionism are very real, as the cases of India, Nigeria and other new nations, so clearly demonstrate.

Bilingualism—a Constructive Force

Bilingualism is potentially at once a powerful disruptive force and a source of enrichment for mankind. The danger is that a nation may attempt to control this force by destroying it. Fishman's work, *Language Loyalty in the United States* (1966), documents the struggle in one country. Aware principally of the disruptive power of language, the United States set about making of its people, drawn from all over the world, a monolingual nation. Now, at last, somewhat aghast at its success, the United States is becoming aware of the riches it has sacrificed to national unity and appreciative of the cultural groups that resisted its conscious, and unconscious, policies of homogenization. The new tendency is seen in educational programs which aim at preserving and fostering what remains of those treasures. (Brault, 1963 and 1964; Center for Applied Linguistics, 1967) and at promoting the learning of foreign languages (Gaarder, 1965). Certainly the United States is now sufficiently influential to give the world an important example of linguistic tolerance. This example is likely to loose much of its force unless there is an understanding of the inspiration which brought it about and the bilingualism which it hopes to achieve.

Bilingualism is so complicated a phenomenon that one has the giddy feeling that in speaking of it one speaks of all things at once. It has been studied by psychologists because it raises problems about the use of two sets of language skills by a single individual and problems about the sometimes conflicting emotions and attitudes associated by the individual with his two languages. It has been studied by educators because of the basic relationship of language to all learning, because of the access which bilingualism allows to two cultures, and because of the administrative problems to which it gives rise. It has been studied by linguists because of its effects on language usage. It has been studied by sociologists and anthropologists because associated with language are attitudes and norms which have an effect on social and cultural institutions. Finally, it has been studied by political scientists who see in it a challenge to political institutions.

It is impossible for any one man to master all the disciplines required for the adequate description and study of bilingualism; so progress depends on the collaboration of representatives of these disciplines. Several contributors appeal for such collaboration. Hymes, in particular points out that the reality to be studied is the use of language for a human purpose in a particular social environment. When the society, the individual and the language are studied in isolation the reality is lost. Nor can the reality be recaptured from the separate parts studied, because the frames of reference for each study were not developed with a view to the subsequent reconstruction of the living speech act. This issue of the *Journal of Social Issues* brings together for the first time articles from scholars in all the relevant disciplines. For this reason alone, and despite the fact that no attempt has been made to cover exhaustively the whole area of research on bilingualism, the contributors are particularly happy to present this issue on Problems in Bilingualism. The issue appears at a time when researches, conferences, and international seminars on bilingualism are more numerous than ever before. It is our hope that it will promote further collaboration between scholars from the fields represented here to their mutual benefit and to the benefit of those bilingual persons and societies who form the object of their studies.

REFERENCES

BERNSTEIN, BASIL. Social class and linguistic development: a theory of social learning. In A. H. Halsey, Jean Floud, and C. Arnold Anderson (Eds.), *Education, economy and society*. Free Press of Glencoe, 1961.

BRAULT, GERARD, J. *Cours de Langue Française Destiné aux Jeunes Franco-Americains*. Philadelphia: University of Pennsylvania, 1963.

BRAULT, GERARD J. Some misconceptions about teaching American ethnic children their mother tongue. *Modern Language Journal*, 1964, 48, 67-71.

BULL, WILLIAM E. The use of vernacular languages in education. In Dell H. Hymes (Ed.), *Language in culture and society*. New York: Harper and Row, 1964, 527-533.

Center for Applied Linguistics. The bilingual American education act. *Information Digest on Government Support for Linguistics and the Language Sciences*, 1967, (2) and (4).

CHRISTIAN, CHESTER C., JR., AND LADO, ROBERT (Eds.), *Our bilinguals; social and psychological barriers; linguistic and pedagogical barriers*. El Paso: Southwest Council of Foreign Language Teachers, 1965.

DARCY, N. T. A review of the literature on the effects of bilingualism upon the measurement of intelligence. *Journal of Genetic Psychology*, 1953, 82, 21-58.

DARCY, N. T. Bilingualism and the measurement of intelligence: review of a decade of research. *Journal of Genetic Psychology*, 1963, 103, 259-282.

Europa Ethnica: a quarterly review for problems of nationality, containing official news of the "Federal Union of European Nationalities". Twenty-fourth volume as of 1967.

FERGUSON, CHARLES A. Diglossia. *Word*, 1959, 15, 325-340.

FISHMAN, JOSHUA A. Planned reinforcement of language maintenance in the United States: suggestions for the conservation of a neglected national resource. In Joshua A. Fishman, *et al.*, *language loyalty in the United States*. The Hague: Mouton, 1966, 369-391.

GAARDER, A. BRUCE, The challenge of bilingualism. In G. Reginald Bishop, Jr. (Ed.), *Foreign language teaching: challenges to the professor*. Princeton: Princeton University Press and Northeast Conference on the Teaching of Foreign Languages, 1965, 54-101.

LABOV, WILLIAM. *The social stratification of English in New York City*. Washington D.C.: Center for Applied Lingusitics, 1966.

MACNAMARA, JOHN. *Bilingualism in primary education*. Edinburgh: Edinburgh University Press, 1966.

PEAL, ELIZABETH AND LAMBERT, WALLACE E. The relation of bilingualism to intelligence. *Psychological Monographs, General and Applied*, 1962, 76, no. 546.

UNESCO. *The Use of vernacular languages in education*. Paris: UNESCO, 1953.

UNESCO. *Bilingualism in education; report of an international seminar, Aberystwyth, Wales*. London: HMSO, 1965.

VILDOMEC, VEROBEJ. *Multilingualism*. Leydon: Sijtnoff, 1963.

MODELS OF THE INTERACTION
OF LANGUAGE AND SOCIAL SETTING

Dell Hymes

JOURNAL OF SOCIAL ISSUES
VOLUME XXIII, NUMBER 2, 1967

Models of the Interaction of Language and Social Setting

Dell Hymes

University of Pennsylvania

Diversity of speech, within the community and within the individual, presents itself as a problem in many sectors of life—in education, in national development, in transcultural communication. When those concerned with such problems seek scientific cooperation, expecting to find a body of systematic knowledge and theory, they must often be disappointed. Practical concern outpaces scientific competence.

The questions which arise from diversity of speech are questions addressed to an understanding of the functional roles of languages. They take for granted a world in which communities have a plurality of languages (or code-varieties) and in which languages have a plurality of roles, the two, codes and roles, often being related in complex and distinctive ways. In expecting to find a scientific theory of such interaction of language and social setting, one in effect expects theory based on successfully asking (at least as a start), what code is used, where and when, among whom, for what purpose and with what result, to say what, in what way; subject to what norms of interaction and of interpretation; as instances of what speech acts and genres of speaking? How do community and personal beliefs, values and practices impinge upon the use of language, and upon the acquisition of such use by children?

No such body of systematic knowledge and theory as yet exists. There is not even agreement on a mode of descriptive analysis of language in interaction with social setting, one which, being explicit and

8

of standard form, could ensure development of knowledge and theory through studies that are full and comparable.

The Phenomenon of Bilingualism

The phenomenon of bilingualism has been the main focus of such interest as has been shown, both in its own right and as medium of linguistic diffusion. (Dialectology in the United States until recently was mostly an abstraction of language from interaction with its immediate social setting, having primarily a geographical and reconstructive orientation of little relevance to contemporary American society.) Thus, the significant work in American linguistics during the 1950's which provides some sociolinguistic orientation to language deals with the description of bilingualism (Weinreich, 1953; Haugen, 1953, 1956).

Yet, bilingualism, it must be said, is not in itself an adequate basis for a model (or theory) of the interaction of language and social setting. From the standpoint of such a model or theory, bilingualism is neither unitary as a phenomenon, nor autonomous. The fact that two distinct languages are present in a community or in a person's communicative competence is compatible with, and may depend on, a great variety of underlying functional relationships. Conversely, it is not necessary that two distinct languages be present for the underlying functional relationships to appear.

Cases of bilingualism par excellence (as for example French and English in Canada, Welsh and English in Wales, Russian and French among pre-revolutionary Russian nobility) are salient, special cases of the general phenomena of variety in code repertoire and switching among codes. No normal person, and no normal community, is limited in repertoire to a single variety of code, to an unchanging monotony which would preclude the possibility of indicating respect, insolence, mock-seriousness, humor, role-distance, etc. by switching from one code variety to another.

Given the universality of code repertoires and of code-switching, then it does not appear decisive that the code-varieties be distinct languages (bilingualism par excellence). Relationships of social intimacy or of social distance may be signalled by switching between distinct languages (Spanish : Guarani in Paraguay), between varieties of a single language (Standard German : dialect), or between a pair of pronouns within a single variety (*tu : vous*). Segregation of religious activity may be marked linguistically by a language not generally intelligible because it is of foreign provenance (e.g., Latin, Arabic), or because it is a lexically marked variety of the common language (Zuni). Conversely, shift between codes may mark a shift between wholly distinct spheres of relationship and activity (Standard Norwegian : Hemnes dialect), or it may simply mark the formal status of talk within a single integral activity (e.g., Siane in New Guinea).

If the community's own theory of code repertoire and code-switching is considered, as it should be in any serious descriptive approach, matters become even more complex and interesting. Among the American Indian peoples, such as the Wishram Chinook of the Columbia River in the state of Washington, it was believed that infants knew first a special language shared with certain guardian spirts and interpretable only by men having those spirits; the *native language*, Wishram, was in native theory a second language to everyone. Furthermore, one pair of communities may strain to maintain mutual intelligibility in the face of great differences in dialect, while another pair of communities may refuse to maintain intellegiblity although the differences seem minor. In native theory, then, cases indistinguishable by objective criteria of linguistic differentiation may be now monolingual, now bilingual, depending on local social relationships and attitudes.

Finally, while it is common to look for specialization in the function, elaboration and value, of a language in a bilingual situation, such specialization is merely an aspect of a universal phenomenon that must be examined in situations dominantly monolingual as well. In doing so it must be borne in mind that language is not everywhere equivalent in communicative role and social value; speaking may carry different functional loads within the communicative economies of different societies. One type of hunting and gathering society, the Paliyans of South India, "communicate very little at all times and become almost silent by the age of 40. Verbal, communicative persons are regarded as abnormal and often as offensive" (Gardner, 1966, 398). Thus the role of language in thought and culture (Whorf's question) cannot be assessed for bilinguals until the functional role of each of their languages is assessed; the same is true for monolinguals, since in different societies language may enter differentially into educational experience, the transmission of beliefs, knowledge, values, practices, the conduct of life (Hymes, 1966b).

What is needed, then, is a general theory and body of knowledge within which code-switching and diversity of code repertoire could find a natural place, and within which salient bilingualism could be properly assessed. Little of such a theory and body of knowledge now exists partly because the social scientists asking the right sort of functional questions have not had the linguistic training and insight to deal with the linguistic face of the problem, and because linguistics, the discipline central to the study of speech, has been occupied almost wholly with analysis of the structure of language as a referential code. In defining such structure as object of study, linguists have tended to dismiss or ignore the functional role. Sometimes as a matter of simplifying assumption, sometimes as a matter of principle, linguistic theory has been almost exclusively concerned with the nature of a single homogeneous code, shared by a single homogeneous community of users, and (by implication) used in a single function, that of referential statement. There have been notable exceptions to such a view, especially among linguists of Prague and London, but only very recently has there emerged something tantamount to a movement to redress the situation. This movement has come to be called sociolinguistics, especially when it focuses attention upon language proper in relation to sociological categories, or ethnography of communication, where there is focus upon verbal art, native taxonomy of speech types and functions, and other features more typically studied by anthropologists (Whiteley, 1966). In point of fact, an adequate study of language in interaction with social setting will enlist scholars from all the social sciences in a common enterprise. Throughout this article I shall use sociolinguistics, intending by it the name of a problem area mediating among disciplines. Ultimately such a term may become redundant, if linguistics comes to accept the sociocultural dimensions of its subject-matter and its theoretical bases; one might then speak simply of linguistics (Hymes, 1964a, 1966a, ms. a.).

The Case for Sociolinguistic Description

For some of the most brilliant workers on the interaction of language and social setting, a general theory and body of knowledge is to be achieved by selecting problems that contribute directly to present linguistic theory and social theory. The mode of progress is direct action: use of multiple working hypotheses and strong constraints on relevance and verification in quite particular problems, intended to satisfy adherents of traditional linguistic theory and social theory. Studies in exotic societies are not particularly valued, since strong control over data and hypothesis-testing cannot be maintained. Information of the sort given (most often incidentally) in reports from other societies is not found to be convincing. A concern to secure reports focused on sociolinguistic information from such societies is thought pointless, since it suggests a prospect of endless descriptions that, whatever their quality and quantity, would not as such contribute to present theory.

My own view is different. I accept that intellectual tradition which since the eighteenth century has sought to understand the unity of mankind through both its ethnographic diversity and its general evolution. In that tradition a theory, whatever its logic and insight, is ultimately unsatisfying if divorced from the natural and existential world of mankind as a whole. The concern is consonant with that of Kroeber, reflecting upon Darwin:

> . . . anthropologists . . . do not yet clearly recognize the fundamental value of the humble but indispensable task of classifying—that

is, structuring—our body of knowledge, as biologists did begin to recognize it two hundred years ago (1960, 14).

One recognizes that communities differ significantly in patterns of code-repertoire, code-switching, and, generally, in the roles assigned to language. Ethnographic reports indicate differences with regard to beliefs, values, reference groups, and the like, as these impinge on the on-going system of language use and its acquisition by children. Since there is at present no systematic understanding of the ways in which communities differ in these respects, we need one. We need, in effect, a taxonomy of sociolinguistic systems.

From this standpoint, each of a variety of diverse cases may be felt to be of value in its own right, as an expression of mankind. In any case, such instances are valued as enlarging and deepening insight. We require a widely ranging series of sociolinguistic descriptions because a particular model, let alone an integrating theory, is not convincing unless it has met the test of many diverse situations, of a mass of systematic data. (Recall that Darwin's exposition of evolution was convincing for such a reason.) A taxonomy and a descriptive model are joint conditions of success.

Information from exotic societies, analyzed with the goals of taxonomy and descriptive models in mind, is in fact interdependent with detailed work in one's own society. Each may provide insight and a test of significance for the other. Thus it has been suggested that there is only a class-linked British relevance to Bernstein's sociological model of elaborated vs. restricted forms of code, governed by personal vs. positional types of social control. [Elaborated codes are largely *now-coding*, adaptive in lexicon and syntax to the ad hoc elaboration of subjective intent, whereas restricted codes are largely *then-coding*, adaptive to the reinforcement of group solidarity through conventional expression. Personal social control appeals to individual characteristics, role discretion, and motivation; positional social control bases itself on membership in categories of age, sex, status, etc.]

From the Standpoint of Taxonomy

From the standpoint of taxonomy, the model takes on a new dimension. It is found to be a valuable set of polar ideal types, applicable to the comparison of whole societies as communicative systems (see the description of Arapesh and Manus by Mead, 1937), and suggestive of new hypotheses linking socialization and adult religious experience. Among the Hopi and Zuni of the American Southwest, for instance, severe socialization pressure is initiated at about two years of age, before the child can have reasons verbally explained, and thus is necessarily experienced as positional control. Among the Wishram Chinook socialization pressure is withheld until the child can talk and have reasons verbally explained; the native view of socialization is explicitly one of personal control through verbal means. Adult religious activity among the Hopi and Zuni is dominated by positional relationship (clan membership, etc.), and its verbal aspect is highly prescribed. Among the Wishram it is dominantly unique to each individual; the verbal aspect is private between person and guardian spirit, and interpreted by the person according to his own life experience.

Furthermore, I believe that failure to postulate a model and taxonomy of sociolinguistic systems as a goal will perpetuate a long-standing, unsatisfactory state of affairs, namely, the failure of scientific study to address itself to the unity of language and social life. This unity is rooted in the use of language in social life, in the integrity of the message as an act. Because of the common divorce of the study of language, as grammar, from the study of society, the unity does not come into view. Each of the separate specialisms abstracts from the speech act its own aspect for its own purposes. A theory of language in society, when envisaged, is usually thought of as uniting the results of such separate enterprises, institution-free grammar and grammar-free institutions. But these enterprises, having made their abstractions in quite disparate frames of reference, and never having been responsible for the study of speech acts as such, are quite incapable of supporting the act of reintegration. What from the standpoint of the actors and the community is an integral act, motivated and subject to shared rules of interpretation, remains invisible. It is both less and more than it was: less, because it lacks its own form and motivation; more, because having been dismembered according to conflicting claims of jurisdiction by specialisms, each concerned to gerrymander speech to its own taste, the parts to be fitted now overlap. The act, still lifeless, has grown grotesque. All approaches in which the relation between language and social life is regarded wholly as a matter of correlation, or of variation, are vitiated by the implicit assumption that integration is a matter of post-hoc putting together of separate results, none obtained with the integral object in view.

In short, there must be a study of speaking that seeks to determine the native system and theory of speaking; whose aim is to describe the communicative competence that enables a member of the community to know when to speak and when to remain silent, which code to use, when, where and to whom, etc. (This view is an application to speaking of the general view of ethnography as the construction of descriptive theory that has been elaborated by Goodenough, Conklin, Frake, Sturtevant, myself and others; for its application to speaking, cf. Hymes 1962, 1964b, 1964c, and ms. b.)

In considering what form sociolinguistic description might take, and what form an integrated theory of such description might take, one needs to show sociologists, linguists, ethnographers and others a way to see data as the interaction of language and social setting. The need for this is clear from the frequency with which researchers have had informal field experience of great sociolinguistic interest, but, lacking precedent and format for its presentation, have let the information lie fallow as at best a matter for anecdotes.

Only a specific, formal mode of description can guarantee the continuation of the present interest in sociolinguistics. Such interest is sustained more by fashion and practical issues, perhaps, than by scientific conviction and accomplishment. It was the development of a specific mode of description that ensured the success of linguistics as an independent discipline in the United States in the twentieth century, and the lack of it that led to the decline and peripheral status of folklore, both having started from a similar base, i.e., the interlocking interest of anthropologists and humanistic scholars in language, in the one case, verbal tradition, in the other.

Such a goal is of concern to practical and applied work as well as to scientific theory. When a problem of bilingualism is to be studied, for example, the componets of speaking that are taken into account will depend upon a model, implicit if not explicit, of the interaction of language with social setting. The significance attached to what is found will vary with the understanding of what is possible, what universal, what rare, what linked, in a comparative perspective. What survey-researchers need to know linguistically about a community, in selecting the code of questioning, and in conducting questioning, is in effect an application of the community's sociolinguistic description. In turn, practical work, if conducted with the needs of taxonomy and theory in mind, can make a special contribution, for it must deal directly with the interaction of language and social setting, and so provide for a test of the relation between theory and practice.

The goal of sociolinguistic description can be put in terms of the present situation in the disciplines whose interests converge in sociolinguistics. Whatever his questions about language, a linguist is clear that there is an enterprise, description of languages, which is central and prerequisite. Whatever his questions about society and culture, a sociologist or an anthropologist is clear that there is an enterprise (whether called ethnography, social structure, social organization) that is concerned with the concepts and methods prerequisite to particular studies and answers, a system that provides a coherent, general guide to inquiry. In other words, such workers understand what it means to describe a language, a social system or the culture of a community. We need to be able to say the same sort of thing, i.e., what it means to describe a sociolinguistic system.

Toward a Descriptive Theory . . .

Sociolinguistic systems may be considered at the level of national states, and indeed, of the emerging world society. The concern of this paper is with sociolinguistic systems at the level of the speech economies of individual communities. The interaction of language with social setting is viewed first of all as a matter of human action and of the knowledge, sometimes conscious, sometimes unconscious, that enables persons to use language in social life. Larger systemᵉ, it is true, may have properties not reducible to those of the speaking competence of persons, just as the world economy has properties not reducible to those of the economies of nations, communities or persons. Such competence, however, underlies communicative conduct, not only within communities, but in encounters between them. Whenever a larger system is dependent upon communication among persons, then the point of departure is persons. The speaking competence of persons may be seen as entering into a series of systems of encounters at levels of different scope. The considerations to be advanced here apply in principle to analysis of any social relationship in which norms of communicative conduct entailing speech have arisen. The examples will typically be from the analysis of relationships characteristic of individual communities.

An adequate descriptive theory would provide for the analysis of individual communities by specifying the technical terms required for such analysis, and by specifying what form the analysis should take. That form would be formal (i.e., would deal with the actual forms of speaking in a wholly explicit way) and standard (in the sense of being subject to general constraints on order, interrelationship and the character of rules). However, only extended empirical work, and extended experimentation with alternative modes of statement, can show what form of descriptive theory is to be preferred. When achieved, such a theory, by providing for the explicit, standard analysis of individual systems will at the same time provide a theory of their universal features.

Some Notions with which the Theory Must Deal

Among the notions with which such a theory must deal are those of speech community, speech situation, speech act, speech event, fluent speaker, native speaker, factors (or components) of speech events, functions of speech, rules of speaking, types of speech event and act. I have sketched a partial approach to such notions, first in "The ethnography of speaking" (1964a, 33-44; 1964b). I shall not repeat the ways in which the approach has already been developed, but show how it has been modified in the course of recent work. It must be emphasized that the discussion at this stage is of a heuristic guide to the analysis of systems, and that an eventual theory will have properties that can emerge only from the results of such analyses.

The recent work has been aimed at analyzing ethnographic data so as to provide at least a preliminary taxonomy of the variety of sociolinguistic systems that impinge upon education and the child. In socialization a child acquires not only language(s), but also sets of attitudes and habits with regard to the value and utilization of language(s). A child capable of any and all grammatical utterances, but not knowing which to use, not knowing even when to talk and when to stop, would be a cultural monstrosity. Often enough a child is confronted not only with more than one code, but also with more than one system for the use of the codes. There may be what linguists have come to call interference (Weinreich, 1953) not only between two sets of code habits, but also between two sets of habits for the use of codes.

In educational situations made complex by diversity of speech, then, whether saliently bilingual or not, one needs to understand the general patterns of communicative competence being acquired by children as background for understanding the outcome of the small fraction of communicative experience encountered by children in school. A comparative perspective may help one to understand problems of a particular case.

In the course of this work a guide to the analysis of socialization, focused on speaking, has been prepared. (Existing guides neglect speech as a variable.) In one sense, such work focuses on the acquisition of a pre-existing system of interaction of language with social setting. In a deeper sense, such work studies the whole system as viewed from the standpoint of the child.

The guide is organized from the more general to the more specific, and is consciously designed to present the acquisition of linguistic codes as but a part of the acquisition of communicative competence as a whole. Its outlines are:

A Guide to Analysis of Speech Socialization

(A.) *General Aspects of Socialization*

    I. Life cycle (the ways in which speed and language enter into the distinguishing and accomplishing of reference points in the life cycle)

    II. Learning and teaching (the place of language and speaking in native conceptions of acquisition of culture and of modes of teaching)

    III. Social control (the relative place of verbal means and verbal explanations)

(B.) *Competence in Speaking*

    IV. Speaking competence (general attitudes toward speaking in relation to valued types of person, satisfactions, normal demeanor; the system of speaking as something in which competence is acquired and evaluated; conceptions of such competence, and its place among other modes of communicative competence)

V. Linguistic code competence (general attitudes toward knowledge of linguistic codes in relation to valued types of person, satisfactions, conduct; the repertoire of codes in the community, their uses, their order and mode of acquisition; conceptions of competence in linguistic codes, and their place among other communicative codes)

(C.) *Processes of Acquisition*

VI. Communicative environment of the infant (what communicative behavior is directed at the infant, in what ways its behavior is interpreted as communicative, differential response to its use of communicative modalities)

VII. Acquisition of speaking competence (conceptions of children's first speech acts, what speaking is directed at children, how their speech is responded to, conceptions of sequence of acquisition of speaking competence, of how competence comes about, what is done)

VIII. Acquisition of linguistic code competence (conceptions of first words, of sequence of acquisition of code(s), of how it comes about, what is done)

(D.) *Generalizations, Typological Contrasts*

The detailed contents of the guide, and the practical procedures for their application to data, must be passed over here. What is directly pertinent is the effect of applying the guide on that part of the guide which sketches the analysis of sociolinguistic systems. As work continues, feedback from data continues too; but certain general formulations have been shown to be necessary and have remained stable. To these I now turn after a brief comment on the background of such efforts.

Most general treatments of language, speech, rhetoric, literature and some treatments of other topics, make assumptions, explicit or implicit, as to notions with which a descriptive theory of speaking must deal. With particular regard to the components of speech events and the functions served in them, there have been important classifications by Karl Bühler, Kenneth Burke, Roman Jakobson, Charles Morris, C. K. Ogden and I. A. Richards and others. With particular regard to code repertoire in relation to social setting there are important classifications and findings in the work of Basil Bernstein (see above), Joshua A. Fishman, H. A. Gleason, Jr., John J. Gumperz, Michael Halliday, William Labov, and others. These studies provide terms and notions that may prove quite useful, and the same is true of studies of other aspects of the field of sociolinguistic description: there is much to be gained heuristically from them. It would not be to the point, however, to review such studies here with the object of picking among them, amalgamating them, or the like. While each suggests a schema that may prove useful in part or in whole, the fundamental problem— to discover the underlying communicative competence that enables members of a community to use and interpret the use of language, and to provide a formal description that is a theory of that competence—cuts deeper than any schema so far proposed.

Concern must now be with terms as heuristic input to descriptive analyses, but just as a theory of language structure must have its universal terms (e.g., sentence, distinctive feature), so must a theory of language use. At least some of the terms now to be discussed will no doubt survive empirical revisions and permanently remain as part of the theory.

Toward a Descriptive Theory . . . *Social Units*

One must first consider the social unit of analysis. For this I adopt the common expression:

Speech Community. Speech is here taken as a surrogate for all forms of language, including writing. The necessity and primacy of the term, speech community, is that it postulates the basis of description as a social, rather than a linguistic, entity. That is, one does not start with a code and look afterward to its context. One starts with a social group and looks within it at the codes present.

Bloomfield (1933) and others have in the past reduced the notion of speech community to the notion of language. Those speaking the same language (or first language, or standard language) were defined as belonging to the same speech community, and this confusion still persists in much social science literature, a quantitative measure of frequency of interaction sometimes being appended. The present approach requires a definition that is qualitative and expressed in terms of the *use* of language. Tentatively, a speech community is defined as a community sharing both rules for the conduct and interpretation of acts of speech, and rules for the interpretation of at least one common linguistic code. The sharing of code rules is not sufficient: there are persons whose English I can interpret, but whose message escapes me. Nor is the sharing of speech rules sufficient: such sharing may characterize a *speech area* (*Sprechbund*—I owe the term to J. Neustupny), comprising several distinct speech communities, not necessarily sharing a common language, but agreeing in patterns of speaking.

The *speech field* (akin to the notion of social field) can be defined as the total range of communities within which a person's knowledge of code and speaking rules enables him to move. Within the speech field must be distinguished the *speech network*, the specific linkages of persons through code and speech rules across communities. To illustrate: one's speech community may be, effectively, a single city or portion of it; one's speech field will be delimited by one's repertoire of codes, sometimes by a single language (say to England, Canada, Australia, and the United States, given a command of English), sometimes not; one's speech network, based for example on the practice of a common profession (say, sociology), may extend across communities, the common profession providing sufficiently common rules of speech. Obviously part of the work of definition is borne by the community, and the difficulties of defining it are here by-passed. Criteria of frequency of interaction, regularity of interaction, focus of interaction, contiguity, degree of commonalty of pattern, etc., may be invoked, each perhaps representing a continuum. The essential thing is that the object of description is an integral social unit. Probably it will be useful to reserve the notion of speech community for the social unit most specifically characterized for a person by common locality and primary interaction (Gumperz, 1962, esp. 30-32). I have essentially drawn distinctions of scale and kind of linkage within Gumperz' wholly general concept of *linguistic community* which amounts to any distinguishable intercommunicating group.

Speech Situation. Within a community one readily detects many situations associated with (or masked by the absence of) speech. Such contexts of situation will often be naturally described as ceremonies, fights, hunts, meals, love-making and the like. It would not be profitable to convert such situations *en masse* into parts of a sociolinguistic description, by the simple expedient of relabelling them in terms of speech. (Notice that the distinctions made with regard to speech community are not identical with the concepts of a general communicative approach, which must note the differential range of communication by speech, film, art object, music.) Such situations may enter as contexts into the statement of rules of speaking as aspects of setting (or of genre). In contrast to speech events, they are not in themselves governed by such rules, or one set of such rules throughout. A hunt, for example, may comprise both verbal and nonverbal events, and the verbal events may be of more than one type.

In a sociolinguistic description, then, it is necessary to deal with activities which are in some recognizable way bounded or integral. From the standpoint of general social description they may be registered as ceremonies, fishing trips, and the like; from particular standpoints they may be regarded as political, aesthetic, etc., situations, which serve as contexts for the manifestation of political, aesthetic, etc., activity. From the sociolinguistic standpoint they may be regarded as speech situations.

Speech Event. The term speech event will be restricted to activities, or aspects of activities, that are directly governed by rules for the use of speech. An event may consist of a single speech act, but will often comprise several. Just as an occurrence of a noun may at the same time be the whole of a noun phrase and the whole of a sentence (e.g., Fire!), so a speech act may be the whole of a speech event, and of a speech situation (say, a rite consisting of a single prayer, itself a single invocation). More often, however, one will find a difference in magnitude: a party (speech situation), a conversation during the party (speech event), a joke within the conversation (speech act). It is of speech events and speech acts that one writes formal rules for their occurrence and characteristics. Notice that the same type of speech act may recur in different types of speech event, and the same type of speech event in different contexts of situation. Thus, a joke (speech act) may be embedded in a private conversation, a lecture, a formal introduction. A private conversation may occur in the context of a party, a memorial service, a pause in changing sides in a tennis match.

Speech Act. The speech act is the minimal term of the set being discussed, as the remarks on speech events have shown. The work on speech acts inspired by British philosophers such as the late J. L. Austin provides many helpful indications of the types of speech acts and the relationships among them. It also contributes to the task of determining for English the membership and meaning of native sets of terms for speech acts.

Toward a Descriptive Theory . . . *Components of Speech*

In discovering the native system of speaking, certain familiar guidelines may be mentioned. One must determine the native taxonomy of terms as an essential although never perfect guide. A shift in any of the components of speaking may mark the operation of a rule (e.g., from normal to another tone of voice, from one code to another). Correction, embarassment, withdrawal and other negative responses may indicate the violation of a rule. There may also be positive evaluation (more in some groups than others) of effective use of speech and its rules.

One must have in addition some schema for the components of speech events. Traditional in our culture is the three-fold one of speaker, hearer and thing spoken about. That has been elaborated upon in various ways, e.g., in information theory. Work with ethnographic data, however, has shown the necessity of a somewhat more detailed schema. The constraints on such a heuristic guide are that it should be ample enough to handle data without arbitrariness, yet compact enough to be kept in mind for use. Being heuristic, rather than at present a theory, there is no harm and a definite advantage in organizing the schema as a mnemonic device. It so happens that in English the letters of the term SPEAKING itself can be used rather naturally for this purpose. (That the analysis of components is not language-bound, determined by the accidents of spelling, can be shown by the possibility of alternative keywords, were the spelling different. Thus what below is I[nstrumentalities] could as well be M[eans], A[gencies]; what below is K[ey] could as well be T[one],, M[anner], W[ay], H[ow]; etc. Changes of terminology, rather than exact translation, may permit an analogous mnemonic device in other languages. (In French, for example, PARLANT could be adapted to the purpose, as will be shown below.))

The criterion for registering a component is that it should be part of the definition of a rule of speaking. Rules of speaking, in other words, entail structured relationships among two or more components.

Organized in terms of the English code-word, components are: *(S) Setting, or Scene.* By setting is intended of course time, and place, of a speech event. In addition, psychological setting, and cultural definition of the setting as a certain type of *scene,* may be implicated here, as when, within a play on the same stage, during the same performance, the dramatic time or place shifts: "ten years later", "a battlefield in France". The types of scene defined by a society may be basic to an analysis of speech events and the role of speaking. For example, among the Subanun of the Philippines, described by Charles O. Frake (ms.), there is a basic division into festive and nonfestive scenes. Thus, the character of Subanun litigation derives from its occurrence in festive scenes and the verbal art appropriate to them. A frequent type of rule is one in which a form of speech act is dependent on an appropriate scene; of equal importance is the use of speech acts or the choice of code to define scenes as appropriate.

(P) Participants or Personnel. Schemes of components usually distinguish Speaker and Hearer (Sender and Receiver, Addressor and Addressee). From the standpoint of explicit rules for speaking, such a categorization is at once too specific and too imprecise. It is too specific in that some rules hold for a participant independent of his role as speaker or hearer. Thus, in conversations among the Abipon of Argentina, if a participant (speaker or listener) is a member of the Hocheri (warrior class), then *-in* is added to the end of every word. It is too imprecise, because societies commonly differentiate a variety of roles for participants in speech events, and these must be specified. The importance of the category of auditor or audience, as a constraint on rules of speaking has recently been emphasized by the sociologist, Allen D. Grimshaw. Among the Wishram Chinook, formal speech events are defined by the relationship between sender, or source (e.g., a chief), a repeater of the sender's words, and an audience constituted as a public; in the major Wishram speech event the addressees at crucial points are not the audience, but the spirits of the surrounding environment.

It is typically in their definitions of the presence or absence of participants in speech events (more generally, communicative events) that societies most differ. Much of religious behavior can be viewed as application of a native theory of communication, often associated with elaboration of a specific code and code-switching.

(E) Ends. Here an English homonymy is exploited, two types of *ends* being meant: *ends* in view (goals, purposes), and *ends* as outcomes. In one sense, intentions and effects; in another, manifest and latent functions. Previous schemata of speech events have most often not provided a place for intention and outcome. (Kenneth Burke, 1945) is the exception, perhaps because of an unconscious behaviorism. Analysis of speech events from several societies shows the category of purpose and that of outcome to be crucial to the distinguishing of varieties of event. Among the Waiwai of Venezuela, for example, the varieties of the central speech event, the *oho*-chant, are to be distinguished as to whether the purpose is a marriage-contract, a trade, a communal work-task, an invitation to a feast, or a composing of social peace after death. Rules for participants and settings vary accordingly. Among the Yakan of the Philippines a taxonomy of four levels of event focused upon speech is to be differentiated in terms of purpose and outcome. Interpreted in a linguistic mode of statement, one has:

(a) [Focus]   [talk about a topic]   / *miting*
    [Outcome] → [no special outcome]

That is, the type of speech event called *miting* has as its focus simply talk about some topic; no special outcome is expected.

(b) [Focus]   [talk about an issue]   / *qisun* ("conference")
    [Outcome] → [decision]

That is, the type of speech event called *qisun* has as its purpose simply talk about something regarded as an *issue*, as when to plant rich, when to take a trip, and a *decision* is expected as the outcome.

(c) [Focus]   [talk about a disagreement] / *mawpakkat*
    [Outcome] → [settlement]   (negotiation)

That is, the type of speech event called *mawpakkat* has as its purpose talk about a *disagreement* involving conflicting interests, and as its expected outcome, a legally binding resolution, or *settlement*.

(d) [Focus]   [talk about a dispute]   / *hukum* (litigation)
    [Outcome] → [ruling]

That is, the type of speech event called *hukum* has as its focus a disagreement arising from a charge that an offense has been committed, and as its expected outcome, a legal ruling, based on precedent and carrying special sanctions. The Yakan examples are from a paper by Frake, *Struck by Speech*, to appear in a volume on the ethnography of communication edited by John Gumperz and myself.

As the varied wording of the Yakan account has shown, where the *focus* of a speech event requires special attention, it seems most naturally to be an aspect of this portion of the heuristic scheme. Contrast in focus is often important for comparative study. Thus litigation among the Subanun (Philippines) has special focus on message-form, in the elaboration of verbal art, in keeping with its occurrence among Subanun festive scenes; whereas Yakan (Philippines) litigation has focus only on topical content, in keeping with its place among Yakan informal scenes.

(A) Art Characteristics. Here two closely linked aspects of acts of speech are grouped together: the form, and the content, of what is said. The technical terms *message-form* and *topic*, respectively, are adopted for these. One context for the distinction is in the reporting of speech events: "He prayed, saying '. . . .'" (preserving message-form) vs. "He prayed that he would get well" (preserving topic only).

Perhaps the gravest and most common defect in most reports of speech events is that it is impossible to recapture the rules for message-form. Without such rules, however, it is impossible to characterize the nature of the competence in speaking of members of the society. Commonly one reads that a certain use of language is important, even crucial to a society—gossip, for example, among the Makah Indians of northwestern Washington or among fox-hunting English aristocrats. If one does not know how to gossip correctly, one cannot be an adequate member of the group. It must, then, be possible to say of an act of speech that it does or does not fit the rules. Possibly the rules for gossip are defined entirely in terms of participants, topics and settings, and not in terms of message-form; but it seems far more likely that some forms of presenting the gossip-content are acceptable and some not. In any case it is certain that where there are genres of speech act, such as gossip, there is differential skill in their accomplishment, and such skill will include handling of the message-form.

A concern for the details of actual form strikes some as picayune and removed from humanistic and scientific importance. Such a view betrays an impatience that is a disservice both to humanistic and scientific purposes. It is precisely the failure to unite form and content in the scope of a single focus of study that has held back scientific understanding of the fundamental human skill, speaking and vitiates so many quasi-scientific attempts to prove the significance of expressive behavior through content categories alone. One can never prescribe in advance the size of signal that will be crucial to content and skill in a communicative genre. The more the genre has become a shared, meaningful expression within a group, the more likely that the crucial cues will be efficient, that is, slight in scale. If one balks at such detail, perhaps because it requires technical skills in linguistics, musicology or the like, one should face the fact that one is simply refusing to take seriously the human meaning of one's object of study and the scientific claims of one's field of inquiry.

A further consideration is that such genres which become shared, meaningful expressions within a group acquire a partial autonomy, an inner logic of their means of expression, that conditions and sometimes even controls their content. For members of the group, then, "freedom is the recognition of necessity"; mastery of the detail and formal logic of the genre is prerequisite to personal expression. Again serious concern for the human meaning of such genres requires analysis that goes beyond gross content to precise, explicit statement of the rules and features of the form.

While such a perspective may seem to apply first of all to genres recognized as conventionally aesthetic, it applies as well to conversation in daily life. Only the most painstaking analysis of form (similar to that of literary criticism) can reveal the fantastic depth and adequacy of the elliptical art that is talk.

(K) Key. This component is introduced to distinguish the tone, manner or spirit in which an act is done. Acts otherwise the same as regards setting, participants, message-form and content, may differ in key, as between *mock : serious; perfunctory : painstaking;* and the like.

The communicative significance of key is underlined by the view that, where the two are in conflict, the manner of an act overrides the content in determining its true significance. The signalling of key may sometimes be a part of the message-form itself, but may be nonverbal such as a wink, gesture, attire, musical accompaniment.

(I) Instrumentalities. Here are grouped together two closely linked components, those of *Channel* and *Code.* By choice of *Channel* is understood the choice of oral, written, telegraphic, semaphore or other medium of transmission. By choice of *Code* is understood a choice at the level of distinct languages. Where the distinction is necessary, varieties within a language may be designated *subcodes.*

For the student of bilingualism, of course, rules linking choice of *Code* (or subcode) with the other components are of primary interest. Each component seems to covary with choice of code in some case or other: setting, participants, ends and outcomes, message-form and topic, key, channel and (to be cited below) norms of interaction and interpretation, and genres.

(N) Norms of Interaction and of Interpretation. By Norms is meant not the normative character that may attach to all rules for choice among components, but specific behaviors and proprieties that may accompany acts of speech—that one must not interrupt, for example; that normal voice must not be used except when scheduled (e.g., in church service). Here, too, may be considered shared rules for the understanding of what occurs in speech acts, e.g., as to what can be ignored or discounted.

In a thoroughgoing analysis of a community, the notion of norms of interaction would implicate the social structure—the members' categories of kinds of person (role, status and the like), and the norms of interaction obtaining between them. Analysis of these norms would be

prerequisite to adequate statement of rules governing modes of address and the symbolic import of other choices, such as choice of code
(see discussion of formal rules below).

The notion of norms of interpretation implicates the belief system
of a community. In the history of ethnographic analysis of language,
the classic precedent is the treatment of symbolic meanings of elements
of Trobrian magical formulae and ritual by Malinowski (1935), under
the heading of *Dogmatic Context*. Malinowski's other rubrics for
analysis are roughly related to those presented here in the following
way: *Sociological Context* and *Ritual Context* subsume information as
to setting, participants, ends in view and outcome, norms of interaction,
higher-level aspects of genre; *Structure* reports salient patterning of
the verbal form of the act or event; *Mode of recitation* reports salient
characteristics of the vocal aspect of message-form.

(G) Genres. By Genres are meant categories or types of speech
act and speech event: conversation, curse, blessing, prayer, lecture,
imprecation, sales pitch, etc.

[With reference to French, the heuristic set of components might
be presented in terms of PARLANT: (P) Participants; (A) Actes
(form, content); (R) Raison, Resultat (= ends, outcomes); (L) Local
(= setting; the English adaptation of the French word, locale); (A)
Agents (channels, codes); (N) Normes; (T) Ton (= Key); Types (=
Genres).]

Toward a Descriptive Theory . . . *Formal Rules*

Rules of speaking do not usually refer to all components of a
speech event, and often to as few as two or three. Choice of code may
be defined in terms of code and interlocutor alone; or code and topic
alone; or code, interlocutor, and setting; etc. It is necessary to distinguish the entire range because in a given case any one may be defining. Moreover, a non-defining component may yet condition the
success or other aspect of the outcome of a speech event.

Many generalizations about rules of speaking will take the form of
statements of relationship among components. It is not yet clear that
there is any priority to be assigned to particular components in such
statements. So far as one can tell at present, any component may be
taken as starting point, and the others viewed in relation to it. When
individual societies have been well analyzed, hierarchies of precedence
among components will very likely appear and be found to differ
from case to case. Such differences in hierarchy of components will
then be an important part of the taxonomy of sociolinguistic systems.
For one group, rules of speaking will be heavily bound to setting; for
another primarily to participants; for a third, perhaps to topic.

Experimentation with the form of statement of rules of speaking has not proceeded very far. Work of Joel Sherzer and myself with some American Indian data suggests the possibility of adapting a linguistic mode of statement. In such a format, generalizations applying throughout a speech event are stated at the outset in a sort of lexicon. The sequential form of the act itself is stated in a sort of syntax by means of context-sensitive rewriting rules (Chomsky, 1965). When prose descriptions of events have been so restated, there has been a considerable gain in understanding of structure. The explicit form of statement makes demands upon description that go beyond what is usually in prose accounts. The form of the event is disengaged, as it were, from the verbal foliage obligatory in prose sentences, and can be more readily *seen*. Such formal restatement is essential, if comparative work is to proceed. One must be able to compare events within a society, and across societies, in concise and standard format. Such comparison cannot depend upon memorizing or shuffling of prose paragraphs vastly different in verbal style. And it is through some formal restatement that one can commit oneself to a precise claim as to what it is a member of a society knows in knowing how to participate in a speech act.

A grave defect in many studies which examine the interaction of language and social setting has been the failure to state precisely (a) the difference and (b) the interrelationship between values pertaining to the sociolinguistic feature, on the one hand, and the values pertaining to the social context in which it can occur.

A related defect has been failure to state precisely the difference, and the interrelationship, between the normal, ordinary, or "unmarked" value of a sociolinguistic feature, on the one hand, and the "marked," or specially loaded values, on the other. Studies of the use of a given code in multilingual situations, like studies of modes of address, may state the range of contexts in which the code can occur, appending information about its use in each, but without contrasting the effects of varying code and context. However, as the Uruguayan linguist, J. P. Rona, has insisted, sociolinguistics deals not only with linguistic facts in contexts, but with linguistic facts having social value in contexts.

Just as the linguistic sign is a relation between a linguistic form and a linguistic value (e.g., the form "*dog*" and meaning "dog"), so a sociolinguistic feature, such as a choice of code, is a sign, a relation between a form (here, the linguistic fact, such as a code) and a sociolinguistic value (say, respect, or formality). The set of code-varieties within a community may thus be analyzed as a semantic set. One may determine for normal contexts the dimensions of meaning along which choice of code-variety implies contrast. To complete the analysis, one must then state separately the domains—settings, role relationships or whatever—across which the normal meanings of code choice are defined. Having done so, one may now state the ways in which code choice may be used to insult, to flatter, to boast—the marked, specially loaded uses—by stating the corresponding, *different* relations between code values and domain values that govern these uses.

All these relationships can take the form of linguistic rules, such as those developed by Chomsky (1965) for handling lexical elements. In effect, one specifies form, content, and context—an overt element, semantic values, and rules governing its selection in those values. Such a form of statement is no more than an elaboration of the form of statement familiar to us in dictionaries now, e.g., *"reach"* (form), "a tack sailed with the wind coming more or less from abeam" (semantic value), with the specification (selection rule), *"in nautical usage"*. To pursue such a form of statement in sociolinguistics, however, will have as consequence *the inseparability of sociolinguistic analysis from the full-scale analysis of social life itself*, for it is in the analysis of social life that the requisite rules of selection for sociolinguistic features are to be found and stated. (For a detailed example of this mode of analysis, see my "Quasi-Korean Modes of Address", submitted to *Anthropological Linguistics*, with the Korean data on Richard Howell (1965), it can be shown that values of authority and intimacy assigned to the modes of address (values often assigned to choice of code in some societies) are in fact properties of the social relationships in terms of which the use of the modes of address is to be defined. The modes of address themselves form a set on a single dimension of social distance. The formal separation of the set of linguistic choices and the set of social relationships reveals the true nature of the relationship between them. For major detailed work on Speech Communities from this standpoint see Gumperz (1964) and Labov (1966).)

Such a mode of analysis permits formal treatment of many of the functions served in acts of speech. The conventional means of many such functions can indeed be analyzed as relations among components, e.g., message-form, genre and key in the case of the *-y* form of the accusative plural of masculine nouns in Polish, which has the value "solemn" in the genre of poetry, and the value "ironic, pejorative" in the genres of non-poetic speech. Functions themselves may be statable in terms of relations among components, such that poetic function, for example, may require a certain relationship among choice of code, choice of topic and message-form in a given period or society.

It would be misleading, however, to think that the definition of functions can be reduced to or derived from other components. Such a thought would be a disabling residue of behaviorist ideology. Ultimately the functions served in speech must be derived directly from the purposes and needs of human persons engaged in social action, and are what they are: talking to seduce, to stay awake, to avoid a war. The formal analysis of speaking is a means to the understanding of human purposes and needs, and their satisfaction; it is an indispensable means, but only a means, and not that understanding itself.

REFERENCES

BLOOMFIELD, LEONARD. *Language*. New York: Henry Holt, 1933.

BURKE, KENNETH. *A Grammar of motives*. New York: Prentice-Hall, 1945.

CHOMSKY, NOAM. *Aspects of the theory of syntax*. Cambridge: M. I. T. Press, 1965.

GARDNER, PETER M. Symmetric respect and memorate knowledge: the structure and ecology of individualistic culture. *Southwestern Journal of Anthropology* 1966, 22, 389-415.

GUMPERZ, JOHN J. Types of linguistic communities. *Anthropological Linguistics* 1962 4,(1), 28-40.

GUMPERZ, JOHN J. Linguistic and Social Interaction in two communities. In John J. Gumperz and Dell Hymes (Eds.), *The Ethnography of Communication*. Washington, D.C.: American Anthropological Association, 1964, 137-153.

HAUGEN, EINAR. *The Norwegian language in America: A study in bilingual behavior* (2 vols). Philadelphia: University of Pennsylvania Press, 1953.

HAUGEN, EINAR. *Bilingualism in the Americas: A bibliography and a research guide*. (American Dialect Society, No. 26.) Montgomery: University of Alabama Press, 1956.

HOWELL, RICHARD. Linguistic Status markers in Korean. *Kroeber Anthropological Society Papers*, 1965, 33, 91-97.

HYMES, DELL H. The ethnography of speaking. In *Anthropology and human behavior*. Washington, D.C.: The Anthropological Society of Washington, 1962, 15-53.

HYMES, DELL H. Directions in (ethno)-linguistic theory. In A. K. Romney and R. G. D'Andrade (Eds.), *Transcultural studies of cognition, Washington, D.C.*: American Anthropological Association, 1964a, 6-56.

HYMES, DELL H. Introduction: toward ethnographies of communication. In John Gumperz and Dell Hymes (Eds.), *The ethnography of communication*. Washington, D.C.: American Anthropological Association, 1964b. 1-34.

HYMES, DELL H. On "Anthropological linguistics" and Congeners. *American Anthropologist* 1966, 68: 143-153.

HYMES, DELL H. Two types of linguistic relativity. In William Bright (Ed.), *Sociolinguistics*. The Hague: Mouton and Co., 1966. 114-165.

HYMES, DELL H. Why linguistics needs the sociologist. *Social Research*, (in press).

HYMES, DELL H. On Communicative competence. (To appear in a volume edited by Stanley Diamond on anthropological approaches to education.)

KROBER, A. L. Evolution, history, and culture. In Sol Tax (Ed.), *Evolution after Darwin*. Chicago: University of Chicago Press, 1960, 1-16.

LABOV, WILLIAM A. *The Social Stratification of English in New York City*. Washington, D.C.: Center for Applied Linguistics, 1966.

MALINOWSKI, BRONISLAW. *Coral gardens and their magic*, Vol. II. London: Allen and Unwin, 1935.

MEAD, MARGARET. Public opinion mechanisms among primitive peoples. *Public Opinion Quarterly*, 1937, 1, 5-16.

WEINREICH, URIEL. *Languages in contact*. New York: Linguistic Circle of New York, 1953.

WHITELY, W. H. Social anthropology, meaning and linguistics. *Man*, new series, 1966, 1, 139-157.

BILINGUALISM WITH AND WITHOUT DIGLOSSIA; DIGLOSSIA WITH AND WITHOUT BILINGUALISM

Joshua A. Fishman

JOURNAL OF SOCIAL ISSUES
VOLUME XXIII, NUMBER 2, 1967

Bilingualism With and Without Diglossia; Diglossia With and Without Bilingualism.

Joshua A. Fishman

Yeshiva University

The psychological literature on bilingualism is so much more extensive than its sociological counterpart that workers in the former field have often failed to establish contact with those in the latter. In the past decade a very respectable sociological (or sociologically oriented) literature has developed dealing with bilingual societies. It is the purpose of this paper to relate these two research traditions to each other by tracing the interaction between their two major constructs: bilingualism (on the part of psychologists) and diglossia (on the part of sociologists).

Diglossia

In the few years that have elapsed since Ferguson (1959) first advanced it, the term diglossia has not only become widely accepted by sociolinguists and sociologists of language, but it has been further extended and refined. Initially it was used in connection with a society that used two (or more) languages for internal (intra-society) communication. The use of several separate codes within a single society (and their stable maintenance rather than the displacement of one by the other over time) was found to be dependent on each code's serving functions distinct from those considered appropriate for the other. Whereas one set of behaviors, attitudes and values supported, and was expressed in, one language, another set of behaviors, attitudes and values supported and was expressed in the other. Both sets of behaviors,

29

attitudes and values were fully accepted as culturally legitimate and complementary (i.e., nonconflictual) and indeed, little if any conflict between them was possible in view of the functional separation between them. This separation was most often along the lines of an H(igh) language, on the one hand, utilized in conjunction with religion, education and other aspects of high culture, and an L(ow) language, on the other hand, utilized in conjunction with everyday pursuits of hearth, home and work. Ferguson spoke of H and L as superposed languages.

To this original edifice others have added several significant considerations. Gumperz (1961, 1962, 1964a, 1964b, 1966) is primarily responsible for our current awareness that diglossia exists not only in multilingual societies which officially recognize several "languages" but, also, in societies which are multilingual in the sense that they employ separate dialects, registers or functionally differentiated language varieties of whatever kind. He has also done the lion's share of the work in providing the conceptual apparatus by means of which investigators of multilingual speech communities seek to discern the societal patterns that govern the use of one variety rather than another, particularly at the level of small group interaction. On the other hand, I have attempted to trace the maintenance of diglossia as well as its disruption at the national level (1964, 1965a, 1965c, 1965d, 1965f, 1966a, 1966b), and in addition have attempted to relate diglossia to psychologically pertinent considerations˙ such as compound and coordinate bilingualism (1965e). The present paper represents an extension and integration of these several previous attempts.

For purposes of simplicity it seems best to represent the possible relationships between bilingualism and diglossia by means of a four-fold table such as that shown in Figure I.

FIGURE I

THE RELATIONSHIPS BETWEEN BILINGUALISM AND DIGLOSSIA

DIGLOSSIA

BILINGUALISM	+	−
+	1. Both diglossia and bilingualism	2. Bilingualism without diglossia
−	3. Diglossia without bilingualism	4. Neither diglossia nor bilingualism

Speech Communities Characterized by Both Diglossia and Bilingualism

The first quadrant of Figure I refers to those speech communities in which both diglossia and bilingualism occur. At times such communities comprise an entire nation, but of course this requires very widespread (if not all-pervasive) bilingualism. An example of this type of nation is Paraguay, where almost the entire population speaks both Spanish and Guarani (Rubin, 1962; 1966). The formerly monolingual rural population has added Spanish to its linguistic repertoire in order to talk and write about education, religion, government, high culture and social distance or, more generally, the status stressing spheres; whereas the majority of city dwellers (being relatively new from the country) maintain Guarani for matters of intimacy and primary group solidarity even in the midst of Spanish urbanity.[1] A further example is the Swiss-German cantons in which the entire population of school age and older alternates between High German (H) and Swiss German (L), each with its own firmly established and highly valued functions (Ferguson, 1959; Weinreich, 1951; 1953).

Below the level of nationwide functioning there are many more examples of stable diglossia co-occurring with widespread bilingualism. Traditional (pre-World War I) Eastern European Jewish males communicated in Hebrew (H) and Yiddish (L). In more recent days their descendents have continued to do so adding to their repertoire a Western language (notably English) for *intragroup* communication as well as in domains of *intergroup* contact (Fishman, 1965c; Weinreich, 1951, 1953; 1962).[2] A similar example is that of upper and upper middle class males throughout the Arabic world who use classical (koranic) and vernacular (Egyptian, Syrian, Lebanese, Iraqui, etc.) Arabic and, not infrequently, also a Western language (French or English, most usually) for purposes of *intragroup* scientific or technological communication (Blanc, 1964; Ferguson, 1959; Nader, 1962.).

All of the foregoing examples have in common the existence of a

---

[1] Note that Guarani is not an official language (i.e.) recognized and utilized for purposes of government, formal education, the courts, etc.) in Paraguay. It is not uncommon for the H variety alone to have such recognition in diglossic settings without this fact threatening the acceptance or the stability of the L variety within the speech community. However, the existence of a single "official" language should not divert the investigator from recognizing the fact of widespread and stable bilingualism at the levels of societal and interpersonal functioning.

[2] This development differs significantly from the traditional Eastern European Jewish pattern in which males whose occupational activities brought them into regular contact with various strata of the non-Jewish coterritorial population utilized one or more coterritorial languages (usually involving H and L varieties of their own, such as Russian, German or Polish on the one hand, and Ukrainian, Byelorussian or "Baltic" varieties, on the other), but did so for *intergroup* purposes almost exclusively.

fairly large and complex speech community in which the members have available to them both a range of *compartmentalized* roles as well as ready *access* to these roles. If the *role repertoires* of these speech communities were of lesser range, then their *linguistic repertoires* would also be(come) more restricted in range, with the result that separate languages or varieties would be(come) superfluous. In addition, were the roles not compartmentalized, i.e., were they not *kept separate* by dint of association with quite separate (though complementary) values, domains of activity and every day situations,[3] one language (or variety) would displace the other as role and value distinctions merged and became blurred. Finally, were widespread access not available to the variety of compartmentalized roles (and compartmentalized languages or varieties), then the bilingual population would be a small, privileged caste or class (as it is or was throughout most of traditional India or China) rather than a broadly based population segment.

These observations lead to the conclusion 'that many modern speech communities that are normally thought of as monolingual are, rather, marked by both diglossia and bilingualism if their several registers (speech varieties related to functional specificity; Halliday, 1964) are viewed as separate varieties or languages in the same sense as the examples listed above. Wherever speech communities exist whose speakers engage in a considerable range of roles (and this is coming to be the case for all but the extremely upper and lower levels of complex societies); wherever access to several roles is encouraged or facilitated by powerful social institutions and processes; and finally, wherever the roles are clearly differentiated (in terms of when, where and with whom they are felt to be appropriate), both diglossia and bilingualism may be said to exist. The benefit of this approach to the topic at hand is that it provides a single theoretical framework for viewing bilingual speech communities and speech communities whose linguistic diversity is realized through varieties not (yet) recognized as constituting separate "languages". Thus, it becomes possible for us to note that while nations characterized by diglossia and widespread bilingualism (the latter term being understood in its usual sense of referring to separate languages) have become fewer in modern times, those characterized by diglossia and diversified linguistic repertoires have increased greatly as a consequence of modernization and growing social complexity. The single theory outlined above enabling us to

---

3 The compartmentalization of roles (and of domains and situations as well) requires the redefinition of roles, domains and situations in any encounter in which a seemingly inappropriate topic must be discussed between individuals who normally stand in a given role-relationship to each other. Under such circumstances one or other factor is altered (the roles are redefined, the topic is redefined) so as to preserve the cultural norms for appropriateness (grammaticality) of behavior between interlocutors.

understand, predict and interrelate both of these phenomena is an instance of enviable parsimony in the behavioral sciences.[4]

Diglossia Without Bilingualism

There are situations in which diglossia obtains whereas bilingualism is generally absent (quadrant 3). Here, two or more speech communities are united religiously, politically or economically into a single functioning unit notwithstanding the socio-cultural cleavages that separate them. At the level of this larger (but not always voluntary) unity, two or more languages or varieties are recognized as obtaining. However, one (or both) of the speech communities involved is (are) marked by relatively impermiable group boundaries such that for "outsiders" (and this may well mean all those not born into the speech community, i.e., an emphasis on ascribed rather than on achieved status) role access and linguistic access are severely restricted. At the same time linguistic repertoires in one or both groups are limited due to role specialization.

Examples of such situations are not hard to find (see, e.g., the many instances listed by Kloss, 1966). Pre-World War I European elites often stood in this relationship with their countrymen, the elites speaking French or some other fashionable H tongue for their *intragroup* purposes (at various times and in various places: Danish, Salish, Provencal, Russian, etc.) and the masses speaking another, not necessarily linguistically related, language for their intragroup purposes. Since the majority of elites and the majority of the masses never interacted with one another *they did not form a single speech community* (i.e. their linguistic repertoires were discontinuous) and their intercommunications were via translators or interpretors (a certain sign of *intragroup* monolingualism). Since the majority of the elites and the majority of the masses led lives characterized by extremely narrow role repertoires their linguistic repertoires too were too narrow to permit widespread societal bilingualism to develop. Nevertheless, the body politic in all of its economic and national manifestations tied these two groups together into a "unity" that revealed an upper and a lower class, each with a language appropriate to its own restricted concerns.

Thus, the existence of national diglossia does *not* imply widespread

---

[4] A theory which tends to minimize the distinction between languages and varieties is desirable for several reasons. It implies that *social* consensus (rather than inherently linguistic desiderata) differentiates between the two and that separate varieties can become (and have become) separate languages given certain social encouragement to do so, just as purportedly separate languages have been fused into one, on the ground that they were merely different varieties of the same language.

bilingualism amongst rural or recently urbanized African groups (as distinguished from Westernized elites in those settings); nor amongst most lower caste Hindus, as distinguished from their more fortunate compatriots the Brahmins, nor amongst most lower class French-Canadians, as distinguished from their upper and upper middle class city cousins, etc. In general, this pattern is characteristic of polities that are economically underdeveloped and unmobilized, combining groups that are locked into opposite extremes of the social spectrum and, therefore, groups that operate within extremely restricted and discontinuous linguistic repertoires. Obviously, such polities are bound to experience language problems as their social patterns alter in the direction of industrialization, widespread literacy and education, democratization, and modernization more generally. Since such polities rarely developed out of initial socio-cultural consensus or unity, the educational, political and economic development of the lower classes is likely to lead to secessionism or to demands for equality for submerged language(s). The linguistic states of Eastern Europe and India, and the language problems of Wales, Canada and Belgium stem from origins such as these.[5] This is the pattern of development that may yet convulse modern African nations if their de-ethnicized Westernized elites and diglossic language policies continue to fail to create bilingual speech communities, incorporating the masses, within their ethnically arbitrary political boundaries.

Bilingualism Without Diglossia

We turn next to those situations in which bilingualism obtains whereas diglossia is generally absent (quadrant 2). Here we see even more clearly than before that bilingualism is essentially a characterization of individual linguistic behavior whereas diglossia is a characterization of linguistic organization at the socio-cultural level. Under what circumstances do bilinguals of similar cultural extraction nevertheless function without the benefit of a well understood and widely accepted social consensus as to which language is to be used between which interlocutors, for communication concerning what topics or for what purposes? Under what circumstances do the varieties or languages involved lack well defined or protected separate functions? Briefly put, these are circumstances of rapid social change, of great social unrest,

---

[5] Switzerland as a whole is not a case in point since it is *not* an example of discontinuous and hierarchically stratified speech communities under a common political regime. Switzerland consists of geographically stratified speech communities under a common regime. Except for the Swiss-German case there is hardly any societally patterned bilingualism in Switzerland. Only the Jura region, the Romansch area and a very few other small areas have (had) a recent history of diglossia without bilingualism.

of widespread abandonment of prior norms before the consolidation of new ones.

Many studies of bilingualism and intelligence or of bilingualism and school achievement have been conducted within the context of bilingualism without diglossia, often without sufficient understanding on the part of investigators that this was but one of several possible contexts for the study of bilingualism. As a result many of the purported "disadvantages" of bilingualism have been falsely generalized to the phenomenon at large rather than related to the absence or presence of social patterns which reach substantially beyond bilingualism (Fishman, 1965b, 1966c).

The history of industrialization in the Western world (as well as in those parts of Africa and Asia which have experienced industrialization under Western "auspices") is such that the means (capital, plant, organization) of production were often derived from one speech community while the productive manpower was drawn from another. Initially both speech communities may have maintained their separate diglossia-with-bilingualism patterns or, alternatively, that of an overarching diglossia without bilingualism. In either case, the needs as well as the consequences of rapid and massive industrialization and urbanization were frequently such that members of the speech community providing productive manpower rapidly abandoned their traditional socio-cultural patterns and learned (or were taught) the language of the means of production much earlier than their absorption into the sociocultural patterns and privileges to which that language pertained. In response to this imbalance some react(ed) by further stressing the advantages of the newly gained language of education and industry while others react(ed) by seeking to replace the latter by an elaborated version of their own largely pre-industrial, pre-urban, pre-mobilization tongue.

Under circumstances such as these no well established, socially recognized and protected functional differentiation of languages obtains in many speech communities of the lower and lower middle classes. Dislocated immigrants and their children (for whom a separate "political solution" is seldom possible) are particularly inclined to use their mother tongue and other tongue for intragroup communication in seemingly random fashion (Nahirny and Fishman, 1965; Fishman, 1965f). Since the formerly separate roles of the home domain, the school domain and the work domain are all disturbed by the massive dislocation of values and norms that result from simultaneous immigration and industrialization, the language of work (and of the school) comes to be used at home (just as in cases of more radical and better organized social change the language of the home comes to be established in school and at work). As role compartmentalization and value complementarity decrease under the impact of foreign models and massive change the linguistic repertoire also becomes less compartmentalized. Languages and varieties formerly kept apart come to influence each other phonetically, lexically, semantically and even grammatically much more than before. Instead of two (or more) carefully separated languages each under the eye of caretaker groups of teachers, preachers and writers, several intervening varieties may obtain, differing in degree of interpenetration. Such fused varieties may, within time, become the mother tongue and only tongue of a new generation. Thus, bilingualism without diglossia tends to be transitional[6] both in terms of the linguistic repertoires of speech communities as well as in terms of the speech varieties involved per se. Without separate though complementary norms and values to establish and maintain functional separation of the speech varieties, that language or variety which is fortunate enough to be associated with the predominant drift of social forces tends to displace the other(s). Furthermore, pidginization is likely to set in when members of the "work force" are so dislocated as not to be able to maintain or develop significantly compartmentalized, limited access roles (in which they might be able to safeguard a stable mother tongue variety) and, furthermore, cannot interact sufficiently with those members of the "power class" who might serve as standard other-tongue models.

Neither Diglossia nor Bilingualism

Only very small, isolated and undifferentiated speech communities may be said to reveal neither diglossia nor bilingualism (Gumperz, 1962; Fishman, 1965d). Given little role differentiation or compartmentalization and frequent face to face interaction between all members of the speech community no fully differentiated registers or varieties may establish themselves. Given self-sufficiency no regular or significant contacts with other speech communities may be maintained. Nevertheless, such groups—be they bands or clans—are easier to hypothesize than to find. All communities seem to have certain ceremonies or pursuits to which access is limited, if only on an age basis. Thus, all linguistic repertoires contain certain terms that are unknown to certain members of the speech community, and certain terms that are used differently by different subsets of speakers. In addition, metaphorical switching (Blom and Gumperz, 1966) for purposes of emphasis, humor, satire or criticism must be available in some form even in relatively undifferentiated communities. Finally, such factors as exogamy, warfare, expansion of population, economic growth and

---

[6] At an individual level this need not be the case since translation bilingualism can be maintained for intragroup communication purposes and for individual vocational purposes without the formation of natural bilingual speech communities.

contact with others all lead to internal diversification and, consequently, to repertoire diversification. Such diversification is the beginning of bilingualism. Its societal normification is the hallmark of diglossia. Quadrant four tends to be self liquidating.

Many efforts are now underway to bring to pass a rapprochement between psychological, linguistic and sociological work on bilingualism. The student of bilingualism, most particularly the student of bilingualism in the context of social issues and social change, may benefit from an awareness of the various possible relationships between individual bilingualism and societal diglossia illustrated in this paper. Since all bilingualism occurs in a social context, and since this context is likely to influence both the manifestations and the concomitants of bilingualism, it is incumbent on the student of bilingualism to differentiate accurately between the particular and the more general phenomena that pertain to his field of study.

REFERENCES

BLANC, HAIM. Communal dialects of Baghdad. Cambridge: Harvard University Press, 1964.

BLOM, JAN-PETER AND GUMPERZ, JOHN J. Some social determinants of verbal behavior. Unpublished paper presented at the annual meeting of The American Sociological Association, 1966a.

FERGUSON, CHARLES A. Diglossia. Word, 1959, 15, 325-340.

FISHMAN, JOSHUA A. Language maintenance and language shift as fields of inquiry. Linguistics, 1964, (9), 32-70.

FISHMAN, JOSHUA A. Yiddish in America. Bloomington, Ind.: Indiana University Research Center in Anthropology, Folklore and Linguistics. Publication 36, 1965c. (Also: International Journal of American Linguistics, 1965a, 31, Part II, (2).)

FISHMAN, JOSHUA A. Bilingualism, intelligence and language learning. Modern Language Journal, 1965b, 49, 227-237.

FISHMAN, JOSHUA A. Language Loyalty in the United States. The Hague: Mouton, 1965c.

FISHMAN, JOSHUA A. Varieties of ethnicity and language consciousness. Monograph Series on Languages and Linguistics (Georgetown University), 1965d, 18, 69-79.

FISHMAN, JOSHUA A. Who speaks what language to whom and when? Linguistique, 1965e, (2), 67-88.

FISHMAN, JOSHUA A. Language maintenance and language shift; The American immigrant case within a general theoretical perspective. Sociologus, 1965f, 16, 19-38.

FISHMAN, JOSHUA A. Billingual sequences at the societal level. On teaching English to speakers of other languages, 1966a, 2, 139-144.

FISHMAN, JOSHUA A. Some contrasts between linguistically homogeneous and linguistically heterogeneous polities. Sociological Inquiry, 1966b, 36, 146-158.

FISHMAN, JOSHUA A. Sociolinguistic perspective on the study of bilingualism. Unpublished manuscript, 1966c.

GUMPERZ, JOHN J. Speech variation and the study of Indian civilization. American Anthropologist, 1961, 63, 976-988.

GUMPERZ, JOHN J. Types of linguistic communities, Anthropological Linguistics, 1962, 4, (1), 28-40.

GUMPERZ, JOHN J. Linguistic and social interaction in two communities. *American Anthropologist,* 1964a, 66, part 2, 137-154.

GUMPERZ, JOHN J. Hindi-Punjabi code-switching in Delhi. In Morris Halle (Ed.), *Proceedings of the International Congress of Linguists.* The Hague: Mouton, 1964b.

GUMPERZ, JOHN J. On the ethnology of linguistic change. In William Bright (Ed.), *Sociolinguistics.* The Hague: Mouton, 1966, 27-38.

HALLIDAY, MICHAEL A. K. The users and uses of language. In M.A.K. Halliday, A. McIntosh, and P. Strevens, *The Linguistic Sciences and Language Teaching.* London: Longmans-Green, 1964, Chap. 4, 75-110.

KLOSS, HEINZ. Types of multilingual communities, a discussion of ten variables. *Sociological Inquiry,* 1966, 36.

NADER, LAURA. A note on attitudes and the use of language. *Anthropological Linguistics,* 1962, 4, (6), 24-29.

NAHIRNY, VLADIMIR C. AND FISHMAN, JOSHUA A. American immigrant groups: ethnic identification and the problem of generations. *Sociological Review,* 1965, 13, 311-326.

RUBIN, JOAN. Bilingualism in Paraguay. *Anthropological Linguistics,* 1962, 4, (1), 52-58.

RUBIN, JOAN. Language and education in Paraguay. Unpublished paper presented at SSRC Conference on Language Problems of Developing Nations, 1966 (to be included in *National Bilingualism in Paraguay.* The Hague: Mouton, in press).

WEINREICH, MAX. Inveynikste tsveyshprakikeyt in a skenaz biz der haskale; faktn un bagrifn. [Intragroup bilingualism in Ashkenaz until the enlightenment; facts and concepts]. *Goldene Keyt,* 1959, No. 35, 3-11.

WEINREICH, URIEL. Research problems in bilingualism, with special reference to Switzerland. Unpublished Dissertation, Columbia University, 1951.

WEINREICH, URIEL. *Languages in contact.* New York: Linguistic Circle of New York, 1953.

WEINREICH, URIEL. Multilingual dialectology and the new Yiddish atlas. *Anthropological Linguistics,* 1962, 4, (1), 6-22.

BILINGUALISM AND NATIONALISM

Heinz Kloss

JOURNAL OF SOCIAL ISSUES
VOLUME XXIII, NUMBER 2, 1967

Bilingualism and Nationalism

Heinz Kloss

Marburg University, Germany

Bilingualism and nationalism are both highly complex phenomena, each of which merits a thorough analysis on its own, yet I have set myself the task of writing about the relationship between the two without the opportunity to describe the real complexity of either. Being short of space my best approach is a rigidly pragmatic one which naively assumes that in spite of differences in outward appearances the various situations described as bilingual have an underlying common core, and that the same holds good for phenomena designated by the term nationalism.

Nationalism and the Role of Link Languages

The first topic I am going to discuss is the role of link languages, i.e., languages of wider communication, in international relations. To begin with, what makes for a language to be employed as a vehicle of international communication? There are many reasons, such as religious importance (Arabic), political and commercial power (English in the 19th and 20th centuries, also Russian), multiplicity of sovereign states sharing a language which enjoys official status in each (Spanish and Arabic).

How does nationalism affect the use and spread of such link languages? There are three ways in which it does: (a) nationalism gives rise to an urge to expand one language as a second tongue across large parts of the globe; (b) it may motivate a nation to reject one foreign

language in favor of another; (c) it may cause some new-born nations to adopt some foreign language as the accepted, acclaimed,
even adored, symbol of their nationhood when none of the indigenous
languages seem to suit the purpose.

The outstanding example of nationalism's backing up the spread
of a link language is that which brought about the almost miraculous
recovery of French as a leading language in the period since 1945.
French was almost bound to recover some lost ground, but its gains
were enormously increased by the tireless and zealous efforts of
France's policy makers. The Soviet Union, too, is endeavouring to make
Russian the second language not only of those 45% of its inhabitants
whose mother tongue is non-Russian, but also of the Communist nations of Eastern Europe. Of course both Frenchmen and Russians
see the spread of their languages as a part of their mission in the service of mankind. Both are convinced that their language represents the
most advanced civilization on earth. While the Russians proudly emphasize their materialism, the French feel that theirs is the last leading
civilization which is primarily spiritual, surmounting the problems
and perspectives, the fruits and the failures of technology and the
natural sciences.

The attitude of the French and Russians is better understood if
compared with that of the Anglo-Saxon nations. Until quite recently
the Anglo-Saxon nations did very little to promote English as a second
language in foreign countries. English grew in importance as a result
of the growth first of British and then of American power. Even today
Great Britain and the United States promote English not to enhance
their influence; their influence is already so enormous that they feel
obliged to help foreigners who wish to learn their language. This is
just the opposite of how the French look at the language problem.

The native language of only a few countries is of sufficient importance to warrant attempts to have it introduced abroad as a second
language. But all nations without exception are faced with the necessity
—more urgent to be sure in the case of the smaller speech communities— of learning one or more foreign languages. Their choice is generally determined by utilitarian considerations, but it is occasionally influenced by emotional nationalism. So, for example, after both world
wars many European nations reduced the time for German in their
school timetables. The diminished stature of Germany in political
and cultural life was not, however, the sole motive for the reduction
in time. This is clearly shown by the fact that Denmark more drastically
reduced the number of German lessons in North Schleswig than elsewhere in Denmark, though North Schleswig is the region adjoining
Germany. Conversely, Germany has occasionally profited since 1945
from the fact that her name had long since ceased to be bound up with

colonialism. Egypt, for example, reacted to French policies in Algeria by attempting to supplant at least in part French with German.

A good many African and Asian nations have adopted as official languages, languages which come from outside their own nations such as English and French. At first glance this setting up of *exoglossic* states[1] seems to follow a uniform pattern. Closer examination, however, reveals two basically different types: (a) a European language is together with indigenous tongues accorded official status; (b) a European language is granted a virtual monopoly. The first phenomenon prevails in India, Ceylon, Pakistan, Malaysia and the Philippines where English is admitted in addition to Hindi, Singhalese, Urdu and Benghali, Malayan and Tagalog respectively. In each of those countries the ancestral language, not the imported one, is considered the symbol of national identity,[2] though of course its status is not always undisputed.[3]

The second type of *exoglossic* state exists chiefly in Africa where French or English have succeeded in ousting the aboriginal tongues. For Gabon, Upper Volta, Malawi and Zambia, the language of the former colonial power seems to be the only conceivable instrument to overcome the numberless tribal loyalties. India grudgingly puts up with English and in doing so hurts its nationalistic feelings: Ghana makes of English the rallying flag of emerging nationhood.

Yet these developments in Africa may yet give rise to a curious paradox. If by employing French or English as *national* languages these new states succeed in overcoming tribalism and tribe-based *lingualism* (to borrow a term used in India), their very success in doing so may be their own undoing as nations. Indeed the success of the present movements would mean that the imported language would become the sole hallmark of national identity; and since many of these states border on other states with the same imported language, they may well be drawn together by their common national symbol to form a new and much larger nation.[4] Thus, for example, Senegal, Mali, the Central African Republic and others, may be irresistibly drawn together by their common possession of French (instead of being separated by Wolof, Bambara and Sango, the principal native lan-

---

[1] The term *exoglossic* was coined by Joshua A. Fishman. He considered it more apt as a description of countries which have adopted a foreign language than the alternative, *teleglossic*, suggested by me.

[2] Notice the change of name from Tagalog and Malayan to Pilipino and Bahasa Indonesia respectively.

[3] Tamil opposition to Hindi is leading to a feeling that Hindi is becoming a wedge dividing Indo-Aryan and Dravidian India.

[4] Linguistically isolated countries like Ghana and Sierra Leone, English enclaves in an ocean of French, would not be affected by this trend.

guages). On the other hand this overriding drift toward unity may in turn give rise to counter-currents re-emphasizing traditions and cultural values linked to the major indigenous languages.

Bilingualism and Nationalism in Multinational States

There are many interpretations of the term *multinational*, but I shall use it here of countries in which two or more languages enjoy equal status. The languages need not be official throughout the nation, but each must at least be official in the region where it is the mother tongue of the bulk of the population. Such countries fall into three classes depending on the type of status they allow the several languages: (a) countries in which the languages enjoy complete equality of status; (b) those which make of one the official national language, but otherwise treat all languages as equal; (c) those which in theory make all languages equal, but in practice discriminate amongst them.

Complete equality of status seems possible only in countries which have two or at most three languages. No country could conduct its affairs in four or more languages without becoming hopelessly muddled. Switzerland has three official national languages, Belgium and Finland have two—but India and the Soviet Union, each with a multiplicitly of indigenous languages, recognize only one of their languages as official (Hindi in India, supplemented by English; Russian in the Soviet Union).

Bilingual and trilingual countries commonly give the appearance of unanimity and equality; yet their present stability can be maintained only if all their separate speech communities are on an equal legal footing and none can be called an underdog. Unfortunately, however, legal equality does not always rule out sociological inequality. In Belgium, for instance, the Flemish who are the numerical majority are conducting an enervating struggle against the superiority complex of their numerically weaker French-speaking compatriots. The latter for their part proclaim that by acquiring a little-known language like Dutch they are wasting time which they could better employ in learning English or even German. Similarly, in Canada French-speakers do not enjoy equal status with English-speakers; while in Switzerland, Italian as a second language, lags hopelessly behind German and French. In other words the number of French-Canadians who know English is far greater than the number of Anglo-Canadians who know French; in Belgium the number of Flemish who know French is far greater than the number of Walloons (French-speakers) who know Dutch; and in Switzerland French-speakers are far more likely to learn German and German-speakers to learn French than to learn Italian, while the Italian-speakers commonly learn French or German or both. As has long been apparent in Belgium, such inequalities make for dissatisfaction and for nationalistic strife. This is becoming apparent in Canada, and may some day become apparent in Ticino, Switzerland's only Italian-speaking Canton.

If even bilingual and trilingual states are not assured of peace amongst their different ethnic groups, how much more quarrelling, bitterness and open discord is to be expected in countries with a greater number of languages, where sheer necessity compels the government to single out one language (at most two languages as in Pakistan where Urdu and Bengali are the official languages), and make it the national language.

No government has ever shown greater willingness to respect and promote all languages within its territories than that of Imperial Austria. But inevitably one language, German, had to remain the universal link-language to be studied by all non-German speakers as their principal second language. This circumstance was by no means the least important in bringing about the disruption of the Empire and the formation of splinter states in which hitherto *minor* languages such as Czech and Slovenian became ruling languages. India in our day is faced with the same problem. She has selected Hindi for preferential treatment to the dismay of other speech communities, notably the Tamils, who interpret the move as discrimination against their own languages. Indeed it is difficult to see how India can arrive at a stable solution of its linguistic problems.

It is important to note that in Imperial Austria, also in present day India, the official national language held no privileges at the regional or local level. In this respect the Soviet Union differs from both. A Ukrainian or Latvian who migrates to Siberia is expected to send his children to a Russian school. A Russian who moves to Riga or Odessa is expected not to send his children to a Latvian or Ukrainian one. Thus in the Soviet Union language equality is nominal rather than real. As some of the national republics are flooded with Russian immigrants, we may suspect that a good deal of nationalistic resentment and even hatred smolders under the surface. Though not every exile's report on the matter is to be swallowed without scrutiny.

Bilingualism and Nationalism in the Nation State

By nation state I mean a country with a single official language which is the mother tongue of the great majority of the inhabitants or of that ethnic group which feels and claims that it possesses some special title to rule and represent the nation as a whole. Examples of the first type of nation state are Denmark, Brazil, Tunisia and Honduras. To the second type belong Ethiopia, Liberia and Bolivia, where native speakers of the official languages form respectively 32%, 5% and 32% of the total populations.

It may be justifiable to call countries of the first type genuine nation states and those of the second type section-based nation states. Obviously in many section-based nation states the ruling minority is bound to clash sooner or later with the nationalism of the nondominant ethnic groups. The awakening and rising of the nondominant groups may be delayed by their backwardness which in turn is often largely due to the fact that they are neglected educationally and politically. Frequently the dominant group tries to have its language established first as a lingua franca with the ultimate aim of having it completely supplant the local vernaculars. While the first goal may be well within reach, the second seems to be largely illusory. Thus most minority-based nation states face the prospect of permanent internal tension, though educational policies may temporarily lull the nondominant majority into long periods of apparant ethnic peace.

In the section-based nation states which I have just described the nondominant ethnic groups are usually subjugated by the minority group. But there exists another type of section-based nation state in which the minority language has been elevated to the dignity of an official national language with the consensus of all the major speech communities in the nation. Thus Bahasa-Indonesia, Swahili (in Tanzania) and Tagalog-Pilipino (in the Philippines), though the native languages of only 8%, 5% and 20% of the populations respectively, have been accepted by the major indigenous speech communities as their common national link-languages. As a rule such a solution is possible only where the languages involved are closely akin.[5] As an exception to this rule may be cited the acceptance of Hebrew by all Israelis.

The genuine nation state is basically different from the section-based nation state. In the former the majority has a real chance of successfully imposing its language not merely as a lingua franca but also in time as the sole language of the entire nation. An ethnic group forming just 2% or 8% of the country's inhabitants will not infrequently surrender to the impact of the dominant language. The minority may even surrender their language voluntarily, as did the Polish-speaking Masurians in Eastern Prussia or the German-speaking Belgians living within the pre-1914 boundaries of Belgium, or the speakers of Pennsylvanish (Pennsylvania Dutch) in Eastern Pennsylvania. In such language shifts a period of replacive bilingualism is bound to occur during which the yielding language becomes laden with loadwords and loanshifts from the overcoming language.

More often than not however ethnic minorities in genuine nation

---

[5] Thus in India it is interesting to observe that Hindi is accepted by speakers of related Indo-Aryan languages but resisted by those who speak Dravidian languages.

states are anxious to retain and defend their ancestral language. (Such minorities may be called *national minorities*, as distinct from minorities which being indifferent to the fate of their ancestral language, might be called *linguistic minorities*.) One of the great disillusionments which ensued upon the break up of multilingual empires was that new governments failed to adopt liberal linguistic attitudes. Successor states to the Turkish, Habsburg and Russian Empires turned out to be more intransigent toward minor ethnic groups than were their predecessors. The Kutzo-Vlachs or Aromunians, an ethnic group speaking a Romanian dialect but living in areas now belonging to Greece, Albania, Yugoslavia and Bulgaria, enjoyed much more cultural freedom under Turkish rule than they did after the Balkan wars. Table 1 which sets out the number of minority schools in certain territories before 1918 and after 1920 throws light on these developments. Nothing of course is to be said against the desire of the new post-1912-13 and post-1920 governments to have linguistic minorities learn the new national language as a second language. But obviously what these governments aimed at was blotting out the minority tongues by means of coercive measures leading first to replacive bilingualism and later to a new monolingualism. That is, the aim was complete language shift.

TABLE I

NUMBER OF MINORIETY SCHOOLS IN CERTAIN TERRITORIES IN CERTAIN YEARS
BEFORE AND AFTER 1920.

Territory	Ethnic Group	Year	Schools	Year	Schools
East Galacia	Ukrainian	1918	2600	1928	400
Poland	Lithuanian	1918	147	1931	2
Lithuania	German	1918	37	1925	14
Bukovina (Romania)	Ukrainian	1914	216	1924	0
Dobrudja (Romania)	Bulgarian	1910	60	1931	0
Greece	Aromunian	1912	45	1939	27
Albania	Aromunian	1912	20	1939	3-4

So ruthlessly did many European governments in the inter-war period pursue an assimilationist policy that many statesmen and scholars came to believe that the nation state, by nature and definition, seeks the linguistic assimilation of all its subjects. That of course is not true. There is no reason why the nation state should not rest content if citizens whose mother tongue is not the official language also learn the official language. In our time Denmark's treatment of her citizens who speak Faroese, or Eskimo (Greenland) or German, is a shining illustration of a genuine nation state's linguistic broad-mindedness.

A Special Aspect of the Problem of Assimilation: "Dialectization"

In the foregoing paragraphs I spoke of assimilationist policy as aiming at replacive bilingualism. Actually the situation is more complex. A linguistic assimilation policy may have to deal with basically different minority tongues some of which are closely related to the national language and others which are not. Therefore, speakers of the dominant language have two ways of doing away with a nondominant language: replacing it, or *dialectizing* it. In other words, the policy may aim at diglossic bilingualism[6] instead of replacive bilingualism. To be sure, diglossic bilingualism is only possible where the dominant and nondominant languages are close relatives. So the Spanish government in trying to establish and maintain the monopoly of Castilian Spanish must (and does) try to blot out the Basque language completely, for there is no possibility that the Basques will ever loose consciousness of the fact that their language is unrelated to Spanish. The position of Catalan is quite different, because both Catalan and Spanish are Romance Languages. There is a chance that speakers of Catalan can be induced to consider their mother tongue as a patois, with Castilian as its natural standard language. As a matter of fact this attitude to Catalan is already to be found not in Catalonia proper but in the province of Valencia and in the Balearic islands. In a similar manner, nearly all speakers of Low Saxon (Low German) and the overwhelming majority of Occitan (Provencal) speakers have lost consciousness of their linguistic identity and consider their folk speech as naturally subordinated to German and French respectively, though linguists continue to group these folk languages with other Gothic and Romance Languages. The spiritual subjugation of speakers of Sardinian, and of Haitian Créole is no less complete. These languages seem never to have been used for literary purposes to any extent; yet all linguists regard them as autonomous systems which have to be classified as languages. Thus these are examples of what have been called *abstand* languages (languages by distance).[7]

It is well known that the Czarist government in the 19th century tried to persuade the Ukrainians that theirs was not an *abstand* language but a Russian dialect, usually called Little Russian, and that the natural thing was that they be educated and governed in Russian. The

---

[6] Each fulfills a function distinct from the other. The most common type is where the standard language is used in government, commerce, education and literature, the dialect being reserved for more intimate discourse, as for instance within the family.

[7] On *abstandsprachen* (languages by distance) and *ausbausprachen* (languages by elaboration) see my book, *Die Entwicklung neuer Germanischer Kultursprachen*, Munich: Pohl, 1952.

Turkish government would like to see the Kurdish language disappear from Turkish soil, but the Persian government plays up the kinship of Persian and Kurdish (both Iranian tongues) in order to pave the way for a diglossic situation with Persian the (near-) dialectized vernacular restricted to oral conversation and, at most, some poetry. Low Saxon, Occitan, Sardinian and Haitian Créole are near-dialectized (or semi-dialectized), since the intrinsic distance between them and the related standard languages remains undiminished. They remain *languages by distance*, or *abstand* languages.

An altogether different category of languages is the *ausbau* language, *language by elaboration*, for example Lallans (Broad Scots) which from the linguistic point of view is merely an offshoot of English. During the centuries before Scotland lost its independence Lallans became, according to the then modest standards, an *ausbau* language which served for all purposes (there were not too many of them) not reserved for Latin. Since the Scottish Act of Union, Lallans has slumped to the level of a mere dialect, thus becoming an example of a dialect which achieved *ausbau* status and returned again to the status of a dialect. A final illustration of complete dialectization is those areas of Southern Sweden which speak a dialect resembling Danish more than Swedish. Danish was once the ruling language of these areas, but nowadays Swedish is, with the result that the dialect speakers feel, and believe, Swedish to be the standard language which naturally corresponds to their folk-speech.[8]

---

8 Similarly, local dialects spoken in Moravia are actually more akin to Slovak than to Czech, yet the Moravians have accepted Czech as their *natural* standard language. Standard Slovak, however, was never the official language of Moravia, so unlike Lallans and the Danish dialects of Southern Sweden, the Slovak dialects of Moravia cannot be said to have been "re"-dialectized.

ON THE LINGUISTIC MARKERS
OF BILINGUAL COMMUNICATION

John J. Gumperz

JOURNAL OF SOCIAL ISSUES
VOLUME XXIII, NUMBER 2, 1967

On the Linguistic Markers of Bilingual Communication*

John J. Gumperz

University of California, Berkeley

A major linguistic problem in the study of bilingual behavior is the description of the verbal skills involved in the speaker's concurrent use of the two languages. Recent ethnographic literature increasingly deals with stable bilingual societies, where several distinct languages are spoken by peoples who in all other respects form part of a single social system (Leach 1954; Salisbury 1962; Ferguson 1964; and Rice 1962).

To the extent that not all members have adequate facility in these languages, language choice is of course affected by requirements of intelligibility. But we also have evidence to show that frequently a majority, or at least a significant minority of residents can communicate effectively in either language, and that they alternate between the two languages for much the same reasons that monolinguals select among styles of a single language (Rubin 1961; Fishman 1965). That is to say, the same social pressures which would lead a monolingual to change from colloquial to formal or technical styles may lead a bilingual to shift from one language to another. Where this is the case, the difference between monolingual and bilingual behavior thus lies in the choice of linguistic symbols for socially equivalent processes. In one instance speakers select among lexical or phonetic variants of

* The research reported herein was supported by grants from the National Science Foundation, Division of Social Science, and from the U.S. Office of Education Language. Thanks are due to Joshua A. Fishman and Roxana Ma for assistance and criticism.

what they regard as the same language; in the other case speakers choose between what they view as two linguistic entities. The question to be asked then is this: what special verbal skills does the process of interlanguage shift require; and how do these skills differ from those needed in the monolinguals' stylistic shift?

Since the classification of speech varieties as belonging to the same or different languages is in fact in large part determined on sociopolitical grounds (Ferguson and Gumperz 1960), it can easily be shown that the purely qualitative distinction between monolingualism and bilingualism is by no means adequate to answer our question. Language pairs like Serbian and Croatian in Yugoslavia, Hindi and Urdu in India, Bokmal and Nynorsk in Norway, all of which have figured prominently in recent accounts of language conflict, are, for example, grammatically less distinct than some forms of upper-and lower-class English in New York. Colloquial and literary varieties of Arabic, on the other hand, would be regarded as separate languages were it not for the fact that modern Arabs insist on minimizing the differences between them. The speakers' view of language distinctions may thus be quite far from linguistic reality.

Even in cases where the languages concerned must be considered separate both on linguistic and social grounds, their separateness is not necessarily absolute. Scholars working in the Balkans, where multilingualism has long been widespread, have frequently noted the considerable overlap in lexicon, phonology, morphology and syntax among local varieties of Slavic and adjoining dialects of Greek, Rumanian and Albanian. They also point out that these relationships are independent of historical relatedness, (Sandfeld 1931). More recently Charles Ferguson (1964) in his discussion of diglossia—the use of grammatically separate varieties among educated residents of several societies—states that the varieties concerned in each case constitute a single phonological structure, in spite of their grammatical differences. Stewart's comparative study of Haitian Creole and French shows similar findings (1964).

The Results of Code Switching

The evidence suggests therefore that bilingualism may correspond to quite diverse linguistic phenomena. The problem is particularly great in bilingual or multilingual societies. Although subgroups within such societies may regard themselves as ethnically and culturally distinct, code switching in everyday interaction sets up cross currents of diffusion which materially change the structure of local speech varieties. The linguistic affinities among such varieties are thus not simply functions of genetic affiliation, but are affected by intensity of communication and speakers' values.

Viewed from the point of view of the standard languages, the peculiarities of bilingual speech constitute deviations from the monolingual norm. They are of interest, for example, to the historical linguist because of the insights they provide into processes of language change. For our purposes, however, it seems more important to consider the effect of internal diffusion on intrasocietal communication. Thus if diffusion in multilingual societies results in structural overlap, to what extent does this affect the difficulties that speakers face in switching from one code to another? Rather than comparing bilingual speech varieties with the monolingual standards it seems more appropriate to deal with them directly as constituent elements of a socially defined system, the linguistic repertoire (Gumperz 1964a). What is needed are empirical measures capable of determining the degree of overlap or language distances of constituent varieties within the repertoire without reference to genetic relationship or to other varieties spoken elsewhere.

Interference Measurements

Much of the linguistic research on bilingualism to date relies on measures of interference, "the use of elements from one language while speaking or writing another" (Mackey 1965). The usual procedure is to search the bilingual performance for features of pronunciation, grammar and lexicon not present in the monolingual standard, which can be attributed to second language influence. Interference analysis has provided important insights into the more general processes of borrowing (Weinreich 1952) and its effect on linguistic change. It also serves as an important tool in language pedagogy, where the object is to study what is involved in the monolinguals' learning of a new language and acculturating to a different monolingual community.

Interference measurements of all kinds, however, assume that the structure of the standard is known and that speakers have direct access to the standard and seriously attempt to imitate it. These assumptions are justified for the ordinary second language learner or for isolated speakers of minority languages, whose significant contacts are largely with the surrounding monolingual community and who can thus be expected to conform to its norms. They do not, however, apply in our case. Members of stable bilingual communities interact largely with other bilinguals and it can be shown that such interaction generates its own norms of correctness (Ervin-Tripp 1964). Although learning through prestige imitation takes place in all societies, the particular linguistic object of this imitation in bilingual societies must be established through empirical research; it cannot be assumed.

Contrastive Analysis

A second technique of inter-language comparison is that of contrastive analysis, which finds extensive application in the preparation of pedagogical language texts (Kufner 1962, Moulton 1962, Stockwell,

Bowen and Martin 1965.) This method consists of a direct point by point comparison of the two grammars at each component of structure. Differences are evaluated according to their place within the respective system (i.e., whether they are phonetic, phonemic, syntactic, etc.). They are then counted under the assumption that "what the student has to learn equals the sum of the differences established by this comparison" (Banathy, Trager and Waddle 1966). The linguist's structural analysis plays an important part in predicting the learner's difficulties. For example, the fact that in Spanish the segments ([d] and [s] are in complimentary distribution, with the former occurring initially in words like *dar* and the latter medially in words like *lado*, whereas they contrast in English words like *dare* and *there*, may lead to the diagnosis that the Spanish-speaking student has the problem of assigning phonemic status to two phonetic entities which are allophones and not phonemes in his own language (Banathy, Trager and Waddle 1966). But the assignment of phonemic status to a linguistic feature is generally based on the performance of "ideal speakers living in a homogeneous community" (Chomsky 1965). Since bilingual speakers are excluded from consideration here, the structural categories of ordinary grammars can hardly be used to predict bilingual performance. Techniques of contrastive analysis, thus, require considerable modification if they are to be applied to the measurement of intrasocietal language distance.

Machine Translation

An alternative approach derives from recent work on machine translation. This approach has the advantage of enabling the investigator to focus directly on speakers' performances without reference to outside information. In some earlier work in machine translation, it had in fact been assumed that grammatical information could be disregarded, but this assumption was soon proved wrong when it was shown that grammatical analysis is the most efficient way of organizing the information required for translation so as to fit into a computer's storage capacity (Lamb 1965). If we then ask what is the minimum coding necessary to translate the speaker's performance in Language A to the same speaker's performance in Language B, we must in fact do a linguistic analysis. But note that a grammar in these terms is merely an information storage device; it is not an independently patterned organic entity. Its categories are justified only to the extent that they facilitate the translation process. This provides the criteria of relevance which enables us to avoid some of the most bothersome questions of linguistic analysis such as segmentation of strings into one or more morphemes. The best solution is simply that which provides the simplest translation rules. Since the greater the grammatical overlap, the easier the translation process, it is simplest to assume that there is a single underlying system from which the differences of the two languages can be derived. Language distance can then be measured as a function of the number of nonshared rules.

If translatability measures are based only on a single set of texts, the number of grammatical rules needed will be an arbitrarily restricted selection. The greater the number of speakers measured, and the greater the variety of contexts in which the texts are collected, the more complete will be the body of rules. Translatability measures thus are akin to sociological forms of measurement in that they depend for their validity on sample size and on interaction processes and are therefore ideally suited for sociolinguistic analysis where interspeaker variation is the central problem.

Some Case Studies . . .

During the last few years, my collaborators and I have experimented with translatability measures in several societies. Although our results are still preliminary, they are of sufficient general interest to warrant reporting here. The following data collection procedure was employed. Tape recorded speech samples in two languages were collected from bilingual speakers interacting in natural settings. Texts originally recorded in Language A were then retold orally in Language B by other native speakers and texts recorded in Language B were retold in Language A. Story retelling in a different language is common in daily interaction, so that informants found it an easy and quite natural task. Most sentences in the derived texts were in fact direct translation equivalents of the originals. Since we were interested in determining the minimum number of differences necessary for utterances to be perceived as distinct languages by their speakers, translations were further edited to substitute translation equivalents so as to minimize the language distance in those instances where different expressions had been used. A third group of bilinguals was asked to check each translated text individually to judge its grammaticality.

Hindi-Punjabi

A preliminary study of Hindi-Punjabi bilingual college students in Delhi shows that varieties of both languages are analyzable in terms of a common set of grammatical categories, e.g., pronouns, adverbs, inflectional patterns, etc., and in terms of identical rules for their combination in sentence structures. They furthermore have the same articulatory base. Our texts in the two languages differ only in morphophonemics, i.e., in the rules which determine the phonetic shape of relevant words and affixes. Here is an extreme example (morpheme boundaries are indicated by a dash, word boundaries by a space).

1. Punjabi	oo	naii	khaa-	nd-	aa
	personal	negative	verb	participle	agreement
	pronoun	adv.	stem	suffix	
Hindi	woo	naii	khaa-	t-	aa
Literal English	he	not	eating		
Idiomatic English	He doesn't eat (it).				

2. Punjabi	oo	kar-	wic	hæ-	g-aa
	personal	noun	post	auxiliary	particle
	pronoun	stem	position		
Hindi	woo	ghar-	me	hæ-	
Literal English	He	house	in	is	
Idiomatic English	He is in the house.				

Note that even content words such as *eat* and *house* are almost identical in the two languages. Differences lie primarily in the function words (i.e., words referring to grammatical relations such as *in*) and inflectional endings. The position of these items within the sentence is the same in each case. Only the Punjabi particle *g-aa* in sentence two does not have a direct Hindi equivalent in the context. However, *g-aa* does occur elsewhere in Hindi (Gumperz 1964b).

Kannada and Marathi

An even more striking example of overlap is found among bilingual speakers of Kannada and Marathi, two genetically unrelated languages along the Maharastra-Mysore boundary in central India. Our data here was collected in the course of approximately three months of field work during which we resided in a local village home. Texts were recorded in a wide variety of settings covering the entire range of everyday village activity. In a more formal test of translatability, the edited material was programmed as if for machine translation using a program devised by Douglas Johnson (1965), based on the work of Sydney Lamb (1965). Here are some sample results:

Kannada:	hog-	i	wand	kudri	turg	maR-	i	aw	tand
	verb stem	partic. suffix	adj.	noun	noun	verb stem	partic. suffix	pro- noun	past verb
Marathi:	ja-	un	ek	ghoRa	cori	kar-	un	tew	anla
Literal English:	go	having	one	horse	theft	take	having	he	brought
Idiomatic English:	Having gone and having stolen a horse he brought it back.								

While on the surface the above two sentences are different in every respect, they have the same constituent structure. We were able to analyze our whole extensive corpus of bilingual texts without having to postulate further grammatical rules in one language which were not present in the other language. Independent phonetic perception tests further showed that native speakers were unable to keep the two languages apart on phonological grounds alone. As in the case of Hindi-Punjabi, therefore, the two languages differ only in their morphophonemics. It is interesting to note that, when examined separately by historical linguists specializing in South Asian languages, our texts are characterized as somewhat deviant but nevertheless easily identifiable specimens of Dravidian and Indo-Aryan, respectively. Genetic relationships among languages are established largely through a process of matching at the morphophonemic level. Since this is the area of structure where the two varieties differ most, it is not surprising that historical linguists in the past have failed to make systematic analyses of the underlying similarities.

To be bilingual in either Hindi-Punjabi or Kannada-Marathi—as these languages are spoken in our experimental community—a speaker simply needs to internalize two sets of terms for the same objects and grammatical relationships. He can switch from one language to the other by merely substituting one item in a pair for the other without having to learn and new grammatical rules other than the ones he already controls. If we contrast this form of bilingual communication with the rather complex selection among phonological, syntactic and lexical variables, which Labov's recent work in New York has revealed (1966), it seems clear that there are at least some circumstances where bilingualism may require less skills than the normal process of communication in some monolingual societies.

In evaluating the significance of the above data, it must be kept in mind, however, that our sample was somewhat biased when compared to what is normally understood as bilingual behavior. In attempting to see whether it is possible for one speaker to speak two languages using the same set of grammatical categories, we confined ourselves only to those speech varieties which are regularly used in bilingual interaction. If we take into account literary varieties or varieties used in religious ritual and other activities that are language specific, a number of new differences arise. In more formal Punjabi, for example, we would have to account for word tone at the phonetic level and for additional differences in lexicon and in the system of function words (Gumperz 1964b). In educated Marathi and Kannada, even when it is used among Marathi-Kannada bilinguals, differences in gender and in rules governing adjective-noun agreement not found in casual village speech will arise. Since the linguist's grammars rely heavily on educated speech, contrastive analysis based on these grammars will show considerably more language distance than our data reveal. The formal varieties concerned, however, are learned primarily through formal education; not all members learn them equally well. Translatability measures can account for this by successively sampling different groups of speakers in different settings. However, language distance when measured in this way is not a constant. It varies both with social context and social class.

New York Spanish-English

Because of the special circumstances of long and continuous contact between speakers of the languages concerned, our Indian examples are not likely to have too many parallels elsewhere. More recent work among Spanish-English bilinguals in New York shows somewhat different results. The two languages in this case are quite distinct phonetically. There are further more obvious differences in syntax. Where, for example, Spanish distinguishes between two verbs of "being," ser and estar, English has only one.

In the realm of verb tenses, Spanish has a number of special subjunctive forms and an inflected future which do not occur in English. It is interesting to note though that in the conversational speech of the uneducated the inflected future is dropped in sentences like "I will write" in favor of the periphrastic construction which, like the English, is formed with the verb ir "go" as the auxiliary. Similarly the only subjunctive form which occurs with any frequency is the conditional which serves as the direct translation equivalent of English constructions with "would". Social interaction seems to lead to increased translatability also with English and Spanish.

On the whole, however, the speech of the Spanish-English bilingual in New York approaches the usual image of bilingual behavior. In spite of some overlap, the systems concerned are distinct in every component. Nevertheless, even in this case, the translatability approach raises some new questions about the nature of bilingual skills. To give a phonological example, much of the difference between the two languages results from the presence in one language of articulations not occurring in the other. Thus Spanish lacks the [š] of English shoe and English lacks the [ñ] of Spanish baño. Further distinctions however emerge when we compare the articulation of phonetically equivalent words. Thus the word photo will be [fowtow] in English and [foto] in Spanish in the same speaker's pronunciation. Whereas in Marathi-Kannada such pairs would be undistinguishable. Spanish-English bilinguals maintain two parallel sets of phonetically similar articulation ranges corresponding to functionally equivalent phones.

It would seem that the necessity of keeping the above ranges separate is an important problem in Spanish-English code switching. Comparison of the formal speech of educated bilinguals with that of uneducated bilinguals or with the same speakers in informal speech shows in fact that these distinctions are frequently collapsed.

Some General Features of Bilingualism

Different as the above bilingual situations are, they nevertheless share certain common characteristics. All repertoires maintain an unusually large number of variants at the morphophonemic level. In actual sentences, moreover, the variants never appear in all combinations. Regardless of how large or small the number of nonshared rules, however, differences in the phonological realizations of morphemes play an important part. Even in Hindi-Punjabi where the list frequency of differences is relatively low, differences are very noticeable because they affect affixes and common function words with high text frequency. Variants furthermore never occur in isolation, but in co-occurrent patterns, so that if a Hindi-Punjabi bilingual begins a sentence with *oo* "he," he must also use the participle affix *-nd-*. The alternate affix *-t-* does not co-occur with *oo*. The rigidity of such co-occurrence rules reinforces the perceptual distinctness of codes. In spite of the underlying grammatical similarities, therefore, the shift between codes have a quality of abruptness which to some extent accounts for the speaker's view of them as distinct languages. Such codes seem ideally suited for communication in societies which stress cultural distinctions, while at the same time requiring regular and frequent interaction. In stylistic switching, co-occurrence rules also exist, but they seem less strictly defined, and transitions between styles are more subtle. Stylistic variation, furthermore, is signalled less by morphophonemic distinctions than by differences at the lexical level.

Our listing of the variant linguistic correlates of bilingualism was intended to be suggestive rather than exhaustive. Nevertheless the view that language distance is a function of social interaction and social contexts raises some interesting general problems. If, in spite of surface appearances, as our Indian examples indicate, language is not necessarily a serious barrier to communication, why do such differences maintain themselves over long periods of time? What is it within the system of roles and statuses or in the norms of social interaction that favors the retention of such overt symbols of distinctness? Under what conditions do such symbols disappear?

Of more direct practical value is the question of the relative importance of social and language barriers to communication. Intralanguage variation clearly plays an important part in bilingual behavior and measures of bilingual competence must account for it if they are to be socially realistic. Furthermore, the common assumption that uneducated speakers of minority languages learn better when instructed through the medium of their own vernacular is not necessarily always justified. Instructional materials in these vernaculars may rely on monolingual norms which are culturally quite alien to the student and linguistically different from his home speech. Considerably more research is needed on these and similar questions. We hope that our discussion highlights the importance of ethnographically oriented linguistic measurement in this task.

REFERENCES

BANATHY, BELA, TRAGER, EDITH, AND WADDLE, CARL D. The use of contrastive data in foreign language course development. In A. Valdman (Ed.), *Trends in language teaching*. New York: McGraw-Hill, 1966. 35-56.

CHOMSKY, NOAM. *Aspects of the theory of syntax*. Cambridge: MIT Press, 1965.

ERVIN-TRIPP, SUSAN. An analysis of the interaction of language topic and listener. In John J. Gumperz and Dell Hymes (Eds.), *The ethnography of communication. American Anthropologist*, 1964, 66, (6), Part 2. 103.

FERGUSON, CHARLES A. AND GUMPERZ, JOHN J. Introduction. In *Linguistic diversity in South Asia*. Indiana University Publications in Anthropology, Folklore and Linguistics, 1960, Publication 13.

FERGUSON, CHARLES A. Diglossia. In Dell Hymes (Ed.), *Language in culture and society*. New York: Harper and Row, 1964. 429-439.

FISHMAN, JOSHUA A. Who speaks what language to whom and when. *La Linguistique*, 1965, 2, 67-88.

GUMPERZ, JOHN J. Hindi- Punjabi code switching in Delhi. In Horace Lunt (Ed.), *Proceedings of the ninth international congress of linguists*. The Hague: Mouton, 1964b. 1115-1124.

GUMPERZ, JOHN J. Linguistic and social interaction in two communities. In John J. Gumperz and Dell Hymes (Eds.), *The Ethnography of communication. American Anthropologist*, 1964a, 66, (6), Part 2, 137-153.

JOHNSON, DOUGLAS. Memorandum on morphologies. *Machine translation project*. University of California, Berkeley, 1965. (mimeo).

KUFNER, HERBERT L. *The Grammatical structures of English and German*. Chicago: University of Chicago Press, 1962.

LAMB, SYDNEY. The nature of the machine translation problem. *Journal of Verbal Learning and Verbal Behavior*, 1965, 4, 196-210.

LEACH, EDMOND. *Political systems of Highland Burma*. London: Harvard University Press, 1954.

MACKEY, WILLIAM F. Bilingual interference: its analysis and measurement. *Journal of Communication*, 1965, 15, 239-249.

MOULTON, WILLIAM. *The sounds of English and German*. Chicago: University of Chicago Press, 1962.

RICE, FRANK A. *Study of the role of second languages*. Washington, D.C.: Center For Applied Linguistics, 1962.

RUBIN, JOHN. Bilingualism in Paraguay. *Anthropological Linguistics*, 1961, 4, 52-58.

SALISBURY, RICHARD. Notes on bilingualism and linguistic change. *Anthropological Linguistics*, 1962, 4, 1-13.

SANDFELD, K. Linguistique Balkanique. In *Ed. for collection linguistique de la societé de linguistique de Paris*, 13, 1930.

STEWART, WILLIAM. Functional distribution of Creole and French in Haiti. In E. P. Woodworth and R. J. diPietro (Eds.), *Linguistics and language study*. Georgetown University, Washington, D.C. 1962, Monograph No. 15.

STOCKWELL, ROBERT P. AND BOWEN, J. DONALD. *The sounds of English and Spanish*. Chicago: University of Chicago Press, 1965.

STOCKWELL, ROBERT P., BOWEN, J. DONALD, AND MARTIN, JOHN W. *The grammatical structures of English and Spanish*. Chicago: University of Chicago Press, 1965.

WEINREICH, URIEL. *Languages in contact*. New York: Linguistic Circle, 1953.

THE BILINGUAL'S LINGUISTIC PERFORMANCE—
A PSYCHOLOGICAL OVERVIEW

JOURNAL OF SOCIAL ISSUES
VOLUME XXIII, NUMBER 2, 1967

The Bilingual's Linguistic Performance–
A Psychological Overview

John Macnamara*
McGill University

The psychologists who first began the study of bilingualism seem not to have been interested in bilingualism so much as in its effect on children's scholastic attainment and intellectual functioning. Before the year 1950 a very large number of studies were carried out to determine the relationship between bilingualism and IQ (Darcy, 1953) on the one hand and between bilingualism and attainment on the other (Macnamara, 1966a). Since 1950, however, there has been a change of interest. Recent studies in general have been aimed at explaining bilingual functioning itself and have led to some revealing discoveries. Specifically, they have tackled problems such as the meaning and measurement of bilingualism, the amount of overlap in the linguistic systems of bilinguals, success and failure in keeping linguistic systems from getting mixed up, the ability to switch from one system to the other and the ability to translate. These are the areas which I propose to review. Before going on to do so, however, it is necessary to make some distinctions in language functioning which are particularly helpful in the interpretation of work on bilingualism.

The educated person can typically speak and write his language

---

* I wish to acknowledge my gratitude to the many friends who commented on a draft of this paper, and my special indebtedness to Dr. Ernest Dalrymple-Alford of the American University of Beirut for permitting me to study an unpublished manuscript which treats of a large part of the area reviewed in this article.

as well as understand it when spoken and written. That is he has two production or encoding skills, speaking and writing, and two reception or decoding skills, listening and reading. In each of these skills four aspects can be distinguished. Thus for example in listening there are the phonological, the lexical, the syntactic and the semantic (meaning) aspects. The complete matrix of four aspects of each of the four skills is set out in Figure 1. Bilingualism, of course, involves two such matrices or, because not all bilinguals possess all four skills, at least

FIGURE I

MATRIX OF FOUR ASPECTS OF EACH OF THE FOUR MAJOR LANGUAGE SKILLS

Encoding		Decoding	
Speaking	Writing	Listening	Reading
Semantics	Semantics	Semantics	Semantics
Syntax	Syntax	Syntax	Syntax
Lexicon	Lexicon	Lexicon	Lexicon
Phonemes	Graphemes	Phonemes	Graphemes

sections from two such matrices. Many bilinguals, of course, possess all four skills, but preschool bilingual children generally cannot read or write either of their languages, while persons who have been educated in only one of their languages may be quite unable to read and write the other, especially if the two orthographies differ greatly. Furthermore, there are instances of bilinguals who can understand but cannot speak one of their languages. This is sometimes called receptive bilingualism and it typically occurs in homes where the parents are immigrants to a country which differs in language from their country of origin.

These distinctions are particularly pertinent to the first section which deals with the description and measurement of bilingualism.

Major Distinctions Among Bilinguals

Degree of Bilingualism[1]

Anyone who wishes to study bilingualism is immediately confronted with the problem of defining bilingualism and then with the further problem of determining who is bilingual and to what extent. Without going deeper into the matter I will use the term *bilingual* of persons who possess at least one of the language skills even to a

---

[1] This term is preferred to the now common *balanced-dominant* usage. The term dominant suggests competition between two languages, and therefore might best be employed to describe two tendencies: (1) the tendency for one of the two languages to be used where, from the point of view of both speaker and topic, the two languages are equally suitable; (2) the tendency for the phonological, syntactic, lexical or semantic systems of one language to intrude on those of the other one.

minimal degree in their second language. That is, I shall consider as bilingual a person who, for example, is an educated native speaker of English and who can also read a little French. This means that we consider bilingualism to be a continuum, or rather a whole series of continua, which vary amongst individuals along a whole variety of dimensions. That there can be variations in an individual's degree of bilingualism from speaking to listening, or from reading to writing is well known (Weinreich, 1953). What is not so commonly considered is that there might also be variations within a single modality, such as listening, from one aspect of linguistic performance to another. For example, it is quite possible for a person to be almost equally skilled in the syntactic analysis of French and English, but not in the ability to perceive spoken French and English. The possibility is not so far-fetched as one might suppose, since an individual might have considerable practice at reading a language such as French without having had much opportunity to hear it spoken, with the result that he might be able to analyze the syntax of spoken French quite well if only he could make out the words which were being used. Nor is the point merely theoretical since some progress has been made in examining bilingual performance in its various linguistic aspects (see Macnamara, this issue).

The term "balanced" has been introduced to described persons who are equally skilled in two languages. Strictly speaking, if a person is described without qualification as balanced he is stated to be equally skilled in two languages in all aspects of the language skills he possesses. Thus if he is an educated person, it is implied that he is balanced in all sixteen cells of Figure 1. Clearly, however, the term is generally intended, implicitly if not explicitly, in a more limited sense: the claim is that a person is balanced in understanding or in speaking two languages, or at least in some particular facet of linguistic performance.

To take for the moment a less analytic point of view, one frequently meets bilinguals who appear to be balanced over a wide range of linguistic skills. However, as Fishman (this issue) points out, such persons are most commonly found in situations characterized by bilingualism without diglossia; that is in situations where both languages are indiscriminately employed across the whole range of human discourse. When bilingualism and diglossia go hand in hand each language is considered appropriate for a certain set of topics, roles, etc. In such situations the vocabulary, phraseology, syntax and literary skills required in one language generally have no exact counterpart in the other. So it is pointless to look for balanced bilinguals—as we have described them—in such a setting. However the bilingual settings most commonly studied by psychologists seem to be those in which bilingualism is not accompanied by diglossia.

How are we to measure degree of bilingualism and categorize bilingual performance along the relevant continua? Lado (1961) shows the complexities involved in composing appropriate tests of skills in a single language; the complexities involved in establishing comparable measures of skills in two languages are, if I may be permitted to quantify, far more than double. To illustrate the point the measurement of vocabulary in two languages will suffice. To begin with, even if standardized vocabulary tests are available in two languages, they may not be appropriate for the population one wishes to test. Thus an English vocabulary test standardized in the United States, and a French vocabulary test standardized in France, may not be valid for use with French-English bilinguals in Quebec. Additionally, vocabulary tests generally assume a vocabulary of about 6000 words, the commonest words in the language, and test for knowledge beyond these. This assumption may be quite invalid when applied to the second language of bilinguals which has been learned in school only. Persons whose knowledge of a language is confined to what they learned in school often fail to learn many words which native speakers of the language picked up as children about their homes and in play with other children. Furthermore, because of the tendency for many European languages to share a learned vocabulary, an educated adult English speaker, for example, may, despite grave deficiencies in French vocabulary, fare better on the more "difficult" items towards the end of a French vocabulary test than on the *simple* ones occurring at the beginning. It is difficult to imagine what effect this might have on the validity of the test. Still further, a bilingual may have received his education at some age level in his second language with the result that he may have a more adequate vocabulary for discussing certain topics in his second than in his first language. Finally, the fact that a bilingual can give an acceptable definition of a word may not reveal whether he is capable of exploiting its full semantic possibilities. Many common words, for example *get* in English or *faire* in French, have extraordinary semantic flexibility which is not tested by conventional vocabulary tests; and yet the ability to use this flexibility seems so typical of the effortless performance of the native speaker.

Difficulties such as these must be considered when testing any bilingual skill, but there is no reason to suppose that they are insurmountable. All that is needed is that the researcher be aware of them.

In order to get around the difficulties involved in directly measuring degree of bilingualism by means of tests of reading, writing, speaking and listening, a number of indirect measures have been devised. These may be loosely classified under four heads: rating scales, tests of verbal fluency, flexibility tests and tests of dominance.

Rating Scales. The technique most frequently employed to determine degree of bilingualism is the language background questionnaire. Most questionnaires of this type derive from the work of Hoffman (1934) and require the subject to estimate the extent to which each of his languages is used in his home. The reliability of such measures is generally quite high, yet it remains to be seen how validly they describe linguistic background and, further, how validly linguistic background can be used to predict language skills. Almost certainly the validity will be found to vary from country to country, owing to varying social pressures to exaggerate or understate the use of a particular language. For example the Irish government makes a grant of £10 per annum per child to parents who make Irish the home language. It is not difficult to imagine the effect of these grants on the validity of responses to language background questionnaires.

A second form of rating scale used to measure bilingualism is self-rating for language skills. Typically such ratings correlate highly with ratings of language background. However, Macnamara (1967a) found them less powerful than a richness of vocabulary test (described below) in distinguishing between groups clearly differing in experience in the two languages. He explained the relative weakness of self-ratings by the influence of examination marks. Many subjects rated their skills in their second language above those in their first language if their marks in the second language were higher than those in the first, although the marks were patently non-comparable.

Fluency Tests. There are a number of economic and convenient tests of speed of responding to verbal stimuli or speed of verbal production in two languages. One such is Ervin's (1961a) picture-naming test which yields times for naming pictures of certain objects. Times thus obtained correlated highly with years of experience in the two languages. A second test is that described by Rao (1964) which measures the speed with which bilinguals follow simple instructions given in their two languages. Several other tests of fluency are due to Lambert and his associates (1955b, 1959, 1967). In one test they measured reaction times in response to instructions to press keys; in another they counted the number of French and English words beginning with a particular pair of letters which bilinguals were able to write. Other fluency tests deserving further study are described by Scherer and Wertheimer (1964), the most interesting of which is their "assimilation of meaning" test in which subjects indicate as quickly as possible whether statements are true or false. Finally, Johnson (1953) and Macnamara (1967b) used a task in which subjects were required to say as many different words as they could in one language (and later in the other) within a limited period.

Many of these tests are ingenious, but their validity as measures of degree of bilingualism remains in doubt. So far, researchers have been content if they found that the data they obtained with such tests correlated with language background questionnaires or estimates of years of experience in the two languages. It remains to be seen how well they correlate with direct measures of language skills.

Flexibility Tests. The easiest way to show what I mean by flexibility tests is to give some examples. Macnamara (1967a) devised a test, which is called a richness of vocabulary test. In this subjects were presented with a series of phrases of the type, "he is *drunk*" (later the same item occurred in translation), and asked to write as many words or expressions as they could which are synonymous or nearly synonymous with the word italicized in the phrase. The idea behind this is that bilinguals seem to have far more ways—some formal, some informal, some humorous—to express a concept in their strong than in their weak language. A possible objection to this test is the fact that languages vary in the number of ways they have to express a particular concept. However this ceases to be important if one can find out the number which native-speakers of each language give in a limited period of time. Macnamara found that results obtained with his test could be used to control 80% of the variance in degree of bilingualism as determined by experience in the languages. A complementary test, a semantic richness test, might also prove worth investigating. This would be a test in which subjects were asked to show in how many senses a given word may be used.

Lambert's word detection test may also be classified as a flexibility test. The test requires subjects to identify as many words (from two languages) as they can in a long nonsense word, for instance the French and English words in the string DANSONODENT. Data obtained with this test correlated highly with ratings obtained by means of language background questionnaires.

Dominance Tests. A dominance test is one in which a bilingual is confronted with an ambiguous stimulus (which could belong to either of two languages) and asked to pronounce or interpret it. The language most frequently used is the dominant one. One example of such a test is that devised by Lambert *et al.* (1959) who presented bilinguals with a list of words to be read aloud of which some items were ambiguous, e.g. *pipe* which is both English and French, but pronounced differently in the two languages. Measures obtained with the test correlated with measures of degree of bilingualism based on linguistic background.

Lambert, Havelka and Gardner (1959) have gone further than others in their studies of how to measure degree of bilingualism and have administered to a group of bilinguals a battery of tests in which all four types of indirect measures were represented: rating scales, fluency, flexibility and dominance tests. They found that all such measures were intercorrelated and could be interpreted as measuring a single factor. This is encouraging because the various tests appear at first sight to measure quite distinct skills. Nevertheless it is necessary to sound a warning note: results of factorial studies of the linguistic performance of monolinguals (Thurstone, and Thurstone, 1941, Carroll, 1941, Vernon, 1961) would suggest that verbal functioning comprises many factors, and that some of these factors, for example verbal fluency, can be subdivided into several factors. However the findings of monolingual studies do not apply directly to work with bilingual measures of the types described. Typically indirect measures of bilingualism have been used to derive difference scores by subtracting scores for performance in one language from those for performance in the other. Thus, from the resulting difference scores the influence of all factors which contribute equally to performance in the two languages has been removed. For this reason a difference score *may be* a better measure of degree of bilingualism than the original measures from which it was derived. However, such difference scores have never been validated by comparing them with direct measures of bilingual skills. To correct this omission is surely the next task in the study of how to measure bilingualism.

Coordinate-Compound

The second major distinction among bilinguals is that between coordinate and compound bilinguals. The distinction, by no means a new one, was brought to the attention of psychologists principally by Weinreich (1953), and was further elaborated by Ervin and Osgood (1954). It refers essentially to the semantic aspects of language. Compound bilinguals are defined as those who attribute identical meanings to corresponding words and expressions in their two languages. The fusion of meaning systems is said to result from their having learned both languages in the same context (e.g., a bilingual home), or one language through the medium of the other (the so-called indirect method). Coordinate bilinguals, on the other hand are defined as those who derive different or partially different meanings from corresponding words and expressions in their two languages. The distinction in the coordinates' meaning systems is said to arise because they acquired their languages in different contexts, e.g., French in France and English in the United States.

Interest in the distinction rests primarily in its implications about the effect of acquisition context on the semantic aspects of language. The distinction also draws attention to cultural differences between language settings and to the possibility of cross-cultural misunderstanding even when fluent bilinguals are available as mediators. Finally the distinction aids us in understanding how coordinate bilinguals manage to keep their languages from becoming mixed up, though it increases our difficulties in explaining how compound bilinguals do so.

The first empirical evidence for the coordinate-compound distinction was produced by Lambert, Havelka and Crosby (1958). They found that two groups of French-English bilinguals, distinguished by the manner in which they had learned their languages, differed in the affective or connotative meanings they attributed to translated equivalents in the two languages. Further, they found that their compound group was better able than their coordinate one to make use of a list of translated equivalents in one language while learning a list of words in the other. However, the groups did not differ in speed of translating words.

The strongest support for the distinction comes from a study by Jakobovits and Lambert (1961) in which a satiation technique was used. Lambert and Jakobovits (1960) had previously found that continuous repetition of a word decreases (satiates) its affective meaning. Jacobovits and Lambert used the technique with bilinguals and found that compounds when satiated in one language also showed satiation effects in the other language; coordinates on the other hand showed no such effects. These results have since been replicated by MacLeod (1966). Further support for the distinction is to be found in the work of Lambert and Fillenbaum (1959), and Lambert (1967).

However two other studies failed to yield the expected support for the theory. Olton (1960) had bilingual subjects read a list of English and French words and note which words signalled an electric shock. He then presented a new list in which some of the words were the translation of the signal words. Contrary to expectations, coordinates did not differ from compounds in their responses to the translations. Similarly, in a task which involved learning a list and later recognizing the items learned, no differences were found between the two groups. It had been expected that compounds would make more "translation errors" than coordinates. However, both studies depended on bilinguals making translation errors. It seems likely that such errors are too rare to show up a difference between the two groups.

Two other studies also serve to temper enthusiasm. Kolers (1963) and Lambert and Moore (1966) made painstaking, though quite different, studies of the word associations of bilinguals in their two languages. The bilinguals examined in each study seem to have been mainly compounds (Kolers describes his Ss as such), yet in each, considerable differences between associational networks in the two languages were observed. These findings probably imply greater differences between the semantic systems of compound bilinguals, at least in relation to individual words and their translations, than has hitherto been considered.[2]

The overall status of the distinction between coordinate and com-

---

[2] Ervin studied the effect on bilinguals' recall of varying the language of learning and language of recall. She found that neither variation affected the recall of compound bilinguals, whereas significant differences associated with such variation were found for coordinate bilinguals. Unfortunately, however, no statistical comparison was made between the two groups, so we do not know whether they differ significantly.

pound bilinguals, and consequently of its theoretical implications, is difficult to assess. The linguistic area in which it has most reliably been found is affective meaning, it has not so been found reliably in the area of denotative and connotative meaning.[3] Furthermore, every study mentioned in this section deals with isolated words, which are certainly convenient materials for study. Yet no evidence derived from such materials is likely to describe adequately so complicated a process as the relating of language and meaning. Even the most cursory acquaintance with dictionaries reveals that there is scarcely a word in any language which has only one meaning. The precise meaning attributed to a word in normal usage is determined by the context, verbal or otherwise. Without such a context the flexibility of word meanings is enormous, and so there is no way of knowing what meanings suggest themselves to bilingual subjects during testing. It would therefore seem that the next logical step is to search for a coordinate-compound distinction among bilinguals with materials in which the meaning of words is determined by a verbal context.

Special Aspects of Bilingual Performance

Linguistic Independence. One of the most remarkable aspects of bilingual performance—so obvious in fact that it has scarcely been mentioned in the literature—is the bilingual's ability to keep his languages from getting mixed up. Many bilinguals know the entire phonological and syntactic systems of two languages and many thousand words in each, yet they manage to function in each language with very little interference from the other. This feat of separate storage, retrieval and processing I shall call linguistic independence. Needless to say, few if any bilinguals are fully successful in maintaining linguistic independence at all times; the ability to do so varies among bilingual communities (Kloss, this issue), among individuals within a com-

---

[3] It may be interesting to refer briefly to studies of the semantic values attributed by bilinguals to color words in two languages which divide the color continuum differently—see, for example, Lenneberg and Roberts (1956) and Ervin (1961a). Particularly instructive is Ervin's finding that bilinguals tend to shift the semantic value of color words to lessen or remove disagreement between the two languages. This phenomenon, so reminiscent of Festinger's (1957) theory that cognitive dissonance tends to disappear, suggests that there is a strong pull in the direction of semantic fusion. Kolers (1963) has pointed out that persons can hardly be categorized for life on the basis of how they originally learned their languages. In a similar vein, Fishman (1964) observes that shifts from coordinate to compound bilingualism, and in the opposite direction, may well be affected by the domains in which the two languages are employed throughout life. Interestingly enough, in all studies where a coordinate-compound distinction was found, Ss were highly educated. By contrast, Ervin's Ss were relatively uneducated. It may be that distinctive semantic systems cannot be maintained without a good deal of education directed at keeping them distinct. See Gumperz (1964).

munity and even within an individual's performance depending on occasion, topic, etc. (Ervin-Tripp, 1964, Gumperz, 1964, Mackey, 1962). In order to explain linguistic independence Penfield and Roberts (1959) proposed the theory that the neurological systems underlying the two languages of bilinguals are functionally separate in such a way that when one is *on* the other must be *off*. This is to propose what may be termed a *single switch* model of bilingual functioning, since it states that the whole system associated with each language is either on or off and so implies a single switching system to control which language is on.

To test this theory Preston (1965) used a bilingual version of the Stroop Color-World Test (1935). In this version a subject is shown a series of color words printed in a variety of colors, the color of the ink always differing from that of which the word is the name (for example, the word, red, printed in blue). The subject's task is to ignore the word and name the color of the ink. Preston's subjects were French-English bilinguals who were asked to respond to series of French color words and series of English ones. Each subject's time to complete the task was taken under four conditions: English stimuli and English responses; English stimuli and French responses; French stimuli and English responses; French stimuli and French responses. Performance times were also taken for control conditions in which noncolor words and patches of color were used. In general, times for the experimental conditions (color words) were appreciably longer than times for the control conditions; times for the four experimental conditions did not vary much. These findings were interpreted as evidence against the Penfield and Roberts theory. This seems reasonable, since the theory would predict that when subjects were set to respond in L_1, the L_1 system would be on and the L_2 system off. In that case, subjects ought to have had no difficulty in ignoring stimuli in L_2, and their times ought to have been the same as if they were merely naming patches of color. The findings, however, were to the contrary.

Preston's study suggests that a slightly more complex theory of functional separation is required, a two switch model. On other grounds, too, such a model seems desirable. A bilingual can decide to speak in one language rather than the other independent of his environment, and so he acts as though he had a language switch controlling his language output system. On the other hand, when he sees some print or hears some words in one of his languages he automatically carries out the decoding process in the appropriate language. In this case he acts as though he had a language switch at the beginning of his input or decoding system which is controlled by the environment. If a *two switch* model is accepted, the Preston findings can be reinterpreted. The requirement to respond in L_1 meant the output system, but not in the input system, of L_1 was on. The input system would automatically and simultaneously be on in the language of the stimuli. If the further reasonable assumption is made that the semantic values of the corresponding English and French color words are either equal or equally disruptive to the subjects' performance, then the results are quite in keeping with the theory.

In order to validate the two switch theory of functional separation and of linguistic independence a series of studies of language switching is required. Such a series of studies would comprise separate investigations of the hypothesized output switch, input switch and of the two in combination. On the assumption that switching takes an observable amount of time, it would probably be possible to determine whether two switches exist, and if they do the relationship between them. This would also throw much light on how linguistic independence is achieved and maintained.

Although no systematic study of linguistic independence along the lines just indicated has been carried out, there are some indications that it would be rewarding. Macnamara (1967b) had bilinguals say as many individual words as they could in a given period while switching (alternating), without translating, from one language to the other. He found that under this condition performance was decidedly poorer than under other conditions when subjects gave words unilingually in either of their languages. Kolers (1966b) studied the performance of bilinguals (French and English) when asked to read and spontaneously produce passages in which two languages were mixed. He found that although comprehension of linguistically mixed passages was not inferior to that of unilingual ones, speeds for reading and spontaneous production were very much slower. Moreover, in the reading and spontaneous production of mixed passages many curious errors of pronunciation and syntax appeared. For example, in reading, subjects showed a marked tendency on coming to the end of a French string to pronounce the English string which followed as though it were French. There was also a tendency, though less marked than the first, to pronounce the last items in a French string as though they were English. That is, subjects seemed, on seeing the English string which followed, to change the pronunciation prematurely. This of course argues that the two switches are not entirely independent. However, taken together, these two studies create the distinct impression that the linguistic performance of the bilingual is similar to that of a musician who observes the notation for key at the beginning of a piece of music and then forgets about it, though in his playing he performs the actions appropriate to the key. Similarly, the bilingual once started in one language can forget about which language he is speaking and yet obey the rules of that language. The two studies mentioned show how much his performance is disrupted if he has to concentrate on the language he is using and switch about from one to the other.

A consistent set of findings from another group of studies throws light on linguistic independence but also raises an unsolved problem. Kolers (1965, 1966a) and Lambert, Ignatow and Krauthammer (1966) examined the free recall of bilinguals for three types of word lists: unilingual word lists in each of the two languages and linguistically mixed lists. Subjects were required to recall the items they had seen in the language in which they were presented. The findings were that subjects recalled items from mixed lists just as well as from unilingual lists and that they made amazingly few translation errors. Kolers (1966a) found further that the repetition of items in translation is just as helpful for recall as repetition in the same language. This suggests that subjects employ a nonlinguistic semantic store for the items; but then, why is no storage space, to borrow a computer term, taken up with assigning the language to the semantic value? We do not know the answer, but it must somehow depend on language being a highly distinctive and overlearned coding system. This in turn helps to explain linguistic independence.

Linguistic Interference. Linguistic interference, the tendency for the phonological, lexical, syntactic and semantic systems of one language to intrude on those of another, is the opposite of linguistic independence. Linguists have studied linguistic indepedence for a long time, but psychologists have paid little attention to it. Apart from those studies already discussed in connection with the coordinate-compound distinction (in essence a distinction between linguistic independence and linguistic interference at the semantic level), there seem to be no relevant studies in the psychological literature. Yet interference in phonology, syntax and vocabulary must surely be related to other types of interference described by psychologists.

Perhaps the best way to approach the matter is to study the performance of persons who are learning a second language or children who are learning two languages simultaneously. Two studies of such children by linguists already exist: Ronjat (1913) and Leopold (1939-49). The difficulties to be anticipated in this approach are (a) particular examples of interference in the learner's performance may have been taught to him by his parents or teachers; (b) sophisticated teaching tends to wipe out as much interference as possible. However, these are not formidable difficulties, and in any case instances of true interference are so abundant in the language of children that the researcher will easily find enough of them for his purpose.[4] In addition, there have been advances recently in techniques for collecting and analysing

---

[4] Frequently interference is so clear that even the most conscientious advocate of the competence-performance distinction will have little scruple in allowing that such instances are more than a mere slip of the tongue. For example, a young German-English bilingual girl once said of the present writer to her mother: "Der can German talken."

the speech of young monolingual children (see Smith and Miller, 1966) which could be adapted to the learning of two languages.

Switching. Part of the bilingual's skill is his ability to switch from one language to the other. I have already dealt to some extent with switching in connection with linguistic independence. Now, however, I wish to focus attention now on the nature and functioning of the switching devices and on the cues which control them.

Switching may take the form of linguistic interference, but in this section I shall confine myself to full code switching without interference.

From the studies of Kolers (1966b) and myself (1967b) it would appear that switching takes an observable amount of time, though it would be premature to suggest actual figures. Differences between individuals in switching time do not appear to be related to degree of bilingualism, since I, while working with groups quite distinguishable in degree of bilingualism, failed to discover a relationship.

If switching takes time, how is it that in normal discourse a bilingual can frequently without seeming to pause have recourse to his other language for a word, a phrase, or an apt quotation? The most likely explanation is that he has the capacity to activate the L_2 system, carry out the semantic encoding, the selection of words and the syntactic organization while more or less mechanically producing in L_1 material which has already been prepared for production.

Support for the above hypothesis is to be found in another study which I made of language switching (1966). Bilingual subjects read two types of lists in three different manners. One type of list consisted of 20 numbers drawn at random from the numbers, 1 to 20; the other consisted of 20 sums of money (e.g., 5s.-8d.) also arranged in random order. Each subject read one number list and one money list in Irish, a similar pair of lists in English; in the third pair he had to switch languages for each new item. Languages were always cued by the color in which the item was written, green for Irish and red for English. A subject was told what type each list was before he came to it and given six practice items. The test items were shown to him one at a time when he completed his response to the previous one. Overall times for reading each list were taken with a stopwatch.

The findings were that unilingual performance on the number lists taken together and unilingual performance on the money lists taken together did not differ significantly. However, times for the mixed lists were decidedly longer than those for the corresponding unilingual lists. Additionally the time which could be attributed to switching when reading numbers was significantly longer than that which could be attributed to switching when reading money lists, though each list involved the same number of switches.

As the main difference between the two types of list was in length of response, the hypothesis was set up that shorter switching times for money lists were due to subjects' ability to anticipate the language of the next item while more or less mechanically naming the item before them. To test this hypothesis two further money lists were presented to the same subjects. Both lists were mixed, both involved the same number of switches, but the pattern of switches in one list was regular and could be anticipated, while in the other list switches occurred in a random pattern. The finding supported the hypothesis: the random order list took significantly longer to read than the regular one.

Two features in these findings deserve particular attention. The improvement in switching times for money lists with a regular pattern of switching occurred, (1) although subjects had to anticipate a switch *while speaking,* and (2) although they did not know what the next response would be—they only knew that it would be in a particular language. The first of these points supports our interpretation of how bilinguals in normal discourse can switch without an apparent pause. They anticipate the switch while speaking and thus avoid disrupting the flow of their speech. The second point is support for some form of the theory of functionally separate language systems (discussed above). It is an advantage to anticipate a language switch even when what is to be said in the other language is still unknown. The most reasonable explanation of this is that a language system can be made ready for a response even before the response has been determined. For this to be possible it must be distinct, at least functionally, from the other language system.

Little is known from a psychological viewpoint about the second aspect of language switching, that is, the cues which guide bilinguals in their choice of language. Bilinguals can of course decide which language to use in the absence of cues or even running counter to available ones. However, it is generally possible to discover in the environment some of the cues which guided a particular choice. The most obvious cues are linguistic: spoken or written language. Sometimes these cues are so powerful that the bilingual is not conscious that he has switched languages (see Graur, 1939). Other cues are nonlinguistic and depend on associations between a particular language on the one hand and certain persons, places and topics on the other. When such associations exist, the persons, places and topics act as cues to language choice and language switches. In fact the study of such cues has been a major interest in sociolinguistics (Hymes, this issue). Bilinguals also seem to become adept at discerning nonlinguistic cues to language choice even among strangers, as daily experience in a city like Montreal testifies. Here, bilinguals seem to be relying on such cues as hair color, facial features, dress and the like. The evidence, however, is only anecdotal.

Translation. Translation is switching with the added limitation that a message already encoded in L_1 be encoded in L_2. The ability to translate, then, involves the ability to map one code on the other in such a way that the new string in L_2 has the same meaning as the original in L_1. The key to the mapping is meaning; and meaning is superordinate to the two languages, although related to them by the semantic networks of the two languages.

This description of translation does not imply that every word and expression in every language has an exact counterpart in every other language. It merely states that whether a word or phrase in one language translates a word or phrase in another language is determined by reference to the meaning. Neither does our description of translation remove the possibility of a coordinate-compound distinction. That distinction rests on the possibility that some bilinguals (compounds) attribute a single meaning to words or phrases in two languages where other bilinguals (coordinates) do not.

The interest of translation for psychologists is the light it can throw on language switching mechanisms, on the semantic aspects of bilingualism, and of course on the problems and possibilities of communication across language boundaries.

There is some evidence that degree of bilingualism and speed of translating are unrelated. Lambert, Havelka and Gardner (1959) presented bilinguals with a list of French and a list of English words and measured the time taken to translate each list. The resulting measures did not correlate with other measures of degree of bilingualism. I (1967b) also measured speed of translating individual words by asking bilinguals to say as many words as they could in a minute in one language following each word by its translation in the other language. Measures thus obtained were not related either to degree of bilingualism as determined by experience in the two languages or to unilingual production (saying distinct words) in either language. Treisman (1965) has a similar finding in a study (described below) of the simultaneous translation of continuous strings.

These findings are surprising because at first sight they imply that speed of decoding and encoding are unrelated to the extent of overall skills in two languages. However, the most likely explanation is that the constant requirement to switch languages has such a disruptive effect on production that it wiped out any differences associated with degree of bilingualism.

Oléron and Nanpon (1964) compared times taken to translate unconnected words presented orally with times taken to repeat them in the same language. They found a difference of about 0.4 seconds. Part of this time may be taken up with the choice of a meaning for the word, since unconnected words are never unambiguous; part is possibly due to language switching[5], and part to the search for the appropriate word in the second language.

I did not find reliable differences due to the direction of translation (L₁ to L₂ or L₂ to L₁), though Lambert *et al.* did find such differences and traced them to different sorts of language settings.

Three Studies . . .

Three studies are particularly interesting in that they go beyond the translation of words and deal with the translation of sentences. Treisman (1965) examined the speed with which bilinguals could carry out simultaneous translation from English to French and vice versa. More specifically, she measured the extent to which her subjects lagged behind the incoming message. She found that the extent of this lag was principally determined by the amount of information (uncertainty or improbability in transition from one item of a string of words to the next) in the incoming message. She also found that translation was slower than repetition in the same language, and, though her subjects varied considerably in degree of bilingualism (some were native French-speakers, others were native English-speakers), that translation from English to French was consistently faster than translation in the opposite direction. This suggests either that there is something about English which makes it easier to decode than French, or something about French which makes for easier encoding. It also suggests that the translation of continuous passages and unrelated words are different processes.

Oléron and Nanpon (1965) also studied delays in simultaneous translation by skilled translators and found that the delays could range from 2 to 10 seconds. The extent of the delay, they suggest, is determined by the difficulty experienced by the translator in organizing the incoming material. The translator must grasp a certain amount of the material before he can begin to translate, the amount varying with the position in the sentence of certain key words such as the verb. On the other hand he cannot afford to fall too far behind because of the limitations of short-term memory. Numerous errors of omission and less numerous errors of addition were also observed.

Hepler (1966) made a systematic and careful study of the effect of combining syntactic transformations with translation on the performance of Russian-English bilinguals. As expected, she found that when her subjects had to combine both tasks (transform and trans-

---

⁵ However, the two switch model of linguistic performance would not suggest a loss of time due to switching in this investigation. The model allows for the input system to be on in the language of the stimuli and the output system to be simultaneously on in the language of the response. Thus no language switch would be required. On the other hand, there might be a tendency for the switches to operate in harmony which would have to be counteracted in the translation test, and thus give rise to a loss of time.

late) their response times were significantly longer than when they carried out transformations within the language of the stimulus. However, the time taken by translation was in general less than that taken by transformation. In general, too, the time added by translation was only about half that observed by Oléron and Nanpon for translating unconnected words. Finally, Hepler found that tasks involving translation from English to Russian were carried out significantly faster than tasks involving translation in the opposite direction.

The studies of Treisman and Hepler suggest that unlike the translation of individual words speed of translation may vary with the pair of languages involved and with the direction in which the translation is made. Treisman's study suggests further that the variables responsible for this are linguistic rather than psychological, but as yet there are no indications as to what these variables may be. Hepler's finding that the translation of simple sentences takes less time than the translation of unconnected words (Oléron and Nanpon) lends support to the view that in the later task subjects lose time in choosing one of the many possible meanings.

So far as I am aware no studies have been made of the quality of translations made by different sorts of bilinguals, for example coordinate and compound bilinguals. The theory behind the distinction would suggest that they would perform translation tasks differently. However this raises the thorny problem of how to evaluate the quality of translations, a problem which is basic to the extension of studies on translation. Fortunately a recent paper by Carroll (1966) takes up this topic.

Carroll thought it unlikely that objective scales would prove useful in the assessment of the quality of translations, so he addressed himself to the development of subjective scales. He personally divided translations into nine bundles using first a subjective scale of fidelity and then one for intelligibility. He then formulated descriptions of each bundle, one set of descriptions for fidelity and one for intelligibility. Next he described the bundles to groups of subjects and had them discriminate among a large number of translations first for intelligibility and then for fidelity. He found high inter-judge reliability on each scale and high inter-scale agreement.

These findings in so complicated an area are very encouraging indeed. They also suggest that a slightly different approach might prove fruitful. A group of highly skilled bilinguals might be divided at random, one half to study the original of a message and one to study a translation. Afterwards they might be set questions on the material they had studied, and the translation assessed in terms of the number of questions answered correctly by the translation group compared with the original group. Repetition of the experiment with various translations might well provide a ranking of the translations for fidelity and intelligibility. If successful, the advantage of this technique over Carroll's is likely to be a considerable saving of time. Carroll's subjects took four and a half hours to assess 144 sentences. In addition, subjects received one hour of instruction on the use of the scales.

In Conclusion—Two Themes

If a broad view is taken of the studies reviewed, one cannot but be impressed at the interest of the problems raised and the progress that has been made in a relatively short time. Even more impressive, however, is the amount of work which still remains to be done. Two themes which run through the review are worth singling out for special attention as they seem so relevant to the further progress of psychological studies of bilingualism: the complexity of language functioning and the complexity of the social settings in which language is employed. Lack of awareness of these very different sets of complexities have frequently led to unjustified generalizations as well as to seeming contradiction between findings.

To offset the disadvantages just referred to, there is the attraction of research on bilingualism, first because of its obvious value to society, and secondly because of the opportunity it affords for elegant and rigorous research designs. In most studies the researcher can use the same subjects as their own controls. In this way it is possible to study such basic problems as for example the relationship between language and thought, because one can study subjects who have a single level of cognitive development and two different levels of language development. To study the same relationship in monolingual subjects is not nearly so easy, since in most tasks language and thought are inextricably confounded. Thus it seems likely that many students will be attracted to bilingualism in the hope of solving some of the most basic problems in human psychology.

REFERENCES

CARROLL, J. B. A factor analysis of verbal abilities. *Psychometrica*, 1941, 6, 279-307.
CARROLL, JOHN B. Quelques mesures subjectives en psychologie: fréquence des mots, significativité et qualité de traduction. *Bulletin de Psychologie*, 1966, 19, 580-592.
DARCY, NATALIE T. A review of the literature on the effects of bilingualism upon the measurement of intelligence. *Journal of Genetic Psychology*, 1953, 82, 21-58.
ERVIN, S. Semantic shift in bilingualism. *American Journal of Psychology*, 1961a, 74, 233-241.
ERVIN, S. Learning and recall in bilinguals. *American Journal of Psychology*, 1961b, 74, 446-451.
ERVIN-TRIPP, S. An analysis of the interaction of language, topic and listener. In John J. Gumperz and Dell H. Hymes (Eds.), *The Ethnography of communication*. American Anthropologist, Special Publication 3, 1964, 86-102.

ERVIN, S., AND OSGOOD, C. E. Second language learning and bilingualism. *Journal of Abnormal and Social Psychology* (Supplement), 1954, 49, 139-146.

FESTINGER, L. *A Theory of cognitive dissonance.* New York: Row, Peterson, 1957.

FISHMAN, JOSHUA A. Language maintenance and language shift as a field of inquiry. *Linguistics,* 1964, 9, 32-70.

GRAUR, A. Notes sur le bilinguisme. *Faculté des Lettres de Bucharest, Bulletin Linguistique,* 1939, 7, 179-180.

GUMPERZ, JOHN J. Linguistic and social interaction in two communities. In John J. Gumperz and Dell H. Hymes (Eds.), *The Ethnography of communication.* American Anthropologist, Special Publication 3, 1964, 137-153.

HEPLER, NORVA K. *Strategies in grammatical transformations.* Unpublished M.A. thesis, McGill University, 1966.

HOFFMAN, MOSES N. H. *The Measurement of bilingual background.* New York: Bureau of Publications, Teachers College Columbia University, 1934.

JAKOBOVITS, L. A., AND LAMBERT, WALLACE E. Semantic satiation among bilinguals. *Journal of Experimental Psychology,* 1961, 62, 576-582.

JOHNSON, G. B. Bilingualism as measured by a reaction time technique and the relationship between a language and a nonlanguage intelligence quotient. *Journal of Genetic Psychology,* 1953, 82, 3-9.

KOLERS, PAUL A. Interlingual word associations, *Journal of Verbal Learning and Verbal Behaviour,* 1963, 2, 291-300.

KOLERS, PAUL A. Bilingualism and bicodalism. *Language and Speech,* 1965, 8, 122-126.

KOLERS, PAUL A. Interlingual facilitation in short-term memory. *Journal of Verbal Behaviour,* 1966a, 5, 314-319.

KOLERS, PAUL A. Reading and talking bilingually. *American Journal of Psychology,* 1966b, 79, 357-376.

LADO, ROBERT. *Language testing.* London: Longmans, 1961.

LAMBERT, WALLACE E. Developmental aspects of second language acquisition. *Journal of Social Psychology,* 1955a, 43, 83-104.

LAMBERT, WALLACE E. Measurement of the linguistic dominance of bilinguals. *Journal of Abnormal and Social Psychology,* 1955b, 50, 197-200.

LAMBERT, WALLACE E. Psychological studies of the interdependencies of the bilingual's two languages. 1967. (mimeo)

LAMBERT, WALLACE E., AND FILLENBAUM, S. A pilot study of aphasia among bilinguals. *Canadian Journal of Psychology,* 1959, 13, 28-34.

LAMBERT, WALLACE E., HAVELKA, J., AND CROSBY, C. The influence of language acquisition contexts on bilingualism. *Journal of Abnormal and Social Psychology,* 1958, 56, 239-244.

LAMBERT, WALLACE E., HAVELKA, J., AND GARDNER, R. C. Linguistic manifestations of bilingualism. *American Journal of Psychology,* 1959, 72, 77-82.

LAMBERT, WALLACE E., IGNATOW, MARIA, AND KRAUTHAMMER, M. Bilingual organization in free recall. McGill University, 1966. (mimeo)

LAMBERT, WALLACE E., AND JAKOBOVITS, L. A. Verbal satiation and changes in the intensity of meaning. *Journal of Experimental Psychology,* 1960, 60, 376-383.

LAMBERT, WALLACE E., AND MOORE, NANCY. Word-association responses: comparisons of American and French monolinguals with Canadian monolinguals and bilinguals. *Journal of Personality and Social Psychology,* 1966, 3, 313-320.

LENNEBERG, E. H., AND ROBERTS, J. M. *The language of experience: a case study.* Indiana University Publications in Anthropology and Linguistics, Memoir 13, 1956.

LEOPOLD, WERNER. F. *Speech development of a bilingual child,* 4 Vols. Evanston, Ill., 1939-1949.

MACKEY, W. F. The description of bilingualism. *Canadian Journal of Linguistics,* 1962, 7, 51-85.

MACNAMARA, JOHN. *Bilingualism in primary education.* Edinburgh: Edinburgh University Press, 1966a.

MACNAMARA, JOHN. The effect of anticipation on the language switching speeds of bilinguals. St. Patrick's College, Dublin, 1966b (mimeo).

MACNAMARA, JOHN. How can one measure the content of a person's bilingual proficiency? Paper read at UNESCO Conference on Bilingualism, 1967a.

MACNAMARA, JOHN. The linguistic independence of bilinguals. *Journal of Verbal Learning and Verbal Behaviour,* 1967b.

MACLEOD, FINLAY. *A study of Gaelic-English bilingualism: The effects of semantic satiation.* Unpublished thesis: Aberdeen University, 1966.

OLÉRON, P., AND NANPON, H. Recherches sur la répétition orale de mots présentés audivement. *Année Psychologique,* 1964, 64.

OLÉRON, P., AND NANPON, H. Recherches sur la traduction simultanée. *Journal de Psychologie Normale et Pathologique,* 1965, No. 1, 73-94.

OLTON, R. M. *Semantic generalization between languages.* Unpublished M.A. thesis, McGill University, 1960.

PENFIELD, W., AND ROBERTS, L. *Speech and brain mechanisms.* Princeton: Princeton University Press, 1959.

PRESTON, M. S. *Inter-lingual interference in a bilingual version of the Stroop color-word test.* Unpublished Ph.D. thesis, McGill University, 1965.

RAO, T. S. Development and use of *Directions Test* for measuring degree of bilingualism. *Journal of Psychological Researches,* 1964, 8, 114-119.

RONJAT, JULES. *Le Développement du Langage Observé chez un Enfant Bilinque.* Paris: Librarie Ancienne H. Champion, 1913.

SCHERER, GEORGE A. C., AND WERTHEIMER, MICHAEL. *A psycholinguistic experiment in foreign-language teaching.* New York: McGraw-Hill, 1964.

SMITH, F., AND MILLER, GEORGE A. (Eds.). *The genesis of language.* Cambridge, Mass.: MIT Press, 1966.

STROOP, J. R. Studies of interference in serial verbal reactions. *Journal Experimental Psychology,* 1935, 18, 643-661.

THURSTONE, L. L., AND THURSTONE, T. G. Factorial studies of intelligence. *Psychometric Monographs,* 1941, 2.

TREISMAN, ANNE M. The effects of redundancy and familiarity on translating and repeating back a foreign and a native language. *British Journal of Psychology,* 1965, 56, 369-379.

VERNON, PHILIP E. *The structure of human abilities* (2nd ed.) London: Methuen, 1961.

WEINREICH, URIEL. *Languages in contact.* New York: Linguistic Circle of New York, 1953.

AN ISSEI LEARNS ENGLISH

Susan Ervin-Tripp

JOURNAL OF SOCIAL ISSUES
VOLUME XXIII, NUMBER 2, 1967

An Issei Learns English

Susan Ervin-Tripp*

University of California, Berkeley

In the years since the second world war, large numbers of American servicemen have brought home Japanese wives. These women, who are Issei, or first-generation, have been exposed to English intensively. Few of their husbands know any Japanese. Few of the women have the intention of teaching their children Japanese. They are scattered about rather than clustered residentially, so that in many cases their friendships are with Caucasians.

They maintain Japanese primarily through reading or friendships with other war brides whom they meet through the war brides clubs or through employment in Japanese restaurants. Since there are two other Japanese communities in the area, comprised of earlier immigrants and of the young business and official groups, one might expect ties with other Japanese. But the other immigrants are mainly older and of rural background. Furthermore, interracial marriages are sufficiently unpopular in Japan to inhibit friendships between the war brides and other Japanese.

I have investigated two aspects of the acquisition of English in this special group of Issei: Why do some learn English faster than

* This research was conducted at the Institutes of Human Development and Human Learning under a grant from the National Science Foundation. I am indebted to Yaeko Nishijima Putzar for a major role in all phases of the study and to Naomi Quenk, David Stimpson, and Jean Goodman as well. Professor Katsuo Sano supervised collection of the norms in Japan.

78

others, and why do some learn what to say as well as how to say it in English?

I will use in this report several different types of measures of English mastery. *Relative fluency* is a measure of comparative speed in naming pictures of simple objects in Japanese and in English. This measure has been found before (Ervin 1961), to be a useful and valid device for assessing purely oral skills, but it does not, of course, take into account any grammatical skills at all. *Morphology* was a test based on a purely verbal version of the device Jean Berko (1958) used with children which asks for the plural, past tense, or possessive of a number of nonsense syllables. For example, one might say "I have a nizz. There are two of them. What are they"? The interest in this measure was whether the speaker inflected the form or not. Japanese does not have inflectional suffixes for nouns so the women often omit them in English. *Prosody* was a score for appropriate stress and intonation patterns in reading sentences designed to test typical contrasts in English. *Phonemes* were measures of the success in distinguishing English phonemes in pictures or in sentences containing key words like *ship* and *sheep*, *light* and *right*, and *hat, hot* and *hut*. *Subphonemes* were allophonic contrasts like vowel length before final consonants, pronunciation of consonant clusters, and syllabic nasals of *wooden* and *mountain*. These were treated separately from phonemic errors on the grounds that subphonemic errors were less likely to lead to misunderstanding of messages.

Many factors should be related to ease in acquiring English. The most important of these are the amount of contact with English including, separately, hearing and speaking the language. In addition it was believed that certain variables of an attitudinal type might be important, in view of Lambert's work (1965) which showed differences between students who varied in level of motivation to learn a second language. Attitudinal variables should have more effect on the features least important for intelligibility.

The number of women in this study was small. Thirty-six Issei women were tested on a variety of tests for a total of around nine hours per woman. In the correlational analysis resulting from the large array of data, there is some problem in sifting causal relations from simple co-occurrences.

Relative Fluency

Basically English dominance, results in terms of naming speed, seems to be a function of exposure to English. There is a relation of .42 to over-all exposure, and both the number of years in the United States and the age of children are related to fluency in English.

On the other hand, some beliefs about oneself are related to low English fluency. The women who judged themselves to be relatively conservative, and those who still yearned to visit or live in Japan, had relatively low fluency in English.

The naming measure is also a relatively good predictor of associate fluency in *both* languages. (Associate fluency refers to the number of word associations given in each language in the test described below.) Evidently the women who have greater verbal fluency in Japanese succeed in learning English more rapidly.

Morphology

Second language learners can successfully communicate in spite of quite deviant grammar in certain respects. Many Japanese women speak English without the usual English inflectional affixes. They omit subjects or objects when these are obvious from context. In many situations of encounter between speakers of two unrelated languages, we find stable pidgins developing. Listening to the "transitional pidgin" of the Issei, and struck by its surprising success in terms of conveying messages, one must ask why these women ever go beyond this stage of learning.

Pidgins typically develop when both parties to a transaction are satisfied with or derive benefit from using this special language. On the other hand, if there is sufficient contact with monolingual norms for the deviance of a pidgin to be disapproved, if there is sufficient contact to allow at least one group to become bilingual, and if there is social equality so that relative rank is not marked by the use of pidgin, bilingualism or even language shift may result from contact. Since the condition of the Issei women is one that makes for bilingualism or language shift, we expect that under the pressure of contact and standard English norms they will gradually shift toward standard English.

Morphological omissions in English are similar to phonemic errors in that they can occasionally result in misunderstanding. Learning of morphology and learning of phonemes go hand in hand ($r = .70$). The strongest predictors of morphological skill are schooling and reading ($p < .05$)[1] which is hardly surprising.

Phonemic System

In every language some sound differences alter messages; others simply indicate dialect, style, accent or mood. Phonemic distinctions are those which can give a different message. The greater variety of word forms and phonemes in English present serious difficulties to Japanese who wish to learn English. Among the most frequent sounds in English are /l/ and /r/, indistinguishable to a Japanese, who imitates both as a flap, as in a stereotyped British *very*. Japanese has

---

1 Unless otherwise indicated Mann-Whitney U-Tests were used.

five vowels; American English has at least nine. The Japanese confuse *ship* and *sheep, pool* and *pull, cat, cot,* and *cut.* Since /v/ and /th/ don't exist in Japanese, substitutes are made.

The astonishing result of this study is that the highest predictor of phonemic mastery, even in naming pictures, is reading, ($p < .01$) though exposure to English in school and on jobs, ($p < .05$), and correction by others are also significant predictors, ($p < .05$). On the other hand, movies, TV and radio are unrelated with phonemic skills and, indeed, phonemic scores are slightly lower for regular moviegoers.

There are two quite different interpretations of the finding that reading is the best predictor of phonemic mastery. One possibility is simply that people who read a lot care more about language, are more motivated to learn, and are more disturbed by failure to be understood, to understand or to meet the norms for English.

Another possibility is that reading helps to supplement oral training. Since many of the phonemic distinctions which cause trouble for the Japanese have spelling correlates, reading is in fact not unrelated to phonemic training. Teachers find that children who have phonemic confusions in discrimination or articulation have trouble reading. If two words have a distinctive spelling, their phonemic distinctiveness in listening could be sought, and in articulation better remembered. In this view, distinctive spelling could accelerate learning. Which of these is the better explanation can only be discovered by experimental manipulation.

Prosody and Accent

In addition to phonemic differences, some measures were included which related to aspects of English less crucial to the intelligibility of messages. One problem with these measures is that they are often more difficult to assess reliably, since the native speaker's ear judges phonemic errors most acutely and tends to disregard features of speech which are not essential to intelligibility. Both of these measures have some relation to phonemic scores (prosody, $r = .41$; phonetic accuracy $r = .55$).

Prosody appears to have some relation to attitudinal variables, in that women with poor prosody scores were more likely to report that it is important to be attractive ($p < .01$) and that jobs are important and may require an accent ($p < .05$). Voices with more Japanese accent were also judged less favorably than samples of American voices ($r = .33$) by women with better English prosodic pattern.

The phonetic scores were better ($p < .05$) for women who said it is important to be a good wife and mother, and if one knows English one can understand the family better. On the whole, prediction of both measures was poor.

Attitudes

I had expected that attitudinal variables might prove to be related closely to the acquisition of prosody and phonetic patterns in English, and included items bearing on both the advantages and disadvantages of an accent and on attitudes about language purity or mixture. Most of the Issei, unlike the French-born bilinguals in an earlier study (Ervin, 1955), do not feel there is anything wrong with language mixture. However, Ss whose pronunciation was poor generally see both more advantages and disadvantages attached to an accent. These findings render the technique suspect because if it had assessed real and possibly effective differences in motivation, I would have expected a relation between good pronunciation and belief that accents are disadvantageous. In conclusion, I think that the attitudes reported arise from the woman's skills at the time of the interview. The French informants who had more language mixture in their speech also approved of it more. Their judgment may rationalize the fact.

Language and Content

Content Shifting

The recent work of Blom and Gumperz (1966) has revealed that language switching is a subtle and pervasive process. In groups of friends in a Norwegian village they found that the introduction of topics of a general sort as opposed to local questions led to an unconscious increase in the use of the standard Norwegian lexicon. One might think that this kind of tie between form and content can only be effective when the forms are not sharply distinct, as in dialect variation where co-occurrence restrictions may be less than in language variation. The observation of the natural speech of many bilinguals belies this belief.

Our concern here will be with the reverse facet of this tie of form and content, i.e., with the effect of language choice upon content. Within the life of a bilingual individual who has moved from one linguistic milieu to another the two languages may have been used in distinctive physical and social environments and at different parts of the life cycle. If there are differences in social experience and beliefs in the two cultural milieux we might expect that language shift will be accompanied by a shift in content. These changes might be due to differences in the perception or recall of experience associated with the two languages, or to differences in verbally expressed values in the two cultures. In other words such a bilingual, in becoming competent in two cultures, learns to associate particular kinds of content with each language.

What might we expect the content differences associated with language to consist of? The simplest possible assumption is that the differences between content in the two languages of a bilingual might be similar to differences between two monolingual groups. This is at least a starting point. In an earlier study with French who came to the United States as adults, predictions were made about content differences in Thematic Apperception Test latent themes. For some variables the themes of the stories changed with language in the direction predicted as likely for monolinguals (Ervin, 1955 and 1964).

In the present study, monolingual norms were obtained for a series of verbal measures. These were Thematic Apperception Test stories, word associations, sentence completions, semantic differentials and story completions. The monolinguals were similar in age, education and social class to the bilingual women. Two groups of bilingual women were studied, the Issei described earlier, and a sample of Kibei Nisei, or second generation Japanese American who returned to Japan for education.

For each type of content, a system was devised for scoring distance from American norms, distance from Japanese norms, and relative dominance of the two distance scores. Thus for stories, sentence completions and word associations, responses were weighted by their frequency in the norm group. For example, on the TAT card MF13, a score of 3 Japanese and 18 American is given for a guilt theme, since 3 Japanese women and 18 Americans said the man felt guilty; in Japan the more common theme was failure. For the semantic differentials a deviation score was devised. While the differences in norms were in some cases surprising, the procedure was completely mechanical and required no judgment about the typicality of the responses.

An analysis of the monolingual norms for story completion led to some curious findings. For example one story ran: "A father died leaving many debts. His only son, earning his own living is studying". One might guess that the Japanese would feel a greater obligation to maintain the family good name in such a case. However, about half the Japanese said that the student finished his studies before repaying, and another 13 per cent never repaid; almost all of the Americans said the student repaid soon by leaving school or working part time. After the fact, one can see that two differences are involved. One is the close tie in the Japanese industrial system between school and job through personal networks, which would make interrupting a highly competitive school career unthinkable; the other is the difference in student economics. The point of the illustration, however, is that the monolingual norms in some cases match a stereotype and in some cases sharply deviate from it.

Content Shifts for Each Task

The most clear-cut effect of language was on word associations and sentence completions. When speaking Japanese, both Issei and Nisei gave associations more typical of women in Japan; when speaking

English, the Issei gave typically American associations. The over-all effect was that content shifted with language for both groups.

Some concepts, of course, are typically more Japanese while others are more American. Thus, *mushrooms* and *New Year's Day* are typically Japanese, while *kitchen, plate* and *marriage* are more typically American. There is not so much shift with language in connection with these words since they reflect a kind of domain specialization. Even in Japan, *kitchens* look American now; but *mushrooms* have, even in English, a rich evocation of the pine forests in the fall in Japan. On the other hand, *tea* evokes lemon and cookies in English, and in Japanese the utensils of the tea ceremony.

As expected, then, shifting was greater for some words. It was also greater for those Issei who were more fluent in English. Evidently learning English brings with it learning appropriate American associates.

Sentence completions also showed a marked relation to language for both groups. In particular the Issei shifted markedly towards the American norms when responding in English. When responding in Japanese both groups increased their Japanese content scores.

Some of the differences are quite subtle. For instance, Japanese women more often say "what I want most in life . . . is peace". Americans say ". . . happiness". "When I am with men . . ." Japanese women are uncomfortable, American women contented. "When a husband finds fault with his wife, the wife . . ." in Japan—is defensive, in America—tries to improve.

For both word associations and sentence completions, though the change in conformity to American norms with language was considerable ($p. < .001$) for the Issei, the Nisei responses, though differing in the two languages, were equally close to American norms in both. Possibly the difference between Issei and Nisei lies in the greater separation of two cultures for the Issei. For the Nisei the American milieu has always been bilingual, since often their families mix languages. But since they were in Japan during the conservative, nationalistic thirties, traditional Japanese culture is uniquely tied to the Japanese language for them, even more than for the Issei who knew post-war Japan.

For story completions, both groups again showed an increase in Japanese solutions when the Japanese language was used. But American solutions did not depend on language. For example, "it is closing time, but the boss is still in his office. An office girl finished her work, but as usual many of the other workers are still remaining". The typical American solution has the girl leave without asking; in the Japanese solutions she waits without asking. Frequently the women commented about the difference in customs. One Issei gave this solution in Japanese: "I think that since she is a working person I guess she will not be able to leave until her boss goes home. She will wait". And in English:

"Well sometimes she have to work, boss say to her . . . I think he say wait, well she does wait". In this case, there is neither a typical American nor a typical Japanese solution at the second session.

The semantic differential results indicated that the effect of language depended on the concept being judged; in the Thematic Apperception Test stories there was no over-all shift with language at all.

Set

One way to account for these effects is to attribute them to self-instructions. If the women can guess what typical responses are, they may be able to shift content with language because the change in language implies a difference in what they ought to say. We sought to separate this feature from language by holding language constant and asking some subjects to give typically Japanese responses at one session and typically American responses at the other.

For some words, set did produce an effect on word association responses. For example, New Year's Day drew quite different responses from one woman under different sets—"New Year's celebration, New Year's greetings, New Year's cards, New Year's house visiting, New Year's eve", vs. "New Year's Eve party, champagne, holiday, New Year's resolution". Most women could simulate typical Japanese responses appropriately but not typically American responses, perhaps because they don't know them. The over-all effect was to increase relative dominance of Japanese under the Japanese set and decrease it under the American set.

For the completions also, the Japanese scores could be increased. In addition there was change for some stories in the American score. Evidently the stereotype of the norms varied from story to story. The two examples we have given of the student with his father's debts and of the office girl leaving at the end of the day illustrate cases where the norms do not conform equally to a stereotype.

In the case of the semantic differential, an American set was effective for some concepts, but not for all. For sentence completions, set affected only American scores, and for the TAT, an American set makes stories more Japanese!

It thus appears that the subjects were able to manipulate proximity only to the Japanese norms on those measures where there had been an effect of language, with the exception of sentence completions. The over-all increase in American score in English testing for word associations and story completions in the Issei is thus unexplained by set.

Individual Differences

I have suggested that learning what is typically American content may be part of the competence to be acquired along with the English language itself. The Issei might be expected to have as wide a range in this kind of mastery as was found in their phonological skills.

What kind of women shifts scores with language? In order to classify them, I ignored how deviant from the norms each woman was and simply looked at how close to each norm group she was at each session, and gave her a relative score.

A woman who moves to the United States might simply learn English and in effect translate her Japanese responses into English. Such a woman should, if she was relatively close to typical Japanese responses in Japan, give such responses in both languages. We shall call her J-dominant. J-dominant women are pictured as shy, conservative and lacking contacts in the United States.

A woman who moves to a different social context in the United States and learns new content appropriate to English would alter content with language. These women are called shifters. They probably have maintained contacts in Japan, and also are fairly acculturated in their behaviour in America, but without strong preferences.

Some women may become (or have become) Americanized even in their behaviour in Japanese. They will be called A-dominant. They probably have a strong identification with American women, show a high degree of acculturation and prefer American contacts.

The J-dominant on word associations do appear to be conservative. They would rather be Japanese than American, they serve Japanese food at home, believe in lucky days ($p < .01$), and wean their children late. But it is hard to distinguish shifters from A-dominant. The shifters wean their children early, have a separate room from the children, like driving a car, and are A-dominant on sentence completions. They are dependent on others and believe it is important to have many acquaintances, ($p < .01$). The A-dominant identify with American women more than the others ($r = .51$), and prefer them as friends ($r = .35$). They go to American movies a lot, and know their neighbors but not their in-laws. They even expect their children to first-name adult friends.

The J-dominant on the TAT were similar in that they weaned their children late, have a typical Japanese New Year's, and are least acculturated. But most of their friends are American. A-dominants have closer friends in America, and have a more American New Year's. Shifters tend to be more acculturated on a few scales. They wean their children early, and have adopted American customs of courtesy and seldom follow such Japanese customs as bowing. They have many Japanese friends, but unlike the A-dominant they lack close friends in America, and are not affectionate. Their high shift score arises largely from being more typically Japanese in responses at the appropriate session.

The problem situations or story completions showed some marked differences between the groups. The J-dominant write to Japan and prefer Japanese friends though they have been married a long time ($p < .01$). They don't read American magazines ($p < .01$) and hence may simply not know American norms for solutions. For them, comfortable living is paramount ($p < .01$). The A-dominant does read American magazines ($p < .01$), is highly dependent ($p < .01$), and was encouraged in her American trends because the closest family member favoured her marriage. Her husband doesn't like her Japanese ties ($r = .66$), doesn't ask her questions about Japan, and doesn't like to hear her speak Japanese. Shifters on the other hand are not dependent.

The J-dominant and shifters on sentence completions have no marked characteristics. The A-dominant are married to men who like the Japanese language, clothes and women, but they have high contact and are relatively acculturated. They have some definite verbal attitudes about values, saying it is important to be attractive, have many acquaintances, do well in a profession, be a good wife and mother and raise children a special way.

Some common themes showed in the results, though there were variations for the different verbal measures. The J-dominant were typically more conservative, more closely tied to Japan, and less acculturated. The particular measures revealing these features varied. Many said they would rather be Japanese than American.

The A-dominant were the reverse. Generally the A-dominant identified with American women more than the others, and preferred them as friends. They had close friends here, and were sometimes quite dependent on them. Their families did not oppose their marriages. They learned a good deal about America from the mass media, going to movies and reading magazines a lot.

The shifters, like the A-dominant, were more acculturated. But they often lacked Caucasian friends here, sometimes lacking any close friends here. Perhaps this is the key difference between shifters and A-dominant who have become completely "Americanized".

It is evident that the knowledge demanded to give American responses varies for the different tests. The word associations could be shifted simply by enumerating different objects; far subtler differences in preoccupations are revealed in the TAT's and sentence completions. The only conspicuous source discovered for American content is American magazines. Women who read them had high scores in both languages for American Content.

The Bilingual and Monolingual Norms

This study began with a model of a bilingual as a person with access to two sets of norms, both of which must be learned. When the norms are linguistic, and the two languages with which he has contact are both standardized languages with which he maintains contact through reading if not orally, such a model may have some appropriateness. But even in language, new norms develop for bilinguals[2] if they use either of their languages primarily with other bilinguals. Their sense of what is "correct" itself changes. Some French informants in the United States even asked me what was correct French. Since actual speech is likely to change even faster than beliefs about language, any group cut off from a monolingual community and low in reading, rapidly loses its ability to shift between two sets of monolingual norms. In the French study every informant, no matter how educated and committed to the maintenance of French and no matter how often he returned to France, showed evidence of English influences in his French, often subtly through semantic categories, frequency of cognates or word order.

In the case of content, there is no norm in the sense of a standard of correctness. Within each monolingual community there is diversity. An Issei who marries an American and emigrates must be deviant herself. Though she might know what average or typical behavior is, there is no reason to assume that she responds this way herself. Besides, of course, it is not clear what *average* she might be reflecting—the Japanese woman of the time she emigrated, or her contemporary in Japan, certainly changed with the years. In some cases I found that Navaho and Anglo monolinguals in the American southwest (Ervin-Tripp, 1964) were more alike than bilinguals on semantic differentials. For example, both Anglos and Navaho monolinguals think highly of doctors. Navaho bilinguals have, like the monolinguals, had contact with doctors in the hospitals, but in addition to recognizing their medical effectiveness, they are aware through their knowledge of English that some Anglo doctors have contempt for Navahos, and speak rudely to and about them. Bilinguals may thus be deviant from both groups.

Secondly, in all bilingual groups there is some specialization of function by language, so that the two languages taken together have the full range of functions for the bilingual individual that a single language has for a monolingual. Thus the bilingual women reported that they knew of their husband's work chiefly through English. The current specialization of functions and topics is closely tied to the fact that in their life histories the two languages were not learned at the same time. It cannot then be expected that they will have acquired knowledge of verbalized values and content in the same way as women who grew up here speaking English. Some content they can learn as

---

[2] Blom and Gumperz (1966), and Gumperz (this issue) show that where bilinguals have been interacting mainly with other bilinguals for a long time the model for each of their languages is not monolingual usage of those languages, but rather the modified forms of those languages as spoken by the bilinguals themselves.

adults; the story completions reflect themes discussed for adults in the women's magazines. But some of the subtle differences in TAT themes, such as the preoccupation with guilt or with failure, may reflect differences which can only be learned through childhood socialization, rearing children here, or decades of close association with Americans. As was pointed out (Ervin, 1964) with the French TAT protocols, the themes that showed most marked shift were those most obvious to adults (e.g., achievement).

In this report of initial results, I sought to characterize why some women learn English faster than others, and why some show more content shift than others. The strongest predictors of simple fluency were found to be contact with the language through the number of years in the United States. But for mastery of English morphological rules and pronunciation, reading of English was important, either because of its relation to values about correct use of language, or because of a direct influence on awareness of distinctions between words.

Marked shifts in content with shift in language were found in a variety of verbal measures. These changes appear to be due to more than self-instruction to give typical responses, because when such instructions were given, the women were unable to make their answers more American, except on sentence completions. Thus set may be a partial but not an adequate explanation for the fact that responses were more typical of the Japanese when given in Japanese and more typical of Americans when given in English.

Women who gave typically American responses in both languages differed on other measures—of conservatism, identification with Americans and acculturation—from women who gave typically Japanese responses in both. Thus the content data were consistent with other differences in these women's behaviour and were not particularly tied to the language being spoken. In one case, story or problem solutions, American themes seem to have been learned from the mass media. At this point in the analysis, the only difference that can be found between those who adopt American content only in English and those who do so also in Japanese is that the latter have stronger friendships here. Since the women who changed content with language were not the same for all the measures of content, I cannot conclude that there is a separate group of women who display two somewhat different selves in the two languages. This kind of shifting with context evidently occurs for most of the women some of the time.

REFERENCES

BERKO, JEAN. The child's learning of English morphology. *Word*, 1958, 14, 150-177.
BLOM, JAN-PETTER AND JOHN GUMPERZ. Some social determinants of verbal behavior. Unpublished paper presented at the annual general meeting of the American Sociological Association, 1966.

ERVIN, SUSAN M. Semantic shift in bilingualism. *American Journal of Psychology,* 1961, 74, 233-241.

ERVIN, SUSAN M. Language and TAT content in bilinguals. *Journal of Abnormal and Social Psychology,* 1964, 68, 500-507.

ERVIN, SUSAN M. *The verbal behavior of bilinguals: The effect of language of report upon the Thematic Apperception Test stories of adult French bilinguals.* (Doctoral dissertation, University of Michigan) Ann Arbor, Mich.: University Microfilms, 1955, MicA 55-2228.

ERVIN-TRIPP, SUSAN M. Navaho connotative judgments: the metaphor of person description. In Hymes, Dell (Ed.), *Southwestern Studies in Ethnolinguistics,* In press.

ERVIN-TRIPP, SUSAN M. An analysis of the interaction of language, topic, and listener. *American Anthropologist,* 1964, 66, No. 6, Part 2, 86-102.

LAMBERT, WALLACE E. Psychological approaches to the study of language. Part II. On second-language learning and bilingualism. *Modern Language Journal,* 1965, 47, 114-121.

A SOCIAL PSYCHOLOGY OF BILINGUALISM

Wallace E. Lambert

JOURNAL OF SOCIAL ISSUES
VOLUME XXIII, NUMBER 2, 1967

A Social Psychology of Bilingualism

Wallace E. Lambert

McGill University

Other contributions in this series have drawn attention to various aspects of bilingualism, each of great importance for behavioral scientists. For instance, we have been introduced to the psychologist's interest in the bilingual switching process with its attendant mental and neurological implications, and his interest in the development of bilingual skill; to the linguist's interest in the bilingual's competence with his two linguistic systems and the way the systems interact; and to the social-anthropologist's concern with the socio-cultural settings of bilingualism and the role expectations involved. The purpose of the present paper is to extend and integrate certain of these interests by approaching bilingualism from a social-psychological perspective, one characterized not only by its interest in the reactions of the bilingual as an individual but also by the attention given to the social influences that affect the bilingual's behavior and to the social repercussions that follow from his behavior. From this perspective, a process such as language switching takes on a broader significance when its likely social and psychological consequences are contemplated, as, for example, when a language switch brings into play contrasting sets of stereotyped images of people who habitually use each of the languages involved in the switch. Similarly, the development of bilingual skill very likely involves something more than a special set of aptitudes because one would expect that various social attitudes and motives are intimately involved in learning a foreign language. Furthermore, the whole process of becoming bilingual can be expected to involve major conflicts of values and allegiances, and bilinguals could make various types of adjustments to the bicultural demands made on them. It is to these matters that I would like to direct attention.

Linguistic Style and Intergroup Impressions

What are some of the social psychological consequences of language switching? Certain bilinguals have an amazing capacity to pass smoothly and automatically from one linguistic community to another as they change languages of discourse or as they turn from one conversational group to another at multilingual gatherings. The capacity is something more than Charles Boyer's ability to switch from Franco-American speech to Continental-style French when he turns from the eyes of a woman to those of a waiter who wants to know if the wine is of the expected vintage. In a sense, Boyer seems to be always almost speaking French. Nor is it the tourist guide's ability to use different languages to explain certain events in different languages. In most cases they are not fluent enough to pass and even when their command is good, their recitals seem to be memorized. Here is an example of what I do mean: a friend of mine, the American linguist, John Martin, is so talented in his command of various regional dialects of Spanish, I am told, that he can fool most Puerto Ricans into taking him for a Puerto Rican and most Columbians into taking him for a native of Bogota. His skill can be disturbing to the natives in these different settings because he is a potential linguistic *spy* in the sense that he can get along too well with the intimacies and subtleties of their dialects.

The social psychologist wants to know how this degree of bilingual skill is developed, what reactions a man like Martin has as he switches languages, and what social effects the switching initiates, not only the suspicion or respect generated by an unexpected switch but also the intricate role adjustments that usually accompany such changes. Research has not yet gone far enough to answer satisfactorily all the questions the social psychologist might ask, but a start has been made, and judging from the general confidence of psycholinguists and sociolinguists, comprehensive answers to such questions can be expected in a short time.

I will draw on work conducted by a rotating group of students and myself at McGill University in Montreal, a fascinating city where two major ethnic-linguistic groups are constantly struggling to maintain their separate identities and where bilinguals as skilled as John Martin are not at all uncommon. Two incidents will provide an appropriate introduction to our work. One involves a bus ride where I was seated behind two English Canadian ladies and in front of two French Canadian ladies as the bus moved through an English-Canadian region of the city. My attention was suddenly drawn to the conversation in front wherein one lady said something like: "If I couldn't speak English I certainly wouldn't shout about it", referring to the French conversation going on behind them. Her friend replied: "Oh, well, you can't expect much else from them". Then one of the ladies mentioned that she was bothered when French people laughed among themselves in her presence because she felt they might be making fun of her. This was followed by a nasty interchange of pejorative stereotypes about French Canadians, the whole discussion prompted, it seemed, by what struck me as a humorous conversation of the two attractive, middle class French Canadian women seated behind them. The English ladies couldn't understand the French conversation, nor did they look back to see what the people they seemed to know so much about even looked like.

The second incident involved my daughter when she was about 12 years old. She, too, has amazing skill with English and two dialects of French, the Canadian style and the European style. One day while driving her to school, a lycée run by teachers from France, I stopped to pick up one of her friends and they were immediately involved in conversation, *French-Canadian* French style. A block or two farther I slowed down to pick up a second girlfriend when my daughter excitedly told me, in English, to drive on. At school I asked what the trouble was and she explained that there actually was no trouble although there might have been if the second girl, who was from France, and who spoke another dialect of French, had got in the car because then my daughter would have been forced to show a linguistic preference for one girl or the other. Normally she could escape this conflict by interacting with each girl separately, and, inadvertently, I had almost put her on the spot. Incidents of this sort prompted us to commence a systematic analysis of the effects of language and dialect changes on impression formation and social interaction.

Dialect Variations Elicit Stereotyped Impressions

Over the past eight years, we have developed a research technique that makes use of language and dialect variations to elicit the stereotyped impressions or biased views which members of one social group hold of representative members of a contrasting group. Briefly, the procedure involves the reactions of listeners (referred to as judges) to the taped recordings of a number of perfectly bilingual speakers reading a two-minute passage at one time in one of their languages (e.g., French) and, later a translation equivalent of the same passage in their second language (e.g., English). Groups of judges are asked to listen to this series of recordings and evaluate the personality characteristics of each speaker as well as possible, using voice cues only. They are reminded of the common tendency to attempt to gauge the personalities of unfamiliar speakers heard over the phone or radio. Thus they are kept unaware that they will actually hear two readings by each of several bilinguals. In our experience no subjects have become aware of this fact. The judges are given practice trials, making them well acquainted with both versions of the message, copies of which are supplied in advance. They usually find the enterprise interesting, especially if they are promised, and receive, some feedback on how well they have done, for example, if the profiles for one or two speakers, based on the ratings of friends who know them well, are presented at the end of the series.

This procedure, referred to as the *matched-guise* technique, appears to reveal judges' more private reactions to the contrasting group than direct attitude questionnaires do (see Lambert, Anisfeld and Yeni-Komshian, 1965), but much more research is needed to adequately assess its power in this regard. The technique is particularly valuable as a measure of *group* biases in evaluative reactions; it has very good reliability in the sense that essentially the same profile of traits for a particular group appear when different samples of judges, drawn from a particular subpopulation, are used. Differences between subpopulations are very marked, however, as will become apparent. On the other hand, the technique apparently has little reliability when measured by test-retest ratings produced by the same group of judges; we believe this type of unreliability is due in large part to the main statistic used, the difference between an individual's rating of a pair of guises on a single trait. Difference scores give notoriously low test-retest reliability coefficients although their use for comparing means is perfectly appropriate (Bereiter, 1963; and Ferguson, 1959, 285f).

Several of our studies have been conducted since 1958 in greater Montreal, a setting that has a long history of tensions between English- and French-speaking Canadians. The conflict is currently so sharp that some French-Canadian (*FC*) political leaders in the Province of Quebec talk seriously about separating the Province from the rest of Canada, comprising a majority of English-Canadians (*ECs*). In 1958-59, (Lambert, Hodgson, Gardner and Fillenbaum, 1960) we asked a sizeable group of EC university students to evaluate the personalities of a series of speakers, actually the matched guises of male bilinguals speaking in Canadian style French and English. When their judgements were analyzed it was found that their evaluations were strongly biased against the FC and in favor of the matched EC guises. They rated the speakers in their EC guises as being better looking, taller, more intelligent, more dependable, kinder, more ambitious and as having more character. This evaluational bias was just as apparent among judges who were bilingual as among monolinguals.

We presented the same set of taped voices to a group of FC students of equivalent age, social class and educational level. Here we were in for a surprise for they showed the same bias, evaluating the EC guises significantly *more* favorably than the FC guises on a whole series of traits, indicating, for example, that they viewed the EC guises as being more intelligent, dependable, likeable and as having more character! Only on two traits did they rate the FC guises more favorably, namely kindness and religiousness, and, considering the whole pattern of ratings, it could be that they interpreted too much religion as a questionable quality. Not only did the FC judges generally downgrade representatives of their own ethnic-linguistic group, they also rated the FC guises much more negatively than the EC judges had. We consider this pattern of results as a reflection of a community-wide stereotype of FCs as being relatively second-rate people, a view apparently fully shared by certain subgroups of FCs. Similar tendencies to downgrade one's own group have been reported in research with minority groups conducted in other parts of North America.

Extensions of the Basic Study

The Follow-up Study. Some of the questions left unanswered in the first study have been examined recently by Malcolm Preston (Preston, 1963). Using the same basic techniques, the following questions were asked: (*a*) Will female and male judges react similarly to language and accent variations of speakers? (*b*) Will judges react similarly to male and female speakers who change their pronunciation style or the language they speak? (*c*) Will there be systematic differences in reactions to FC and Continental French (*CF*) speakers?

For this study, 80 English Canadian and 92 French Canadian first year college age students from Montreal served as judges. The EC judges in this study were all Catholics since we wanted to determine if EC Catholics would be less biased in their views of FCs than the non-Catholic EC judges had been in the original study. Approximately the same number of males and females from both language groups were tested, making four groups of judges in all: an EC male group, an EC female, a FC male and a FC female group.

The 18 personality traits used by the judges for expressing their reactions were grouped, for the purposes of interpretation, into three logically distinct categories of personality: (a) *competence* which included intelligence, ambition, self-confidence, leadership and courage; (b) *personal integrity* which included dependability, sincerity, character, conscientiousness and kindness; (c) *social attractiveness* which included sociability, likeability, entertainingness, sense of humor and affectionateness. Religiousness, good looks and height were not included in the above categories since they did not logically fit.

Results: Evaluative Reactions of English-Canadian Listeners. In general it was found that the EC listeners viewed the female speakers more favorably in their French guises while they viewed the male speakers more favorably in their English guises. In particular, the EC men saw the FC lady speakers as more intelligent, ambitious, self-confident, dependable, courageous and sincere than their English counterparts. The EC ladies were not quite so gracious although they, too, rated the FC ladies as more intelligent, ambitious, self-confident (but shorter) than the EC women guises. Thus, ECs generally view FC females as more competent and the EC men see them as possessing more integrity and competence.

Several notions came to mind at this point. It may be that the increased attractiveness of the FC woman in the eyes of the EC male is partly a result of her inaccessibility. Perhaps also the EC women are cognizant of the EC men's latent preference for FC women and accordingly are themselves prompted to upgrade the FC female, even to the point of adopting the FC woman as a model of what a woman should be.

However, the thought that another group is better than their own should not be a comfortable one for members of any group, especially a group of young ladies! The realization, however latent, that men of their own cultural group prefer another type of women might well be a very tender issue for the EC woman, one that could be easily exacerbated.

To examine this idea, we carried out a separate experiment. The Ss for the experiment were two groups of EC young women, one group serving as controls, the other as an experimental group. Both groups were asked to give their impressions of the personalities of a group of speakers, some using English, some Canadian style French. They were, of course, actually presented with female bilingual speakers using Canadian French and English guises. Just before they evaluated the speakers, the experimental group was given false information about FC women, information that was designed to upset them. They heard a tape recording of a man reading supposedly authentic statistical information about the increase in marriages between FC women and EC men. They were asked to listen to this loaded passage twice, for practice only, disregarding the content of the message and attending only to the personality of the speaker. We presumed, however, that they would not likely be able to disregard the content since it dealt with a matter that might well bother them—FC women, they were told, were competing for EC men, men who already had a tendency to prefer FC women, a preference that they possibly shared themselves. In contrast, the control group received quite neutral information which would not affect their ratings of FCs in any way. The results supported the prediction: The experimental Ss judged the FC women to be reliably more attractive but reliably less dependable and sincere than did the control Ss. That is, the favorable reactions toward FC women found previously were evident in the judgments of the control group, while the experimental Ss, who had been given false information designed to highlight the threat posed by the presumed greater competence and integrity of FC women, saw the FC women as men stealers—attractive but undependable and insincere. These findings support the general hypothesis we had developed and they serve as a first step in a series of experiments we are now planning to determine how judgments of personalities affect various types of social interaction.

Let us return again to the main investigation. It was found that *FC* men were not as favorably received as the women were by their *EC* judges. *EC* ladies liked *EC* men, rating them as taller, more likeable, affectionate, sincere, and conscientious, and as possessing more character and a greater sense of humor than the *FC* versions of the same speakers. Furthermore, the *EC* male judges also favored *EC* male speakers, rating them as taller, more kind, dependable and entertaining. Thus, *FC* male speakers are viewed as lacking integrity and as being less socially attractive by both *EC* female, and, to a less marked extent, *EC* male judges. This tendency to downgrade the *FC* male, already noted in the basic study, may well be the expression of an unfavorable stereotyped and prejudiced attitude toward *FCs*, but, apparently, this prejudice is selectively directed toward *FC* males, possibly because they are better known than females as power figures who control local and regional governments and who thereby can be viewed as sources of threat or frustration, (or as the guardians of *FC* women, keeping them all to themselves).

The reactions to Continental French (*CF*) speakers are generally more favorable although less marked. The *EC* male listeners viewed *CF* women as slightly more competent and *CF* men as equivalent to their *EC* controls except for height and religiousness. The *EC* female listeners upgraded *CF* women on sociability and self-confidence, but downgraded *CF* men on height, likeability and sincerity. Thus, *EC* judges appear to be less concerned about European French people in general than they are about the local French people; the European French are neither downgraded nor taken as potential social models to any great extent.

Evaluative Reactions of French-Canadian Listeners. Summarizing briefly, the *FC* listeners showed more significant guise differences than did their *EC* counterparts. *FCs* generally rated European French guises *more* favorably and Canadian French guises *less* favorably than they did their matched *EC* guises. One important exception was the *FC* women who viewed *FC* men as more competent and as more socially attractive than *EC* men.

The general pattern of evaluations presented by the *FC* judges, however, indicates that they view their own linguistic cultural group as *inferior* to both the English Canadian and the European French groups, suggesting that *FCs* are prone to take either of these other groups as models for changes in their own manners of behaving (including speech) and possibly in basic values. This tendency is more marked among *FC* men who definitely prefered male and female representatives of the *EC* and *CF* groups to those of their own group. The *FC* women, in contrast, appear to be guardians of *FC* culture at least in the sense that they favored male representatives of their own cultural group. We presume this reaction reflects something more than a preference for FC marriage partners. FC women may be particularly anxious to preserve FC values and to pass these on in their own families through language, religion and tradition.

Nevertheless, FC women apparently face a conflict of their own in that they favor characteristics of both CF and EC women. Thus, the FC female may be safe-guarding the FC culture through a preference for FC values seen in FC men, at the same time as she is prone to change her own behavior and values in the direction of one of two foreign cultural models, those that the men in her group apparently favor. It is of interest that EC women are comfronted with a similar conflict since they appear envious of FC women.

The Developmental Studies. Recently, we have been looking into the background of the inferiority reaction among FC youngsters, trying to determine at what age it starts and how it develops through the years. Elizabeth Anisfeld and I (1964) started by studying the reactions of ten year old FC children to the matched guises of bilingual youngsters of their own age reading French and English versions of *Little Red Riding Hood*, once in Canadian style French and once in standard English. In this instance, half of the judges were bilingual in English and half were essentially monolingual in French. Stated briefly, it was found that FC guises were rated significantly *more* favorable on nearly all traits. (One exception was height; the EC speakers were judged as taller.) However, these favorable evaluations of the FC in contrast to the EC guises were due almost entirely to the reactions of the monolingual children. The bilingual children saw very little difference between the two sets of guises, that is, on nearly all traits their ratings of the FC guises were essentially the same as their ratings of EC guises. The results, therefore, made it clear that, unlike college-age judges, FC children at the ten year age level do not have a negative bias against their own group.

The question then arises as to where the bias starts after age ten. A recent study (Lambert, Frankel and Tucker, 1966) was addressed to solving this puzzle. The investigation was conducted with 375 FC girls ranging in age from 9 to 18, who gave their evaluations of three groups of matched guises, (a) of some girls about their own age, (b) of some adult women, and (c) of some adult men. Passages that were appropriate for each age level were read by the bilingual speakers once in English and once in Canadian style French. In this study attention was given to the social class background of the judges (some were chosen from private schools, some from public schools and to their knowledge of English (some were bilingual and some monolingual in French). It was found that definite preferences for EC guises appeared at about age twelve and were maintained through the late teen years. There was, however, a marked difference between the private and public school judges: the upper middle class girls were especially biased after age 12, whereas the pattern for the working class girls was less pronounced and less durable, suggesting that for them the bias is short-lived and fades out by the late teens. Note that we probably did not encounter girls from lower class homes in our earlier studies using girls at *FC* collèges or universités.

The major implication of these findings is that the tendency for certain subgroups of college-age *FC*s to downgrade representatives of their own ethnic-linguistic group, noted in our earlier studies, seems to have its origin, at least with girls, at about age 12, but the ultimate fate of this attitude depends to a great extent on social-class background. Girls who come from upper middle class *FC* homes, and especially those who have become bilingual in English, are particularly likely to maintain this view, at least into the young adult years.

The pattern of results of these developmental studies can also be examined from a more psychodynamic perspective. If we assume that the adult female and male speakers in their *FC* guises represent parents or people like their own parents to the *FC* adolescent judges, just as the same-age speakers represent someone like themselves, then the findings suggest several possibilities that could be studied in more detail. First, the results are consistent with the notion that teen-age girls have a closer psychological relation with their fathers than with their mothers in the sense that the girls in the study rated *FC* female guises markedly inferior to *EC* ones, but generally favored or at least showed much less disfavor for the *FC* guises of male speakers. Considered in this light, social-class differences and bilingual skill apparently influence the degree of same-sex rejection and cross-sex identification: by the mid-teens the public school girls, both monolinguals and bilinguals, show essentially no rejection of either the *FC* female or male guises, whereas the private school girls, especially the bilinguals, show a rejection of both female and male *FC* guises through the late teens. These bilinguals might, because of their skill in English and their possible encouragement from home, be able to come in contact with the mothers of their *EC* associates and therefore may have developed stronger reasons to be envious of *EC* mothers and fathers than the monolingual girls would have.

Similarly, the reactions to "same-age" speakers might reflect a tendency to accept or reject one's peer-group or one's self, at least for the monolinguals. From this point of view, the findings suggest that the public school monolinguals are generally satisfied with their *FC* image since they favor the *FC* guises of the same-age speakers at the 16 year level. In contrast, the private school monolinguals may be expressing a marked rejection of themselves in the sense that they favor the *EC* guises. The bilinguals, of course, can consider themselves as being potential or actual members of both ethnic-linguistic groups represented by the guises. It is of interest, therefore, to note that both the public and particularly the private school bilinguals apparently favor the *EC* versions of themselves.

Two Generalizations

This program of research, still far from complete, does permit us to make two important generalizations, both relevant to the main argument of this paper. First, a technique has been developed that rather effectively calls out the stereotyped impressions that members of one ethnic-linguistic group hold of another contrasting group. The type and strength of impression depends on characteristics of the speakers—their sex, age, the dialect they use, and, very likely, the social-class background as this is revealed in speech style. The impression also seems to depend on characteristics of the audience of *judges*—their age, sex, socio-economic background, their bilinguality and their own speech style. The type of reactions and adjustments listeners must make to those who reveal, through their speech style, their likely ethnic group allegiance is suggested by the traits that listeners use to indicate their impressions. Thus, *EC* male and female college students tend to look down on the *FC* male speaker, seeing him as less intelligent, less dependable and less interesting than he would be seen if he had presented himself in an *EC* guise. Imagine the types of role adjustment that would follow if the same person were first seen in the *FC* guise and then suddenly switched to a perfect *EC* guise. A group of *EC* listeners would probably be forced to perk up their ears, reconsider their original classification of the person and then either view him as becoming too intimate in "their" language or decide otherwise and be pleasantly amazed that one of their own could manage the other group's language so well. Furthermore, since these comparative impressions are widespread throughout certain strata of each ethnic-linguistic community, they will probably have an enormous impact on young people who are either forced to learn the other group's language or who choose to do so.

The research findings outlined here have a second important message about the reactions of the bilingual who is able to convincingly switch languages or dialects. The bilingual can study the reactions of his audiences as he adopts one guise in certain settings and another in different settings, and receive a good deal of social feedback, permitting him to realize that he can be perceived in quite different ways, depending on how he presents himself. It could well be that his own self-concept takes two distinctive forms in the light of such feedback. He may also observe, with amusement or alarm, the role adjustments that follow when he suddenly switches guises with the same group of interlocutors. However, research is needed to document and examine these likely consequences of language or dialect switching from the perspective of the bilingual making the switches.

Although we have concentrated on a Canadian setting in these investigations, there is really nothing special about the Canadian scene with regard to the social effects of language or dialect switching. Equally instructive effects have been noted when the switch involves a change from standard American English to Jewish-accented English (Anisfeld, Bogo and Lambert, 1962); when the switch involves changing from Hebrew to Arabic for Israeli and Arab judges, or when the change is from Sephardic to Ashkenazic style Hebrew for Jewish listeners in Israel (Lambert, Anisfeld and Yeni-Komshian, 1965). Our most recent research, using a modified approach, has been conducted with American Negro speakers and listeners (Tucker and Lambert, 1967). The same type of social effects are inherent in this instance, too: Southern Negroes have more favorable impressions of people who use what the linguists call *Standard Network Style* English than they do of those who speak with their own style, but they are more impressed with their own style than they are with the speech of educated, Southern whites, or of Negroes who become too "white" in their speech by ex-aggerating the non-Negro features and over-correcting their verbal output.

Social-Psychological Aspects of Second-Language Learning

How might these intergroup impressions and feelings affect young people living in the Montreal area who are expected by educators to learn the other group's language? One would expect that both French-Canadian youngsters and their parents would be more willing, for purely social psychological reasons, to learn English than ECs to learn French. Although we haven't investigated the French-Canadians' attitudes toward the learning of English, still it is very apparent that bilingualism in Canada and in Quebec has long been a one-way affair, with FCs much more likely to learn English than the converse. Typically, this trend to English is explained on economic grounds and on the attraction of the United States, but I would like to suggest another possible reason for equally serious consideration. FCs may be drawn away from Canadian style French to English, or to bilingualism, or to European style French, as a psychological reaction to the contrast in stereotyped images which English and French Canadians have of one another. On the other hand, we would expect EC students and their parents in Quebec, at least, to be drawn away from French for the same basic reasons. It is, of course, short-sighted to talk about groups in this way because there are certain to be wide individual differences of reaction, as was the case in the impression studies, and as will be apparent in the research to be discussed, but one fact turned up in an unpublished study Robert Gardner and I conducted that looks like a group-wide difference. Several samples of Montreal EC, high school students who had studied French for periods of up to seven years scored no better on standard tests of French achievement than did Connecticut high schoolers who had only two or three years of French training.

Instrumental and Integrative Motivation

When viewed from a social-psychological perspective, the process of learning a second language itself also takes on a special significance. From this viewpoint, one would expect that if the student is to be successful in his attempts to learn another social group's language he must be both able and willing to adopt various aspects of behavior, including verbal behavior, which characterize members of the other linguistic-cultural group. The learner's ethnocentric tendencies and his attitudes toward the other group are believed to determine his success in learning the new language. His motivation to learn is thought to be determined by both his attitudes and by the type of orientation he has toward learning a second language. The orientation is *instrumental* in form if, for example, the purposes of language study reflect the more utilitarian value of linguistic achievement, such as getting ahead in one's occupation, and is *integrative* if, for example, the student is oriented to learn more about the other cultural community, as if he desired to become a potential member of the other group. It is also argued that some may be anxious to learn another language as a means of being accepted in another cultural group because of dissatisfactions experienced in their own culture while other individuals may be as much interested in another culture as they are in their own. In either case, the more proficient one becomes in a second language the more he may find that his place in his original membership group is modified at the same time as the other linguistic-cultural group becomes something more than a reference group for him. It may, in fact, become a second membership group for him. Depending upon the compatibility of the two cultures, he may experience feelings of chagrin or regret as he loses ties in one group, mixed with the fearful anticipation of entering a relatively new group. The concept of *anomie* first proposed by Durkheim (1897) and more recently extended by Srole (1951) and Williams (1952), refers to such feelings of social uncertainty or dissatisfaction.

My studies with Gardner (1959) were carried out with English-speaking Montreal high school students studying French who were evaluated for their language learning aptitude and verbal intelligence, as well as their attitudes and stereotypes toward members of the French community, and the intensity of their motivation to learn French. Our measure of motivation is conceptually similar to Jones' (1949 and 1950) index of interest in learning a language which he found to be important for successful learning among Welsh students. A factor analysis of scores on these various measures indicated that aptitude and intelligence formed a common factor which was independent of a second one comprising indices of motivation, type of orientation toward language and social attitudes toward FCs. Furthermore, a measure of achievement in French taken at the end of a year's study was reflected equally prominently in both factors. This statistical pattern meant that French achievement was dependent upon both aptitude and verbal intelligence as well as a sympathetic orientation toward the other group. This orientation was much less common among these students than was the instrumental one, as would be expected from the results of the matched-guise experiments. However, when sympathetic orientation was present it apparently sustained a strong motivation to learn the other group's language. Furthermore, it was clear that students with an integrative orientation were more successful in learning French than were those with instrumental orientations.

A follow-up study (Gardner, 1960) confirmed and extended these findings. Using a larger sample of EC students and incorporating various measures of French achievement, the same two independent factors were revealed, and again both were related to French achievement. But whereas aptitude and achievement were especially important for those French skills stressed in school training, such as grammar, the development of such skills, skills that call for the active use of the language in communicational settings, such as pronunciation accuracy and auditory comprehension, was determined in major part by measures of an integrative motivation to learn French. The aptitude variables were insignificant in this case. Further evidence from the intercorrelations indicated that this integrative motive was the converse of an authoritarian ideological syndrome, opening the possibility that basic personality dispositions may be involved in language learning efficiency.

In this same study information had been gathered from the parents of the students about their own orientations toward the French community. These data suggested that integrative or instrumental orientations toward the other group are developed within the family. That is, the minority of students with an integrative disposition to learn French had parents who also were integrative and sympathetic to the French community. However, students' orientations were not related to parents' skill in French nor to the number of French acquaintances the parents had, indicating that the integrative motive is not due to having more experience with French at home. Instead the integrative outlook more likely stems from a family-wide attitudinal disposition.

Language Learning and Anomie

Another feature of the language learning process came to light in an investigation of college and postgraduate students undergoing an intensive course in advanced French at McGill's French Summer

School. We were interested here, among other matters, in changes in attitudes and feelings that might take place during the six-week study period (Lambert, Gardner, Barik and Tunstall, 1961). The majority of the students were Americans who oriented themselves mainly to the European-French rather than the American-French community. We adjusted our attitude scales to make them appropriate for those learning European French. Certain results were of special interest. As the students progressed in French skill to the point that they said they "thought" in French, and even dreamed in French, their feelings of anomie also increased markedly. At the same time, they began to seek out occasions to use English even though they had solemnly pledged to use only French for the six-week period. This pattern of results suggests to us that these already advanced students experienced a strong dose of anomie when they commenced to *really* master a second language. That is, when advanced students became so skilled that they begin to think and feel like Frenchmen, they then became so annoyed with feelings of anomie that they were prompted to develop strategies to minimize or control the annoyance. Reverting to English could be such a strategy. It should be emphasized however, that the chain of events just listed needs to be much more carefully explored.

Elizabeth Anisfeld and I took another look at this problem, experimenting with 10-year old monolingual and bilingual students (Peal and Lambert, 1962). We found that the bilingual children (attending French schools in Montreal) were markedly more favorable towards the "other" language group (i.e., the ECs) than the monolingual children were. Furthermore, the bilingual children reported that their parents held the same strongly sympathetic attitudes toward ECs, in contrast to the pro-FC attitudes reported for the parents of the monolingual children. Apparently, then, the development of second language skill to the point of balanced bilingualism is conditioned by family-shared attitudes toward the other linguistic-cultural group.

These findings are consistent and reliable enough to be of general interest. For example methods of language training could possibly be modified and strengthened by giving consideration to the social-psychological implications of language learning. Because of the possible practical as well as theoretical significance of this approach, it seemed appropriate to test its applicability in a cultural setting other than the bicultural Quebec scene. With measures of attitude and motivation modified for American students learning French, a large scale study, very similar in nature to those conducted in Montreal, was carried out in various settings in the United States with very similar general outcomes (Lambert & Gardner, 1962).

One further investigation indicated that these suggested social psychological principles are not restricted to English and French speakers in Canada. Moshe Anisfeld and I (1961) extended the same experimental procedure to samples of Jewish high school students studying Hebrew at various parochial schools in different sectors of Montreal. They were questioned about their orientations toward learning Hebrew and their attitudes toward the Jewish culture and community, and tested for their verbal intelligence, language aptitude and achievement in the Hebrew language at the end of the school year. The results support the generalization that both intellectual capacity and attitudinal orientation affect success in learning Hebrew. However, whereas intelligence and linguistic aptitude were relatively stable predictors of success, the attitudinal measures varied from one Jewish community to another. For instance, the measure of a Jewish student's desire to become more acculturated in the Jewish tradition and culture was a sensitive indicator of progress in Hebrew for children from a particular district of Montreal, one where members of the Jewish sub-community were actually concerned with problems of integrating into the Jewish culture. In another district, made up mainly of Jews who recently arrived from central Europe and who were clearly of a lower socio-economic level, the measure of desire for Jewish acculturation did not correlate with achievement in Hebrew, whereas measures of pro-Semitic attitudes or pride in being Jewish did.

Bilingual Adjustments to Conflicting Demands

The final issue I want to discuss concerns the socio-cultural tugs and pulls that the bilingual or potential bilingual encounters and how he adjusts to these often conflicting demands made on him. We have seen how particular social atmospheres can affect the bilingual. For example, the French-English bilingual in the Montreal setting may be pulled toward greater use of English, and yet be urged by certain others in the FC community not to move too far in that direction, just as EC's may be discouraged from moving toward the French community. [In a similar fashion, dialects would be expected to change because of the social consequences they engender, so that Jewish accented speech should drop away, especially with those of the younger generation in American settings, as should Sephardic forms of Hebrew in Israel or certain forms of Negro speech in America.] In other words, the bilingual encounters social pressure of various sorts: he can enjoy the fun of linguistic spying but must pay the price of suspicion from those who don't want him to enter too intimately into their cultural domains and from others who don't want him to leave his "own" domain. He also comes to realize that most people are suspicious of a person who is in any sense two-faced. If he is progressing toward bilingualism, he encounters similar pressures that may affect his self-concept, his sense of belonging and his relations to two cultural-linguistic groups, the one he is slowly *leaving*, and the one he is *entering*. The conflict exists because so many of us think in terms of in-groups and out-groups, or of the need of showing an allegiance to one group or another, so that terms such as own language, other's language, *leaving* and *entering* one cultural group for another seem to be appropriate, even natural, descriptive choices.

Bilinguals and Ethnocentrism

Although this type of thought may characterize most people in our world, it is nonetheless a subtle form of group cleavage and ethnocentrism, and in time it may be challenged by bilinguals who, I feel, are in an excellent position to develop a totally new outlook on the social world. My argument is that bilinguals, especially those with bicultural experiences, enjoy certain fundamental advantages which, if capitalized on, can easily offset the annoying social tugs and pulls they are normally prone to. Let me mention one of these advantages that I feel is a tremendous asset.[1] Recently, Otto Klineberg and I conducted a rather comprehensive international study of the development of stereotyped thinking in children (Lambert and Klineberg, 1967). We found that rigid and stereotyped thinking about in-groups and out-groups, or about own groups in contrast to foreigners, starts during the pre-school period when children are trying to form a conception of themselves and their place in the world. Parents and other socializers attempt to help the child at this stage by highlighting differences and contrasts among groups, thereby making his own group as distinctive as possible. This tendency, incidentally, was noted among parents from various parts of the world. Rather than helping, however, they may actually be setting the stage for ethnocentrism with permanent consequences. The more contrasts are stressed, the more deep-seated the stereotyping process and its impact on ethnocentric thought appear to be. Of relevance here is the notion that the child brought up bilingually and biculturally will be less likely to have good versus bad contrasts impressed on him when he starts wondering about himself, his own group and others. Instead he will probably be taught something more truthful, although more complex: that differences among national or cultural groups of peoples are actually not clear-cut and that basic similarities among peoples are more prominent than differences. The bilingual child in other words may well start life with the enormous advantage of having a more open, receptive mind about himself and other people. Furthermore, as he matures, the bilingual has many opportunities to learn, from observing changes in other peo-

---

1 For present purposes, discussion is limited to a more *social* advantage associated with bilingualism. In other writings there has been a stress on potential intellectual and *cognitive* advantages, see Peal and Lambert (1962) and Anisfeld (1964); see also Macnamara (1964) as well as Lambert and Anisfeld (1966). The bilingual's potential utility has also been discussed as a linguistic mediator between monolingual groups because of his comprehension of the subtle meaning differences characterizing each of the languages involved, see Lambert and Moore (1966).

ple's reactions to him, how two-faced and ethnocentric *others* can be. That is, he is likely to become especially sensitive to and leery of ethnocentrism.

Bilinguals and Social Conflicts

This is not to say that bilinguals have an easy time of it. In fact, the final investigation I want to present demonstrates the social conflicts bilinguals typically face, but, and this is the major point, it also demonstrates one particular type of adjustment that is particularly encouraging.

In 1943, Irving Child (1943) investigated a matter that disturbed many second-generation Italians living in New England: what were they, Italian or American? Through early experiences they had learned that their relations with certain other youngsters in their community were strained whenever they displayed signs of their Italian background, that is, whenever they behaved as their parents wanted them to. In contrast, if they rejected their Italian background, they realized they could be deprived of many satisfactions stemming from belonging to an Italian family and an Italian community. Child uncovered three contrasting modes of adjusting to these pressures. One subgroup rebelled against their Italian background, making themselves as American as possible. Another subgroup rebelled the other way, rejecting things American as much as possible while proudly associating themselves with things Italian. The third form of adjustment was an apathetic withdrawal and a refusal to think of themselves in ethnic terms at all. This group tried, unsuccessfully, to escape the conflict by avoiding situations where the matter of cultural background might come up. Stated in other terms, some tried to belong to one of their own groups or the other, and some, because of strong pulls from both sides, were unable to belong to either.

Child's study illustrates nicely the difficulties faced by people with dual allegiances, but there is no evidence presented of second-generation Italians who actually feel themselves as belonging to both groups. When in 1962, Robert Gardner and I (1962) studied another ethnic minority group in New England, the French-Americans, we observed the same types of reactions as Child had noted among Italian-Americans. But in our study there was an important difference.

We used a series of attitude scales to assess the allegiances of French-American adolescents to both their French and American heritages. Their relative degree of skill in French and in English were used as an index of their mode of adjustment to the bicultural conflict they faced. In their homes, schools and community, they all had ample opportunities to learn both languages well, but subgroups turned up who had quite different patterns of linguistic skill, and each pattern was consonant with each subgroup's allegiances. Those who expressed a definite preference for the American over the French culture and who negated the value of knowing French were more proficient in English than French. They also expressed anxiety about how well they actually knew English. This subgroup, characterized by a general rejection of their French background, resembles in many respects the rebel reaction noted by Child. A second subgroup expressed a strong desire to be identified as French, and they showed a greater skill in French than English, especially in comprehension of spoken French. A third group apparently faced a conflict of cultural allegiances since they were ambivalent about their identity, favoring certain features of the French and other features of the American culture. Presumably because they had not resolved the conflict, they were retarded in their command of both languages when compared to the other groups. This relatively unsuccessful mode of adjustment is very similar to the apathetic reaction noted in one subgroup or Italian-Americans.

A fourth subgroup is of special interest. French-American youngsters who have an open-minded, nonethnocentric view of people in general, coupled with a strong aptitude for language learning are the ones who profited fully from their language learning opportunities and became skilled in *both* languages. These young people had apparently circumvented the conflicts and developed means of becoming members of both cultural groups. They had, in other terms, achieved a comfortable bicultural identity.

It is not clear why this type of adjustment did not appear in Child's study. There could, for example, be important differences in the social pressures encountered by second-generation Italians and French in New England. My guess, however, is that the difference in findings reflects a new social movement that has started in America in the interval between 1943 and 1962, a movement which the American linguist Charles Hockett humorously refers to as a "reduction of the heat under the American melting pot". I believe that bicultural bilinguals will be particularly helpful in perpetuating this movement. They and their children are also the ones most likely to work out a new, nonethnocentric mode of social intercourse which could be of universal significance.

REFERENCES

ANISFELD, ELIZABETH. A comparison of the cognitick functioning of monolinguals and bilinguals. Unpublished Ph.D. thesis, Redpath Library, McGill University, 1964.

ANISFELD, ELIZABETH, AND LAMBERT, W. E. Evaluational reactions of bilingual and monolingual children to spoken language. *Journal of Abnormal and Social Psychology*, 1964, 69, 89-97.

ANISFELD, M., BOGO, N., AND LAMBERT, W. E. Evaluational reactions to accented English speech. *Journal of Abnormal and Social Psychology*, 1962, 65, 223-231.

ANISFELD, M., AND LAMBERT, W. E. Social and psychological variables in learning Hebrew. *Journal of Abnormal and Social Psychology*, 1961, 63, 524-529.

BEREITER, C. Some persisting dilemmas in the measurement of change. In Harris, C. W. (Ed.), *Problems in measuring change*. Madison: The University of Wisconsin Press, 1963.

CHILD, I. L., *Italian or American? The second generation in conflict*. New Haven: Yale University Press, 1943.

DURKHEIM, E. *Le suicide*. Paris: F. Alcan, 1897.

FERGUSON, G. A. *Statistical analysis in psychology and education*. New York: McGraw-Hill, 1959.

GARDNER, R. C. AND LAMBERT, W. E. Motivational variables in second-language acquisition. *Canadian Journal of Psychology*, 1959, 13, 266-272.

GARDNER, R. C. Motivational variables in second-language acquisition. Unpublished Ph.D. thesis, McGill University, 1960.

JONES, W. R. Attitude towards Welsh as a second language. A preliminary investigation. *British Journal of Educational Psychology*, 1949, 19, 44-52.

JONES, W. R. Attitude towards Welsh as a second language, a further investigation. *British Journal of Educational Psychology*, 1950, 20, 117-132.

LABOV, W. Hypercorrection by the lower middle class as a factor in linguistic change. Columbia University, 1964. (Mimeo)

LAMBERT, W. E., HODGSON, R. C., GARDNER, R. C., AND FILLENBAUM, S. Evaluational reactions to spoken languages. *Journal of Abnormal and Social Psychology*, 1960, 60, 44-51.

LAMBERT, W. E., GARDNER, R. C., OLTON, R., AND TUNSTALL, K. A study of the roles of attitudes and motivation in second-language learning. McGill University, 1962. (Mimeo)

LAMBERT, W. E., GARDNER, R. C., BARIK, H. C., AND TUNSTALL, K. Attitudinal and cognitive aspects of intensive study of a second language. *Journal of Abnormal and Social Psychology*, 1963, 66, 358-368.

LAMBERT, W. E., ANISFELD, M., AND YENI-KOMSHIAN, GRACE. Evaluational reactions of Jewish and Arab adolescents to dialect and language variations. *Journal of Personality and Social Psychology*, 1965, 2, 84-90.

LAMBERT, W. E., FRANKEL, HANNAH, AND TUCKER, G. R. Judging personality through speech: A French-Canadian example. *The Journal of Communication*, 1966, 16, 305-321.

LAMBERT, W. E., AND ANISFELD, ELIZABETH. A reply to John Macnamara. Mimeographed and submitted to *Studies*, 1966.

LAMBERT, W. E., AND MOORE, NANCY. Word-association responses: Comparison of American and French monolinguals with Canadian monolinguals and bilinguals. *Journal of Personality and Social Psychology*, 1966, 3, 313-320.

LAMBERT, W. E., AND KLINEBERG, O. *Children's views of foreign peoples: A cross-national study*. New York: Appleton, 1967.

MACNAMARA, J. The Commission on Irish: Psychological aspects. *Studies*, 1964, 164-173.

McDAVID, R. I. The dialects of American English. In Francis, W. N. (Ed.), *The structure of American English*, New York: Ronald, 1958.

PEAL, ELIZABETH, AND LAMBERT, W. E. The relation of bilingualism to intelligence. *Psychological Monographs*, 1962, 76, Whole No. 546.

PRESTON, M. S. Evaluational reactions to English, Canadian French and European French voices. Unpublished M.A. thesis, McGill University, Redpath Library, 1963.

SROLE, L. Social dysfunction, personality and social distance attitudes. Paper read before American Sociological Society, 1951, National Meeting, Chicago, Ill. (Mimeo)

TUCKER, G. R., AND LAMBERT, W. E., White and Negro listeners' reactions to various American-English dialects. McGill University, 1967. (Mimeo)

WILLIAMS, R. N. *American society*. New York: Knopf, 1952.

ORGANIZATION OF THE BILINGUAL SCHOOL

A. Bruce Gaarder

JOURNAL OF SOCIAL ISSUES
VOLUME XXIII, NUMBER 2, 1967

Organization of the Bilingual School

A. Bruce Gaarder*

U. S. Office of Education

A *bilingual school* is a school which uses, concurrently, two languages as mediums of instruction in any portion of the curriculum
except the languages themselves. Thus, for example, arithmetic taught
in both English and Irish, or arithmetic in English and history in Irish,
or all subjects (except Irish and English) in both tongues would constitute bilingual schooling. English through English and all other subjects in Irish would not. The teaching of a vernacular solely as a bridge
to another, the official language, is not bilingual education in the sense
of this paper, nor is ordinary foreign language teaching.

Bilingual schools of several kinds and varied purpose are now and
have long been in operation worldwide. This paper assumes that there
are at present sound reasons, which will become increasingly more
compelling, for establishing many more such schools and seeks to set
forth some guidelines for their organizers. These reasons, briefly stated,

for *adding the mother tongue* as a teaching medium are
  a. to avoid or lessen scholastic retardation in children whose mother
     tongue is not the principal school language
  b. to strengthen the bonds between home and school
  c. to avoid the alienation from family and linguistic community
     that is commonly the price of rejection of one's mother tongue
     and of complete assimilation into the dominant linguistic group
  d. to develop strong literacy in the mother tongue in order to make
     it a strong asset in the adult's life

for *adding a second tongue* as a teaching medium are
  a. to engage the child's capacity for natural, unconscious language
     learning (Anderson, 1960; Penfield 1956; and Stern, 1963,
     chapter 11)
  b. to avoid the problems of *method, aptitude,* etc., which beset the
     usual teaching of second languages

---

* This article was written by the author in his private capacity. No official support or endorsement by the U.S. Office of Education is intended or should
be inferred.

110

c. to make the second language a means to an end rather than an end in itself (Stern, Chapter 9)

d. to increase second language experience without crowding the curriculum

e. plus other well-known reasons which do not concern us here: to teach the national language, to provide a lingua franca or a *world status* language, for cultural enrichment, and economic gain.

The literature on bilingualism gives virtually no information on the organization of bilingual schools. Furthermore it generally omits consideration of the teaching-learning process itself: what happens in the classroom—the interaction of teacher, pupils, methods and materials—and the theories of language and language learning underlying those happenings. This paper gives central importance to what happens in the classroom, and it is largely based on such a body of theory (Moulton, 1963). The position taken here is that however desirable—or undesirable—bilingual schooling may be, its effectiveness can neither be assessed nor assured without full consideration of school organization and classroom practices.

The following chart shows some basic features that differentiate bilingual schools (Stern, 1963, Part II; UNESCO, 1953).

One-way school: one group learning in two languages	Mother tongue added	Equal time and treatment	(no example known)
		Unequal time and treatment	. . . Hiligayon in the Philippines; Welsh in Wales, in some schools.
	Second tongue added	Equal time and treatment	. . . In some Welsh-English schools, one language alone on alternate days.
		Unequal time and treatment	. . . Irish in southern Ireland; Russian in non-Russian USSR; most bilingual schools in Latin America; English in Nigeria; French in Madagascar; English in Wales in some schools; French or Spanish in grade 12 in nine Virginia high schools.
Two-way school: two groups, each learning in its own and the other's language	Segregated classes	Equal time and treatment	. . . Spanish-English, Miami, Florida (mixed classes in grades 4-6).
		Unequal time and treatment	. . . (no example known)
	Mixed classes	Unequal time and treatment	. . . Spanish-English, Laredo, Texas; English-Swedish, Viggbyholmsskolan, Sweden; German-American Community School, Berlin-Dahlem.
		Equal time and treatment	. . . English-French, Ecole Active Bilingue—Ecole Internationale de Paris; L'Ecole Internationale SHAPE, St. Germain; the European School, Luxembourg.

The dynamics and pedagogy are not at all the same in a school which adds the mother tongue as in one which adds a second tongue. In the *two-way* model both the mother tongue and the second tongue are added.

Organization is here viewed as process and product. That is to say, organization is taken as (a) the process or course of action followed in bringing a bilingual school into existence and (b) as the educational structure which follows upon and is to some extent determined by (a). The view taken here is that the most important factors entering into the structure of bilingual schools are the time allowed for each of the languages, the treatment and use of each language and whether the language which is added to the previously existing system is the mother tongue or not. Other factors, too, can make a great deal of difference to the school's effectiveness, e.g., whether individual teachers teach in one or in both languages, whether one or two languages are employed within an individual class period, the relative socio-economic status of native speakers of each of the languages and the relative prestige of each (Carroll, 1963; Fishman, 1966).

Organization as Product

Coral Way Elementary School

A bilingual school which can be used to illustrate the major organizational patterns and the problems of bilingual schooling is the Coral Way Elementary School in Miami, Florida.[1] In operation since 1963, in a neighborhood broadly representative of all economic levels but mostly lower middle class, it is a six grade school with normally four classes at each grade level and a total of approximately 720 pupils. Half of the pupils enter the school as monolingual speakers of English; half are native speakers of Spanish (Cubans), some of whom know bits and pieces of English. Coral Way Elementary is a *two-way* bilingual school, since each group learns through its own and the other's tongue. Since Coral Way has segregated classes (the language groups are not mixed in grades 1-3 and only to a limited extent in grades 4-6), it is in effect two *one-way* schools. For the Cubans (in this United States setting) Coral Way adds the mother tongue; for the Anglos[2] it adds Spanish, a second tongue. It gives as nearly as possible *equal time and treatment* to the two mediums. Finally, since either of the two halves, the Anglo or the Cuban, could function alone as a *one-way* school with complete effectiveness, Coral Way exemplifies all the organizational possibilities except that of *unequal time and treatment*.

---

[1] The Coral Way project was established with Ford Foundation support. The director of the Ford Foundation Project was Dr. Pauline M. Rojas.

[2] A term widely used to differentiate native English speakers from native speakers of Spanish.

Equal Time, Equal Treatment

Equal time, equal treatment means curriculum-wide (except for the languages themselves) use of both languages as mediums. Coral Way presents all subjects in grades 1-3 through the mother tongue for approximately half the day, and all are taught again through the other tongue during the following half. These are segregated classes. There is, however, free interchange of both languages for physical education, art, music and supervised play, during which periods the groups are mixed.

There are two sets of teachers, native English and native Spanish (four teachers in all, one for each of the four classes at each grade level), plus four bilingual teaching aides. The aides perform two kinds of teaching task: they are responsible for the physical education, art, music and supervised play; and they give special help to slow learners and transfer students. Even more importantly, they allow the regular teachers free time every day for consultation and planning for the purpose of coordinating the two halves of each child's program.

The Coral Way bilingual school program was initiated in grades 1-3 simultaneously, work in the second language being increased by stages until by approximately mid-year each child was receiving half of his instruction through each of the languages. After the initial year this procedure was followed in the first grade only. As noted above, in grades 1-3 new concepts and skills are learned first through the vernacular and then reinforced by being taught again through the second tongue. This is not slavish imitation of the first teacher by the second one, but rather the presentation of the same content and concepts in a fresh, somewhat different way by a teacher with the varied perspective of another country[3] and another language. In the fourth and fifth grades (the third year of operation of the school) it was found that the pupils' command of the second language was such that they could learn through it alone without need of a duplicate class in the vernacular.

Despite the carefully coordinated dual-perspective double teaching of each subject, the basic methodological principle is that of expecting the instructors in each language to act in the classroom as if that were the only language in the world and the children's entire education depended on it. This means that work in one language is not presented in terms of or with reference to the other one.

One of the most difficult problems at Coral Way arose from the need to provide the same curricular time allotments as in other Miami schools. Although the reinforcing procedure gives maximum second language experience with minimum crowding of the curriculum, some

---

[3] The Spanish medium teachers at Coral Way were born and educated in Cuba.

114   A. BRUCE GAARDER

time inevitably goes to the second language per se. This reduces the amount of extra-curricular activities during school hours.

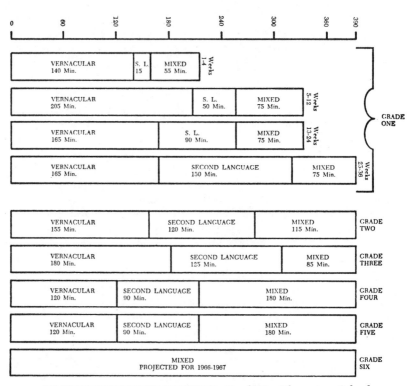

TIME DISTRIBUTION PATTERN—Coral Way Elementary School

Vernacular and second language (S. L.) mean the use of these as mediums of instruction. Mixed in grades 1-3 means physical education, art and music only. In grades 4-6 mixed also means combined classes of Anglos and Cubans alternating 3 weeks of each grading period working through English only, and 3 weeks working through Spanish only, in all subjects.

The most crucial teaching problem is the proper initiation of pupils (in grades 1-3 during the first year of the school and in grade one thereafter) to the second language. The same problem occurs with latecomers and with transfer pupils who enroll initially above grade one. The Coral Way solution has two special features: (a) close coordination of each day's second language experience with the preceding experience in the vernacular, and (b) careful structuring of the second language experience so that although the teacher-class interaction gives the impression of complete spontaneity, the teacher's portion is in fact worked out in advance to introduce and review constantly a specified corpus from the form and order systems and from the lexicon of the new tongue. Detailed linguistic sequences for English and Spanish *as second languages* were developed in order to meet the needs of the several content areas of the curriculum. The oral lesson material is supplemented by a great many pictures of objects and activities. As an additional precaution to assure a good second language beginning without detracting from the other curricular areas, the school day is lengthened one hour during the last twelve weeks in grade one, and one hour throughout the year in grade two. In grade one the second language is taught by the regular second medium teacher. Transfer pupils get special help with their second language from the aides. These pupils sit with their grade-mates all day except during the regular class in the second language, when they receive semi-private instruction from the aides. This special help, 30-45 minutes daily, may be required for only a few weeks or it may go on for an entire year.[4]

Indications of Success . . .

There are several indications that the Coral Way bilingual school has been successful. The introduction at the fourth and fifth grade levels of mixed classes in each language without reteaching in the other was based on the teachers' judgment that learning had become equally effective through either language alone.[5] Those Anglo pupils who entered Coral Way in the first grade in September 1963 (and who therefore have been exposed for the longest time to the possibly harmful effects of receiving half of their schooling through a foreign tongue) have been the object of close attention. On the Stanford achievement tests, administered in the spring of 1966, their median percentile ranking was as follows: paragraph meaning, 85; word meaning, 93; spelling, 99; arithmetic reasoning, 93; and arithmetic computation, 60. Their median score on the Otis Alpha test of mental maturity was 89. These pupils are not a selected group. Thus far the scores of the Cubans on these tests (all given in English) are generally lower than those of the Anglos, despite the fact that fluency in English is a prerequisite for taking them. Expert observers have noted that the Anglo children

---

[4] Similar concern for developing readiness for second language work in the newly-enrolled pupil is reported from the Ecole Active Bilingue (Ecole Internationale de Paris), L'Ecole Internationale SHAPE St. Germain, and the German-American Community School, Berlin-Dahlem. See Stern, *op. cit.*, 58, 59, 61.

[5] Preliminary findings of a three-year doctoral study of pupil achievement at Coral Way, scheduled for completion in 1967, show that on successive administrations of the Cooperative Inter-American Tests (H. Manuel, University of Texas), which have equated forms in English and Spanish, the learning curves for each group in its two language are coming very close together. (Communicated by the researcher, Mrs. Mabel Richardson.)

acquire excellent pronunciation of Spanish, while the English of some of the Cuban children shows interference from Spanish. This is attributed to the fact that the former group hears nothing but native Spanish, while in the homes of the latter one hears a good deal of heavily-accented English spoken by adult immigrants.[6]

It is scarcely surprising that the Cubans' scores on tests of achievement given through the medium of their second language are lower than those of the Anglos. A fair comparison could be made only if both groups were tested through both languages. Extensive testing of Puerto Rican children by the International Institute of Teachers College, Columbia University, using comparable Spanish and English forms of the Stanford achievement tests showed this to be true (International Institute of Teachers College, 1926).

Unequal Time, Unequal Treatment

Unequal time, unequal treatment for each of the languages characterizes most bilingual schooling throughout the world. Typically, the added language (i.e., taught in addition to the national, official or regular school language), whether it is the mother or the other tongue, is kept in a subordinate position. This is commonly true of the mother tongue, as when rising nationalism forces the introduction of history through Spanish in Mexican French-language schools, or when African vernaculars are introduced in the early primary grades as a mere bridge to the eventual exclusive use of English. It is true of the other tongue, as in the USSR where several hundred high schools were to teach some academic or scientific subjects—especially physics and mathematics—through English, French, or German, (New York Times, 1964) or in the United States, where there is a movement currently under way in a few high schools and colleges to teach such courses as history and geography through the medium of the second language to advanced students of that language.

One of the most promising unequal time and treatment programs in the United States is for schools where some of the students at each grade level have in common a mother tongue other than English. The program is simple. Instead of ignoring or deploring the children's home language the school provides regular instruction in and through it for something like a period a day in all grades. The course material may be,

---

[6] These data and much of the other description of Coral Way school were furnished by Mr. Lee Logan, the school principal. His help is here gratefully acknowledged. An incidental fact of interest is that the annual cost at Coral Way attributable to its being a bilingual school is about $17,000 in excess of what it would cost as a monolingual school. This is a four per cent increase of the school's annual budget. The extra money goes to pay the teaching aides and to buy Spanish language teaching materials.

for example, Spanish language arts and literature[7] or it may be a sampling of all areas of the regular school curriculum. The latter seems better, for it takes virtually no time away from the regular curriculum and has the added advantage of employing the language as a means to ends other than achievement in the language itself. The latter system also contributes more to curriculum-wide literacy in the mother tongue. The question of time and treatment, equal or unequal, is central to the larger question of the alleged handicap of bilingualism most often reported in the literature in school situations where the mother tongue is the subordinate language, given markedly unequal time and treatment, ignored completely, or even made the object of official censure. There is increasing awareness that the cause of any handicap may not be the existence of bilingualism per se, but school policy regarding the teaching of both languages and sociological factors extrinsic to the school itself (Jensen, 1962; Lambert, 1962).

Organization as Process

Wherever bilingual education is to be an innovation great care should be exercised to inform and orient all sectors of the community —particularly parents, pupils and all persons officially concerned with the school—to the rationale, procedures and goals of the program. In addition to general meetings of all parents, separate grade-level meetings have been found desirable.

The teachers should have native-like command of the language taught, with academic preparation and experience through that medium. In order to maximize the dual perspective pupils can get from bilingual schooling, the teachers should be native speakers educated in the country where the language is native. A special feature of the Coral Way program commends itself to this writer. During the summer preceding the opening of the school and the two following summers a six-weeks workshop on teaching methods and materials and for program planning was conducted for the Coral Way teachers. The first summer there was a required course in descriptive linguistics and another in the structure of the English language, for all teachers. As noted above, the use of teacher aides frees time every day for the regular teachers to coordinate work in the two languages.[8]

Regarding teaching materials little can be said in the brief space of this essay. In some vernaculars books and other materials are inadequate or non-existent. As for the added second language, if suit-

---

[7] Such a program, Spanish-S, is established in Dade County, Florida. Course of study bulletins may be secured from the Superintendent, Dade County Public Schools, in Miami.

[8] In the opinion of the Coral Way principal, Mr. Lee Logan, the first requisite for success is that the school principal have the privilege of selecting every member of the staff. The second requisite is that aides be employed as noted above.

able texts are available from the language's home country a healthful biculturism can result from the chance to use them in addition to texts prepared for use in the country where the school is situated, but over-emphasis or exclusive use of books based on a foreign environment can divorce the school from the reality of the child's home and community.

The course of action to be followed to bring a bilingual school into existence should be set with full awareness of the essential differences between teaching the mother tongue and teaching a second language.

Deep Grammar

The native speaker of a language (including the native speaker-teacher) usually has no awareness of the deep grammar (Twaddell, 1962) of his own language, i.e., the interdependent systems of phonology, morphology and syntax which comprise it, and the extent to which the native speaker-child brings virtually complete, thoughtless mastery of the systems to school with him at the age of six. As with his own regional accent and the complex body motion which accompanies his own speech, he doesn't know or knows only vaguely that the deep grammar is there and is concerned in the classroom with the niceties of usage (Say "as a cigarette should," not "like a cigarette should".), with grammatical nomenclature (This is a verb, and this is its direct object.) and with orthography (i before e except after c). Usage, nomenclature and orthography, whatever their importance, are of the surface alone; they are applied on top of the deep, thoughtless mastery which the native speaker-child acquired at home.

Grammatical nomenclature and the niceties of usage are at best a sort of polish on the surface of the deep grammar, the language itself. This polish can be applied quite effectively when the pupils speak an acceptable variant of the subject language, especially if theirs is the same variant as the teacher's. The polish is largely ineffective with the speaker of an unacceptable variant; the configuration of his deep grammar is so different that the polish, applied in the traditional ways, doesn't even touch the surface. Finally, there is the situation of the child who is not a speaker of the language to which the teaching is applied. In the sense of the figure used here, he has no deep grammar in the new language, hence no surface to be polished.

The point is that for pupils who speak unacceptable variants of their school language (e.g., English-based Jamaican Creole or Liberian Pidgin English) just as for pupils who are learning a second or foreign language, the normal materials and methods and orientation of the mother tongue class are not very effective.

Another common weakness in the teaching of a second language derives from the assumption that language is composed of words and that teaching is therefore teaching words. The grain of truth in this assumption gives the child no clue to any of the structural or paralinguistic differences among, for example, these utterances (which would be enormously more complex if presented orally, as they must be to the neophyte):

1. I haven't seen him for five years.
2. Hace cinco años que no lo veo.
   (It makes five years that not him I see.)
3. Seit fünf Jahren habe ich ihn nicht mehr gesehen.
   (Since five years have I him not more seen.)

Yet visits to the classrooms reveal teachers who, irrespective of the materials that are being used, are concerned largely with the *names of things* and word-correspondence from language to language.

Next, there is the teacher who is overly aware of the traps described above, particularly the importance of developing in the child a sense and command of the stuff of language itself, what we are calling deep grammar. Here the most serious weakness lies in over-structuring the course materials at too early an age, i.e., too early and overt dependence upon pattern drills based on contrastive analysis of the two languages, or upon the strict sequencing of the order of presentation of the features of the new language. Such drills and sequencing are not in themselves bad. The harm seems to come when their use requires that children 3-7 years old focus their attention on the language itself rather than beyond language, on their involvement in events or situations. The way out of the dilemma is suggested above in the description of Coral Way. If the child is to acquire the intuitive sense of deep grammar which he lacks, the teacher must know how to give it to him in ways which, however structured and systematized they may be, have the appearance and effect of complete spontaneity. For as Penfield says, speaking of the child's learning of a second tongue, ". . . language is not a subject to be studied nor an object to be grasped. It is a means to other ends, a vehicle, and a way of life" (Penfield, 1956, 257).

Finally, there is the question of whether or not to allow teacher and pupils to use both of the languages of a bilingual school during a given class period (as opposed to confining each to its own class periods or its own part of the day). In the United Nations Nursery School in Paris children three to five years old are mixed without regard to mother tongue and the teachers use both languages, a sentence in one then the same sentence in the other, especially at the beginning of the year with three-year-olds. This practice is implicitly justified on the grounds that two thirds of the school population is transient and that the children need above all security and understanding. Four- and five-year-olds are allowed to hear each language alone for increasingly longer periods of time (Dartigue, 1966). But the weight of opinion seems to favor the one-language-one person principle.

Unquestionably a young child learns a second language quickly and effectively if it is the unavoidable means to his full-time involvement in all the affairs of his life. Much less than full-time involvement will suffice for him to learn the new language. The minimum time, the optimum kind of involvement, and the affairs most conducive to this learning process *in a school* are still largely unknowns. Water falling drop by drop into a bucket will fill it, unless, of course, the conditions are such that each drop evaporates before the next one strikes.

REFERENCES

ANDERSSON, THEODORE: The optimum age for beginning the study of modern languages. *International Review of Education*, 1960, 6, 298-306.

CARROLL, JOHN B. Research problems concerning the teaching of foreign or second languages to younger children. In *Foreign languages in primary education: the teaching of foreign or second languages to younger children* (Report on an International Meeting of Experts 9-14 April, 1962, International Studies in Education), H. H. Stern, Ed. Hamburg: UNESCO Institute of Education, 1963, 72-80.

DARTIGUE, ESTHER. Bilingualism in the nursery school. *French Review*, 1966, 4.

FISHMAN, JOSHUA. Bilingual sequences at the societal level. In Carol J. Kreidler (Ed.), *On teaching English to speakers of other languages* Series II. Champaign, Illinois: National Council of Teachers of English, 1966, 139-144.

(The) International Institute of Teachers College. *A survey of the public educational system of Porto Rico*. New York: Bureau of Publications, Teachers College, Columbia University, 1926, 93-149.

JENSEN, J. VERNON. *Bilingualism—effects of childhood bilingualism*. (Reprinted from *Elementary English*, Feb. 1962, 132-143; April 1962, 358-366) Champaign, Illinois: National Council of Teachers of English, 1962.

LAMBERT, WALLACE AND ELIZABETH PEAL. The relation of bilingualism to intelligence. In Washington, D.C.: American Psychological Association, *Psychological Monographs: General and Applied*, 1962, No. 546, 76, No. 27.

MOULTON, WILLIAM G. *Linguistics and language teaching in the United States, 1940-1960*, Utrecht, Netherlands: Spectrum. (Also available from Superintendent of Documents, U.S. Government Printing Office, Washington, D.C. 20402. 1963.)

New York Times, October 11, 1964.

PENFIELD, WILDER AND L. ROBERTS. *Speech and brain mechanisms*. Princeton: Princeton University Press, 1956, chapter 9.

STERN, H. H. (Ed.) *Foreign languages in primary education: the teaching of foreign or second languages to younger children.* (Report on an International Meeting of Experts 9-14 April, 1962, International Studies in Education), Hamburg: UNESCO Institute of Education, 1963.

TWADDELL, W. FREEMAN. Does the FL teacher have to teach English grammar? *PMLA*, **57**, (2), May, 1962, 20.

UNESCO. *The use of vernacular languages in education*. (Monographs on Fundamental Education—VIII), Paris: UNESCO, 1953.

THE EFFECTS OF INSTRUCTION
IN A WEAKER LANGUAGE

John Macnamara

JOURNAL OF SOCIAL ISSUES
VOLUME XXIII, NUMBER 2, 1967

The Effects of Instruction in a Weaker Language

John Macnamara
McGill University

Millions of students throughout the world are being taught sub- jects such as mathematics, history and geography (i.e., subjects other than languages) in the medium of their weaker language. The reasons for this are as numerous as the reasons for language maintenance and language shift (Fishman, 1964). Many African countries, for example, have made English or French the language of instruction, not only be- cause they have adopted English or French as their *lingua franca*, but also because the native languages have not developed a vocabulary suited to the expression of sophisticated Western concepts and sche- mata especially in the technological subjects. Furthermore, suitable literature in the native languages is for the most part either insufficient or nonexistent (Unesco, 1953; Bull, 1955). Some countries such as Israel and Ireland have for cultural and poltical reasons made a dead or a minority language the favored medium of instruction. Immigrant stu- dents form another large group who are frequently obliged to follow courses in what is to them a foreign language. Many children, too, who are born in a country like the United States speak Spanish or Italian or Japanese at home, and yet are taught mainly or exclusively in English. Finally, even in essentially monolingual settings, there is a growing tendency to use teaching in a foreign language as a means of teaching that language (Stern, 1963).

For most students the major advantage in taking courses in their weaker language is that they receive an education which they could

121

not otherwise receive. However, the practice raises several problems. How successful are students' attempts to learn and understand material in a weaker language? Does instruction through the medium of a weaker language improve students' knowledge of that language, and is such instruction associated with losses in their stronger language? I propose to review studies in which these problems have been investigated and also to present for the first time some new data of my own.

School Achievement and Language of Instruction

Studies of bilinguals' school achievements throw light on the effects of teaching through the medium of a weaker language. Most of such studies were conducted in settings where bilinguals were a minority and could be compared with a monolingual majority. In almost all of these studies (Macnamara, 1966a) bilinguals were found to be weaker than monolinguals in the monolinguals' language which was of course the language of instruction. Thus, whether or not this was the bilinguals' weaker language, the results show up the relationship between grasp of the language of instruction and attainment. The majority of the twenty-two studies in which attainment in arithmetic was investigated (Macnamara, 1966a, Chap. 5) found that bilinguals were inferior to monolinguals in problem arithmetic (reasoning) but not in mechanical arithmetic (computation). The difference between the two sets of findings is probably due to the fact that in mechanical arithmetic the student is simply required to carry out an arithmetical operation indicated by an arithmetical symbol, whereas in tests of problem arithmetic he is required to read and interpret prose passages. Language, therefore, plays a much larger role in the latter type of test.

A further question is whether the retardation in problem arithmetic is found only at the initial stages of being taught in a weaker language. The indications are that it is of longer duration. A careful study conducted by the Department of Education, Manila (1953) revealed such a retardation over the two years of primary schooling investigated. Macnamara (1966a) found a retardation of about one year of problem arithmetic age amongst fifth standard primary school children in Ireland. The Irish children who were native speakers of English with only a school knowledge of Irish had been taught arithmetic in Irish for six years. The International Institute of Teachers College, Columbia (1926) found even greater retardation at the twelfth grade level amongst Puerto Rican children who had been taught arithmetic in English (the second language) from the beginning of the fifth grade. Running counter to these findings is a report of a South African study by Malherbe (1946). He claims that South African children taught arithmetic through the medium of their weaker language, English or Afrikaans, quickly recover from an initial handicap to draw level with those being taught in their mother tongue. Perhaps the reason for this divergence in findings is that the South African children had a better grasp of the second language than those studied elsewhere. Malherbe suggests that they had. However his report is extremely inadequate, and the study seems to have been poorly controlled. Several other sets of findings are now coming from individual schools which support Malherbe. However, the results of studies conducted in individual schools, with programs which in their setting are exceptional, cannot be extrapolated to more general situations without a good deal of caution.

What of students who in the middle of their schooling change from being taught arithemetic in their mother tongue to being taught in a second language? (There seem to be no studies of children who made the opposite switch.) The Puerto Rican and Manila investigations indicate that such a switch is accompanied by a falling off in attainment, but, as one would expect, there is a good deal of transfer from learning in the mother tongue to learning in the second one.

There is practically no information about the attainment of students who are being taught subjects other than arithmetic in their weaker language. One would expect to find that here, too, retardation results, and, as in the case of arithmetic, that it depends principally on two factors: the extent to which a subject involves language and the extent of the students' weaknesses in the language of instruction. However, there is very little evidence about the second factor. There is no evidence at all about the influence of another possible factor, the teacher's command of the language of instruction; though obviously it could be crucial if the language of instruction is also the teacher's weaker language.

Problem Solving in Two Languages

The student's difficulty in following courses in his weaker language might seem at first sight to lie solely in his ignorance of certain words, phrases or syntactic structures. However, there is probably more to it than that. Those of us who read a second language poorly will probably from time to time have experienced difficulty in following the meaning of complex passages in that language, even though we could have translated each individual word and expression used. This we may have attributed to inadequate *grasp of language*. The studies now to be described derive from this observation and attempt to clarify what is meant by the term, grasp of language.

Preliminary studies (Macnamara, 1963) revealed that bilinguals take longer to solve written problems when they are presented in their weak rather than in their strong language. In subsequent studies of problem solving no time limits were set; speed of performance was examined separately (see below).

After several attempts the following technique was developed for investigating the difficulties encountered by bilinguals when attempting to solve problems presented in their weaker language (Macnamara and Kellaghan, in press). The crucial thing was to obtain problems which, though involving relatively complex reasoning processes, could be expressed in both languages in terms that were familiar to the subjects. The solution was to devise (or borrow) what appeared to be suitably complex problems, and test for children's ability to understand the language in which they were expressed, by devising in addition a series of simple problems which made use of the same vocabulary and syntactic structures. An example of a problem in complex form was:

If the letters of the word BAD[1] were removed from the alphabet, what would be the fifth letter of the alphabet?

The set of simple questions into which this was broken in order to test children's understanding of each of its components was:

a What is the fifth letter of the alphabet?
b What is the eighth letter of the alphabet?
c If the letter A were removed from the alphabet, what would be the first letter of the alphabet?

In all, eight complex problems and eight sets of appropriate simple questions were devised. The subjects were all children in sixth standard (N = 341) in six Irish primary schools. All the children were native speakers of English, but all had been taught Irish for about 37%, and English for about 20%, of the school time over their seven years at school. Half the children in each school (randomly chosen) took the tests in Irish, the other half in English. The complex problems were presented first in each case.

Results were analysed separately for each problem. We were interested only in those children who understood a problem, that is, those who answered all the relevant simple problems correctly. The chief interest lay in comparing, of those who understood, the proportion which solved a complex problem in Irish with the proportion which solved it in English. As there were no reliable differences between boys and girls, the data for all children were combined. For all eight problems the results lie in the expected direction. On a two-tailed Chi² = χ^2 test, four of them are significant at the 5% level of probability, while on a one-tailed test, five are significant at that level. It is not clear, however, why some problems yielded significant results, while others did not.

---

1 In Irish the letters BAD mean *boat*.
2 These problems were taken from the Schonell Essential Problem Arithmetic Test, Form A, which had been translated into Irish for the purpose of the Irish investigation reported in Macnamara (1966a). For details about this translation see *op cit.* Chap. 7.

These findings indicate that in some instances, the problem solving ability of bilingual children is poorer when information is provided in their weaker language, even when the components of the problem are separately understood.

Speed of Reading in Two Languages

What precisely is the nature of the difficulty indicated in the problem solving studies described above? Where in the process of assimilating and dealing with the information might it occur? From the results of the preliminary study which showed that bilinguals took longer to solve problems in their weaker language it seemed likely that the difficulty could be located, at least partly, in the assimilation of the problem. This idea gave rise to a series of studies of reading.

First (Macnamara, 1966b), primary school children comparable with those who worked on the problems were asked to read lists of numbers and lists of quantities of money (e.g., 5s.-6d.) in each of their languages. The reason for doing so was that several of the problems contained figures or sums of money, and it was necessary to see whether they could name them equally quickly in the two languages. The finding was that they could.

Next (Macnamara and Kellaghan, in press), three arithmetical problems expressed in both Irish and English[2] were presented to two groups of sixth standard primary school boys, all native speakers of English. One group consisted of 20 boys who had been taught all subjects in Irish, the other consisted of 20 boys who had been taught all subjects in English. Each boy read aloud each version of the three problems three times, and his time for each problem was recorded. Irish and English versions of a problem never differed in length by more than a single word. The order in which the versions were presented was counterbalanced. For both groups, the first reading of the Irish version took significantly longer than the first reading of the English version. In fact, the Irish version took from 1.4 to 1.7 times as long. Improvement from first to best (usually third) reading was also examined and found to be significantly greater in Irish than in English for both groups on all three problems. The groups did not differ significantly in this respect.

The general finding that reading in a weaker language takes longer than reading in the stronger one is supported by Lambert, Havelka and Gardner (1959) and by Kolers (1966). The finding that reading times improve more in Irish than in English suggests that the boys came nearer on their first reading in English than on their first reading in Irish to the speed at which they could comfortably handle semantic information.

This study of reading yielded overall time differences for reading aloud in two languages, but did not reveal where in the input and output processes the difficulties which accounted for the overall differences were located. My colleague, Dr. Thomas Kellaghan, and I then began to analyse this process into its components. We thought that on the input side, the difference might be in part at the perceptual level, in part at the syntactic and semantic analyses levels. On the output side the same sort of analysis does not quite apply since the semantic encoding and the syntactic organization are already done for the reader. We felt, however, that a reader might not be able to make as much use of the sequential or transition probabilities in the sentences of his weaker language as in those of his stronger one. We also felt that the articulation of individual words might take longer in the weaker language and that bilinguals might not be able to string words together (catenation in linguistic terminology) as effectively in articulating sentences in their weaker language. We had some success in validating certain sections of our analysis. However, Miss Marie Feltin[3] and I have recently replicated and extended the studies carried out with Dr. Kellaghan, so I shall describe only the recent study, which is presented here for the first time.

Analysis of Bilinguals' Reading Skills

Materials. Eighteen feminine French nouns were selected all naming common objects of which pictures could easily be drawn. In English these nouns are: bulb, car, cow, crown, door, dress, flower, girl, hen, house, lamp, leaf, leg, mouse, queen, tail, wheel, wing. To these were added two other words in each language, *a* and *has*, so that the original words might be combined to form sentences of which half were true and half were false; e.g., *a hen has a wing* and *a hen has a door*. Words and sentences were printed on cards. Filmstrips were also prepared in which the same words were printed beneath pictures. In 50% of the combinations the word named the picture and in 50% it did not. In one filmstrip all the words were French, in the other they were all English. Two other filmstrips were prepared, one containing the French sentences, and one the English sentences.

Finally, the true sentences were combined, by using the word *and*, which in turn were made into two 50 word paragraphs, one English and one French. These were typed on cards. Scrambled versions of each paragraph were also typed on cards.

Ss and procedure. The Ss who took part in the experiment were 24 English-speaking girls from Marianopolis College.[4] All had taken

---

[3] At present a student in the University of California at Berkeley. The research reported here was supported by a generous grant from the French-Canada Studies Programme, McGill University.

[4] Miss Feltin and I are grateful to the authorities of Marianopolis College for helping us to obtain Ss for this study.

high school French and one year of college French. One half of the individual words and sentences, chosen at random, were presented tachistoscopically to each S and perceptual thresholds recorded. The filmstrips were projected on a screen with a Dukane Projector (Model 576-47B) which operates so rapidly that the stimulus is steady on the screen within a twentieth of a second of pressing the switch which operates the projector. Ss were asked to press a key marked (+) if the word matched the picture or if a stimulus sentence was true, to press a key marked (−) if the word did not match the picture or if the sentence was false. A clock was set in motion by the switch which operated the projector and stopped by the key which S pressed. Cumulative times were recorded for each S.

The Ss were asked to read the paragraphs of text and scrambled passages in two ways, aloud and silently, and their times were recorded with a stopwatch. In silent reading they indicated the words they were reading with a pointer.

Eight measures were obtained for each S in each of the two languages: mean perceptual thresholds for (1) words, (2) sentences; mean reaction times for (3) words on the screen, (4) sentences on the screen; times for (5) silent reading of text, (6) reading text aloud, (7) silent reading of scrambled passages, (8) reading scrambled passages aloud.

The order in which the four tasks involved in (1) and (2) were presented was counterbalanced across all Ss. The order of the four tasks involving filmstrips (3 and 4) were presented was counterbalanced in a similar manner. Twelve Ss, chosen at random, completed the tachistoscopic tasks first, and twelve completed the filmstrip tasks first. Tasks (5), (6), (7) and (8) came last for all Ss, and they were counterbalanced in the same way as the earlier tasks.

Results. The results are set out in Table 1. In analysing them the

TABLE 1
MEAN TIMES IN MILLISECONDS FOR TACHISTOSCOPE AND FILMSTRIP
TASKS; MEAN TIMES IN SECONDS FOR READING TASKS

| | Tachistoscope | | Film | | Silent Reading | | Reading Out Loud | |
	Words	Sentences	Words	Sentences	Scrambled Passages	Text	Scrambled Passages	Text
English	69	236	1089	1448	12.01	7.37	17.70	9.64
French	75	270	1230	1704	12.92	10.00	20.54	14.80

method of paired differences was used throughout. That is, each S's time for a task in one language was subtracted from his time for the corresponding task in the other language. From the resulting difference scores has been removed the influence of all factors which contributed equally to scores in the two tasks. Thus, these difference scores are purer measures than the original scores from which they were derived of the factor which produces a difference between performance in the two languages. Further, where appropriate one set of difference scores was deducted from another set. The second order difference scores which result provide data for testing the null-hypothesis that the two sets of first order difference scores can be interpreted as measuring the same factor.

The mean difference between perceptual thresholds for English and French words (tachistoscope) is not significant ($df = 23$, $t = 1.52$, $p > .05$). Perceptual thresholds for English and French sentences differ significantly ($df = 23$, $t = 2.49$, $p < .05$). If, however, they are corrected for individual differences in thresholds for words, the difference for sentences falls far short of significance ($df = 23$, $t = .95$, $p > .05$). Thus, it is reasonable to conclude that the recognition of sentences brought into play no skill not involved in the recognition of words.

Mean times for matching words and pictures (filmstrip) were corrected for individual differences in perceptual thresholds for words. The resulting mean difference between performance in the two languages is 135 msecs which is significant ($df = 23$, $t = 4.76$, $p < .05$). Mean times taken to decide whether sentences were true or false were corrected for perceptual thresholds for sentences. The resulting mean difference between performance in the two languages is 243 msec, which is significant ($df = 23$, $t = 2.73$, $p < .05$). However when times taken to decide whether sentences were true or false are corrected for times taken to match words and pictures, the resulting mean difference of 115 msecs falls well short of significance ($df = 23$, $t = 1.13$, $p > .05$). Thus these two tasks can be interpreted as calling into play the same skills.

In analysing the times taken to read the sequences of text and scrambled passages four components were isolated. These may be loosely called: (a) perception of individual words, (b) pronunciation of individual words, (c) use of transition probabilities, (d) catenation. The various reading times contain the following components:

Silent reading of scrambled passages   = (a)
Reading of scrambled sentences aloud = (a) + (b)
Silent reading of text   = (a) − (c)
Reading of text aloud   = (a) + (b) − (c) − (d)

Note that (c) and (d) contribute to a reader's speed and are therefore entered as negative quantities. By simple arithmetic the value of each component can be calculated for each S.

Four analyses were carried out. In each, the mean "French" value of a component was compared with its mean "English" value. The mean difference for (a), which is 0.91 seconds, is not significant ($df = 23$, $t = 1.57$, $p > .05$). The mean difference for (b), which is 1.94 seconds, is significant ($df = 23$, $t = 2.19$, $p < .05$). The mean difference for (c), which is 1.72 seconds, is significant ($df = 23, t = 2.58, p < .05$). The mean difference for (d), which is 0.59 seconds, is not significant ($df = 23, t = 0.66, p > .05$).

Discussion. In interpreting these findings it is important to bear three things in mind. Ss knew all the words used; each S read the same words eight times in each language; only one, very simple, syntactic structure was employed.

It is hardly surprising, then, that no difference in perceptual thresholds for English and French words was observed. Since the order of tachistoscopic and filmstrip tasks was counterbalanced, mean perceptual thresholds represent performance at a stage when, on an average, the words had already been encountered four times in one or other of the languages. It is likely, then, that differences in perceptual threshold are obscured by a considerable familiarity factor. Where in the series of comparisons differences were found to be significant, the factors being investigated must have been robust enough to withstand the effect of such familiarity.

Differences in perceptual thresholds for sentences cease to be significant when corrected for individual differences in perceptual threshold for words. This means that it is reasonable to interpret both tasks as involving nothing but the recognition of words. This ceases to be surprising when we recall that all sentences had the same syntactic structure. Once S had become familiar with this structure he could ignore it and concentrate on recognizing the particular pair of nouns in which alone the sentences differed. The next step in our research program will be to test for a syntactic component with sentences in which the syntax is systematically varied.

It is quite revealing that times taken to determine the semantic values of English words and sentences were significantly faster than those for French words and sentences, even when corrected for individual differences in perceptual thresholds for the same words and sentences. It might at first appear that in matching words and pictures Ss employed different strategies in French and English. When responding to the French series they might, for example, have recalled the French word which named the pictured object and then seen whether it matched the word printed beneath the picture. On the other hand, when responding to the English series, they might simply have read the English word, decoded it, and compared the semantic value thus obtained with their interpretation of the picture. However, the findings for speed in determining the truth or falsehood of sentences makes this interpretation rather improbable. The difference between French and English speeds for the latter task ceases to be significant when corrected for individual differences in speed of matching French and English words and pictures. In other words, the two tasks seem to involve very similar skills. It would be impossible to perform the true-false task without decoding both nouns in each sentence, French and English, and testing for a part-whole relationship. Because of the close similarity of this and the task of matching words and pictures, it is unlikely that Ss employed different strategies in the two tasks. Thus the most satisfactory interpretation of the data is the one suggested earlier: Ss decoded the semantic values of French words more slowly than those of English ones. This conclusion has the support of some studies carried out by Lambert *et al.* (1955, 1959). They required Ss to press keys in response to written directions in French or in English. They found that response times were slower when the directions were in a S's weaker language.

The first finding in the analysis of times for reading the longer sequences is in keeping with the rest of the study: the perception of individual words, as determined by speed of reading scrambled passages silently, does not differ signficantly from French to English. Though the method of timing the movement of a pointer from the beginning to the end of a passage is rough and ready, there is no reason to believe that it differentially affected the measurement of times for silent reading in French and English. The finding that individual French words are articulated more slowly than English ones is not unexpected. It implies, of course, that Ss such as those tested generally take longer to articulate messages in French than in English. However, the observed difference is slight, coming on an average to about 40 msecs per word. On the other hand in the simple texts on which they were tested Ss appeared to string words together in articulation as effectively in French as in English. Finally they made less use of the sequential probabilities in French sentences than of those in English ones, thus adding about 30 msecs per word to their French reading times.

Can the above analysis be applied to overall reading times in French and English in such a way as to obtain the relative weight of each? It is certainly hazardous to do so in view of the number of times Ss read these words. However if attention is focused on the relative rather than the absolute size of the quantities observed, the danger of being misled is greatly reduced. The largest difference between performance in French and English is that for semantic decoding of nouns, which yields a figure of 110 msecs per word. The second largest difference is that for articulation of individual words, which comes to about 40 msecs per word. The third largest is that associated with the differential use of sequential probabilities in French and English, which comes to about 30 msecs per word. Taken together the three differences come to a sizeable time difference, even when reading simple and much practised words. The likelihood also remains that this difference would have been even larger if a variety of syntactic structures had been introduced.

To return for a moment to the point of departure, the relative difficulty experienced by bilinguals in solving written problems presented in their weaker language, it is interesting to reflect on the fact that of the differences noted the greatest was that associated with the semantic decoding of words. This suggests at least a partial explanation of the bilinguals' problem solving difficulties. Longer decoding times in the weaker language imply greater difficulty with that task and also an added burden on a short-term memory which is extremely limited both in the quantity of information it can store and in the length of time for which it can store it. The normal manner in which persons cope with the limitations of short-term memory is to reduce the amount of information and *chunk* it in such a way that a single stored item stands for several original items (Miller, 1956). For most purposes the most parsimonious way of chunking language is to decode it and store the meaning, or such parts of the meaning as are relevant. The present findings prompt the conjecture that the bilingual has greater difficulty in making out the meaning, and, because of the extra attention he must pay to that task, greater difficulty in recalling other parts of the message while decoding a particular section. Consequently he has greater difficulty in picking out what is relevant to his purpose and discarding the remainder. All this would amount to greater difficulty in solving problems expressed in the weaker language.

Verbal Interchange in the Classroom

Much remains to be done to complete the analysis of bilingual's reading abilities, yet enough has been done to show which lines are likely to prove fruitful. The results will surely cast light not only on reading but also on linguistic functioning generally. Similar studies of verbal interchange in two languages are urgently required. The indications of the reading study are that articulation, and consequently communication, is slower in the weaker language. It is also likely that bilinguals encode ideas[5] and carry out syntactic organization more slowly in their weaker language. However, the process of oral production needs to be thoroughly investigated before the bilingual's difficulties are clearly understood. Similar investigations of listening comprehension and of writing are needed to complete the picture of what it means to take a course in a weaker language.

One effect of a thorough and comprehensive series of investigations along the lines suggested would be to create understanding for

---

[5] Ervin (1961), reports that relative speed of naming pictures in two languages is related to degree of bilingualism. Unfortunately, however, it is not clear from the report cited whether she separated time for recalling names from time for articulation.

persons who have to work in a weaker language. As things stand they are frequently made to look stupid, particularly if their accent is reasonably good, because then their deficiencies are not so apparent. Hopefully, a second effect would be to provide indications as to how they might be helped over their difficulties. All that can be said at present is that such students, and their teachers, must resign themselves to a slower pace of work.

Another whole area that requires study is the inner speech employed by the bilingual student. Does he, for example, *think* in his weaker language when he is given a problem to solve in that language, or does he translate it into his stronger one? I attempted to answer this question (Macnamara, 1965) by asking bilingual primary school children what language they thought in. The children were 24 native speakers of English in sixth standard, and had been taught all subjects in Irish throughout their schooling. I saw them individually and gave them three problems to solve in Irish, and when they had given their answers I asked them, to their surprise, what language they had been thinking in. They all found the question a difficult one, but all replied that to the best of their knowledge they had been thinking in Irish. I noticed three of them muttering to themselves as they worked over the problems, and so far as I could judge they muttered only in Irish. This encouraged me to believe the children's answer to my question.

The assumption that the children I questioned were thinking in Irish, raises further problems. At what stage in their learning of the second language do they begin to think in it, and what are the factors which affect this? What are the effects on their thinking of expressing their thoughts to themselves in a language they grasp only poorly? At present there is no answer to these questions; but a technique similar to that used by psychologists working on computer simulation might prove fruitful in investigating such problems. The technique is to train subjects to vocalize their thoughts. Recordings of such vocalizations might well furnish some answers to questions about inner speech.

Linguistic Effects of Teaching in a Weaker Language

What effect does teaching in a weaker language have on the bilingual's two languages? The most obvious effect is that he learns the technical terms employed in a subject only in the language in which the subject is taught. But it is quite reasonable to ask whether, apart from this, teaching in a foreign language has a more general effect on language skills. The difficulty in answering this question is that in the majority of studies (Macnamara, 1966a) two factors were confounded: the effect of teaching the language or languages, and the effect of teaching other subjects in the medium of one of these languages. Malherbe (1946) claims to have isolated the effect of the second factor and that it was beneficial to the second language without impoverishing the first. He also claims that the lower the child's I.Q. the greater the benefit to his weaker language. However, it seems quite unlikely that Malherbe succeeded in isolating the effect of the second factor from that of the first and from those of other factors such as teaching skill, social class, etc. Two other South African reports, Logie (Bovet, 1935) and McConkey (1951) arrive at conclusions similar to Malherbe's without the addendum that the dull child benefits most. In addition to the South African studies there are now numerous reports from individual bilingual schools (see, for example, Gaarder, this issue) that support the South African findings. However, in my own study in Ireland (Macnamara, 1966a) which attempts to control for differences in I.Q., social class and quality of teaching, I found no significant differences in Irish or in English between children who had been taught throughout their six years of primary schooling in Irish and those taught in English. This study differed from the reports from individual schools in two ways: it was a fairly large study in which children in 100 schools, selected at random from all Irish primary schools, were tested and the various bilingual programmes had been in operation in the Irish schools for about 40 years. Thus in the Irish study the Hawthorne effect, which may have had an influence on the individual schools mentioned, had long since disappeared. The Irish study also differs from the South African ones in the type of bilingual setting in which it was conducted. In Ireland, Irish is no more than a school subject for about 97% of the school population; in South Africa, English and Afrikaans are widely used, and it would appear from Malherbe's report that South Africans who attend bilingual schools typically have a far better knowledge of their second language than Irish children have of theirs. It must be admitted that the Irish findings are unexpected. One would predict that extensive teaching in a second language would have some general beneficial effect on the second language and some general detrimental effect on the first one. However, in view of the lack of satisfactory evidence, perhaps the wisest counsel to follow at the present time is to say that the linguistic effects of teaching in a second language are unknown.

In Conclusion

Considering the magnitude of the problem and the nature of the difficulties involved for students it is surprising that so little work has been done on teaching through the medium of a second language. The topic is surely one of the most neglected in the whole of educational psychology. What is required first of all is a detailed analysis of the four major language skills, speaking, listening, writing and reading, along the lines indicated above. This means that each skill should be examined in each of two languages at the perceptual, syntactic, lexical and semantic levels in the decoding of messages, and at the semantic, lexical, syntactic and motor levels of encoding messages. As a bilingual's difficulties will vary with the pair of languages involved, the whole investigation of his difficulties would be greatly aided by a contrastive analysis of those languages. When the chief difficulties are sufficiently clear the next task is to devise and assess programs of instruction to improve the student's language skills and lessen the burden he has to carry. Hopefully, these programs could be incorporated in existing language programs. After that, several problems of a less pressing nature might be broached. One of these is the effect on language skills of teaching through the medium of a second language. Undoubtedly if the plan of campaign I am outlining were followed, such teaching would be associated with improvement in the weaker language, although the researcher's task of showing a causal link between the two might well increase in difficulty. Another problem which merits attention is the possible effect of teaching in a weaker language on the student's emotions and attitudes. Undoubtedly the student who finds himself being outstripped by his contempories who have the advantage of working in their strong language—especially if that student is unaware of the full extent of his deficiencies in the language of instruction—will experience frustration and perhaps grow less confident of his own abilities. Additionally, he may come to feel increasingly cut off from his own family and other members of his own linguistic community if he is unable because of a language barrier to discuss with them his academic studies and interests. Something of this sort happens to many students even without the complication of studying in a foreign language, but the feeling of alienation may well be heightened for the student who does have that complication. There were indications in the Philippine study (Department of Education, Manila, 1953) that children were happier studying in their native Hiligaynon than in English, and that they attended school more regularly. However, so far as I am aware, no investigation has been made of the other emotional aspects which I mentioned. Yet in the long run, these may prove just as important to the welfare of the students I have been discussing as the more obvious cognitive difficulties with which this paper was principally concerned.

REFERENCES

Bovet, P. Les problèms scolaires posés par le bilinguisme. Zurich: Pour L'Ere Nouvelle, No. 105, 1935.

Bull, William E. The use of vernacular languages in education. In Dell H. Hymes (Ed.), Language in culture and society. New York: Harper and Row, 1964, 527-533.

Department of Education, Manila. The relative effectiveness of the vernacular and of English as media of instruction. Manila: Bureau of Public Schools. *Bulletin nos. 9, 12, 14, 16*, 1953.

ERVIN, S. Semantic shift in bilingualism. *American Journal of Psychology*, 1961, 74, 233-241.

FISHMAN, JOSHUA A. Language maintenance and language shift as a field of inquiry. *Linguistics*, 1964, 9, 32-70.

International Institute of Teachers College, Columbia University. *A survey of the public educational system of Puerto Rico.* New York: Bureau of Publications, Teachers College, Columbia University, 1926.

KOLERS, PAUL A. Reading and talking bilingually. *American Journal of Psychology*, 1966, 79, 357-376.

LAMBERT, WALLACE E. Measurement of the linguistic dominance of bilinguals. *Journal of Abnormal and Social Psychology*, 1955, 50, 197-200.

LAMBERT, WALLACE E., HAVELKA, J., AND GARDNER, R. C. Linguistic manifestations of bilingualism. *American Journal of Psychology*, 1959, 72, 77-82.

McCONKEY, M. G. An experiment in bilingual education. *Journal of Social Research*, Pretoria, 1951, 2, 28-42.

MACNAMARA, JOHN. *The use of Irish in teaching children from English-speaking homes: A survey of Irish National Schools.* Unpublished Ph.D. thesis, University of Edinburgh, 1963.

MACNAMARA, JOHN. The problem solving difficulties of bilingual children. Paper read to Northern Ireland branch of the British Psychological Society, 23 January, 1965. *Bulletin of the British Psychological Society*, 1965, 18, 58-59 (Abstract).

MACNAMARA, JOHN. *Bilingualism in primary education.* Edinburgh: Edinburgh University Press, 1966a.

MACNAMARA, JOHN. The effect of anticipation on the language switching speeds of bilinguals. St. Patrick's College, Dublin, 1966b. (Mimeo)

MACNAMARA, JOHN AND KELLAGHAN, THOMAS P. Reading in a second language. In Marion D. Jenkinson (Ed.), *Improving reading throughout the world.* Newark, Delaware: International Reading Association, in press.

MALHERBE, E. G. *The bilingual school.* London: Longmans, Green, 1946.

MILLER, G. A. The magical number seven, plus or minus two: some limits on our capacity for processing information. *Psychological Review*, 1956, 63, 81-97.

STERN, H. H. *Foreign languages in primary education.* Hamburg: Unesco, 1963.

UNESCO. *The use of vernacular languages in education.* Paris, Unesco, 1953.

THE MEASUREMENT AND DESCRIPTION OF WIDESPREAD AND RELATIVELY STABLE BILINGUALISM

Joshua A. Fishman

Bilingualism in the Barrio

Preface

JOSHUA A. FISHMAN

THE March and April, 1969, issues of *The Modern Language Journal* contain excerpts from a study of a bilingual neighborhood that several of my students, a few of my colleagues and I recently completed. Although we studied only a single, predominantly lower class, Puerto Rican *barrio* (and aspects of the larger network of communication media and communication elites through which it is tied to the Puerto Rican community of the Greater New York Metropolitan Area) our sociolinguistic interests, both theoretical and practical, extended considerably beyond the immediate community under study.

In the realm of theory we wanted to explore bilingualism as a *societal* manifestation, i.e. as a type of *social behavior* the regularity of which could be recognized, measured and described, whether at the individual, the small group, the large aggregate or even the national level of analysis, in *societally meaningful and entirely commensurable terms*; in terms that searched for the orderly but yet necessarily differential functions of languages and language varieties in any fully bilingual speech community.

In practical terms we were concerned with the economic poverty and lack of dignity or appreciation that so unfortunately impinge on bilingualism in the United States. As a result we wanted to explore more deeply than before the richness of societal bilingualism in order to reveal to teachers, social workers and community activists alike that bilingualism is a mark of great communal sophistication and subtlety, of interpersonal stability and cultural sensitivity, rather than the badge of backwardness and disorganization that it has so mistakenly been taken to be. A teacher aiming at sociolinguistic competence in a bilingual speech community, whether for himself or for his pupils, is setting high goals indeed and should, therefore, do so with both pride and awareness.

The papers that follow constitute an educationally relevant selection from a report to the Department of Health, Education and Welfare, Office of Education, which, in its original version, numbered six times as many papers and totaled over 1200 pages of text. Other papers from this report will, within a period of six months or so, begin to appear in psychological, sociological, anthropological, linguistic and educational journals published primarily in the United States but also, to some extent, in Europe, Latin America, Africa and Asia. Finally, the full report, entirely recast as an integrated whole from its initial appearance as a string of separate (and, therefore, necessarily somewhat redundant) papers, will appear as a volume in the Indiana University Language Sciences Series during the 1970–71 academic year. In view of the fact that two years normally elapse between the completion of a technical report and its partial or complete publication via journal articles and book presentations, I must express not only my own sincere gratitude but also that of my invaluable major associates (Robert L. Cooper and Roxanna Ma, both of whom are at this moment engaged in pioneering studies of bilingualism in East and West Africa respectively) to Dr. Robert F. Roeming for enabling parts of our work to come before the readers of this distinguished *Journal* within six to eight months of the release of our voluminous report. It is my sincere hope that our studies will be of interest and of use to language teachers since they, more than any other professional group, hold in their hands, heads and hearts the future of bilingualism in the United States.

151

The Measurement and Description of Widespread and Relatively Stable Bilingualism

JOSHUA A. FISHMAN, *Yeshiva University*

A RATHER small number of definite and interrelated purposes prompted the study of *Bilingualism in the Barrio* and served as guideposts during the two years of collective labors on this project. The enumeration and discussion of these purposes or goals at the very outset will aid in understanding the articles selected from the complete report and in evaluating the success obtained in answering the questions that initially stood before us.

1. *Intra-group Bilingualism: Micro-processes and Macro-structures*

The measurement and description of bilingual populations is everywhere undergoing an exciting rebirth or revitalization. The young discipline of sociolinguistics is largely responsible for this excitement since it has emphasized a number of stimulating propositions and concepts (doing so largely on the basis of theoretical considerations as well as on the basis of qualitative studies of small groups) that require substantiation and refinement in connection with the study of such larger societal contexts as neighborhoods, towns, cities, regions or even countries.

Among the major messages of sociolinguistics is that which states that the *individual should be viewed as a member of a speech community*. A speech community is characterized by definite norms of language and behavior. These norms not only encompass the varieties or languages that exist within the speech community for its own internal communicative needs but also relate them to the types of other-than-speech behaviors (e.g. the interactions, the mutual rights and obligations, the roles and statuses, the purposes and identifications) in which various networks within the community are engaged. Thus, the description and measurement of an individual's bilingualism, as of an individual's repertoire range with respect to the language varieties that exist even within monolingual communities of any com-

plexity, should reflect and disclose the socio linguistic norms of the speech networks and the speech community of which he is a part, precisely because the latter (the sociolinguistic norms) underlie the former (the individual' bilingualism).

The sociolinguistic study of bilingualism focuses not on *language acquisition*, since bilingualism is presumably acquired much as all other socially normed behavior is acquired by exposure to and interaction with a community that lives in accord with the norms of usage and that is involved in the normal process of change to which most communities and most norms are exposed, but on *communicative appropriateness*. The sociolinguist investigating a bilingual speech community must ask not "How well do they speak X and Y?" but primarily: "What are the different varieties of X and Y, who uses them and when?". Thus the sociolinguist assumes that each "language" utilized in a bilingual speech community itself merely an abstraction from several varying lexical, grammatical and phonological realizations. However, these variations are far from random or idiosyncratic. Indeed, they are governed by norms which are implicitly understood by native members of the communities in question and which the investigator must elicit or discover. These norms imbed the variation in language usage within variation other concomitant social behavior. A valid sociolinguistic description of a bilingual speech community is one which faithfully reflects the norms of bilingual usage that exist within the community as a whole. Individuals or small networks may then be described in terms similarity or dissimilarity of their usage profile to the profile that obtains for the speech community or larger networks more generally.

The foregoing goal of describing the bilingualism of a speech community in terms the sociolinguistic norms that exist within is complicated enough even when we deal on with small networks of individuals. Even when the actual speech and behavior can be meticulously recorded and exhaustively examined the processes of human interaction and variety switching are so subtle and complex that the investigator's task is a formidable and, as yet, an unmastered one. However, our task, in the presently reported study, was an even more complicated one, namely, to describe sociolinguistic norms on the basis of data representative of larger societal contexts.

In going from the small group to the larger societal context we inevitably go from the immediate context of speech, and from the immediate corpus of speech, to the larger contexts of behavior that surround both speech contexts and speech samples. However, just as the individual's bilingualism is structured in accord with his network's and his community's norms, so is the process and the corpus of speech structured in accord with higher level regularities. In both cases we must utilize the performance of individuals to recognize the norms that obtain. However, when we generalize from individuals to small network, we can reserve the direct and exhaustive analysis of the language and behavior that are of concern to us. When we need to generalize from individuals to entire neighborhoods or countries we must frequently find larger contexts than the immediate context of individual speech and more suggestive or parsimonious data than the individual's corpus of speech. However, if the guidance provided by sociolinguistic theory is not to be lost, the large scale studies that we have in mind must continue to seek counterparts, at their own level, to the small group notions that have thus far been proposed.

One goal of this project was to maintain as close a link to small-group sociolinguistics as possible while developing data gathering and data analyzing techniques that might be of value in the study of widespread and relatively stable bilingualism in large and complex social environments. Population and behavioral sampling methods, quantitative analyses of mass data, multiple and interrelated measurements—all of these concerns and pursuits that are common to social science inquiry on large populations were to be part and parcel of our work; at the same time we were to struggle to maintain contact with such micro-sociolinguistic notions as repertoire range in language and behavior, compartmentalization of language and behavior, situational and metaphorical variation, etc. Our purpose, then, was to conduct a large scale study, but yet an intensive study; to go beyond the limitations of small-group sociolinguistics but yet not to break with the theoretical stimulation that it has provided.

2. The Contextualization of Bilingualism

If our first charge derived from challenges *within* the field of sociolinguistics, our second charge derived from challenges in a number of *neighboring* fields that have long been interested in bilingualism. Our second goal was to involve various disciplines in the study of widespread and relatively stable bilingualism and, in the process of bringing to bear on this matter disciplines that had traditionally gone their separate ways, to subject each of them to sociolinguistic criticism and revision.

Psychological study of bilingualism has, in recent years, produced a number of interesting findings, methods and theories. All of these might be considerably enriched if the sociolinguistic notion of contextualization of verbal interaction were taken into account. Thus, while the psychologist interested in bilingualism is likely to ask "Which language is stronger (or weaker) in this individual (or population)?" or "Which is used more fluently?," the sociolinguist is likely to restate this question in contextual terms and to ask "When and by whom is one language used primarily and when the other?." Does this sociolinguistic restatement of the problem represent an improvement? It does, if it can be shown that individuals or communities can appear to be bilingually balanced (i.e., using each language equally fluently) when viewed from the psychologist's overall perspective and yet reveal marked and reliable imbalances when viewed in different sociolinguistic contexts. Can traditional psychological measures of bilingualism be contextualized so as to reveal differences in degree of proficiency when these exist between one societal context and the next? If so, what relationship will exist between such measures and others that are more naturalistically sociolinguistic to begin with, in that their concern is with usage rather than with proficiency identified with fluency, output, correctness?

Sociology's interest in bilingualism has traditionally been limited to self-report measures (such as the questions utilized in language censuses). The longstanding difficulty with such measures has been that they have not been validated with respect to either proficiency or usage, and that they, too, have not been sufficiently contextualized to either recognize or yield societal patterns with respect to the functional allocation of codes in bilingual speech communities. Our goal, therefore, was to plan a number of new and revised self-report measures, drawing explicitly upon sociolinguistic theory in the process of instrument design, and then to compare the data obtained via such instruments with direct and indirect measures of bilingual proficiency and bilingual usage.

Obviously, it is easier to ask a person about his language behavior than to gather sufficient data in order to extract the regularities in such behavior from the data alone. The easier route is exactly the one that sociology has traditionally followed in studying societal bilingualism. However, now that sociolinguistics has sharpened sociological sensitivities for nuances in language usage, we are doubly obliged to face the questions of reliability and validity with respect to self-report data. What kinds of questions concerning their own language behavior can individuals drawn from different kinds of speech networks answer, and what is the reliability and the validity of the answers they give? Only by answering such basic questions can we know where and when it is most crucial to replace self-report methods with more difficult measures of usage and proficiency in future studies of large populations that are not amenable to exhaustive small-group research.

Linguistics, too, has traditionally treated bilingualism in a parochial fashion. It has primarily asked how two proportedly pure and independent codes have interfered with or influenced each other. It has usually not asked *when* these "pure" varieties are used (or by whom) nor when the "interfered" varieties are employed. Indeed, in quite recent days, "im-

maculate linguistics" has retreated even further from usage or performance and, in so doing, has adopted the pretense that neither usage nor performance are of real interest, but, rather, that the linguistic capacity of the human species and the ideal structure of the pure code that underlies speech usage and speech corpuses are the only matters that deserve attention. Sociolinguistics, on the other hand, stresses the reality of performance and the equal reality of the linguistic and behavioral norms that apply to performance. Thus, sociolinguistics asks the linguist to go beyond his usual interest in the standard speech variety and his usual satisfaction with a single informant, to concern with non-standard varieties, with the representativeness of informants and with differential performance within as well as between informants. Sociolinguistics also impels the linguistic analysis of bilingual corpuses toward greater quantification, toward a more frequent concern for the reliability of transcription, and toward more frequent curiosity as to the agreement between linguistic and other disciplinary analyses.

All in all, then, the second major purpose of this study was to devise new and better means of measuring and describing widespread and relatively stable bilingualism and of doing so in as contextualized and as interdesciplinary a fashion as possible.

3. *Utility Considerations*

If we believe that "nothing is as practical as a good theory" (Kurt Lewin) then we should admit that the test of good theory is that it is adequate to the demands of application. While our studies were not addressed to immediate applied concerns several such concerns were sufficiently close to consciousness to interact with our theoretical and methodological involvements.

The valid description of "language situations" in various multilingual areas of the world is itself a serious applied problem. All such censuses, surveys and investigations, even the most adequately financed among them, are severely limited in time, funds and manpower relative to the complexity of the task that faces them. All of them must be concerned with selecting from among alternative methods those calculated to yield the most reliable and valid data, given research time, research funds and subject time available. It was our constant hope that we might be able to recommend the subset of "best" methods for future language surveys to employ, at least under socio-political circumstances roughly similar to those which obtained in the area and at the time of our work.

Another applied interest of which we were frequently aware is that represented by the teaching of languages in general and by the teaching of languages that are normally utilized in a bilingual context more specifically. In both of these cases valid and insightful sociolinguistic description would not only enable teachers and pupils to recognize the varieties that local communicative appropriateness presupposes, but also to recognize the societal norms that govern the use or non-use of particular varieties between particular (types of) persons in particular (types of) situations. Language instruction is not a particularly successful venture at the present time, even given the simplified assumptions concerning linguistic and role repertoires under which it currently labors. The addition of sociolinguistic sensitivity to the tasks currently facing and baffling language teachers may be asking for much more refinement than can normally be handled. Nevertheless, some teachers and some students could doubtlessly strive for and attain sociolinguistic sensitivity (communicative appropriateness) in their respective teaching and learning tasks. They were not altogether forgotten as we collected, analyzed and interpreted our data.

The immediately above comments concerning language learning pertain not only to foreign languages, nor even only to languages that co-occur in multilingual speech communities. The problem of teaching standard English to speakers of non-standard varieties of English certainly requires sociolinguistic sensitivity on the part of teachers and administrators, if they are not to commit the error of seeming to wish to estrange students from their normal speech communities. Students and teachers alike must recognize that even speakers of standard English belong to a variety of speech networks and that their usage is *not* equally and unvaryingly standard in each of them. Even na-

tive-born teachers of standard English do not always speak that variety of their mother tongue and it alone to all their interlocutors and under all circumstances. They, too, have come to realize—albeit unconsciously in most cases—that native communicative appropriateness is based upon utilizing a repertoire of varieties of English as the situation demands. It is exactly this kind of sensitivity that speakers of non-standard varieties of English require if standard English is to be *added* to their linguistic repertoire without pretending to displace entirely those varieties that are already there. It is only the prospect of repertoire expansion, including role repertoire expansion, that can legitimize standard English for those for whom it is thus far little more than a silly abstraction. It was our hope that our work might indirectly contribute to the efforts to describe the usage of speech networks that utilize *both* standard and non-standard varieties of English.

4. *Study Design and Report Design*

Our attempts to devise and interrelate measures of widespread and relatively stable bilingualism focused on a single Puerto Rican neighborhood in Jersey City, New Jersey. On the one block on Ninth Street and on the intersecting two blocks on Grove Street we located some 431 individuals of Puerto Rican birth or extraction. These constituted our target or core population. In order to study them more exhaustively we rented and furnished a walk-up apartment in the study neighborhood. Some of our study team lived there practically all of the four summer months that we required in order to obtain the data we sought. All team members used "the apartment" as their headquarters during their daily data gathering visits. Interviews and tests administered to members of the target population were commonly administered in "the apartment," since it was sometimes quieter there than in the apartments of our subjects or in the neighborhood anti-poverty center, all of which were frequently available to us for data gathering purposes as needed. "The apartment" was also our equipment storage center, our rest and refreshment center and a place where neighborhood residents—adults and children alike—

could, and did, just drop in on us to chat, to have some coffee or some coke.

Our first formal data gathering venture in the study neighborhood was to conduct a language census. As is usually the case when language censuses are conducted our census-takers were still strangers to the target population at the time of the census. This strangeness did not last long after the census was completed, however. Several staff members came to be well known neighborhood "characters" as they trudged around the streets or sat around on the stoops with tape recorders of various sizes, as they were invited to dinners, attended funerals, helped rush neighbors to hospitals, baby-sat, fed children whose parents were at work, went to anti-poverty meetings and church services, attended picnics at the beach, made parties for the local children, and, in general, missed no opportunity to interview, to record and to observe.

In addition to our target population, three contrast populations were also examined in order that we might understand our Jersey City data more fully. One such contrast population consisted of Puerto Rican intellectuals in the greater New York area—writers, singers, artists, poets, musicians, and organizational leaders. Their language performance and their language views enabled us to see our Jersey City respondents in sharper relief. A second contrast population consisted of college oriented high school students of Puerto Rican birth or parentage. These were all members of ASPIRA (an organization that sponsors clubs in New York City public and parochial high schools) and, as such, they enabled us to understand what was usual and unusual about the Puerto Rican attitudes and behaviors of the less academically oriented youngsters in our Jersey City study neighborhood. Finally, the two Spanish dailies that appear in the New York City area also constituted a study population of sorts for us since we made a careful content analysis of their every reference to Puerto Ricans and to the Spanish language during a six month period that included our four month stay in Jersey City. In this fashion we sought to determine what views regarding Puerto Ricans and the Spanish language were impinging upon and possibly influencing our target population during the time of our study.

All of these studies are genuinely socio-linguistic in theory and in purpose and their authors were far less concerned with disciplinary labels than with interdisciplinary clarification.

It is always a little sad to find, on the completion of many months of work, that what one has learned is less than what needs to be known. Indeed, in the current case, we seem to have progressed primarily in our understanding of how the problem should be put and how its solution should be approached. The future measurement and description of widespread and relatively stable bilingualism in larger populations should benefit as much from our improved understanding of what still needs to be known as from the actual instruments and findings that we present.

PUERTO RICANS IN OUR PRESS

Joshua A. Fishman
and
Heriberto Casiano

Puerto Ricans in Our Press*

JOSHUA A. FISHMAN, *Yeshiva University*
AND
HERIBERTO CASIANO, *Pace College*

INTRODUCTION

THIS study reports on the treatment of Puerto Ricans in four New York City dailies, two published in English and two in Spanish, during the six-month period March–August, 1967, inclusive. It seeks to answer such questions as the following:

How frequently were Puerto Ricans referred to?

What was the major focus of the references to Puerto Ricans?

How often is the Spanish language referred to in connection with Puerto Ricans?

Are needs or problems of the Puerto Rican community discussed and if so, are these viewed as remediable?

Are particular characteristics ascribed to Puerto Ricans individually or as a group and, if so, are these positive or negative?

Are Puerto Ricans viewed as Americans also or is their dual status ignored?

In all of these connections two matters are of primary interest:

(1) Are there any differences between the English language and the Spanish language dailies in the consideration of these questions?

(2) Is the treatment accorded the Spanish language and Puerto Rican culture related to the treatment accorded other topics pertaining to Puerto Ricans or are these matters substantially unrelated?[1]

FREQUENCY OF MENTION

During the six-month period covered by this study 722 items mentioning individuals or groups referred to as Puerto Rican(s)[2] were encountered in the four dailies selected for study. Of these, 658 were encountered in the two Spanish dailies and 64 in the two English dailies.[3] The Spanish dailies revealed a rather constant number of references to Puerto Ricans during each of the six months studied. The English dailies showed a more irregular pattern, jumping from 5% of all of their mentions of

Puerto Ricans in June (the month before several incidents of looting and rioting in Spanish Harlem) to 53% of all mentions in July (the month of the incidents), and falling back to 16% in August. Thus, Puerto Ricans seemed to be of little interest to the English press either before or after the brief flare-up of violence in July.

MAJOR FOCI OF INTEREST

An analysis of all 722 items dealing with Puerto Ricans revealed that the major focus of

---

* The research reported in this paper was financed by the Language Research Section, Department of Health, Education and Welfare (Contract No. OEC-1-7-062817-0297). Data processing in connection with this research was supported by a grant from the College Entrance Examination Board.

[1] The major focus of the entire project of which this report is a part was upon Puerto Rican bilingualism in the Greater New York City area. The initial questions which prompted the newspaper study in connection with this project were: What is the saliency of the Spanish language in comparison with other references to Puerto Ricans in the local Spanish and English press?; Is Spanish viewed as important or unimportant, positive or negative in comparison to other Puerto Rican concerns and characteristics? Thus this study was viewed as one of several seeking to establish the general climate of opinion surrounding Puerto Rican bilingualism. The degree and nature of that bilingualism was simultaneously studied by a team of psychologists, sociologists, and linguists.

[2] The following permissible synonyms for "Puerto Rican(s)" were recognized in perusing the Spanish dailies: *boricua* and *borinquen*. In view of the purposes of this study, items dealing with individual acts of crime or violence were omitted unless they pertained to community leaders or to community-wide concerns or problems. The elimination of items dealing with individual acts of crime or violence restricted the number of Spanish press items included in this study much more than it restricted the number of English press items. News items, features, editorials and, in general, all items other than paid advertisements were included in the scope of this study.

[3] Both Spanish dailies (*El Diario* and *El Tiempo*) publish 6 issues per week. One English daily (*The New York Times*) publishes 7 issues per week and the other (*The Post*), 6. Item size in square inches did not prove to be a factor that differentiated between the Spanish and English dailies.

TABLE 1

FOCI OF INTEREST

Focus	Items in Spanish Dailies	Items in English Dailies
1. Individual affairs	17.8%	7.7%
2. Organizational events	23.2	1.6
3. Cultural topics	14.3	9.3
4. Puerto Rican/Anglo relations	41.3	76.5
5. Puerto Rican/Negro relations	1.2	5.0
6. Puerto Ricans and other Hispanic groups, Puerto Ricans and international affairs, etc.	2.3	—
N	658	64

interest, for both English and Spanish dailies, was in the area of intergroup relations between Puerto Ricans and the dominant Anglo society. As Table 1 reveals, 76% of all English references to Puerto Ricans were coded as belonging to this category.[4] On the other hand, 41% of the Spanish references to Puerto Ricans were coded as belonging to this category. The only other category in which there were proportionately more English than Spanish items was that dealing with Puerto Rican/Negro relations.

By way of contrast it should be pointed out that Puerto Rican organizational events, the attainments of individual Puerto Ricans, and Puerto Rican cultural affairs receive very little attention in the English dailies and far less than in the Spanish dailies. Thus, for the English dailies, Puerto Ricans are of interest primarily as they impinge upon the surrounding Anglo society. The internal life of the Puerto Rican community, its leaders, its functions, its holidays, its creativity, are not brought to the attention of the readers of the English press. As in the case of the extended coverage accorded Puerto Ricans during the July, 1967, disturbances, Puerto Ricans are discussed and reported in the English press primarily in the context of the problems or difficulties that they pose for Anglo society, whereas their cultural activity and creativity is by and large overlooked.

THE SPANISH AND ENGLISH LANGUAGES

Only a quarter of the Spanish items and some 42% of the English items referring to

Puerto Ricans contain any reference to th Spanish language. In the English press sucl references are largely of an identifying natur ("Spanish speaking individuals...," "... h said in Spanish."). In the Spanish press identi fying references also predominate but th relative proportion of positive references whicl encourage retention, interest and utilization o Spanish is greater.

In conjunction with English the tw emphases are reversed. Once again there i little overall concern with the topic but thi time it is the English press that has relativel; more positive references.

In general, neither the English nor th Spanish press seemed to be much concerne with language as a group symbol or cultura value during the months under study. Th United States Congress was engaged i debating the Bilingual Education Act and botl Senators from New York State and severz Congressmen from New York City sought t impress the Puerto Rican community witl their favorable actions on behalf of this act Nevertheless, it cannot be said that any grea interest was manifested among rank-and-fi' Puerto Ricans in the New York City are; although several Puerto Rican cultural an organizational leaders testified on behalf c this Act and arranged to have their view publicized in the Spanish press.

Puerto Ricans in New York are not ye language conscious or organized on behalf c language use, language recognition, or languag maintenance. Their use of Spanish is largel traditional, in connection with the daily rounc of family and neighborhood life, rather tha in terms of an ideology or an organized point view. Although the Spanish press tends reveal a different view of Spanish than does th

---

[4] Each investigator coded separately. The senior i vestigator spot-checked 20% of the classifications of tl junior author throughout the coding period and discuss with him all disagreements encountered. The agreeme rate was constantly above 90%.

[5] The Bilingual Education Act was finally adopted t Congress in December, 1968. For texts of the hearings connection with this act see Yarborough, Ralph (Chmn *Hearings before the Special Subcommittee on Bilingual Educ tion of the Committee on Labor and Public Welfare, Unie States Senate, 90th Congress, First Session, on S. 428.* Was ington, U. S. Government Printing Office, 1967.

English press the difference is more one of relative emphasis than of clearcut distinction or major saliency.[6]

PUERTO RICAN NEEDS AND PROBLEMS

The English dailies are much more likely to view Puerto Ricans in terms of their needs or problems than are the Spanish dailies. Over 85% of the references to Puerto Ricans in the English dailies were problem-connected. In the Spanish dailies this association obtains for only 50% of all references to Puerto Ricans. Spanish dailies see Puerto Rican as more than merely carriers of problems. For them Puerto Ricans also have leaders, organizations, customs, celebrations, creative figures, etc. For the English dailies the association of Puerto Ricans and problems is practically complete.

However, even if we examine only references to Puerto Rican problems a major difference obtains between the English and the Spanish dailies. The Spanish dailies indicate the programs or steps that are needed in order to overcome the problems of Puerto Ricans in 79% of the cases in which such problems are noted. The English dailies, on the other hand, recommend solutions or remedial steps only in 56% of the cases in which they discuss the problems of Puerto Ricans. Thus, in the English dailies the Puerto Rican is not only more frequently problem ridden but the action implications or remediation recommendations with respect to these problems are less frequently forthcoming. The English dailies do not show the concern for remedying the problems or needs of Puerto Ricans that is shown by the Spanish dailies.

However, the above difference may, in part, be due to a difference in journalistic tradition. The Spanish dailies may generally be more amenable than are the English dailies to making recommendations or evaluations, and to doing so in the news columns rather than only on the editorial page. Thus, in connection with the needs or problems of Anglo-Americans vis-a-vis their interactions with Puerto Ricans, the Spanish dailies are again more inclined to recommend solutions and remedial steps than are the English dailies, even though the English dailies feel free to mention relatively more

TABLE 2

CHARACTERISTICS OF PUERTO RICANS
AS INDIVIDUALS OR AS A GROUP

		Spanish Dailies	English Dailies
Characteristics mentioned		62%	64%
	N	658	64
Balance between positive and negative traits		14%	46%
	N	410	41
Positive traits only		82%	37%
	N	410	41
Negative traits only		4%	18%
	N	410	41

needs and problems of Anglo-Americans vis-a-vis Puerto Ricans than do the Spanish ones.

CHARACTERISTICS AND TRAITS OF PUERTO RICANS

Slightly over a third of the items from both groups of dailies made *no* mention of the traits or characteristics of Puerto Ricans, whether as individuals or as a group (Table 2). However, when such mention *is* made the English dailies are far more likely to attempt either a "balanced" (negative plus positive) presentation or an entirely negative presentation than are the Spanish dailies. The Spanish dailies are far more likely than are the English dailies to make entirely positive comments about Puerto Ricans.

CHARACTERISTICS AND TRAITS OF ANGLO-AMERICANS

Anglo-Americans who interact with Puerto Ricans are far less frequently characterized by both sets of dailies than are Puerto Ricans. Once again, however, we note that the English dailies are much more inclined toward *balanced* characterizations whereas the Spanish dailies

[6] This statement applies equally well to treatment of Puerto Rican culture. Here again we find a slight tendency for the Spanish press to treat this topic more frequently and more favorably than does the English press, rather than any dramatic difference between them. This may be taken as further evidence that the Spanish press does not serve a readership that actively seeks to maintain or to develop Hispanic culture in New York in any ideologically mobilized fashion.

are more inclined toward positive characterizations. However, Anglo-Americans are less
frequently viewed positively and more frequently viewed negatively or in a balanced
fashion than are Puerto Ricans. It is in this
roundabout way that it becomes evident that
both sets of dailies tend to be relatively critical
of Anglo-Americans in so far as their interaction
with Puerto Ricans is concerned. The increment
in negative characterizations is particularly
noticeable for the Spanish dailies.

NEGRO/PUERTO RICAN RELATIONS

The English dailies are much more inclined
to discuss Negro needs and problems as part of
their treatments of Puerto Ricans than are
the Spanish dailies. "Negroes and Puerto
Ricans" is often a stock phrase in the English
dailies whereas it is anything but that in the
Spanish dailies. However, the Spanish dailies
are, once again, more inclined to offer recommendations or solutions to the Negro problems
that they do discuss. Finally it should be noted
that the English dailies are more inclined to
make recommendations with respect to Negro
problems and needs than they were with respect
to Anglo-American problems and needs. This
is not the case for the Spanish dailies.

As for the characterization of Negroes, they
are less frequently viewed positively and more
frequently viewed negatively or in a "balanced"
fashion than are either Anglo-Americans or
Puerto Ricans by both sets of dailies.[7] The
increase in the proportion of negative characterizations of Negroes is particularly noticeable for the Spanish dailies.

COMPARISON BETWEEN NEGROES AND
ANGLO-AMERICANS VIS-A-VIS INTERACTIONS
WITH PUERTO RICANS

Since the items under study were selected because of their reference to Puerto Ricans it
should come as no surprise that Puerto Rican
needs and traits are mentioned more frequently
than are those of either Anglo-Americans or
Negroes. However, it is exactly the comparison
between Anglo-Americans and Negroes that is
of interest to us at this point. It is quite clear
that the English dailies more frequently recognize that both of these groups have problems
or needs in connection with their interaction

with Puerto Ricans. It is equally clear that the
Spanish dailies suggest solutions to these needs
or problems relatively more often.

As far as traits are concerned it is clear that
the English dailies more frequently describe Negroes and Anglo-Americans with "balanced"
terms whereas Spanish dailies more frequently
describe them with positive terms. Negroes receive the largest proportion of negative descriptions in both sets of dailies, the proportion of
such negative descriptions for Negroes being
somewhat higher in the Spanish dailies than in
the English. All in all, the Spanish dailies reveal
a lower relative frequency of mention of Negro
problems, a higher relative frequency of suggested solutions to Negro problems, and a
higher relative frequency of negative characterizations of Negroes. These may all be considered indicative of growing Puerto Rican/Ne-
gro polarization in the New York City area.

PUERTO RICANS AS AMERICANS

The American citizenship that all Puerto
Ricans possess receives different treatment in
the two types of dailies under consideration. It
is mentioned in 31% of the items from the
Spanish dailies but only in 20% of the items in
the English dailies. Of those items that mention
it in the Spanish dailies 37% do so with advocacy and positive references (e.g., pointing to
Puerto Rican contributions to American life,
demanding additional assistance for them as
American citizens, etc.) and 63% do so merely
in an identifying fashion (Puerto Rican residents of New York are entitled to participate
in tomorrow's elections, Puerto Ricans constitute x% of American servicemen in Viet Nam).
The corresponding percentages in the English

---

[7] With some numbers (n's) as small as 12 or 18 (and even
smaller n's in some subsequent tables and computations)
the requirements of statistical significance, in an inferential
sense, may not be met. However, the requirements of inferential statistics do not present a valid claim upon our analysis since the entire "population" of items relating to Puerto
Ricans has been examined in the four dailies selected for
study, rather than merely a sample of such items, as is the
practice in inferential studies. Whether or not the six
month period, March–August, 1967, is characteristic of
other periods, before or since, is a matter that requires
separate study. As of this writing (July, 1968), it is our impression that the dailies studied have not changed their
views or emphases with respect to Puerto Ricans.

lailies are 23% and 77%. The American citizenship of Puerto Ricans is more frequently viewed n a positive and noteworthy light in the Spansh dailies than it is in the English dailies.

PUERTO RICAN GAINS IN THE UNITED STATES

While the American citizenship of Puerto Ricans is more frequently applauded (or exploited) in the Spanish dailies than in the English ones, the topic of progress, gains, and accomplishments of Puerto Ricans in the United States is more frequently mentioned in the atter than in the former. In the Spanish dailies only 17% of all items were concerned with this opic whereas in the English dailies 36% dealt with this matter. This difference in relative concern with whether Puerto Ricans are or are not making progress in their "war against poverty" is related to the greater readiness of English dailies to view Puerto Ricans in a context of needs and problems.

While the Spanish dailies are less inclined to raise the question of progress or gains among Puerto Ricans in the United States they are somewhat more inclined to mention this topic with satisfaction when it is raised. Thus 28% of the mentions of this topic in the Spanish dailies express satisfaction whereas only 22% of the mentions in the English dailies do so. It should be underscored that not only is this difference a small one but that the lion's share of all references to Puerto Rican gains, whether in the Spanish or in the English dailies, are negative rather than positive ones.

THE CONTEXT OF REFERENCES TO SPANISH

In the Spanish dailies 47% of the references to the Spanish language are in connection with Puerto Rican/Anglo-American intergroup relations (Table 3). In the English dailies the corresponding figure is 80%. English dailies are much more likely to view the Spanish language as a barrier to intergroup communication or Puerto Rican gains and progress in the United States. Spanish dailies by no means overlook the problematic nature of the Spanish language in both of these contexts. However, for the Spanish dailies the Spanish language is also related to Puerto Rican cultural events, to organizational activities and to individual de-

TABLE 3

THE CONTEXT OF REFERENCES TO SPANISH

Context		Spanish Dailies	English Dailies
Intergroup (Puerto Rican/ Anglo-American)		47%	80%
	N	658	64
Other (cultural, organizational, individual, etc.)		53%	20%
	N	658	64
Puerto Rican needs and problems		27%	45%
	N	396	35
Positive mention in connection with Puerto Rican needs/ problems		44%	24%
	N	108	25
Positive mention concerning Puerto Ricans as Americans		22%	00%
	N	55	8
Positive mention concerning advocacy of Puerto Ricans as Americans		50%	00%
	N	24	2
Puerto Rican gains/progress viewed negatively		26%	53%
	N	80	18

scriptions, none of which obtain more than very rare mentions in the English dailies.

This difference in the contextualization of references to the Spanish language is equally noticeable if we examine only those items that deal with Puerto Rican needs and problems. In the Spanish dailies 27% of these items contain a reference to the Spanish language whereas in the English dailies 45% do so. Furthermore, of the references to the Spanish language in the context of Puerto Rican needs and problems carried in the Spanish dailies 44% are positive and 56% identifying. In the English dailies only 24% of the references to the Spanish language in the context of Puerto Rican needs and problems are positive and 76% are identifying. Thus it becomes quite clear that the English press references to the Spanish language lack the positive and compensatory connotations that they have in the Spanish press.

The Spanish dailies refer to the Spanish language positively in 22% of their references to Puerto Ricans as Americans and in 50% of their advocatory references to Puerto Ricans as Americans. The English dailies have no positive references to the Spanish language in either of these connections. On the other hand, the Spanish dailies mention the Spanish language in only 26% of their negative comments concerning Puerto Rican gains or progress in the United States. The English dailies do so in 53% of such comments. Obviously the Spanish language among Puerto Ricans is viewed as also being something positive and valuable in the Spanish dailies whereas it is viewed as being something primarily negative and harmful in the English ones.[8]

SUMMARY

Content analyses of references to Puerto Ricans in two English and two Spanish dailies in New York City during a six month period revealed that the English dailies showed little interest in Puerto Ricans either before or after the month of July during which there was a flare-up of violence in Spanish Harlem.

In comparison with the Spanish dailies, the English dailies: were more concerned with Puerto Rican/Anglo-American intergroup relations, referred more frequently to the Spanish language but did so more frequently for identifying purposes rather than in a positive vein, more frequently referred to Puerto Ricans in connection with their needs or problems, less frequently offered solutions or remedial steps in conjunction with these problems, less frequently attributed positive traits to Puerto Ricans and more frequently attributed negative traits to them, more frequently mentioned Negro needs and problems together with their references to Puerto Ricans, less frequently characterized Negroes in either negative or positive terms, less frequently referred to Puerto Ricans

as Americans, less frequently made positive or advocatory comments about Puerto Ricans as Americans even when they were referred to as such, more frequently raised the topic of Puerto Rican gains or progress in the United States but did so with fewer positive references, more frequently referred to the Spanish language in connection with Puerto Rican/Anglo-American intergroup relations, Puerto Rican needs and problems and the absence of Puerto Rican gains and improvements in the United States, and less frequently referred to the Spanish language positively in conjunction with Puerto Ricans as Americans.

Whereas the saliency of the Spanish language was rather low in the Spanish press this topic as such was normally referred to in the context of positive evaluations and intra-group cultural values and activities. There were some indications of Puerto Rican/Negro tension, primarily in terms of competition for anti-poverty funds as well as in terms of Puerto Rican reluctance to being classified together with Negroes in most Anglo-American references.

[8] In terms of the basic purposes of the project of which this study is a part it seems clear that we are dealing with a Spanish press that currently seeks to sustain a low-keyed but generally positive view of the Spanish language among its readers. Spanish language maintenance (the continued *use* of Spanish) and language loyalty (feelings of *pride and devotion* toward the language) are not frequently mentioned, and Spanish language purity, the avoidance of Anglicisms is mentioned hardly at all. However, relative to the English press the Spanish press fosters and reinforces a view of the Spanish language as being the normal and entirely desirable vehicle of communication of Hispanic New Yorkers. In addition, it relates Puerto Ricans to other Hispanic residents of the Greater New York Area and implies the need for Spanish as an *inter*-Hispanic bond, in addition to its functions *within* the Puerto Rican community alone. If Puerto Ricans in New York react to the Spanish language in the same terms and in the same key as does the Spanish press that they read we would expect general positiveness with little conscious stridency or overt advocacy.

WORLD FREQUENCY ESTIMATION
AS A MEASURE OF DEGREE
OF BILINGUALISM

Robert L. Cooper
and
Lawrence Greenfield

Word Frequency Estimation as a Measure of Degree of Bilingualism*

ROBERT L. COOPER, *Yeshiva University*
AND
LAWRENCE GREENFIELD, *Trenton State College*

PSYCHOLOGISTS have developed a number of indirect measures of degree of bilingualism or of the relative skill with which bilingual speakers employ their languages. These measures have been classified under four headings: rating scales, tests of verbal fluency, tests of flexibility and tests of dominance.[1] The rating scales most frequently used are language background questionnaires and self ratings of language use. On the other hand, tests of verbal fluency are usually either measures of speed of response to verbal stimuli or of the number of responses produced within time limits. Ervin,[2] for example, compared the speed with which bilinguals were able to name pictures in each language and Johnson[3] and Macnamara[4] contrasted the number of different words produced in each language within equal time limits. An example of a flexibility measure is Macnamara's richness of vocabulary tests in which subjects (Ss) are presented with a series of phrases in each language, of the type "he is *drunk*", and are asked to write as many words or expressions as possible that are synonymous with the word underlined in the phrase. In dominance tests the bilingual is confronted with an ambiguous stimulus and is asked to pronounce or interpret it. It is assumed that his behavior indicates the language which he controls most fully.

Recently, the possibility of using word frequency estimation as a measure of bilingual proficiency has been suggested by the finding that individuals can accurately estimate the frequencies with which words appear in print. Thus Carroll[5] reported that rankings of printed word frequencies obtained from monolingual Ss had substantial correlations with the rankings found in the Thorndike-Lorge frequency counts.

The present study was designed to determine the utility of a word frequency estimation task as a measure of degree of bilingualism. The task employed in the present study differs from the one used by Carroll in that the respondents were asked not *how often individual words appeared in print* but instead *how often they were encountered*, i.e., heard or spoken.

METHOD

Procedure

As the experimenter (E) read successive lists of 75 common Spanish and English words, S rated each item in terms of the frequency with which he heard or said it. The order in which the lists were read was randomized. In each language 15 words were selected by E to represent each of 5 domains of social interaction. These were family, education, religion, work and neighborhood. Of the 15 words in each language that were associated with each domain between 8 and 12 were translation equivalents. For example, some of the words associated with the family domain were home (*casa*), grandmother (*abuela*) and spoon (*cuchara*). The English

* The research reported in this paper was supported under Contract No. OEC-1-7-062817-0297, "The Measurement and Description of Language Dominance in Bilinguals," Joshua A. Fishman, Project Director. Data analysis was supported by a grant to the Project Director from the College Entrance Examination Board. The authors wish to thank Dr. Joshua A. Fishman for his advice and encouragement during all stages of the work reported here.

[1] John Macnamara, "The Bilingual's Linguistic Performance—a Psychological Overview," *Journal of Social Issues*, Vol. XXIII, No. 2 (April, 1967), pp. 58–77.

[2] Susan M. Ervin, "Semantic Shift in Bilingualism," *American Journal of Psychology*, Vol. LXXIV, No. 2 (June, 1961), pp. 233–241.

[3] Granville B. Johnson, Jr., "Bilingualism as Measured by a Reaction-Time Technique and the Relationship Between a Language and a Non-Language Intelligence Quotient," *Journal of Genetic Psychology*, Vol. XXXII, No. 1 (March, 1953), pp. 3–9.

[4] John Macnamara, "The Linguistic Independence of Bilinguals," *Journal of Verbal Learning and Verbal Behavior*, Vol. VI, No. 5 (October, 1967), pp. 729–736.

[5] John B. Carroll, "Quelques mesures subjectives en psycholinguistique: Fréquence des mots, significativité et qualité de traduction," *Bulletin de Psychologie*, Vol. XIX, 8–12 (Janvier, 1966), pp. 580–592.

words were drawn from the Thorndike-Lorge word frequency count[6] and the Spanish ones from Eaton's word frequency dictionary.[7] For each domain the mean frequency of occurrence of the printed words in each language was equal. The words were rated on a seven-point scale which ranged from "more than once a day" to "never." The task was individually administered along with a number of other instruments during a tape-recorded interview. The interviews, which lasted between two and four hours, were conducted in the respondent's home or in a project field office in his neighborhood. The interviewers were bilingual in Spanish and in English and conducted the interview in whatever language or combination of languages was desired by S.

Subjects

The Ss who participated in the study were residents of a four-block area in the "downtown" section of Jersey City, New Jersey. Living in this area were 431 persons of Puerto Rican background. Of those 13 or older, who constituted 50% of the population, 48 participated in the interviews in which our data were obtained.[8] Of the latter Ss, the word frequency estimation task was administered to 40.

Scoring

For each domain a mean difference was obtained between word frequency estimation ratings given for Spanish and English (S-E).

Criterion Variables

The obtained word frequency estimation difference scores were studied in relation to a number of criterion variables, including two self-rating scales, one fluency measure, and two linguistic variables.

Self ratings. In a sociolinguistic census of the community[9] Ss were asked to report 1) the degree to which they used each language at home, and 2) their speaking facility in the two languages.

Fluency. During the course of the same interview in which word frequency estimates were obtained a Word Naming task was administered.[10] This task required Ss to name within 60 seconds as many objects as possible that were found at home. Word Naming was conducted

once in Spanish and once in English with each S. Word Naming performance was scored as the number of Spanish minus the number of English words produced.

Linguistic variables. The linguistic criterion variables were (a) an Accentedness score and (b) an English Repertoire Range score. The linguistic scores were assigned by two linguists who had completed a phonetic analysis of the speech produced by the same Ss during the course of two to four hour interviews.[11] In the Accentedness scale, the Ss were rated in terms of the degree to which the phonological and syntactic structures of one language appeared to influence speech produced in the other. A seven-point scale was used on which high scores indicated Spanish influence on English speech, low scores indicated English influence on Spanish speech and intermediate scores indicated no influence of either language upon speech produced in the other. In the English Repertoire Range scale, respondents were rated in terms of the number of English speech styles which they appeared to use and the fluency with which they were employed. A six-point scale was used ranging from knowledge of only a few English words and phrases at one extreme, to the ability to employ both careful and casual English speech styles, in a maximally fluent manner, at the other.

RESULTS

Table 1 shows the correlations of the Word

[6] Edward L. Thorndike and Irving Lorge, *The Teacher's Word Book of 30,000 Words*, New York: New York Teachers College, Columbia University, 1944.

[7] Helen S. Eaton, *An English-French-German-Spanish Word Frequency Dictionary*, New York: Dover, 1961.

[8] Joshua A. Fishman, Robert L. Cooper, Roxana Ma et al., *Bilingualism in the Barrio*, Final Report: Yeshiva University, Contract No. OEC-1-7-062817-0297, U.S. Department of Health, Education, and Welfare, 1968.

[9] Joshua A. Fishman, "A Sociolinguistic Census of a Bilingual Neighborhood," in Joshua A. Fishman, Robert L. Cooper, Roxana Ma, et al., *op. cit.*, pp. 260–299 and in *American Sociological Review*, in press.

[10] Robert L. Cooper, "Two Contextualized Measures of Degree of Bilingualism," in Joshua A. Fishman, Robert L. Cooper, Roxana Ma, et al., *op. cit.*, pp. 505–524, and also in *The Modern Language Journal*, Vol. LIII, No. 3 (March, 1969), pp. 172–178.

[11] Roxana Ma and Eleanor Herasimchuk, "Linguistic Dimensions of a Bilingual Neighborhood," in Joshua A. Fishman, Robert L. Cooper, Roxana Ma, et al., *op. cit.*, pp. 636–835.

TABLE 1

CORRELATIONS BETWEEN WORD FREQUENCY ESTIMATION DIFFERENCE SCORES AND CRITERION VARIABLES BY DOMAIN

Criterion Variables	Domain				
	Family	Education	Religion	Work	Neighborhood
Self ratings of language used at home	−58**	50**	62**	45**	49**
Self rating of speaking skill	41**	28	54**	28	37*
Word Naming (home)	54**	39**	32	09	54**
Accentedness	52**	39*	51**	33*	40**
English Repertoire Range	−69**	−42**	−44**	−27	−56**

* $p < .05$
** $p < .01$

Frequency Estimation difference scores with the various criterion variables. The Word Frequency Estimation difference scores for family and neighborhood best predicted the criterion variables, being significantly correlated with all 5 of them. Significant correlation coefficients (r's) were observed between 4 of the criterion variables and the Word Frequency Estimation difference scores for the domains of education and religion, however, only 2 of the criterion variables were significantly correlated with the Word Frequency Estimation difference scores for the domain of work.

Self ratings of language use at home and Accentedness scores were each significantly correlated with Word Frequency Estimation difference scores in all 5 domains. English Repertoire Range scores were significantly correlated with Word Frequency Estimation difference scores in 4 domains, while self ratings of language skills and Word Naming difference scores were each correlated with only 3 Word Frequency Estimation difference scores.

Thus, in general, reports of greater use of Spanish than English words were associated with reports of greater facility in speaking Spanish than English, reports of more frequent use of Spanish than English at home, greater word production in Spanish than in English, predominance of Spanish accent in English and use of fewer speech styles in speaking English.

DISCUSSION

The fact that the obtained Word Frequency

Estimation difference scores for words related to family and neighborhood correlated significantly with all 5 criterion variables and that those obtained for words related to religion and education correlated significantly with 4 of the criterion variables, suggests that such difference scores are valid indices of degree of bilingualism. While the magnitude of these correlations equaled those obtained for more traditional global or noncontextual measures,[12] even higher correlations might have been found if the stimulus words had been supplied by a group of native speakers instead of by E, since it is possible that some of the words were unrepresentative of the domains in the community studied.

The Word Frequency Estimation task may fill several gaps left by other measures of degree of bilingualism. For example, since it may be possible to disguise its purpose, the Word Frequency Task might be used if S is reluctant to be truthful about his language usage or skill, whereas self-rating scales, whose purpose cannot be hidden, are unlikely to be valid. Furthermore, as it is likely that attitudes toward speed of response vary from culture to culture, Word Frequency Estimation, which is non-speed dependent, may be more valid for making cross-cultural comparisons of degree of bilingualism than are fluency measures, since the latter mea-

12 W. E. Lambert, J. Havelak, and R. C. Gardner, "Linguistic Manifestations of Bilingualism," *American Journal of Psychology*, Vol. LXXII, No. 1 (March, 1959), pp. 77–82.

sures are heavily dependent on speed of response. Also, Word Frequency Estimation seems likely to be more easily designed to reflect the existence of domain related differences in degree of bilingualism than are either flexibility or dominance tests. This fact may be of importance in studying communities in which bilingualism is characterized by diglossia, i.e.,

where differential patterns of language use exist in different domains of social interaction.[13]

[13] Joshua A. Fishman, *op. cit.*, Robert L. Cooper, *op. cit.*, and Martin Edelman, "The Contextualization of Schoolchildren's Bilingualism," in Joshua A. Fishman, *op. cit.*, pp. 525–537, Robert L. Cooper, Roxana Ma, *et al.*, *op. cit.*, pp. 525–537, and also in *The Modern Language Journal*, Vol. LIII, No. 3 (March, 1969), pp. 179–182, as well as in *The Irish Journal of Education*, Vol. II (1968), pp. 109–114.

LANGUAGE USE
IN A BILINGUAL COMMUNITY

Robert L. Cooper
and
Lawrence Greenfield

Language Use in a Bilingual Community*

ROBERT L. COOPER, *Yeshiva University*

AND

LAWRENCE GREENFIELD, *Trenton State College*

THE use of two languages for purposes of intragroup communication has been studied in relation to a variety of factors. The variables studied have often differed with respect to level of analysis, as some have pertained to individual differences among the members of the community under investigation and others to more general features of the social or sociocultural context in which linguistic behavior takes place. As yet, no systematic attempt has been made to integrate these different levels of description.

Among the individual characteristics which have been found helpful in describing language use in a bilingual community are the linguistic proficiency, age, sex, occupation and education of the speaker and listener.[1] For example, in a study of language use in Paraguay, Rubin found that in intimate conversation bilingual speakers of Spanish and Guarani tended to choose the language in which they were most proficient, namely, the first language learned. She also found that in choosing a language, the speaker would often estimate the linguistic ability of the listener, as in the case of a doctor who said that he used the language in which he thought his patients were most proficient.[2] Similar behavior was observed by Herman[3] who reported that in the absence of external pressures to use Hebrew, immigrants to Israel most often used the language in which they were most proficient, namely, the "mother" tongue.

One construct pertaining to the socio-cultural context of speech events which has been employed in the study of this problem is that of social domain.[4] According to Fishman, social domains identify the major spheres of activity in a culture, e.g., familial, religious, educational, and are defined by the co-occurrence of a cluster of congruent role relationships, topics, and locales of communication. For example, in the U.S. the domain of education would be composed of interactions among occupants of specific statuses, e.g., teacher-student, student-stu-

* The research reported herein was supported under DHEW Contract No. OEC-1-7-062817-0297, "The Measurement and Description of Language Dominance in Bilinguals," Joshua A. Fishman, Project Director. Data analysis was made possible by a grant to the Project Director by the College Entrance Examination Board. The authors wish to thank Dr. Joshua A. Fishman for his advice and encouragement during all stages of the work reported here.

[1] Clifford Geertz, "Linguistic Etiquette," in *The Religion of Java*, Glencoe, Illinois: Free Press, 1960, pp. 248-260, Simon N. Herman, "Explorations in the Social Psychology of Language Choice," *Human Relations*, Vol. XIV, No. 2 (May, 1961), pp. 149-164, and Joan Rubin, "Bilingualism in Paraguay," *Anthropological Linguistics*, Vol. IV, No. 1 (1962), pp. 52-58. Each of these three studies is also included in Joshua A. Fishman, editor, *Readings in the Sociology of Language*, The Hague: Mouton, 1968.

[2] Joan Rubin, *op. cit.*

[3] Simon N. Herman, *op. cit.*

[4] Joshua A. Fishman, "Language Maintenance and Language Shift as Fields of Inquiry," *Linguistics*, Vol. IX (November, 1964), pp. 32-70, Joshua A. Fishman, *Language Loyalty in the U.S.*, The Hague: Mouton, 1966, J. R. Reimen, "Esquisse d'une situation plurlingue, le Luxembourg." *Linguistique*, No. 2 (1965), pp. 89-102, and Joshua A. Fishman, "Sociolinguistic Perspective on the Study of Bilingualism," *Linguistics*, Vol. XXXIX (1968), pp. 21-49.

dent; during specified hours, e.g., school hours; and in specified locales, e.g., classroom, principal's office.

Using this concept, Fishman has distinguished between stable bilingual situations which are characterized by language maintenance and unstable ones which are characterized by language shift. Under conditions of stable bilingualism, the "mother" and "other" tongues are reserved for different domains of life in the community, the former typically being used in the domains of family and friendship and the latter being used in domains such as education and employment. Under conditions of unstable intra-group bilingualism, on the other hand, domain separation in language use vanishes as the "mother" tongue becomes displaced by the "other" tongue in the family and friendship domains. In general, unstable intragroup bilingualism has occurred in cases of immigrant languages in the context of rapid industrialization, urbanization, or other rapid social change, as for example, in the cases of Yiddish, Ukrainian, Hungarian and German in the United States.[5]

Examples of more stable intragroup bilingual situations, or diglossia,[6] have been described by Barker, Fishman, and Rubin.[7]

Recent studies have suggested the possibility that in contrast to most immigrant languages in the United States, Spanish in the Puerto Rican community of New York is being maintained in a relatively stable manner.[8] One factor that has been cited in favor of such a possibility is that unlike most of the former immigrant groups in the United States, Puerto Ricans in New York continue to maintain close physical contact with their homeland.

In the present investigation language use was studied among bilingual Puerto Ricans in an urben community near New York City. Data was gathered pertaining to each of five hypothesized domains of social interaction, namely, family, neighborhood, religion, education, and work. Data was also gathered pertaining to the linguistic abilities of interlocutors. It was hypothesized that if Spanish was preferred over English in at least some domains, especially that of the home, evidence for language maintenance would be provided. On the other hand, if it was found that English is preferred in all domains of

life, the hypothesis of language shift would be supported.

METHOD

Procedure

Language use. The data on language use was collected by means of individual interviews in which respondents were asked to rate what proportion of their talk at school, at work, in the neighborhood, at church and at home was in Spanish, when speaking to other Puerto Ricans who knew both languages. For example, respondents were asked to rate the degree to which they used Spanish with parents, grandparents, aunts and uncles and other older relatives, or with brothers and sisters and other relatives of the same age, or with children and grandchildren and other younger relatives at home. In all domains but that of education, subjects (*S*s) were asked to rate their usage with interlocutors who were younger, older and of the same age as themselves. Age of interlocutor was not asked in connection with usage in the education domain since only the young *S*s were attending school.

Ratings were made on an 11-point scale, with speaking only in Spanish at one extreme (10) and speaking only in English at the other (0). The Spanish Usage Rating questions were asked during the course of an interview in which a number of other instruments were also administered. The interviews were held in the respondent's home or in a field office in his neighborhood and lasted from between two to four hours. The interviewers were bilingual and the

[5] Joshua A. Fishman, "Sociolinguistic Perspective on the Study of Bilingualism," *Linguistics*, Vol. XXXIX (1968), pp. 21–49.

[6] Charles A. Ferguson, "Diglossia," *Word*, Vol. XV, No. 2 (1959), pp. 325–340.

[7] George C. Barker, "Social Function of Language in a Mexican-American Community," *Acta Americana*, Vol. V, No 3 (July/September, 1947), pp. 185–202, Joshua A. Fishman, *Language Loyalty in the U.S.*, The Hague: Mouton, 1966 and Joan Rubin, *op. cit.*

[8] Elena Padilla, *Up from Puerto Rico*, New York: Columbia University, 1958, Clarence Ollson Senior, *The Puerto Ricans*, Chicago: Quadrangle, 1965 and Gerard Hoffman, "Puerto Ricans in New York: A Language-Related Ethnographic Summary," in Joshua A. Fishman, Robert L. Cooper, Roxana Ma, *et. al.*, *Bilingualism in the Barrio*, Final Report: Yeshiva University, Contract No. OEC-1-7-062817-0297. U.S. Department of Health, Education, and Welfare, 1968, pp. 20–76.

language of the interview was the language or combination of languages that seemed to be most acceptable to the respondent.

Linguistic variables. A phonetic analysis of representative portions of the respondent's speech as recorded during the interview was completed by Ma and Herasimchuk.[9] As a by-product of their work, they developed two measures of linguistic proficiency on which they rated all respondents. One of these measures is referred to as the Spanish-English Accent Scale and the other, as the English Repertoire Range scale. In the first of these measures, the respondents were rated in terms of the degree to which the phonological and syntactic structures of one language appeared to influence speech produced in the other. A 7-point scale was used, on which high scores indicated Spanish influence on English speech, low scores indicated English influence on Spanish speech and scores in between indicated no influence of either language on speech produced in the other. In the second measure, respondents were rated in terms of the number of English speech styles which they appeared to use and the fluency with which these were employed. A 6-point scale was used ranging from knowledge of only a few words and phrases at one extreme, to the ability to employ both careful and casual speech styles, in a maximally proficient manner, at the other.

Scores on these "linguistic scales" were obtained for each speaker who responded to the Spanish Usage Rating questions.

Demographic variables. Information on certain demographic variables was obtained from a language census of the community which was conducted by Fishman[10] a few weeks before the interviews on which the current study is based were given. The demographic variables studied in relation to language use were: sex, age, birthplace, occupation, education and years in the United States.

Subjects

The Ss who participated in the study were residents of a four-block area in the "downtown" section of Jersey City, New Jersey. Living in this area were 431 persons of Puerto Rican background. Of those 13 or older, who constituted 50% of the population, 48 participated in the interviews in which our data was

obtained. Of the latter Ss, 38 were asked the Spanish Usage Rating questions.

For purposes of data analysis, the Ss were divided into three subgroups: 1) the 9 Ss who were attending school and who thus responded to the school items; 2) the 21 Ss who were working[11] and who were therefore able to answer the work items; and 3) the 9 remaining Ss who neither worked nor went to school and so were not asked questions about language usage in these domains. All Ss responded to questions about usage at home and in the neighborhood and almost all of them responded to questions about usage in church.

The Ss who responded to educational items were younger than those in the other two groups, as the School group included Ss who ranged in age from 13–19, while the other groups included Ss who ranged in age from 19–65. For the most part, those in the School group were also born in the United States or arrived here by the average age of 3, while most of those in the two older groups were born in Puerto Rico. These older Ss arrived in the United States at a mean age of 30. Furthermore, the three groups were also found to differ in scores obtained on the Spanish-English Accent scale, $F(2, 36) = 13.6$ (p < .01) as well as on the English Repertoire Range scale, $F(2, 36) = 3.86$ (p < .05). These differences indicated that the younger or School group was more proficient in English than either of the two older groups.

Data Analysis

For each S, mean Spanish usage ratings were computed for each domain, and the resulting domain scores were correlated with the linguistic and demographic variables which have been

---

[9] Roxana Ma and Eleanor Herasimchuk, "Linguistic Dimensions of a Bilingual Neighborhood," in Joshua A. Fishman, Robert L. Cooper, Roxana Ma, *et al.*, *Bilingualism in the Barrio,* Final Report: Yeshiva University, Contract No. OEC-1-7-062817-0297, U.S. Department of Health, Education, and Welfare, 1968, pp. 636–835.

[10] Joshua A. Fishman, "A Sociolinguistic Census of a Bilingual Neighborhood," in Joshua A. Fishman, Robert L. Cooper, Roxana Ma, *et. al.*, *Bilingualism in the Barrio,* Final Report: Yeshiva University, Contract No. OEC-1-062817-0297, U.S. Department of Health, Education, and Welfare, 1968, pp. 260–299 and in the *American Journal of Sociology,* in press.

[11] One S worked and attended school and was therefore included in both School and Work groups.

TABLE 1

PEARSON-PRODUCT MOMENT CORRELATIONS (r) OBTAINED BETWEEN 5 DOMAIN SCORES IN SPANISH USAGE RATING
AND VARIOUS DEMOGRAPHIC AND LINGUISTIC VARIABLES

	Domain				
	Family	Neighborhood	Religion	Education	Work
Sex	00	−02	−25	−29	−14
Age	32	52**	43*	52	−05
Birthplace	29	50**	55**	−50	21
Occupation	−30	−35*	−39*	00	−18
Education	−20	−13	−23	−51	03
No. years in U.S.	−30	−31	−29	38	-37
Spanish-English Accent Scale	59**	61**	61**	03	12
English Repertoire Range Scale	−37*	−39*	−45**	−19	−16

* p<.05
** p<.01

described. In addition, the domain scores were subjected to three analysis of variance, one for each subgroup. In each domain, three additional scores were computed for each S, namely, his mean usage ratings for interlocutors who were older, the same age, and younger than himself. The interlocutor scores, when totalled across for the domains of family, neighborhood, and religion, were also subjected to analysis of variance.

RESULTS

Table 1 shows the correlations of the six demographic and two linguistic variables with the Spanish usage ratings in each of five domains. Of the demographic variables age and birthplace correlated positively and occupation negatively with Spanish Usage Ratings in region and neighborhood. Thus, the respondents who said they used more Spanish in these domains were older, more often born in Puerto Rico, and of a lower occupational status than those who said they used less Spanish.

None of the demographic variables correlated significantly with Spanish Usage Ratings for family, employment or education. Noteworthy, however, is the fact that the correlations of the demographic variables with ratings for family were consistently similar in directions to the correlations of these variables with ratings for religion and neighborhood.

The Spanish-English Accent scale scores correlated positively with ratings of Spanish usage in three of the five domains, namely, family, neighborhood and religion. These correlations were of the order r=.60. Furthermore, negative correlations were found between ratings of amount of Spanish use in these domains and position on the English Repertoire Range scale (r= −.37 to r= −.45). Thus, the less Spanish-accented a S's English and the more styles he commanded with fluency in English, the less likely he was to claim Spanish in the domains of family, neighborhood and religion.

The absence of significant correlations between the rating of Spanish usage in the work and educational domains and any of the linguistic and demographic variables is probably due to the fact that the Ss who responded to questions for these domains were restricted in range of age (since those who responded to education were below 19 years of age, while those who responded to work were above this age). In addition, the number of Ss included in these domains was relatively small, i.e., N=9 in educa-

TABLE 2

SPANISH USAGE RATINGS BY GROUP AND DOMAIN

Group	Domain				
	Family	Neigh-borhood	Religion	Education	Work
School	5.2	5.3	4.38	3.01	NR
Work	8.16	7.76	7.19	NR	7.65
Others	6.9	8.5	6.8	NR	NR

NR = No response.

tion and N = 21 in work. In the remaining domains, on the other hand, responses were obtained from almost all of the Ss.

Table 2 shows the mean ratings in the five domains which were obtained for each of the three subgroups, namely, the School group, the Work group and the No School/No Work group (others).

Whereas for the School group significant differences between domains were obtained in ratings of Spanish usage, F(3, 17) = 3.23 (p <.05), no such differences between domains were found for the remaining groups. Using *t* tests, it was found that the School group reported that they used significantly less Spanish in the domain of education than in the family or neighborhood domains. The remaining intra-group differences in reported usage were not found to be significant.

When similar comparisons were made, with age of interlocutor controlled, somewhat different results were found. Table 3 shows for each of the three subgroups the mean Spanish ratings obtained for Older, Younger and Same age interlocutors in each of the five domains. It was reported by all three groups that they used more Spanish with older people than with younger people. The School group reported that it used the least amount of Spanish with people of the same age, next-to-least amount with younger and most Spanish with older people. The two older groups reported that they used most Spanish with older people, next-to-most with people of the same age and least with younger people. Similar trends were found in all domains for which data were obtained.

Of particular importance is the finding that in talking to people of the same age, the School group reported that they used mostly English in all domains including family. Thus, when age of listener was controlled, no substantial differences in amount of Spanish used were noted between domains.

The interlocutor scores, when combined across the domains of family, religion, neighborhood (See Table 4) were subjected to analysis of variance, which as Table 5 shows, yielded significant between group effect, F(2, 36) = 9.2 (p <.01), a significant Age of Interlocutor effect F(2, 36) = 30.6 (p <.01), and a significant Group x Age of Interlocutor interaction, F(4, 72) = 9.2 (p <.01). The results indicate that less

TABLE 3

SPANISH USAGE RATINGS BY DOMAIN, AGE OF INTERLOCUTOR AND GROUP

Groups	Age of Interlocutor	Domain				
		Family	Neighborhood	Religion	Education	Work
School n=9	Older	6.8	8.1	7.3	NR	NR
	Same	3.5	2.6	3.3	3.0	NR
	Younger	5.7	4.9	4.3	NR	NR
Work n=21	Older	8.7	8.8	9.9	NR	8.6
	Same	8.1	7.9	9.2	NR	7.8
	Younger	7.4	7.2	6.4	NR	7.1
Others n=9	Older	8.1	9.6	8.2	NR	NR
	Same	7.4	8.2	8.0	NR	NR
	Younger	5.1	7.7	6.8	NR	NR

NR = No response.

Spanish was used by the School group than by the two older groups, more Spanish was used with older than with younger interlocutors, and the difference in amount of Spanish used by the School group in talking to older and same age interlocutors was larger than the corresponding differences in amount of Spanish used by the two non-school groups in talking to these types of interlocutors.

DISCUSSION

Since in talking to other bilinguals, younger members of the community both used and received less Spanish than older people, and since younger people were also relatively more proficient in English than older people, it would seem that the linguistic proficiency of the speaker and interlocutor each played a role in determining language use in this community. Specifically, speakers who were dominant in English used it more often than those who were more proficient in Spanish. Similarly, interlocutors who were dominant in English tended to receive it more often than those who were dominant in Spanish.

The fact that the School group showed a slight tendency to use more Spanish with younger people, i.e., people below age 13, than with people of the same age, i.e., between the ages 13–19, would seem to be in accord with these trends, since it is likely that children below 13 years of age are less proficient in English than those between the ages of 13–19. This possibility

TABLE 4

SPANISH USAGE RATINGS BY GROUP AND AGE OF INTERLOCUTOR*

Group	Age of Interlocutor			
	Older	Same	Younger	Total
School (n=9)	7.4	2.8	4.9	5.0
Work (n=21)	9.0	8.3	6.9	8.1
Others (n=9)	8.6	7.7	6.6	7.7
Total	8.5	6.9	6.4	7.3

* Based on scores in Family, Neighborhood and Religion.

TABLE 5

ANALYSIS OF VARIANCE OF SPANISH USAGE RATING SCORES BY GROUP AND AGE OF INTERLOCUTOR

Source	Sums of Squares	df	Mean Square	Fisher's Ratio*
Between Groups	52,226	38		
(A) Groups	17,733	2	8,866.5	9.26**
Ss w Groups	34,493	36	95.8	
Within Groups	27,860	78		
(B) Age of Interlocutor	9,973	2	4,986.5	30.6**
A×B	6,134	4	1,533.2	9.2**
B×Ss w Groups	11,753	72	163.2	
Total	80,086	116		

* The mean square for the effect being tested divided by the appropriate error variance term.
** $p < .01$.

seems likely, since Spanish is the first language learned by these youngsters.

No evidence for the *independent* influence of socio-cultural context upon language use was found inasmuch as no differences in ratings of Spanish usage appeared between domains *when differences in age of interlocutor were controlled.* Such a conclusion received support from a recent study by Fishman and Greenfield,[12] who found that a group of bilingual Puerto Rican teenagers in New York reported that although they would use more Spanish with parents, than with friends, priests, teachers, and employers, they also reported that they would use the same amount of Spanish with each of these people regardless of differences in the topic or place in which the conversation occurred. The differences obtained between these interlocutors was probably due to the fact that parents were less proficient in English than the others. Thus, when language use is studied in relation to difference in the socio-cultural context in which communication takes place, it must also be studied in relation to individual differences in

[12] Lawrence Greenfield and Joshua A. Fishman. "Situational Measures of Language Use in Relation to Person, Place, and Topic among Puerto Rican Bilinguals," in Joshua A. Fishman, Robert L. Cooper, Roxana Ma, *et. al.*, *Bilingualism in the Barrio*, Final Report: Yeshiva University, Contract No. OEC-1-7-062817-0297, U.S. Department of Health, Education, and Welfare, 1968, pp. 430–458.

linguistic ability. If the former is more significantly related to language use then diglossia may be said to obtain. If the latter is the major determinant of usage then language shift may be said to be taking place.

The finding that young people, in speaking among themselves, use English more often than Spanish in all domains, including family, suggests that bilingualism in the community under study is characterized by language shift. Moreover, the finding that these youngsters use Spanish primarily in talking to older members of the community suggests that it is used by these Ss principally as a tool for communicating with people who are less proficient in English than themselves. Furthermore, the fact that the two non-school groups, who speak primarily in Spanish, used somewhat more English with younger than with older people would seem to exclude the possibility that the use of English among the young is merely a form of teenage deviation from adult standards and suggests instead that it is accepted among adults as well. Therefore, it might be expected that as proficiency in English increases among the members of the community, less Spanish will be used in all domains of life including family. Thus, with respect to the phenomenon of language maintenance, the Puerto Ricans in the community studied would seem to be headed in the same direction as previous immigrant groups in the United States, as they appear to be undergoing displacement of the "mother" tongue by English in all domains of life.

TWO CONTEXTUALIZED MEASURES
OF DEGREE OF BILINGUALISM

Robert L. Cooper

Two Contextualized Measures of Degree of Bilingualism*

ROBERT L. COOPER, *Yeshiva University*

TRADITIONAL measures of degree of bilingualism typically yield a single difference score, computed by subtracting a score obtained in one language from a score obtained in another. A respondent whose performance or score is the same in each language is said to be a "balanced" bilingual, *i.e.*, he is said to be equally skilled in two languages with respect to that aspect of linguistic performance required by the task.[1] Lambert,[2] for example, has compared the speed with which bilinguals can respond to directions given in each language, and Johnson[3] and Macnamara[4] have contrasted the number of different words in each language produced within equal time limits.

The use of the resulting difference scores to express degree of bilingualism may be insufficiently revealing of relative proficiency inasmuch as bilingual speakers may use each language under socially differentiated circumstances.[5] Thus, for example, language A may be used more often than language B at home but less often than B at school or at work.[6] The techniques for the measurement of degree of bilingualism which are described in this paper

can be distinguished from the traditional ones in being differentiated with respect to such

* The research reported in this paper was supported by a grant from the U.S. Office of Education, Contract No OEC-1-7-062817-0297, "The Measurement and Description of Language Dominance in Bilinguals." Data analysis was made possible by a grant from the College Entrance Examination Board. The author wishes to thank Dr Joshua A. Fishman for his advice and encouragement during all stages of the work reported here and Mr. Lawrence Greenfield for his comments on an earlier draft of this paper

[1] John Macnamara, "How Can One Measure the Extent of a Person's Bilingual Proficiency?" in *Preprints*, International Seminar on the Description and Measurement of Bilingualism, Ottawa: Canadian National Commission for UNESCO, 1967, pp. 68–90.

[2] Wallace E. Lambert, "Measurement of the Linguistic Dominance of Bilinguals," *Journal of Abnormal and Social Psychology*, Vol. L, No. 2 (March, 1955), pp. 197–200.

[3] Granville B. Johnson, Jr., "Bilingualism as Measured by a Reaction-Time Technique and the Relationship Between a Language and a Non-Language Intelligent Quotient," *Journal of Genetic Psychology*, Vol. XXXII, No. 1 (March, 1953), pp. 3–9.

[4] John Macnamara, "The Linguistic Independence of Bilinguals," *Journal of Verbal Learning and Verbal Behavior*, Vol. VI, No. 5 (October, 1967), pp. 729–736.

[5] Johsua A. Fishman, "Who Speaks What Language to Whom and When?" *Linguistique*, Vol. I, No. 2 (1965), pp

societal domains or contexts. The present techniques were designed to yield a set of scores in order to reveal those differences in bilingual proficiency which might be associated with the differential societal usage of two languages. Some evidence for the validity of such scores as well as the description they give of a specific bilingual community are presented in this report.

METHOD

Two techniques, word naming and word association, were adapted for use with Puerto Rican bilinguals living in Greater New York. The techniques yielded Spanish and English scores corresponding to five hypothesized societal domains. These were family, neighborhood, religion, education, and work.

Techniques

On the word naming task, subjects (Ss) were asked to name, in one minute, as many different words referring to a specified context as they could. This was done in each language for each domain. For family, they were asked to name things seen or found in a kitchen; for neighborhood, things seen or found in a neighborhood; for religion, things seen or found in a church; for education, subjects taught in schools; and for work, jobs, occupations, or professions. Responses were elicited for all five domains in one language followed by all five domains in the other language. The language in which responses were first given was randomly chosen for each S. The order of domains was kept the same for all Ss, this being family, neighborhood, religion, education, and work. Directions were of the order: "Tell me as many English (Spanish) words as you can that name things you can see or find in a kitchen—your kitchen or any other kitchen. Words like salt (sal), spoon (cuchara), rice (arroz)." Two practice runs were given, one in English before the five domains were presented in English, and one in Spanish before the domains were presented in Spanish. In the trial runs, Ss were asked to name as many different words as possible without restriction.

On the word association task, Ss were asked to give, within one-minute periods, as many continuous associations as possible to the following English and Spanish stimulus words:

factory, school, church, street, home, factoría, escuela, iglesia, calle, and casa. Responses were restricted to the language of the stimulus word. Directions were of the order: "Tell me as many English (Spanish) words as come to mind when you hear the word home (casa)." Before the presentation of the first domain stimulus word, Ss were asked to respond to a series of practice stimuli until it was clear that they understood the task. The order in which the domains were presented was work, education, religion, neighborhood, and family. The order in which the language response was elicited from each S was always opposite to that followed on the word naming task.

Both tasks were individually administered along with a number of other instruments during a tape-recorded interview. The interviews, which lasted between two and four hours, were conducted in the respondent's home or in a field office in his neighborhood. More than one session was sometimes required to complete the interview. The word naming task always preceded the word association task. Between the administration of the two, a ten-minute interval elapsed, during which time Ss were asked to read some Spanish and English materials. Interviewers were bilingual in Spanish and in English and gave instructions in whichever language or combination of languages the respondent preferred.

Subjects

The tasks were administered as part of an intensive study of Spanish-English bilingualism within a four-block Puerto Rican area of the "downtown" section of Jersey City.[7] Living there were 431 persons of Puerto Rican background who comprised 90 households. Half of this group consisted of children under the age of 13. Of those who were 13 or older, over one-

67-88 and "Sociolinguistic Perspective on the Study of Bilingualism," Linguistics, Vol. XXXIX (1968), pp. 21-49.

[6] Charles A. Ferguson, "Diglossia," Word, Vol. XV, No. 2 (1959), pp. 325-340 and Joan Rubin, "Bilingualism in Paraguay," Anthropological Linguistics, Vol. IV, No. 1 (1962), pp. 52-58, also included in Joshua A. Fishman, editor, Readings in the Sociology of Language, The Hague, Mouton, 1962.

[7] Joshua A. Fishman, Robert L. Cooper, Roxana Ma, et al., Bilingualism in the Barrio, Final Report: Yeshiva University, Contract No. OEC-1-7-062817-0297, U.S. Department of Health, Education, and Welfare, 1968.

fifth ($N=48$) voluntarily participated in interviews of which the reported tasks formed a part.
An attempt was made to obtain both male and
female respondents who would represent the
range of ages of those 13 or older and the range
of occupational and educational backgrounds
to be found in that community. Not all respondents completed all portions of the interview. The word naming task was administered
to 38 Ss and the word association task to 29 Ss.
All those who took the word association task
also took the word naming task.

Scoring

The taped responses were orthographically
transcribed and the number of each S's different
responses for each domain-language combination was counted for each task. Thus, Ss who
completed all subtests received 10 scores on
each of the two tasks.

Criterion Variables

Performance on the word naming and word
association tasks was studied in relation to six
criterion variables. These are described below.
The first two were obtained from a language
census of the community.[8] The census variables
were demographic characteristics that were
expected to be positively related to degree of
exposure to English. The third and fourth
variables were global ratings of linguistic
performance. The ratings were made by the
linguists who had performed a phonetic analysis
of representative portions of each respondent's
speech recorded during the extended interview.[9]
The fifth and sixth variables were listening
comprehension scores obtained from a technique employing tape-recorded, naturalistic
conversations between bilingual Puerto Ricans
in New York.[10]

The six criterion variables were as follows:
1. Number of years on the mainland. Recency
of arrival was rated on a 7-point scale with "less
than one year" at one extreme and "U.S. born"
at the other.
2. Occupation. Occupational status was
rated on a 4-point scale ranging from "operative, service worker, laborer, or usually unemployed" to "professional, manager, or college
student." Housewives and students enrolled in
grades below the college level were not rated.

3. Accentedness. Respondents were rated in
terms of the degree to which the phonological
and syntactic structures of one language appeared to influence speech produced in the
other. A 7-point scale was used on which high
scores indicated Spanish influence upon English
speech, low scores indicated English influence
upon Spanish speech, and scores in between
indicated maximum language distance, or no
influence by either language upon speech produced in the other.
4. English repertoire range. Based on the
notion of verbal repertoire,[11] respondents were
globally rated in terms of the number of
English speech styles which they appeared to
use and the fluency with which these were employed. A six-point scale was used, ranging from
knowledge of only a few words and phrases, at
one extreme, to the ability to employ both
careful and casual speech styles, in a maximally
fluent manner, at the other.
5. Listening comprehension (English). Subjects were assessed with respect to their ability
to understand a taped conversation among
four Puerto Rican college students who were
engaged in a "bull session" about the political
status of Puerto Rico. This conversation was
almost entirely in rapid, excited English.
6. Listening comprehension (Spanish and
English). Subjects were assessed with respect
to their ability to understand a taped conversation between a parish priest and a parishioner
who had come to the rectory to ask for a letter
of recommendation. Each speaker used both
English and Spanish. For each respondant, the
percentage of correct responses to items testing

[8] Joshua A. Fishman, "A Sociological Census of a
Bilingual Neighborhood," in Joshua A. Fishman, Robert L.
Cooper, Roxana Ma, *et al., op. cit.,* pp. 260–299 and in the
American Journal of Sociology, in press.
[9] Roxana Ma and Eleanor Herasimchuk, "Linguistic
Dimensions of a Bilingual Neighborhood," in Joshua A.
Fishman, Robert L. Cooper, Roxana Ma, *et al., op. cit.,*
pp. 636–835.
[10] Robert L. Cooper, Barbara Fowles, and Abraham
Givner, "Listening Comprehension in a Bilingual Com-
munity," in Joshua A. Fishman, Robert L. Cooper,
Roxana Ma, *et al., op. cit.,* pp. 577–597 and also in *The
Modern Language Journal,* Vol. LIII, No. 4 (April, 1969),
forthcoming.
[11] John L. Gumperz, "Linguistic and Social Interaction
in Two Communities," *American Anthropologist,* Vol.
LXVI, No. 6, Part 2 (December, 1964), pp. 137–153.

TABLE 1

CORRELATIONS BETWEEN DIFFERENCE SCORES AND CRITERION VARIABLES

Difference Score				Criterion		
	Years in the United States	Occupation	English Repertoire Range	Listening Comprehension (English)	Listening Comprehension (Spanish-English)	Accentedness
Word Naming						
Family	−.57**	−.52*	−.54**	−.33	.47**	.53**
Neighborhood	−.34*	−.26	−.45**	−.23	.48**	.50**
Religion	−.41*	−.63**	−.23	−.39*	.15	.42**
Education	−.41*	−.70**	−.52**	−.63**	.31	.57**
Work	−.17	−.45*	−.34*	−.33	.14	.49**
Word Association						
Family	−.31	.00	−.29	−.48*	.36	.20
Neighborhood	−.19	−.56**	−.52**	−.35	.47*	.25
Religion	.10	−.59*	−.44*	.11	.32	.30
Education	.17	−.24	−.33	−.28	.28	.09
Work	−.05	−.05	−.30	−.14	.11	.32

* $p<.05$
** $p<.01$

comprehension of the English portions of the conversation was subtracted from the percentage of correct responses to items testing comprehension of the Spanish portions. Thus, positive difference scores indicated that the respondent understood more of the Spanish portions than of the English portions and negative difference scores indicated the reverse.

Data Analysis

Each S's English domain scores were subtracted from the corresponding Spanish domain scores on the word naming and word association tasks. Intercorrelations were obtained between the resulting 10 difference scores and the criterion scores. Since positive difference scores represented greater fluency in Spanish than in English, evidence for the validity of the techniques would be obtained if positive correlations were observed between the difference scores and those criterion variables on which high or positive scores reflected greater relative proficiency in Spanish (the accentedness scale and the listening comprehension difference score). Similarly, evidence for the validity of the techniques would be obtained if negative correlations were observed between the difference scores and those criterion variables

reflecting proficiency in English (the English repertoire range scale and the English listening comprehension score) and between the difference scores and the two demographic variables which reflected degree of exposure to English. As a complement to the correlation analysis, an analysis of variance was performed for the ten word naming scores, and one was performed for the 10 word association scores as well. For the analyses of variance, Ss were classified in terms of six demographic subgroups based on the intersection of three age groups (13–18, 19–34, and 35 and above) with two groups differing in length of residence on the mainland (less than 11 years, more than 11 years). Support for the validity of the techniques would be found if these subgroups displayed different degrees of bilingualism and if these differences varied by domain.

RESULTS

Table 1 presents the correlations obtained between the criterion variables and the word naming and word association difference scores. In general, the word naming difference scores were significantly correlated with the criterion variables, and in the expected direction, whereas the word association difference scores

TABLE 2

INTERCORRELATIONS BETWEEN WORD NAMING AND WORD ASSOCIATION DIFFERENCE SCORES

Variable	1	2	3	4	5	6	7	8	9	10
1. WN-Family	—	.61	.57	.63	.42	.23	.49	.46	.19	.09
2. WN-Neighborhood		—	.43	.51	.26	.29	.42	.32	.26	.41
3. WN-Religion			—	.62	.55	.34	.42	.20	.26	.19
4. WN-Education				—	.59	.40	.53	.20	.54	.42
5. WN-Work					—	.10	.50	.43	.36	.42
6. WA-Family						—	.40	.07	.45	.31
7. WA-Neighborhood							—	.43	.27	.18
8. WA-Religion								—	.20	.15
9. WA-Education									—	.43
10. WA-Work										—

were not. Whereas 21 of 30 coefficients were statistically significant for the word naming difference scores, only 6 of the 30 word association coefficients reached statistical significance. Word naming coefficients ranged from .17 to .70 with the median coefficient at .44. Highest word naming coefficients were obtained with the occupational status scale. The fewest significant word naming coefficients were obtained with the two listening comprehension scores. Performance on each listening comprehension test was predicted by a different set of word naming difference scores. The education and religion difference scores were significantly correlated with the scores which measured comprehension of the college students' conversations in English ($p < .01$ and $< .05$, respectively), whereas the family and neighborhood difference scores were significantly correlated with the scores which measured comprehension of the Spanish and English conversation in a parish rectory ($p < .01$). Of the word naming difference scores, the home and education scores yielded statistically significant correlations with the greatest number of criterion variables (5 of 6), and the work scores yielded significant correlations with the fewest.

Intercorrelations between the word naming and word association difference scores are presented in Table 2. For the intercorrelations of word naming difference scores with each other, coefficients ranged from .26 to .63 with a median of .56. The range for the correlations of word association difference scores with each other was from .07 to .45 with a median of .29.

The analysis of variance of the English and

Spanish word naming scores is presented in Table 3. No difference was observed between the total number of English and Spanish words (all domains combined) given by the respondents as a total group. However, a significant interaction was observed between language and domain, indicating that there was signifi-

TABLE 3

ANALYSIS OF VARIANCE OF WORD NAMING SCORES

Source	df	ms	F
Between subjects	37		
Age (C)	2	245.53	1.33
Years in U. S. (D)	1	530.02	2.88
CD	2	366.49	1.99
Error (b)	32	183.85	
Within subjects	316		
Domain (A)	4	999.71	92.74**
Language (B)	1	18.08	.50
AB	4	14.92	2.55*
AC	8	19.38	1.80
AD	4	6.68	.62
BC	2	25.95	.72
BD	1	349.98	9.65**
ABC	8	11.99	2.05*
ABD	4	21.65	3.71**
ACD	8	24.78	2.30*
BCD	2	80.67	2.23
ABCD	8	15.17	2.60*
Error (w)	262		
Error₁ (w)	117	10.78	
Error₂ (w)	29	36.25	
Error₃ (w)	116	5.84	
Total	353		

* $p < .05$
** $p < .01$

TABLE 4

MEAN WORD NAMING SCORES OF SIX DEMOGRAPHIC SUBGROUPS

Subgroup	N	Age	Years in U. S.	Language	Family	Neighborhood	Religion	Education	Work
I	6	13–18	<11	Eng	11.66**	11.83	6.50*	10.00	8.00
				Span	18.83	13.83	9.66	12.16	9.50
II	6	13–18	>11	Eng	24.50**	21.00**	14.00	16.33**	15.16
				Span	20.16	16.50	12.83	8.16	12.83
III	7	19–34	<11	Eng	15.71*	13.00	6.71**	8.14*	7.86
				Span	18.29	12.43	10.71	11.14	9.29
IV	7	19–34	>11	Eng	16.57	12.86	11.00	8.00	8.14
				Span	16.43	10.57	9.00	6.86	8.29
V	4	35+	<11	Eng	12.67**	5.33**	3.00	4.00	3.50
				Span	17.67	13.33	5.50	2.33	4.50
VI	8	35+	>11	Eng	20.25	13.57	7.86	10.83	7.66**
				Span	18.75	13.29	9.86	11.33	12.33

* $p < .05$ for difference between means of English and Spanish domain scores (t test).
** $p < .01$ for difference between means of English and Spanish domain scores (t test).

cant differences between average English and Spanish scores for some domains. To describe the performance of the group as a whole would be misleading, however, inasmuch as significant subgroup differences were observed. There was, for example, a significant interaction between language and length of residence in the United States. T tests indicated that those respondents with the shorter residency had a higher average total score in Spanish than in English ($p < .01$) whereas there was no significant difference between the average total language scores for those respondents with the longer residency. More importantly a significant four-way interaction was obtained. This indicated that the six subgroups varied with respect to the relationships between English and Spanish average scores as observed over the five domains. That is to say, relative proficiency varied as a function of domain, and the pattern of this variation, the dominance configuration,[12] varied from subgroup to subgroup. Note, however, that there was no significant interaction between language, age, and recency of arrival. Thus, the six subgroups cannot be said to differ with respect to their relative proficiency in terms of *total* English and

Spanish scores. However, they can be said to differ with respect to the pattern of language dominance as exhibited by domain.

The pattern of dominance as it varied from subgroup to subgroup can be seen in Table 4, which presents the average English and Spanish word naming scores for each of the six subgroups. For example, subgroup II, which consisted of school age respondents who had received their formal education via the medium of English, showed a significantly higher education score in English than in Spanish ($p < .01$), whereas subgroup I, which consisted of school age respondents who had received their education via both languages, showed no significant difference between their average language scores for that domain. In the word naming task there was one domain for which more than two subgroups exhibited a significant difference between English and Spanish means. This was the domain of family, for which three of the four significant differences favored Spanish. Of the three domains for which two subgroups exhibited significant differences between language means, in only one did both differences

[12] Joshua A. Fishman, "Who Speaks What Language to Whom and When?" *Linguistique*, No. 2 (1965), pp. 67–88.

favor the same language. This was the domain of religion, for which Spanish again was favored.

Unlike the analysis of variance of word naming scores, the analysis of variance of the word association scores yielded no significant differences between subgroups. Like the former, however, the latter yielded a significant interaction between language and domain (p <.01) while showing a nonsignificant main effect for language.

DISCUSSION

The word naming difference scores' significant correlations with the criteria and the ability of the word naming subtests to distinguish varying patterns and levels of performance of demographic subgroups suggest that word naming represents a promising technique for the contextualized description of degree of bilingualism. The moderate correlations among the word naming subtests, the subtest difference scores' differentially successful prediction of contextually and linguistically differing listening comprehension passages, and the coherent pattern of between-domain language differences, as seen in the performance of the different subgroups, suggest that the word naming subtests did tap somewhat different contextual skills.

The continuous word association subtests, on the other hand, were not successful inasmuch as they neither predicted the criterion variables very well nor did they distinguish among demographic subgroups that one would expect to be different with respect to degree of bilingualism, whether globally or contextually defined. The reason for the failure of these subtests is by no means clear, although it may be hypothesized that the task, in being relatively less focussed than the word naming task, resulted in a lower level of performance, which

reduced the opportunity for reliable differences to emerge. Indeed, there were fewer total words produced in response to the word association task than in response to the word naming task.

The between-group differences in dominance configurations, obtained by means of the contextualized word naming tasks, supports the contention by Fishman[13] that global measures of degree of bilingualism may provide inadequate descriptions of bilingual performance. For example, the performance of the six demographic subgroups on the word naming task would have been described as "balanced" in terms of the differences between their English and Spanish average total scores inasmuch as a nonsignificant main effect for language was observed and the triple interaction between language, age, and recency of arrival was also nonsignificant. Yet all but one of these groups exhibited significant differences between English and Spanish average scores in one or more domains. The use of such contextualized measures may be useful not only in describing the relative proficiency of bilinguals as realized in varying contexts but also in describing the direction of generational shift in these abilities where the tasks are administered to subgroups differing in age or in the opportunity to learn both languages. Thus, the word naming scores suggest that in the community studied, the tradition-oriented domains of home and religion are the most resistant to the erosion of Spanish, or stated positively, that these domains are, as predicted by Fishman,[14] the ones in which the use of Spanish is most likely to be maintained.

[13] Joshua A. Fishman, "Sociolinguistic Perspective on the Study of Bilingualism," *Linguistics*, Vol. XXXIX (1968), pp. 21–49.

[14] Joshua A. Fishman, *Language Loyalty in the U.S.*, The Hague: Mouton, 1966.

THE CONTEXTUALIZATION
OF SCHOOL CHILDREN'S BILINGUALISM

Martin Edelman

The Contextualization of Schoolchildren's Bilingualism*

MARTIN EDELMAN, *Yeshiva University*

IN RECENT years there has been increasing recognition of the need to view bilingualism not as a global capacity but as one which could be described in terms of various components.[1] This view has led to the consideration that bilingual proficiency might vary over a range of social settings. For example, a bilingual individual might be more proficient in one language when discussing matters of an academic nature and more proficient in another language when talking about household matters.

Drawing upon this assumption, Cooper and Greenfield[2] and Cooper[3] developed a series of instruments designed to measure degree of bilingualism in various domains or institutional contexts in which language behavior occurs, e.g., family, education, religion. In the work reported in the present paper, two contextualized measures of degree of bilingualism were adapted for use with children. One measure was designed to tap bilingual *proficiency* in each of several domains. The other was constructed to assess the relative *use* of two languages in different settings. The proficiency measure seeks to indicate what a bilingual individual can do. The use measure seeks to indicate what that individual typically does do.

METHOD

Subjects

The subjects tested were 34 children of Puerto Rican background who lived in the "downtown" area of Jersey City, an area in which Puerto Rican bilingualism has been intensively studied.[4] The children, whose ages ranged from 6 to 12 and who were evenly divided by sex, attended a parochial school within the neighborhood. All children had been born on the Mainland.

Procedure

The children were interviewed individually. Each interview was tape recorded. A modified version of a Spanish usage rating schedule developed by Cooper and Greenfield[5] for use with adults was administered to each subject. The modified inventory consisted of a series of structured questions designed to assess the degree to which respondents used Spanish and English with various bilingual interlocutors in school, at church, in the neighborhood, and at home to represent usage in the domains of education, religion, neighborhood, and family, respectively. For example, students were asked to indicate the extent to which they used Spanish with other Puerto Rican bilingual children when playing outside in the street near

* The research reported herein was supported under DHEW Contract No. OEC-1-7-062817-0297, "The Measurement and Description of Widespread and Stable Bilingualism," Joshua A. Fishman, Project Director. Data analysis was made possible by a grant to the Project Director from the College Entrance Examination Board. The author is indebted to Sister Julia of St. Michael's School, Jersey City, and to Sister Patricia and Brother Patrick of Holy Name School, New York City, for their very kind and gracious assistance. This article also appears in *The Irish Journal of Education*, Vol. II (1968) pp. 109–114.

[1] Joshua A. Fishman, "Who Speaks What Language to Whom and When?" *Linguistique*, No. 2 (1965), pp. 67–88 and "Sociolinguistic Perspective on the Study of Bilingualism," *Linguistics*, Vol. XXXIX (1968), pp. 21–49.

[2] Robert L. Cooper and Lawrence Greenfield, "Language Use in a Bilingual Community," in Joshua A. Fishman, Robert L. Cooper, Roxana Ma, *et al.*, *Bilingualism in the Barrio*, Final Report: Yeshiva University, Contract No. OEC-1-7-062817-0297, U.S. Department of Health, Education, and Welfare, 1968, pp. 485–504 and also in *The Modern Language Journal*, Vol. LIII, No. 3 (March, 1969), pp. 166–172.

[3] Robert L. Cooper, "Two Contextualized Measures of Degree of Bilingualism," in Joshua A. Fishman, Robert L. Cooper, Roxana Ma, *et al.*, *Bilingualism in the Barrio*, Final Report: Yeshiva University, Contract No. OEC-1-7-062817-0297, U.S. Department of Health, Education, and Welfare, 1968, pp. 505–524 and also in *The Modern Language Journal*, Vol. LIII, No. 3 (March, 1969), pp. 172–178.

[4] Joshua A. Fishman, Robert L. Cooper, Roxana Ma, *et al.*, *Bilingualism in the Barrio*, Final Report: Yeshiva University, Contract No. OEC-1-7-062817-0297, U.S. Department of Health, Education, and Welfare, 1968.

[5] Robert L. Cooper and Lawrence Greenfield, *op. cit.*

179

their home. Following the administration of the Spanish usage rating scale the pupils were presented with a modified version of a word naming task developed by Cooper[6] for use with adults. In the modified word naming task, subjects were asked to name, within 45-second periods, as many objects as could be found in each of four settings: kitchen, school, church, and neighborhood, to represent the domains of family, education, religion, and neighborhood, respectively. The children named objects for all four domains in one language and then named objects for all four domains in the other language. Half the children first named the objects in English and the other half first named them in Spanish.[7]

Scoring

Responses on the Spanish usage rating schedule were scored on a five-point scale, with the exclusive use of Spanish at one end of the scale and the exclusive use of English at the other. A rating for the use of Spanish across various interlocutors was computed for each subject for each setting or domain. For the word naming test the number of different words produced in each domain in each language was counted for each respondent.

Data Analysis

The childrens' responses on the word naming test and Spanish usage rating schedule were each subjected to an analysis of variance. For the purpose of these analyses, subjects (Ss) were divided into four groups based on the intersection of age (6–8, 9–11) and sex.

RESULTS

Spanish Usage Rating Scores

The analysis of variance for the Spanish usage rating schedule is summarized in Table 1. A significant main effect was observed for domain ($p < .01$). That is to say, children reported that on the average, they used more Spanish in some domains than in others.

Table 2 shows the mean rating for the use of Spanish in each of the four domains. Most Spanish was reported for family and least for education. A Newman-Keuls test of the significance of the differences between the domain means indicated that the ratings for family and neighborhood were significantly higher than

TABLE 1

ANALYSIS OF VARIANCE OF SPANISH USAGE RATING SCORES

Source	df	ms	F
Between Subjects	33		
Age (B)	1	395.76	2.08
Sex (C)	1	152.46	.80
BC	1	147.17	.77
Error (b)	30	189.95	
Within Subjects	100		
Domain (A)	3	1242.54	15.98**
AB	3	20.00	.26
AC	3	176.55	2.27
ABC	3	297.85	3.83*
Error (w)	88	77.75	
Total	133		

* p < .05
** p < .01

those for education and religion. There was no difference between the family and neighborhood ratings and no difference between the education and religion ratings.

These findings are in general agreement with those of Greenfield and Cooper[8] who found that older children (ages 13–18) in that neighborhood used less Spanish in the domains of education and religion and more Spanish in the domains of neighborhood and family.

Word Naming Scores

The analysis of variance of the word naming scores is summarized in Table 3. Significant effects were observed for age, domain, language, and for the interaction of language with domain.

The significant F for age indicates that word naming fluency (the number of words produced when both languages are combined) was related to the age of the respondents, the older children producing more words. This suggests a developmental trend of increasing proficiency in terms of productivity.

[6] Robert L. Cooper, op. cit.

[7] Due to a procedural error, the original scores of six subjects were lost, and these children had to be retested. Mean score comparisons of the Spanish usage rating scale and the word naming task between the second scores of this group and the original scores of the other children of the same age and sex showed no differences. The second set of scores of the six retested children were retained for the analyses that followed.

[8] Robert L. Cooper and Lawrence Greenfield, op. cit.

TABLE 2

MEAN SPANISH USAGE RATING SCORE
(N=34)

Domain			
Education	Religion	Neighborhood	Family
2.08	2.30	3.15	3.30

The main effect for domain, on the other-hand, indicates that when words given in both languages are combined, a greater number of words were produced in some domains than in others. The mean scores for each domain were subjected to a Newman-Keuls test of significance. The results showed overall language fluency for the domains of education, family and neighborhood to be the same and that this fluency was superior to that for the domain of religion. Thus, the first three contexts appear to be equally salient for children as stimuli for the production of speech, whereas the religious domain proved to be a less salient stimulus.

TABLE 3

ANALYSIS OF VARIANCE OF WORD NAMING SCORES

Source	df	ms	F
Between subjects	33		
Age (C)	1	689.30	19.67**
Sex (D)	1	15.54	.44
CD	1	87.87	2.51
Error (b)	30	35.05	
Within subjects	235		
Domain (A)	3	64.18	9.30**
Language (B)	1	123.13	11.11**
AB	3	21.71	6.66**
AC	3	20.51	2.97*
AD	3	.96	.14
BC	1	16.50	1.49
BD	1	42.08	3.80
ABC	3	8.00	2.45
ABD	3	2.23	.68
ACD	3	4.51	.65
BCD	1	14.62	1.32
ABCD	3	2.66	.82
Error (w)	207		
Error₁ (w)	89	6.90	
Error₂ (w)	29	11.08	
Error₃ (w)	89	3.26	
Total	268		

* p<.05
** p<.01

The significant effect for language indicates that on the average more words were produced in one language than in the other when all domains are combined, with the greater number of words being produced in English. However, the significant language by domain interaction indicates that relative proficiency varied as a function of domain. This variation can be seen in Table 4, which presents the average number of words named in each language and domain. It can be observed that English was favored over Spanish for the domains of neighborhood, religion, and education. However, with respect to the domain of family, no difference between English and Spanish averages was observed.

A ratio of language dominance was computed for the performance of each child in each domain. The formula used was

$$\left(\frac{\text{Spanish}-\text{English}}{\text{Larger of the two}}+1\right)/2.$$

This formula yields a score which indicates the degree to which Spanish is dominant. Spanish dominance scores can range theoretically from 0 to 1, with a score of .50 indicating "balance." The average language dominance ratios for the domains of religion, neighborhood, family and education were .42, .42, .50, and .37, respectively. Thus, the greatest Spanish dominance was observed for family and the least for education. These results correspond in general to those obtained from the Spanish usage rating scale (see Table 2). A difference between the two instruments, however, is found for the domain of neighborhood. In this domain children's self ratings indicated slightly more Spanish than English. However, their

TABLE 4

MEAN NUMBER OF WORDS NAMED BY LANGUAGE
AND DOMAIN

Language	Domain			
	Education	Religion	Neighbor-hood	Family
English	10.5**	7.7**	9.6**	9.0
Spanish	7.8	6.5	8.0	9.0

** p<.01 for difference between pairs of English and Spanish means.

performance on the word naming test revealed the opposite tendency.

SUMMARY

Two contextualized degree of bilingualism measures, one designed to assess relative proficiency in two languages, the other to assess the extent to which each is used, were administered to 34 bilingual children of Puerto Rican background who attended a parochial school in Jersey City. The children reported that they used more Spanish, when talking to other bilingual Puerto Ricans, in the contexts of family and neighborhood, than they did in those of education and religion. Their relative proficiency scores were in general agreement with their usuage scores: the greatest difference between English and Spanish proficiency scores being observed for the domain of education and the smallest difference for the domain of family.[9]

[9] These results were approximated by Gerard Hoffman with a group of 32 Puerto Rican children, aged 6–13, randomly selected from a parochial school in New York City. Hoffman used the same modified versions of the word naming task and the Spanish usage rating scale, with the following modification. The presentation of domain-related stimuli were randomized to eliminate the possibility of bias from a fixed order of presentation. Both analyses of variance yielded the same significant main effects and interactions as in the original study (except for the triple interactions, inasmuch as Hoffman substituted a socioeconomic status rating for sex as one of the between group variables). Hoffman's Ss gave significantly more English than Spanish words in each domain, with the smallest difference being observed for the domain of family. The Spanish usage means of the two groups were quite similar, the same rank order being observed.

SEMANTIC INDEPENDENCE AND DEGREE
OF BILINGUALISM IN TWO COMMUNITIES

Tomi D. Berney
and
Robert L. Cooper

Semantic Independence and Degree of Bilingualism in Two Communities*

TOMI D. BERNEY AND ROBERT L. COOPER, *Yeshiva University*

PSYCHOLOGISTS interested in bilingual functioning have devised a number of relatively quick and inexpensive measures of degree of bilingualism such as the number of words named in each language within equal time periods[1] the speed of response to directions given in each language[2] and the speed with which pictures are named in each language.[3] The present report describes a measure of semantic independence which can be derived from verbal fluency measures of degree of bilingualism.

METHOD

Two bilingual fluency techniques, word naming and continuous word association, were administered to 38 and 31 respondents respectively as part of an intensive study of bilingualism conducted within a four-block Puerto Rican neighborhood in the "downtown" section of Jersey City.[4] Each of these techniques elicited a series of discrete words, in English and in Spanish separately, for each of five semantic contexts representing the in-stitutional domains of family, neighborhood, religion, education, and work. These techniques were administered primarily to obtain an

* The research reported in this paper was supported by DHEW Contract No OEC-1-7-062817-0297, "The Measurement and Description of Language Dominance in Bilinguals," Joshua A. Fishman, Project Director. Data analysis was made possible by a grant to the Project Director by the College Entrance Examination Board.

[1] Granville B. Johnson, Jr., "Bilingualism as Measured by a Reaction-Time Technique and the Relationship Between a Language and a Non-Language Intelligence Quotient," *Journal of Genetic Psychology*, Vol. XXXII, pp. 3–9 (March, 1953), pp. 3–9 and John Macnamara, "The Linguistic Independence of Bilinguals," *Journal of Verbal Learning and Verbal Behavior*, Vol. VI, No. 5 (October, 1967), pp. 729–736.

[2] Wallace E Lambert, "Measurement of the Linguistic Dominance of Bilinguals," *Journal of Abnormal and Social Psychology*, Vol. L, No. 2 (March, 1955), pp. 197–200.

[3] Susan M. Ervin, "Semantic Shift in Bilingualism," *American Journal of Psychology*, Vol. LXXIV, Nc. 2 (June, 1961), pp. 233–241.

[4] Joshua A. Fishman, Robert L. Cooper, Roxana Ma, et al., *Bilingualism in the Barrio*, Final Report: Yeshiva University, Contract No. OEC-1-7-062817-0297, U.S. Department of Health, Education, and Welfare, 1968.

estimate of relative bilingual fluency in each domain, by comparing the number of words produced in each language. It was also possible, however, to subject the responses to another analysis in terms of the proportion of translation equivalent responses which were observed. This proportion could serve as an index of the degree of semantic independence exhibited in each domain by respondents in their two languages.

A Puerto Rican Spanish-English bilingual translated all Spanish responses into English. For any domain, a translation equivalent pair was counted for a respondent when an English response was identical to the English translation of one of his Spanish responses. The number of translation equivalent pairs in each domain was counted for each respondent and expressed as a ratio to the total number of words observed in the weaker language for that domain. For example, if for a given domain a respondent produced 20 words in Spanish and 15 words in English, and if 5 of his English responses had equivalent responses in Spanish, his translation equivalent ratio for that domain would be $5/15 = .33$.

To provide a contrast to the responses of the Jersey City group, the word naming and word association tasks were administered to 41 residents of Yauco, a small town a few miles away from Ponce, Puerto Rico. These responses were also analyzed in terms of translation equivalent ratios. The translation equivalent ratios of both groups were then compared via two analyses of variance, one for the word naming task and one for the word association task.

RESULTS

Tables 1 and 2 summarize the analyses of variance of the word naming and word association equivalent ratios respectively. Each analysis showed significant main effects for group ($p < .05$) and for domain (word naming, $p < .01$; word association, $p < .05$), but no significant interaction between the two. That is to say, one group, the Yauco respondents, gave significantly larger translation equivalent ratios on the average than did the other, and some domains exhibited significantly greater average ratios than did others, but no difference was

TABLE 1

ANALYSIS OF VARIANCE OF WORD NAMING TRANSLATION EQUIVALENT RATIOS

Source	df	ms	F
Between subjects	78		
Group (B)	1	36.75	4.21*
Error (b)	77	8.73	
Within subjects	285		
Domain (A)	4	19.54	4.79**
A×B	4	7.53	1.85
Error (w)	277	4.08	
		—	
Total	359		

* $p < .05$
** $p < .01$

observed between the two groups' patterns of domain differences.

On the word naming task, when the responses of both groups were pooled, the domains with the smallest ratios of translation equivalent responses or conversely the domains with the greatest semantic independence were those of family and neighborhood, and the domains with the largest ratios were those of religion and education. A Newman-Keuls multiple range test of these word naming differences indicated that the differences between the ratios for religion and neighborhood, religion and family, and education and neighborhood were statistically significant ($p < .01$, .05, .05, respectively). On the word association task, only one difference between domains,

TABLE 2

ANALYSIS OF VARIANCE OF WORD ASSOCIATION TRANSLATION EQUIVALENT RATIOS

Source	df	ms	F
Between subjects	71		
Group (B)	1	34.60	4.02*
Error (b)	70	8.87	
Within subjects	270		
Domain (A)	4	10.12	2.44*
A×B	4	1.90	.46
Error (w)	262	4.14	
		—	
Total	341		

* $p < .05$

TABLE 3

MEAN TRANSLATION EQUIVALENT RATIOS* ON TWO BILINGUAL FLUENCY TASKS

Group	Domain					
	Family	Neighborhood	Religion	Education	Work	Total
	Word Naming					
Jersey City	.46	.41	.60	.51	.52	.50
Yauco, P. R.	.53	.53	.60	.65	.56	.57
Total	.50	.47	.60	.58	.54	.54
	Word Association					
Jersey City	.37	.45	.49	.49	.49	.46
Yauco, P. R.	.47	.54	.50	.55	.53	.52
Total	.42	.50	.50	.52	.51	.49

* Ratio of translation equivalent pairs to the number of words produced in the weaker language.

with both groups' responses pooled, approached significance ($p < .05$) when assessed by the Newman-Kuels multiple range test, this being the difference between the domains of family and education, the former domain exhibiting the smallest ratio and the latter the largest. On both tasks the domains of family and neighborhood showed the two lowest translation equivalent ratios and the domain of education showed either the highest or the second highest. Thus, it might be argued that the least public domains, those upon which it is plausible that English is likely to impinge the least, were the

ones which exhibited the greatest semantic independence. Table 3 presents the translation equivalent ratios of both groups for each domain on each task.

With respect to the relationship between semantic independence and relative proficiency, it did not appear that the former was a function of the latter. When the difference between the average number of Spanish and English words produced by all respondents for a given domain was expressed as a ratio to the number of words produced in the weaker language, it was found that on both tasks the domains of family and

TABLE 4

MEAN RELATIVE PROFICIENCY RATIOS* ON TWO BILINGUAL FLUENCY TASKS

Group	Domain					
	Family	Neighborhood	Religion	Education	Work	Total
	Word Naming					
Jersey City	.05	−.03	.12	−.07	.11	.04
Yauco, P. R.	.48	.24	.38	.27	.26	.33
Total	.27	.11	.24	.10	.19	.19
	Word Association					
Jersey City	.14	−.11	.14	.00	−.04	.03
Yauco, P. R.	.32	.23	.44	.13	.31	.29
Total	.24	.09	.30	.08	.16	.18

* The number of Spanish words minus the number of English words divided by the larger number of words.

religion exhibited the greatest ratios (Table 4). However, it can be seen that while the domain of religion exhibited the greatest translation equivalent ratio on the word naming task, the domain of family showed the second lowest. Similarly, on the word association task, the lowest translation equivalent ratio was observed for the domain of family, while the highest was observed for the domain of education. Thus, it is likely that semantic independence and relative proficiency are at least partially independent dimensions.

The greater average total translation equivalent ratio obtained by the Yauco group can be explained not in terms of their greater Spanish dominance (since the difference between their proficiency ratios and those of the Jersey City respondents was much greater than the difference between the two sets of translation equivalent ratios) but rather in terms of the compound-coordinate distinction.[5] The bilingualism of the Yauco group was more likely to have been school-based and hence compound than that of the Jersey City group. Thus, the finding of greater semantic interdependence in the former groups is not surprising. Such an interpretation is consistent with the finding of greater semantic independence in those domains, the family and the neighborhood, in which the compound use or compound acquisition of English and Spanish would be least likely.

SUMMARY

The Spanish and English word naming and word association responses of two groups of Puerto Rican respondents, one living on the Island and the other on the mainland, were analyzed in terms of the proportions of translation equivalent pairs to the number of words produced in the weaker language for each of five domains. The respondents living on the Island gave significantly higher translation equivalent ratios than did those living on the mainland. The domains of family and neighborhood exhibited the smallest translation equivalent ratios and the domain of education either the second largest or the largest. It was concluded that semantic independence and relative proficiency are probably largely independent dimensions and that the former may reflect the coordinateness of the bilingual's language systems.

[5] Susan M. Ervin and Charles E. Osgood, "Second Language Learning and Bilingualism," *Journal of Abnormal and Social Psychology*, Vol. XLIX, No. 4, Part 2 "Psycholinguistics, a Survey of Theory and Research Problems" (October, 1954), pp. 139–146. This supplement was also published as Memoir 10 in Indiana University Publications in Anthropology and Linguistics.

BILINGUAL NEED AFFILIATION
AND FUTURE ORIENTATION IN EXTRAGROUP
AND INTRAGROUP DOMAINS

Joav Findling

Bilingual Need Affiliation and Future Orientation in Extragroup and Intragroup Domains*

Joav Findling, *Yeshiva University*

THE purpose of the work here reported was to determine whether need affiliation and future orientation are differentially reflected in the languages of Spanish-English bilinguals and whether such differences, if found, are explainable in terms of domain characteristics. Two experiments were conducted to answer these questions, one having to do with need affiliation and the other with future orientation.

Central to both of these experiments is the construct of domain. Domains are defined as institutionalized spheres of activity in which language behavior occurs (i.e., family, education, religion, etc.). Each domain is extrapolated from and denotative of more concrete situations, the common attributes of which make them conceptually congruent and socially distinguishable from other spheres of activity.[1]

Domains may be characterized in terms of different dimensions, one of which is the intragroup to extragroup continuum. Intragroup domains are institutionalized spheres of activity over which members of the speech community have relatively greater control than outsiders to the speech community. In contrast, extragroup domains may be defined as institutionalized spheres of activity over which outsiders to the speech community enjoy relatively greater control than members of the speech community. Between these extremes there may also be intermediate domains over which control is mixed. In such domains the proportion of control positions (positions of authority or power) occupied by members of the speech community is approximately equal to the proportion of control positions occupied by outsiders to the speech community.

Underlying the future orientation experiment was the notion that, from the viewpoint of members of the speech community, intragroup domains are less ambiguous and more closely representative of the traditional ways of life of a given speech community than extragroup domains. The need affiliation experiment was based on the notion that members of the speech community are more likely to feel welcomed in situations denoted by intragroup domains than in situations denoted by extragroup domains.

Experiment 1: Need Affiliation

Need affiliation has been defined by Atkinson[2] as "concern over establishing, maintaining and restoring positive relationships with others." Modeled after physiological needs, need affiliation is said to be a function of *social deprivation* in much the same way as hunger is a function of food deprivation. Thus, the degree of one's need affiliation is positively related to the frequency of rejecting attitudes aimed at frustrating one's desire to be accepted by others.[3]

It was reasoned that in the case of Spanish-English bilinguals of Puerto Rican descent who are largely confined to an urban, Spanish speaking ghetto, English is commonly used in extragroup domains which, in turn, are more likely to be associated with social deprivation

* This study was supported under DHEW Contract No. OEC-1-7-062817-0297, "The Measurement and Description of Widespread and Stable Bilingualism," Joshua A. Fishman, Project Director. Data analysis was supported by a grant to the Project Director from the College Entrance Examination Board. I am indebted to Dr. R. Cooper whose interest, fruitful criticism and clarity of thought helped guide this work to completion.

[1] Joshua A. Fishman, "Sociolinguistic Perspective on the Study of Bilingualism," *Linguistics*, Vol. XXXIX (1968), pp. 21–49.

[2] John W. Atkinson, *An Introduction to Motivation*, Princeton, New Jersey: Van Nostrand, 1964, p. 227.

[3] John W. Atkinson, Roger W. Heyns, and Joseph Veroff, "The Effect of Experimental Arousal of the Affiliation Motive on Thematic Apperception," *Journal of Abnormal and Social Psychology*, Vol. XLIX, No. 3 (July, 1954), pp. 405–410.

than are intragroup domains. It was, consequently, hypothesized (1) that Spanish-English bilinguals (of the kind just described) would exhibit greater need affiliation in English than in Spanish, and (2) that Spanish-English bilinguals would exhibit progressively greater need affiliation in both languages as they shift from typically intragroup domains such as familial relationships to more extragroup domains such as the sphere of work or education. The third and final hypothesis in this experiment stated that people with less responsible jobs would show greater need affiliation in either language and in all domains than people with more responsible jobs. This prediction was based on the belief that in the American minority group context, people with higher occupational status are less likely to be rejected by others than are people with lower occupational status.

METHOD

To test these hypotheses, use was made of word association (WA) scores obtained by Cooper[4] from a group of 32 Puerto Rican bilinguals from a Spanish-speaking urban ghetto near New York.

Cooper administered the WA test in English and in Spanish using 10 stimulus words, each of which referred to a behavioral domain. The words used were school, home, factory, church, street, escuela, casa, factoría, iglesia, and calle. Each stimulus word was presented separately with the instructions to say as many different words as the stimulus word brought to mind. Responses were confined to the language of the stimulus word, allowing one minute per domain.

To these series of WA responses, a measure based on Henley's index of need affiliation was applied. Henley[5] analyzed published literary works and found that the frequency of plural nouns referring to persons was positively correlated with the need affiliation imagery of the society in which the works were published. It was therefore decided to represent the subject's (S's) degree of need affiliation in each language and domain by the proportion of his "human" responses (responses referring to persons, such as "teacher," "uncle," "policeman," etc.) to the total number of his WA responses in the relevant series.

Subjects were divided into two groups based on occupational status. Respondents in the High status group were either working at jobs requiring relatively high degrees of skill or they were full time students at the high school level or beyond. Respondents in the Low status group were either housewives or working at relatively routine and unskilled jobs or unemployed or they were students below the high school level.

RESULTS

The need affiliation scores were subjected to an analysis of variance, presented in Table 1. Significant main effects were found for language and for domain but not for occupational status. As expected, greater need affiliation ratio scores were obtained in English than in Spanish. Furthermore, the size of need affiliation proportions, when words for both languages were combined, varied by domain, suggesting that need affiliation is revealed not only by language but by sphere of activity as well. The average need affiliation scores by language and domain are presented in Table 2. The largest average need affiliation ratios were obtained for the domains of work and education and the smallest for religion, neighborhood and home. The direction of these domain differences supports the hypothesis that extragroup domains are more socially depriving and need affiliation producing than intragroup domains.

Experiment 2: Future Orientation

Future orientation has been defined as the extent to which one's preoccupation with things and events that may (or may not) happen exclude one's preoccupation with things and events that have already taken place. Ac-

[4] Robert L. Cooper, "Two Contextual Measures of Degree of Bilingualism," in Joshua A. Fishman, Robert L. Cooper, Roxana Ma, *et al.*, *Bilingualism in the Barrio*, Final Report: Yeshiva University, Contract No. OEC-1-7-062817-0297, U.S. Department of Health, Education and Welfare, 1968, pp. 505–524 and also in *The Modern Language Journal*, Vol. XLIII, No. 3 (March, 1969), pp. 172–178.

[5] Nancy M. Henley, "Achievement and Affiliation Imagery in American Fiction, 1901–1961," *Journal of Personality and Social Psychology*, Vol. VIII, No. 2 (October 1967), pp. 208–211.

TABLE 1

ANALYSIS OF VARIANCE OF HUMAN RATIO
(NEED AFFILIATION) SCORES

Source of Variance	Sum of Squares	df	Mean Square	F	F_{95}	F_{99}
Between subjects	19,573.09	31				
Occupation (C)	110.73	1	110.73	.17	4.17	7.56
Error (b)	19,463.08	30	648.77			
Within subjects	65,904.10	288				
Language (A)	701.69	1	701.69	3.78*	4.17	7.56
Domain (B)	12,043.27	4	3,010.82	12.10**	2.44	3.47
AB	239.49	4	59.87	.48	2.44	3.47
AC	181.84	1	181.84	.98	4.17	7.56
BC	1,855.50	4	463.87	1.86	2.44	3.47
ABC	446.16	4	111.54	.89	2.44	3.47
Error (w)	50,436.15	270				
Error₁ (w)	5,571.17	30	185.71			
Error₂ (w)	29,851.83	120	248.77			
Error₃ (w)	15,013.15	120	125.11			
Total	85,477.19	319				

* $p > .07$
** $p > .01$

cording to May[6] and Rokeach and Bonier,[7] "preoccupation with the future" is related to cognitive ambiguity (that is, to emotionally charged, incongruent or vague plans of action) and to conflicting world views causing a person to be anxiously undecided as to what scale of values to adapt and what scale of values to reject.

It was reasoned that to Puerto Rican Spanish English bilinguals living in the modern and highly complex urban society of New York, English would be associated with newer, more changeable, less predictable and, in general, more ambiguous social expectations than the

TABLE 2

MEAN NEED AFFILIATION RATIO SCORES BY
LANGUAGE AND DOMAIN

Language	Domain					
	Work	Educa-tion	Re-ligion	Neigh-borhood	Home	Total
English	33	24	20	17	14	22
Spanish	28	23	17	13	14	19
Total	30	23	18	15	14	20

traditional ones associated with Spanish. It was therefore predicted that Spanish-English bilinguals would show greater future orientation in English than in Spanish.

Presumably, Puerto Rican Spanish speaking ghettos in this country are communities in transition, experiencing severe socio-cultural tension. It is felt that the younger and more educated members of such communities are in conflict with the traditional Puerto Rican way of life (viewing it as being old-fashioned) as well as with the modern world whose scale of values they have not as yet fully accepted. Fluctuating between two world views, these young people are expected to be critical of traditional authorities when involved in intragroup domains whereas—when involved in extra-group domains—they are expected to be critical of modern authorities. It was, consequently, hypothesized that young Puerto Rican Spanish-English bilinguals in New York would exhibit

[6] Rollo, May, The Meaning of Anxiety, New York: Ronald, 1950.

[7] Milton Rokeach and Richard Bonier, "Time Perspective, Dogmatism, and Anxiety," in Milton Rokeach, The Open and Closed Mind, New York: Basic Books, 1960, pp. 366–375.

greater future orientation in both extragroup domains (school, work sphere) and intragroup domains (home, friendship) than in inter-mediate domains over which control is mixed.

METHOD

To test these hypotheses, an experiment was conducted with 18 Spanish-English bilinguals. The subjects were all male teenagers who at-tended the same high school and were members of the same Puerto Rican Youth Club. The experiment was conducted in a classroom and it took about 45 minutes to complete.

Future orientation scores were obtained as follows. Each subject (*S*) was presented with a page containing six pairs of incomplete sen-tences and instructed to complete one sentence from each pair in writing. The six pairs of incomplete sentences referred to six different domains: home, friendship, neighborhood, re-ligion, education, and work. The two incom-plete sentences in each pair differed from each other with respect to time. One sentence was oriented to the future and the other to the past. Thus, for example, the pairs of incomplete sentences referring to the domains of friendship and education respectively, were:

It is good to make new friends, because...

It is good to keep old friends, because...

Last year school was very difficult for some students, because...

Next year school will be very difficult for some students, because...

The incomplete sentences were presented in two forms: Spanish and English. Out of the 18 subjects in the group, nine were randomly selected to complete the Spanish sentences in Spanish and the other nine to complete the English sentences in English. Future orienta-tion scores (number of "future oriented" sen-tences chosen) were determined for each *S*, domain, and language.

In order to see whether future orientation scores varied with respect to need affiliation, *S*s were also presented with a written version of Cooper's WA test. The test was administered in English to those who took the English form of the future orientation test, and in Spanish to those who took the Spanish form. The stimulus words in this test were each printed on a separate page and presented with the instruc-tions to write the first ten different words that the stimulus word brought to mind. To these series of WA responses (ten in each series) the modified version of Henley's index of need affiliation was later applied and need affiliation ratio scores calculated.

RESULTS

An analysis of variance of future orientation scores by language, domain and need affiliation was performed. The analysis is presented in Table 3. Significant main effects were observed for language and for domain. The need affilia-tion effect approached significance ($p < .10$). The average number of future oriented sen-tences chosen by language and domain are presented in Table 4. Greater future orientation ratio scores were observed in English than in Spanish. Higher future orientation scores were observed in the more extragroup domains (work, education) and the more intragroup domains (home, friendship) than in the inter-mediate domains over which control is mixed (religion, neighborhood). The higher need af-filiation group had higher future orientation scores than did the lower need affiliation group.

SUMMARY AND CONCLUSIONS

In the two experiments reported in this paper, hypotheses relating future orientation and need affiliation to language, domain and job responsibility were tested on two groups of Spanish-English bilinguals of Puerto Rican descent living in or around the city of New York.

It was found that both future orientation and need affiliation were greater in English than in Spanish. Inasmuch as need affiliation is viewed as a function of social deprivation and future orientation as a symptom of congni-tive ambiguity or conflicting world views, these findings suggest that to these subjects English is associated with stronger social rejection and more difficult-to-comprehend social expecta-tions than is Spanish.

Need affiliation and future orientation also varied significantly along the extragroup to intragroup continuum of domains yielding, however, uniquely different patterns of varia-

TABLE 3

ANALYSIS OF VARIANCE OF FUTURE ORIENTATION RATIO SCORES

Source	ss	df	ms	F	F_{90}	F_{95}	F_{99}
Between Subjects	6.63	17					
Language (B)	1.33	1	1.33	4.75*		4.60	
Need Affiliation (C)	.92	1	.92	3.29†	3.10		
BC	.41	1	.41	1.46			
Error (b)	3.97	14	.28				
Within Subjects	20.33	90					
Domain (A)	3.96	2	.79	4.38**			3.29
AB	1.23	5	.25	1.39			
AC	1.64	5	.33	1.83			
ABC	.72	5	.14	.78			
Error (w)	12.78	70	.18				
Total	26.96	107					

† $p < .10$
* $p < .05$
** $p < .01$

TABLE 4

MEAN NUMBER OF FUTURE ORIENTED SENTENCES CHOSEN BY LANGUAGE AND DOMAIN

Language	Intergroup		Mixed		Intragroup		Total
	Work	Education	Religion	Neighborhood	Friendship	Home	
English	4	8	4	4	7	5	32
Spanish	4	6	1	0	3	6	20
Total	8	14	5	4	10	11	52

tion. While need affiliation decreased progressively from extragroup domains over which control is largely in the hands of community outsiders to intragroup domains over which community members are predominantly in control, future orientation was found to be higher at both extremes of the continuum and lower in intermediate domains over which control is mixed. The pattern of distribution of need affiliation ratios supported the notion that social deprivation is more likely to be felt in extragroup than in intragroup domains. On the other hand, the distribution of future orientation ratios supported the notion that the intensity of the conflict between traditional and modern world views is likely to be greater in either extra-group or intra-group domains than in intermediate domains in which traditional and modern authorities co-exist.

Contrary to expectation, need affiliation scores did not vary significantly with respect to job responsibility. The overall results obtained, however, supported the general notion that need affiliation and future orientation vary in degree from spheres of activity in which Spanish is most commonly used to spheres of activity in which English is most commonly used, and that these variations are capable of being differentially reflected in the language of Puerto Rican Spanish-English bilinguals.

WORD NAMING AND USAGE SCORES
FOR A SAMPLE
OF YIDDISH-ENGLISH BILINGUALS

Judah Ronch
Robert L. Cooper
and
Joshua A. Fishman

Word Naming and Usage Scores for a Sample of Yiddish-English Bilinguals*

Judah Ronch, Robert L. Cooper, and Joshua A. Fishman,

Yeshiva University

THE purpose of this study is to explore the importance of societal domains of verbal interaction in connection with two measures of the bilingual performance of a sample of Yiddish-English speakers in New York City. The methods employed have been adapted from those used by Cooper[1] and Cooper and Greenfield[2] with Puerto Rican bilinguals. Their adaptation for Jewish bilinguals should be of importance for researchers studying Jewish populations in various parts of the world in terms of their distance-proximity to co-territorial populations.

Subjects

The subjects of the present study were a group of 15 (8 Male and 7 Female) European-born Jewish adults who spoke Yiddish as children while living in Europe, and who continued to use Yiddish actively after they arrived in the United States. Their ages ranged from 55 to 80 years, with the greatest number of individuals clustering around the 67–70 year age range. All of these individuals had come to the United States between 1900 and 1929, and, as a result, had been in the United States for 40 to 60 years by the time they served as Subjects (Ss) for this research.

All Ss were active in Jewish organizational and cultural work on behalf of Yiddish language and literature. The societal domains hypothesized as being of importance in their bilingual usage were: (a) home, (b) ethnic behavior: Passover Seder celebration, (c) work, (d) neighborhood, and (e) Jewish cultural activities.

Procedures

All Ss were given a Word Naming test in Yiddish and in English and a Yiddish Usage Rating scale in English. The language in which the Word Naming scale was administered first (i.e., Yiddish or English) was randomly varied. In each case the Word Naming task always

preceded the Usage Rating scale.

All responses were tape recorded to facilitate subsequent data analysis and to enable the Experimenter (E) to make the testing situation as informal as possible.

1. *Word Naming.* Each subject was asked to give as many different English and Yiddish words as he could which name objects or other items appropriate to a given domain. For example, for the domain of home, Ss were asked to name as many English (Yiddish) words as they could that represent things that could be seen or found in a kitchen. The number of individual words a subject gave in 60 seconds were counted as his score for that domain in that language. The subject received the entire series first in one language and then in the other, with the instructions, questions and examples in Yiddish being direct translations of those in English. Thus, each S received 10 scores, 5 in each language.

2. *Usage Rating.* All Ss were asked how much of their talk was in Yiddish when the spoke to particular people (e.g., husband, co-worker,

* The research reported in this paper was supported by a grant from the U.S. Office of Education, Contract No. OEC-1-7-026817-0297, "The Measurement and description of language dominance in bilinguals," Joshua A. Fishman, Project Director. Data analysis was supported by a grant to the Project Director by the College Entrance Examination Board.

1 Robert L. Cooper, "Two Contextualized Measures of Degree of Bilingualism," in Joshua A. Fishman, Robert L. Cooper, Roxana Ma, *et al.*, *Bilingualism in the Barrio*, Final Report: Yeshiva University, Contract No. OEC-1-7-062817-0297, U.S. Department of Health, Education and Welfare, 1968, pp. 505–524 and also in *The Modern Language Journal*, Vol. LIII, No. 3 (March, 1969), pp. 172–178.

2 Robert L. Cooper and Lawrence Greenfield, "Language Use in a Bilingual Community," in Joshua A. Fishman, Robert L. Cooper, Roxana Ma, *et al.*, *Bilingualism in the Barrio*, Final Report: Yeshiva University, Contract No. OEC-1-7-062816-0297, U. S. Department of Health, Education, and Welfare, 1968, pp. 485–504 and also in *The Modern Language Journal*, Vol. LIII, No. 3 (March, 1969), pp. 166–172.

232

children, friends) who knew both English and Yiddish. The suggested settings for their interactions with these interlocutors were the home, the Passover Seder, the Yiddish-oriented cultural club, the neighborhood, and the place of employment. Ss were asked to rate the relative amount of Yiddish they spoke with each interlocutor on a 7-point scale that ranged from speaking only in Yiddish to speaking only in English with the specified interlocutor in the specified setting.

A total score for each subject in each domain was obtained by summing responses across interlocutors within settings.

DATA ANALYSIS

1. *Word Naming*. Table I presents the mean scores for English and Yiddish. An analysis of variance yielded a significant language by domain interaction [$F(14, 56) = 17.67$ (p $<$.001)], indicating that the ratio of English to Yiddish words named varied as a function of domain.

Further analysis of the data (t-test) showed that for the domains of cultural activity (number of authors named) and the Passover Seder, the mean number of words named in each language differed significantly (p $<$.01), there being a greater number of words named in Yiddish than in English in these domains. In addition, for the home domain, there was a significant difference between mean number of words named in each language (p $<$.05), but in the opposite direction, that is, more words were given in English than in Yiddish in this domain. The remaining domains showed no significant between-language differences.

2. *Yiddish Usage Rating*. Table 2 shows the

TABLE 1

WORD NAMING SCORES

Language	Domain				
	Home	Neigh-borhood	Cul-tural	Seder	Work
English	18.8*	13.5	6.2**	10.8**	13.9
Yiddish	16.7	12.8	12.6	15.4	13.1

* p $<$.05 for difference between means for English and Yiddish.

** p $<$.01 for difference between means for English and Yiddish.

TABLE 2

MEAN YIDDISH USAGE RATING ($\times$10)

	Domain				
	Home	Seder	Cul-tural	Neigh-borhood	Work
Rating	45.0	37.7	76.5*	38.9	34.2

(Note—Raw scores were multiplied $\times$10 for computational purposes.)

* p $<$.01 difference between rating for cultural domain and other domains.

mean Yiddish usage rating scores for the five domains. An analysis of variance revealed that the effect of domain on language usage rating was significant [$F(4, 56) = 10.31$(p $<$.01)]. This significant main effect was due to the cultural domain which was different from the other domains studied (Newman-Keuls test on 5 means). That is, Ss rated themselves as using more Yiddish in the Yiddish cultural domain than in any of the other domains investigated.

Finally, Pearson product-moment correlations between Usage Rating scores and differences in Word Naming scores (Yiddish-English) for each domain, and for the sum of the Usage Rating scores and sum of the difference scores, were computed to ascertain the relationship between those two aspects of verbal behavior. These correlations were all small and nonsignificant. It would appear then that these two measures, one "self-report" and the other "proficiency" in nature, are substantially independent in the population under study.

DISCUSSION

From the above results, certain patterns of bilingual usage for the group under study can be noted. First, this group tends to report its greatest amount of Yiddish usage in Yiddish cultural activities, and second, their ability to name words in English and Yiddish differs most in domains related to such Yiddish cultural activity. Thus, the results obtained by the two instruments were consistent. However, in general these two types of measures seem to be substantially independent for this group. That is, for a given individual, one cannot predict a score obtained from one technique from that obtained from the other.

In general, our *S*s indicated that they felt comfortable enough using English but that they were more comfortable using Yiddish. This is evidenced by the fact that the domains in which mixed usage is possible (e.g., home, Seder [because of the presence of children], neighborhood, and work) all were rated between the 34% to 45% level of Yiddish usage, while the cultural domain, in which the positive attitude and interest that the people have toward Yiddish gets institutionalized expression, was rated at about 75% Yiddish usage. Despite the fact that these people have been here for so many years, they have fought cultural assimilation through deep involvement in a broad range of Yiddish-language cultural organizations and activities, including choral groups, theater groups, literary and cultural clubs, and schools for the education of their children and grandchildren. It would therefore seem that their language behavior has come to exist on two levels, the first being a bilingual Yiddish-English interaction with others in their everyday life, and a second, more intensely Yiddish-oriented and Yiddish-preserving level of cultural activity.

COMPARISON OF WORD NAMING RESULTS WITH JERSEY CITY PUERTO RICAN SAMPLE

The Word Naming results obtained from the group under study were compared with the results obtained by Cooper[3] using a group of Spanish-English bilinguals who were drawn from the Puerto Rican population of Jersey City. Cooper divided his sample into six subgroups based on age and number of years in the United States. The group which most closely resembles the Yiddish-English bilinguals used in the present study were those Puerto Rican bilinguals who had been in the U.S. for more than 11 years and were 35 years of age or older (N = 8). For that group only the domain of work yielded a significant difference between Spanish and English Word Naming scores, with more words named in Spanish than in English. This finding differs from our finding for the Yiddish-English group, for which no significant difference was found for the work domain. There were, however, results obtained by Cooper which are congruent with ours.

In the home domain, more words were named in English than in Spanish, though this difference was not statistically significant. In the Yiddish-English sample, we found a significant difference in the same direction. For the religion domain, which is roughly parallel to the culture domain used in the present study, Cooper found that more Spanish than English words were named. This difference was again not statistically significant. This difference was significant, however, for the total Puerto Rican sample given the Word Naming task (N = 38), and was the only significant difference in either direction for all of the domains tested, for the total group, all subgroups combined.

The congruities between the two sets of results are best understood in terms of length of residence in the United States and consequent degree of interaction with monolingual English speakers. Our Yiddish sample has spent many more years in the United States and has learned much more English than have most Puerto Ricans in the New York Area. As a result, our Yiddish-English bilinguals have maintained Yiddish dominance only in distinctly Jewish ethnic-cultural domains. While tending toward English at home, older Puerto Ricans are still Spanish dominant at work and in church with no significantly English dominant domain yet in evidence. That older Puerto Ricans, too, are moving toward greater use of English is indicated by the fact that home is no longer Spanish dominant for them insofar as this is revealed by the Word Naming tsak.

CONCLUSION

A sample of Yiddish-English bilinguals active in Yiddish cultural work was tested on Word Naming and Usage Rating techniques previously developed for a study of Puerto Rican Spanish-English bilinguals. The Yiddish-English bilinguals proved to be significantly stronger in Yiddish in the cultural domain on both techniques. They also proved to be significantly stronger in Yiddish in the ethnic behavior domain and in English in the home domain on Word Naming.

In comparison with older Puerto Rican Spanish-English bilinguals who have been in

[3] Robert L. Cooper, *op. cit.*

he United States for 11 years or more the Yiddish-English bilinguals produce proportionally more English words in the home domain and proportionally less mother-tongue words in the work domain. Both groups are dominant in their mother tongues in the ethnic domains of cultural and religious activity.

Our impression of the utility of the Word Naming and Usage Rating techniques is strengthened as a result of the face validity of the findings obtained on two different bilingual populations.

LISTENING COMPREHENSION
IN A BILINGUAL COMMUNITY

Robert L. Cooper
Barbara R. Fowles
and
Abraham Givner

Listening Comprehension in a Bilingual Community*

ROBERT L. COOPER, BARBARA R. FOWLES, AND ABRAHAM GIVNER,
Yeshiva University

PSYCHOLOGISTS have developed several methods for the measurement of degree of bilingualism, or relative proficiency in two languages. For the most part, these techniques are "indirect."[1] That is, the performances they describe, such as speed of naming pictures[2] or the number of discrete words produced within time limits[3] have a less than obvious relationship to the criterion behavior of relative linguistic proficiency. Furthermore, with the notable exception of a measure devised by Lambert, who compared the speed of responding to directions given in each of two languages,[4] most of these techniques have described various aspects of verbal production, although relative proficiency can also vary along other dimensions, such as listening, reading, and writing.

The technique which is described in the present paper was designed to yield not only a more direct estimate of bilingual proficiency than those reported in the past but also a measure of bilingual listening comprehension ability. It differs from other listening comprehension techniques not only in offering a measure of relative proficiency (instead of a score in one language or the other) but also in being devised to reflect bilingual proficiency in varying types of social context. The attempt to construct a listening comprehension test in terms of differing social contexts was made on the assumption that speakers vary with respect to the number and kinds of social situation in which they can communicate effectively.[5] It was believed that a technique which was designed to reflect com-

municative competence would provide a more adequate estimate of the bilingual person's rel-

* The research reported in this paper was supported by a grant from the U.S. Office of Education, Contract No. OEC-1-7-062817-0297, "The Measurement and Description of Language Dominance in Bilinguals." Data analysis was made possible by a grant from the College Entrance Examination Board. The authors wish to thank Mr. Charles Blake, New Rochelle High School, and Mr. Milton Saltzer, New York University, for their cooperation. The authors are most grateful to Dr. Joshua A. Fishman for his advice and encouragement during all stages of the research reported here.

[1] John Macnamara, "How Can One Measure the Extent of a Person's Bilingual Proficiency?" in *Preprints*, International Seminar on the Description and Measurement of Bilingualism, Ottawa: Canadian National Commission for UNESCO, 1967, pp. 68–90

[2] Susan M. Ervin, "Semantic Shift in Bilingualism," *American Journal of Psychology*, Vol. LXXIV, No. 2 (June, 1961), pp. 233–241.

[3] Granville B. Johnson, Jr., "Bilingualism as Measured by a Reaction-Time Technique and the Relationship Between a Language and a Nonlanguage Intelligence Quotient," *Journal of Genetic Psychology*, Vol. XXXII, No. 1 (March, 1953), pp. 3–9.

[4] Wallace E. Lambert, "Measurement of the Linguistic Dominance of Bilinguals," *Journal of Abnormal and Social Psychology*, Vol. L, No. 2 (March, 1955), pp. 197–200.

[5] Joshua A. Fishman, "Who Speaks What Language to Whom and When?" *Linguistique*, No. 2 (1965), pp. 67–68 and Joshua A. Fishman, "Sociolinguistic Perspective on the Study of Bilingualism," *Linguistics*, Vol. XXXIX (1968), pp. 21–49.

John J. Gumperz, "Linguistic and Social Interaction in Two Communities," *American Anthropologist*, Vol. LXVI, No. 6, Part 2 (December, 1964), pp. 137–153.

Dell Hymes, "Models of Interaction of Language and Social Setting," *Journal of Social Issues*, Vol. XXIII, No. 2 (April, 1967), pp. 8–28.

ative proficiency than one which was confined to a single context.

The present report describes the performance on a contextualized bilingual listening comprehension task of members of a Puerto Rican neighborhood near New York City. The paper also compares their performance to that of two contrasting groups. In addition, the relationship between bilingual listening comprehension ability and other bilingual skills, as observed in this neighborhood, is described.

METHOD

Stimuli

Five tape-recorded, natural conversations, between Spanish-English bilingual residents of New York, were obtained. The participants in all but one of the conversations were Puerto Rican college students who spoke fluent, native English and Spanish and who were adept at style switching. In one conversation, one of the participants was a parish priest, who played himself in that role, and whose Spanish was fluent but not native.

Each conversation was obtained in the following manner. First, the "actors" agreed upon a social situation in which switching between English and Spanish would be appropriate among Puerto Ricans in New York. Second, they mapped out a story-line which determined the general direction of the conversation in that situation, i.e., who would say what to whom. No scripts were prepared, however. The actors then assigned the roles to one another and "role played" or ad libbed the scene, using Spanish when they felt Spanish was appropriate and English when they felt English was appropriate. Finally, they played back the conversation to themselves to determine whether or not it sounded natural. If parts of the conversation struck them as unnatural, those portions were re-recorded and at a later time spliced into the tape. Each completed conversation lasted between two to three minutes.

Each conversation was intended to represent a different type of social context. Consequently, the relationships between speakers (e.g., mother-daughter, priest-parishioner), the locales or settings (e.g., home, rectory), the topics of conversation (e.g., the Puerto Rican Parade, the health of an uncle), and the purposes of the

interactions (e.g., offering an invitation, dictating a letter) all varied from conversation to conversation.

Subjects

The conversations were played to Ss as part of an intensive study of Spanish-English bilingualism within a four-block Puerto Rican area of the "downtown" section of Jersey City.[6] Living there were 431 persons of Puerto Rican background who comprised 90 households. Half of this group consisted of children under the age of 13. Of those who were 13 or older, over one-fifth (N=48) agreed to participate in interviews of which the listening comprehension test formed a part. An attempt was made to obtain both male and female respondents who would represent the range of ages (of those 13 or older) and the range of occupational and educational backgrounds to be found in that neighborhood. Although not all respondents completed all portions of the interview, 35 Ss heard and responded to all five of the taped conversations.

Procedure

After a conversation had been played twice to the respondent, he was asked a series of questions designed to assess his comprehension of the passage. In addition to questions which were asked to test comprehension of the English and Spanish portions of each conversation, questions were asked to assess the respondent's interpretation of various aspects of the social situation represented by the conversation as a whole. For example, respondents were asked to identify the role-relationships between speakers (e.g., boss-secretary), the degree of social distance or intimacy between speakers, the motivation underlying certain remarks made by the speakers, the conversation's setting and for some conversations, the educational and occupational status of the speakers.

The listening comprehension test was administered as part of an individual, tape-recorded interview which lasted from two to four

[6] Joshua A. Fishman, Robert L. Cooper, Roxana Ma, et al., *Bilingualism in the Barrio*. Final Report: Yeshiva University, Contract No. OEC-1-7-062817-0297, U. S. Department of Health, Education, and Welfare, 1968.

nours. Interviewers were bilingual in English and Spanish and were able to conduct the interview in whatever language or combination of languages that was preferred by the respondent. Interviews were held in the respondent's home or in a field office in his neighborhood.

Scoring

For each subtest, the percentage which each respondent correctly answered of items assessing comprehension of the English portion was subtracted from the percentage which he correctly answered of items assessing comprehension of the Spanish portion. As a result, positive difference scores indicated that the respondent understood more of the Spanish than the English portion and negative difference scores indicated the reverse. The percentage correct of the other types of items, assessing interpretation of various components of the conversation as a whole, such as the role-relationships among the speakers, was also computed. Correctness was scored in terms of the impression intended by the actors in their formulation of the social situation.

Other Variables

The five comprehension difference scores, one for each subtest, and a total difference score based on all five subtests, were studied in relationship to the following five variables, reflecting skills in speaking, reading, and writing. Scores on these variables were obtained independently of the authors of this paper.

1. Accented Speech. Respondents were rated by independent judges in terms of the degree to which the phonological and syntactic structures of one language appeared to influence speech produced in the other, as observed during the interview. A seven-point scale was used on which high scores indicated Spanish influence upon English speech, low scores indicated English influence upon Spanish speech, and scores in between indicated maximum language distance, or no influence by either language upon speech produced in the other.

2. Reading. During the extended interview, respondents were asked to read an English word list, a Spanish word list, and two short paragraphs in English and in Spanish. Based on their performance on these tasks, respondents were rated by independent judges on a five-point scale, in terms of their ability to read in the two languages. High scores indicated that the respondent could read only in Spanish (or not at all), low scores indicated that he could read only in English, and intermediate scores indicated that he could read in both languages.

3. Writing. During a language census of the neighborhood[7] a representative of each household was asked whether each member of that household could write in English and in Spanish. A three-point scale was used to rate claimed writing proficiency in each language. The English rating was subtracted from the Spanish rating for each respondent so that positive scores indicated Spanish dominance and negative scores indicated English dominance.

4. Spanish repertoire range. Based on the notion of verbal repertoire which has been advanced and elaborated by Gumperz[8] respondents were globally rated by independent judges in terms of the number of Spanish speech styles they were observed to use during the interview and the fluency with which they used them. A four-point scale was employed, which ranged from the use of only a single, casual style to the fluent use of several speech styles, including more careful, formal Spanish.

5. English repertoire range. Respondents were also rated by independent judges in terms of the number and fluency of English speech styles which were observed during the interview. A six-point scale was used, ranging from knowledge of only a few words and phrases, at one end of the dimension, to the ability to employ both careful and casual speech styles, in a maximally fluent manner, at the other.

Ratings on the English and Spanish repertoire range scales and on the reading and accent scales were made by the linguists who had performed a phonetic analysis of representative portions of each respondent's speech, as re-

[7] Joshua Fishman, "A Sociolinguistic Census of a Bilingual Neighborhood" in Joshua A. Fishman, Robert L. Cooper and Roxana Ma, et al., Bilingualism in the Barrio. Final Report: Yeshiva University, Contract No. OEC-1-7-062817-0297, U.S. Department of Health, Education and Welfare, 1968, pp. 260–299 and also in American Sociological Review, in press.

[8] John J. Gumperz, "On the Linguistic Markers of Bilingual Communication," Journal of Social Issues, Vol. XXIII No. 2 (April, 1967), pp. 48–57.

corded during the interview.[9] The accent, reading, and writing scales, as well as the listening scale (total score), can be regarded as degree of bilingualism scales on which high or positive scores indicate Spanish dominance, low or negative scores English dominance, and intermediate scores no difference or "balance." The Spanish and English repertoire range scales, on the other hand, are unilingual scales, reflecting performance in a single language only.

Data Analysis

Correlations were obtained among the listening comprehension difference scores and between these difference scores and the other scales. In addition, an analysis of variance was performed on the respondents' comprehension scores in terms of the five conversations and the several types of item, including identification of relationships, comprehension of English content, and comprehension of Spanish content.

Subsidiary Administrations

The listening comprehension test was individually administered to two groups of Ss whose backgrounds differed from those of the Jersey City respondents. One group (N = 20) consisted of students at a suburban high school near New York City. These Ss had all completed three or four years of high school Spanish courses. The other group (N = 19) consisted of Latin American, Spanish-speaking students enrolled in an advanced course in English as a second language at a university in New York City. It was expected that each of these groups would differ from the Jersey City respondents with respect to their performance on the listening comprehension test. Each group's performance was compared to that of the Jersey City respondents by means of analysis of variance.

RESULTS

Relationships among Bilingual and Unilingual Scales

Table 1 presents the intercorrelations among the bilingual and unilingual scores for the Jersey City respondents. Substantial correlations were observed among the four degree of bilingualism scales, ranging from .41 to .77, with a median coefficient of .59. Thus, the different dimensions of degree of bilingualism

were related to one another. The correlations were not so high, however, that an individual's rank on one dimension could be substituted for his rank on another with a high degree of confidence. The dimensions were, in other words, at least partially independent.

Substantial correlations were also observed between the English repertoire range scale and the degree of bilingualism scales, ranging from −.54 to −.69. The Spanish repertoire scale, on the other hand, was not significantly related to any of these variables. Its lack of relationship to the other scales can be attributed to its relatively small variance, as can be seen from the standard deviations presented in Table 1. The respondents were much more alike in terms of their Spanish repertoire range ratings than they were in terms of their scores on the other variables (p < .01 for the difference between the variance of the Spanish repertoire ratings and that of four of the five scales). The greater homogeneity of the Spanish repertoire range ratings is consistent with the fact that for most of the respondents, Spanish was the first language learned and was primarily a home and neighborhood language. Thus, there was more opportunity for the respondents to vary with respect to their English skills, due to differential exposure to English at school and at work. It is likely, therefore, that the significant relationships that were observed among the degree of bilingualism scales were caused primarily by an underlying common variation in English competence.

Listening comprehension and English repertoire range. The correlations obtained between the individual listening comprehension subtest difference scores and the English repertoire range ratings were all significant, varying from −.36 to −.47 (p < .05 for the lowest coefficient, p < .01 for the others). These correlations were substantially lower, however, than that obtained between the total listening comprehension score and the English repertoire range scale (r = −.68). The improvement in prediction ob-

[9] Roxana Ma and Eleanor Herasimchuk, "Linguistic Dimensions of a Bilingual Neighborhood," in Joshua A. Fishman, Robert L. Cooper and Roxana Ma, et al., *Bilingualism in the Barrio,* Final Report: Yeshiva University, Contract No. OEC-1-7-062817-0297, U. S. Department of Health, Education, and Welfare, 1968.

TABLE 1

INTERCORRELATIONS AMONG BILINGUAL AND UNILINGUAL SCALES,
JERSEY CITY RESPONDENTS (N = 35)

			Variable					
	L	AS	R	W	SRR	ERR	x̄	S.D.
Bilingual scales								
Listening	.50**	.41*	.44**	−.06	−.68**		2.16	.94
Accented Speech		.74**	.77**	.27	−.69**		2.03	1.68
Reading			.67**	.19	−.61**		2.57	1.38
Writing				.29	−.54**		2.29	1.39
Unilingual Scales								
Spanish repertoire range					.04		2.03	.77
English repertoire range							3.11	1.54

* p < .05
** p < .01

tained by using the total score was not primarily due to the difference in length between a single subtest and a group of subtests, inasmuch as the intercorrelations among the comprehension subtests were quite low, ranging from .04 to .41, with a median coefficient of .24. Rather, the improved prediction of the English repertoire range ratings was probably due to the fact that the total comprehension score was based on a set of conversations that represented range not only of social situations but also of the speech styles appropriate to them.

Analysis of Variance: Jersey City and Comparison Groups

Table 2 summarizes the analysis of variance of the Jersey City respondents' performance on items assessing comprehension and interpreta-

TABLE 2

ANALYSIS OF VARIANCE OF LISTENING SCORES:
JERSEY CITY RESPONDENTS

Source	df	ms	F
Subjects (S)	35		
Item types (A)	6	40.07	33.12**
A×S	210	1.21	
Conversations (B)	4	45.04	25.89**
B×S	140	1.74	
A×B	24	8.04	8.74**
A×B×S	840	.92	
Total	1259		

** p < .01

tion of the taped conversations. Significant main effects were observed for conversations and for item types. That is to say, some conversations were more difficult to interpret and some types of items more difficult to answer than others. The most difficult conversation was one which represented a bull session among college students and which was carried on almost entirely in rapid, excited English. Not surprisingly, among the most difficult types of item was that assessing comprehension of the English portions of the conversations, and among the easiest was that assessing comprehension of the Spanish portions. A significant interaction between conversation and item type was also observed, indicating that the difficulty of item types, relative to each other, was not constant across stories. For example, there was a greater difference between the average English and Spanish comprehension scores for conversations which took place outside the home and neighborhood than for conversations which took place within such settings. Similarly, the relationship between the ability to comprehend the manifest content (what was said) and the ability to interpret the social content (what was meant) differed by conversation. For example, respondents correctly answered a greater proportion of social content items than manifest content items for a conversation taking place within a home, whereas the reverse was true for a conversation taking place within an office. Thus, knowing what was

TABLE 3

ANALYSIS OF VARIANCE OF LISTENING SCORES:
HIGH SCHOOL STUDENTS V. JERSEY CITY RESPONDENTS

Source	df	ms	F
Between Subjects (S)	62		
Groups (C)	1	17.86	30.27**
Error (b)	61	.59	
Within Subjects	2072		
Item types (A)	6	2.64	22.00**
A×C	6	4.07	33.92**
A×S	354	.12	
Conversations (B)	4	4.13	25.81**
B×C	4	1.44	9.00**
B×S	236	.16	
A×B	24	1.34	33.50**
A×B×C	24	1.88	47.00**
A×B×S	1414	.04	
Total	2134		

** $p < .01$

said did not necessarily enable listeners to absorb the full communicative impact of a conversation, and, conversely, missing the details of manifest content did not necessarily prevent listeners from grasping the speakers' intent.

As expected, the performance of each comparison group differed from that of the respondents in Jersey City, which can be seen in the analyses of variance summarized in Tables 3 and 4. In each analysis, a significant effect was observed for the difference between groups. Both the high school students and the Latin American students, probably due to their superior educational background, had higher average total scores than did the Jersey City respondents. However, the comparison groups were not uniformly superior in performance as can be seen from the significant interactions involving group differences. The high school students, for example, who understood more of the English portions of the conversations, understood less of the Spanish portions than did the Jersey City respondents. The high school students also differed in the expected direction from the Jersey City Ss with respect to the interpretation of role relationship involved in one of the conversations. The Jersey City respondents more often than the high school students correctly identified the participants in one conversation as a priest and parishioner, a relationship which the high

school students most often identified as that of teacher and student.

The Latin American students did not differ from the Jersey City group with respect to the amount of Spanish and English understood. That is, both groups correctly answered about the same proportion of the English items and about the same proportion of the Spanish items. However, the Latin American students differed from the Jersey City respondents in terms of some of their interpretations of the social situations represented by the conversations. For example, the Latin Americans were better than the Jersey City Ss in interpreting the role relationships between speakers in conversations taking place at school and at work. The Jersey City respondents, on the other hand, were better able than the Latin Americans to interpret the relationships involved in conversations representing the more local and intragroup domains of home and church. The Latin Americans also consistently gave lower educational and occupational ratings to those speakers who were intended to occupy relatively prestigeful statuses than did the Jersey City respondents. Thus, the similarity between the Jersey City and Latin American respondents' understanding of manifest content did not prevent the two groups from interpreting the conversations' social meaning in divergent ways. These differences are indicative of the

TABLE 4

ANALYSIS OF VARIANCE OF LISTENING SCORES:
LATIN AMERICAN STUDENTS V.
JERSEY CITY RESPONDENTS

Source	df	ms	F
Between Subjects (S)	61		
Groups (C)	1	11.18	13.15**
Error (b)	60	.85	
Within Subjects	2046		
Item types (A)	6	4.52	34.77**
A×C	6	.52	4.00**
A×S	349	.13	
Conversations (B)	4	4.51	112.75**
B×C	4	1.09	27.25**
B×S	233	.04	
A×B	24	1.28	11.64**
A×B×C	24	.38	3.45**
A×B×S	1396	.11	
Total	2107		

** $p < .01$

extent to which speech community membership and knowledge of communicative appropriateness go beyond language competence per se.

DISCUSSION

The moderate correlations which were observed among the degree of bilingualism scales supports the argument that bilingual proficiency can vary along several partially independent dimensions.[10] Thus, reliance upon performance in a single modality may yield an inadequate estimate of bilingual ability. Inadequate appraisals can also result from confining one's attention to a narrow range of contexts. The sharply increased prediction of English repertoire range ratings, which were obtained by combining comprehension scores based on a range of speech styles, testifies to the usefulness, as maintained by Fishman, of a contextualized approach to the measurement and description of bilingual skills.

The listening comprehension technique described in this report promises to be useful in several ways. First, it should prove useful in assessing bilingual skills in those situations of language contact in which a second language is known primarily on a receptive basis. Second, the use of bilingual tapes should be helpful in describing the abilities of those who claim, either from a mistaken estimate of their own competence or from a reluctance to be identi-fied with a language of lesser prestige, that they are unable to understand a given language. Some of the women in the Jersey City group, for example, told the interviewers that they did not know any English, and some of the Latin Americans professed not to be able to understand the variety of Spanish that was presented on the tapes. Nonetheless, all respondents understood at least some of the material that was presented in each language. Finally, the technique should enable us to learn more about the components of communicative competence, the ability which enables a speaker to know what to say, with whom, in what language, in what manner, and at what time.[11] The analysis of the responses of sociolinguistically contrasting groups to recorded conversations may help us to learn what elements in the conversation distinguish those who are members of a given speech community from those who are not. That is, the technique may help us to distinguish between the linguistic and sociolinguistic abilities which are necessary before one can fully understand the meaning of a conversation.

[10] John Macnamara, "The Bilingual's Linguistic Performance—a Psychological Overview," *Journal of Social Issues*, Vol. XXIII, No. 2 (April, 1967), pp. 58–77.

[11] Dell Hymes, "Models of Interaction of Language and Social Setting," *Journal of Social Issues*, Vol. XXIII, No. 2 (April, 1967), pp. 8–28.

THE EVALUATION OF LANGUAGE VAR

Stuart H. Silverman

The Evaluation of Language Varieties*

STUART H. SILVERMAN, *Yeshiva University*

THE purpose of this study was to determine whether certain linguistically based differences in speech as observed by trained workers could also be observed by ordinary members of a bilingual community in the greater New York area.

METHOD

Stimuli

Speech samples of four female Puerto Rican bilingual residents of a neighborhood whose Spanish-English bilingualism has been intensively studied[1] were utilized in this experiment.

Two were chosen by trained linguists because they represented optimally contrastive verbal abilities in English and two because they represented optimally contrastive abilities in

* The research reported in this paper was supported under Contract No. OEC-1-7-061817-0297, "The Measurement and Description of Language Dominance in Bilinguals," Joshua A. Fishman, Project Director. Data analysis was supported by a grant to the Project Director by the College Entrance Examination Board.

[1] Joshua A. Fishman, Robert L. Cooper, Roxana Ma, *et al.*, *Bilingualism in the Barrio*, Final Report: Yeshiva University, Contract No. OEC-1-7-062817-0297, U.S. Department of Health, Education, and Welfare, 1968.

Spanish.[2] These contrasts are in terms of verbal repertoire range.[3] Speakers with a narrow range in English or in Spanish commanded a single casual style in that language. Speakers with a wide range commanded several styles, including more formal ones. The narrow range English speakers also spoke English with a decided Spanish accent. For each speaker two twenty-second segments of tape were chosen. One segment contained speech that was elicited in a formal manner (paragraph reading) and the other segment contained casual or "free" conversation. Thus there were eight tape segments in all, permitting a $2 \times 2 \times 2$ analysis of variance design. The three factors to be studied were: language (English and Spanish), repertoire range (wide and narrow) and formality (casual and careful speech). The order of presentation for the segments was randomized. The segments were re-recorded and then spliced together on a single tape. Each segment was presented twice in succession before the next segment was presented.

Subjects

Twenty-two students at a public high school served as subjects. All of the students were speakers of Spanish and English and were members of the school's Puerto Rican youth group. Most subjects were American born or had lived for more than 10 years in the continental United States.

Rating Scale

A rating scale was administered to each of the respondents.[4] After listening to each segment the subjects were required to judge the highest grade in school completed by the speaker. In addition, for each segment, the subject was asked to rate the speech on fourteen bipolar scales based upon Osgood's "semantic differential technique."[5]

Investigators such as Osgood, Lambert, Anisfeld and Yeni-Komshian, Anisfeld and Lambert, Lambert, Hodgson and Fillenbaun and Triandis, Loh and Levin have all found significant differences in respondents' attitudes towards various groups based upon replies to semantic differential scales.[6] Lambert, Hodgson and Fillenbaun,[7] reported that subjects' percep-

tions of speakers changed when the latt changed from one dialect to another. Obvious then the dialect differences themselves mu have been discriminated by the subjects, whet er or not they were fully aware of the diffe ences. Thus, it seems clear that the semant differential technique, when used to measure a titudinal changes in connection with speech di ferences, also indicates the absence or presen of perceived dialect (or language) differences the part of respondents.

Three semantic differential factors have bee empirically determined from numerous invest gations of a large variety of stimuli, namely, Evaluation, 2) Potency and 3) Activity. F each factor three of the total number of bi-pol dimensions have been found to be represent tive of that factor. For the Evaluative fact these are nice/awful, pleasant/unpleasant ar rough/smooth. For the Potency factor they ar strong/weak, masculine/feminine and seriou /humorous. For the Activity factor they ar

[2] Roxana Ma and Eleanor Herasimchuk, "Linguis Dimensions of a Bilingual Neighborhood," in Joshua Fishman, Robert L. Cooper, Roxana Ma, *et al.*, *op. cit.*, p 636-835.

[3] John J. Gumperz, "Linguistic and Social Interaction Two Communities," *American Anthropologist*, Vol. LXV No. 6, Part 2 (December, 1964), pp. 137-154.

[4] The exact text and layout of the rating scales is show in Appendix VIII-2 of Joshua A. Fishman, Robert Cooper, Roxana Ma, *et al.*, *op cit.*, pp. 1198-1199.

[5] Charles E. Osgood, "Semantic Differential Techniqu in the Comparative Study of Cultures," *American Anthr pologist*, Vol. LXVI, No. 3, Part 2 (June, 1964), pp. 171-20

[6] Charles E. Osgood, *op. cit.*, Wallace E. Lamber Moshe Anisfield, and Grace Yeni-Komshian, "Evaluation Reactions of Jewish and Arab Adolescents to Dialect an Language Variations," *Journal of Personality and Soci Psychology*, Vol. II, No. 1 (July, 1965), pp. 84-90, an Elizabeth Anisfield and Wallace E. Lambert, "Evalu tional Reactions of Bilingual and Monolingual Children Spoken Languages," *Journal of Abnormal and Social Ps chology*, Vol. LXIX, No. 1 (July, 1964), pp. 89-97, Wallac E. Lambert. R. C. Hodgson, and S. Fillenbaum, "Evalu tional Reactions to Spoken Languages," *Journal of A normal and Social Psychology*, Vol. LX, No. 1 (1960), p 44-51, and Harry C. Triandis, Wallace D. Loh, and Lesl Ann Levin, "Race, Status, Quality of Spoken English, an Opinions about Civil Rights as Determinants of Interpe sonal Attitudes," *Journal of Personality and Social Ps chology*, Vol. III, No. 4 (April, 1966), pp. 468-472.

[7] Wallace E. Lambert, R. C. Hodgson, and S. Fille baum, *op. cit.*

TABLE 1

ANALYSES OF VARIANCE OF RATINGS OF
EIGHT STIMULUS TAPES

Source	df	ss	F
Activity			
Language (A)	1	81.57	11.91**
Range (B)	1	.36	.06
Formality (C)	1	.82	.09
A×B	1	.01	.0009
A×C	1	1.68	.19
B×C	1	129.07	23.26**
A×B×C	1	49.86	5.59*
Evaluative			
Language (A)	1	27.84	6.68*
Range (B)	1	.01	.00
Formality (C)	1	1.12	.06
A×B	1	.82	.05
A×C	1	.82	.12
B×C	1	2.02	.25
A×B×C	1	70.37	7.24*
Potency			
Language (A)	1	2.50	.65
Range (B)	1	9.09	3.06
Formality (C)	1	.73	.16
A×B	1	88.84	21.51**
A×C	1	26.25	9.02**
B×C	1	82.97	42.55**
A×B×C	1	14.73	2.91
Formality			
Language (A)	1	1.45	.13
Range (B)	1	8.21	1.07
Formality (C)	1	10.03	1.10
A×B	1	2.28	.20
A×C	1	.01	.00
B×C	1	16.56	1.81
A×B×C	1	52.35	3.40
Level of Education			
Language (A)	1	32.82	1.37
Range (B)	1	32.82	6.76*
Formality (C)	1	23.27	3.51
A×B	1	16.56	1.14
A×C	1	127.84	24.76**
B×C	1	6.57	1.58
A×B×C	1	36.37	5.95*

excitable/calm, fast/slow and fancy/plain. For the purposes of this study a fourth factor, Formality, was devised. The bi-polar dimensions used for this factor were: formal/informal, tense/relaxed, good/bad, soft/loud and careful/sloppy. Each dimension was presented on a seven-point bi-polar scale. One scale, for example, read: extremely good, quite good, slightly good, indifferent, slightly bad, quite bad, extremely bad. The order of the dimensions was randomized eight times (once for each segment of tape) and the subjects were required to rate each segment of tape on each demension. Fourteen dimensions in all were utilized: 3 evaluative, 3 potency, 3 activity, and 5 formality.

Scoring and Data Analysis

Scoring was done on a seven-point basis corresponding to the seven term scale of each dimension. For the evaluative factor, for example, extremely nice, extremely pleasant, and extremely smooth were assigned the value "seven" while extremely awful, extremely unpleasant and extremely rough were assigned the score "one." Values in between "one" and "seven" were assigned to intermediate terms in accord with their distance from the extreme terms. For the educational level rating, the score used was the grade which the respondent circled as his choice for the speaker. For each subject, five scores per tape were obtained. They were: Evaluative, Potency, Activity, Formality and Educational Level. An analysis of variance was performed on each of these variables.

RESULTS

Table 1 summarizes the five analyses of variance. These results show that one language was seen as being significantly more "active" than the other and one was seen as being significantly "better" than the other. An examination of the raw data means indicated that English was rated by most respondents as higher on both the Evaluative and Activity factors. Further, speakers in one range were perceived as having higher educational levels than speakers in the other range. An examination of the ly, the Formality scale yielded no significant results, probably because the dimensions used therein actually belonged in one or more of the other factors.

CONCLUSIONS

The results seem to indicate that linguistically based differences in bilingual repertoires do have interpretable correlates for the naive listener. These findings are in accord with others in the literature as reported earlier in this paper.

Most interesting, however, is the fact that subjects were able to perceive different repertoire *ranges*. These are the first findings to pro-

vide experimental verification of the communicative function of differential repertoire ranges in speech. Further, they suggest that in previous studies which have utilized the semantic differential technique, some of the results obtained may also have reflected changes in repertoire rather than merely changes in variety or language. These earlier findings should certainly be re-examined with this thought in mind. Finally, this study implies that the linguistic variables initially used to determine differences in language, range and formality are, indeed, adequate in terms of their application to "real world" situations.

SOME MEASURES
OF THE INTERACTION
BETWEEN LANGUAGE, DOMAIN AND SEMANTIC
DIMENSION IN BILINGUALS

Sheldon Fertig
and
Joshua A. Fishman

Some Measures of the Interaction Between Language, Domain and Semantic Dimension in Bilinguals*

SHELDON FERTIG AND JOSHUA A. FISHMAN, *Yeshiva University*

THERE is currently a growing need for contextualized measures of bilingualism that are not as susceptible to respondent bias as are census claims or usage ratings. Measures of bilingualism that are both contextualized as well as relatively bias-free are needed in order to validate and interrelate such constructs as domain and value cluster,[1] as well as in order to refine the diglossic notion of differential functional allocation of languages, which is so basic to sociolinguistics more generally. A method that shows promise for determining which language or speech variety is predominantly viewed as congruent with which societal domain or which value cluster is Osgood's semantic differential.[2] The present paper utilizes semantic differential scales in these very connections and compares the finding obtained from such scales to findings derived from other contextualized measures of bilingualism.

Osgood has taken his lead for measuring meaning from factorial studies of traits, abilities, and attitudes. Underlying the semantic differential as a measuring instrument is the basic assumption that any term or concept is locatable in a multidimensional "semantic space" analogous to the description of a color in terms of its hue, brightness, and saturation.

In order to test the "marriage" of the semantic differential with the sociolinguistic construct of language and domain, an analysis of variance design will be utilized to determine the significance of the main effects of language and domain as well as the significance of their interaction. Our hypotheses are as follows:

Hypothesis 1 (Part I and Part III).

While significant overall differences between *languages* may exist with respect to *absolute* measures of frequency of language use in bilingual populations, significant *domain* differ-

* The research reported in this paper was supported under Department of Health, Education, and Welfare Contract No. OEC-1-7-062817-0297, "The Measurement and Description of Language Dominance in Bilinguals," Joshua A. Fishman, Project Director. Data analysis was made possible by a grant to the Project Director by the College Entrance Examination Board.

[1] Joshua A. Fishman, "Sociolinguistic Perspective in the Study of Bilingualism," *Linguistics*, Vol. XXXIX (1968), pp. 21–49.

[2] Charles E. Osgood, George J. Suci, and Percy H. Tannenbaum, *The Measurement of Meaning*, Urbana: University of Illinois Press, 1957.

ences exist with respect to *relative* measures of frequency of language use. Specifically, while English may, on the whole, be used more than Spanish by Puerto Rican adolescents in New York City, Spanish is used relatively more frequently with home domain words and English is used relatively more frequently with school domain words.

Hypothesis 2 (Part IIa).

A significant interaction exists between language and domain, i.e., Spanish stands significantly higher on the home domain and significantly lower on the school domain on the semantic differential evaluative and dynamism dimensions. Conversely, English stands lower on the home domain and significantly higher on the school domain on these two dimensions. Schematically, we can illustrate our expected results in the following way:

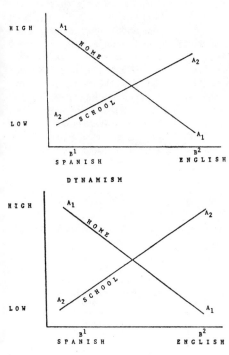

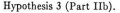

Hypothesis 3 (Part IIb).

The home domain is rated more positively than the school domain on the evaluative dimension, while on the dynamism dimension the school domain is rated more positively than the home domain.

Hypothesis 1 relates to Parts I and III of this three part study. Its rationale is derived from reports of various diglossic communities which imply that one language is primarily associated with home and family whereas another is primarily associated with education and other High Culture pursuits. The distinction between absolute and relative measures of bilingualism in diglossic settings is primarily a methodological one. Relative measures can not directly reveal overall language differences, as absolute measures can. However, both types of measures can reveal language by domain interaction and, therefore, their results should be in harmony with each other if the measures utilized are valid.

Hypotheses 2 and 3 relate to Part II of this study. Its rationale derives directly from Fishman's theory that different value clusters are enacted in and serve to differentiate between the domains of societal interaction. Fishman hypothesizes that fewer value clusters than domains are needed in the analysis of diglossic speech communities since most value clusters subsume several domains. The semantic differential *evaluative* dimension is assumed to be an approximation of Fishman's *intimacy* value cluster. The semantic differential *dynamism* dimension is assumed to be an approximation of Fishman's *status stressing* value cluster. Intimacy (Evaluative Dimension) is assumed to be more closely related to home and to Spanish whereas status (Dynamism Dimension) is assumed to be more closely related to school and to English in accord with Fishman's earlier discussion. As a result we expect language and domain to interact significantly on each of these dimensions if we can first successfully demonstrate that home is indeed more related to the evaluative dimension and that school is indeed more related to the dynamism dimension.

METHOD

Three different instruments[3] (designated as

[3] All instruments utilized in Parts I, II, and III of this study are shown in full in Appendix VIII-2 of Joshua A. Fishman, Robert L. Cooper, Roxana Ma, *et al.*, *Bilingualism in the Barrio*, Final Report: Yeshiva University, Contract No. OEC-1-7-062817-0297, U. S. Department of Health, Education and Welfare, 1968.

TABLE 1

ANALYSIS OF VARIANCE FOR ABSOLUTE FREQUENCY OF USE

Source	ss	df	mss	F
Total	24,325.914	183	—	
Between subjects	12,724.414	45	—	
Years in United States (A)	15.848	1	15.848	<1
Subject w Year (E₁)	12,708.566	44	288.830	
Within subjects	11,601.500	138	—	
Language (B)	1,140.021	1	1,140.021	17.37**
Domain (C)	4.261	1	4.261	<1
Language×Domain (B×C)	665.759	1	665.759	10.14**
Years×Language (A×B)	704.347	1	704.347	10.73**
Years×Domain (A×C)	420.020	1	420.020	6.40*
Years×Language×Domain (A×B×C)	4.262	1	4.262	<1
Groups w Subject (E₂)	8,662.830	132	65.627	

* p<.05
** p<.01

Part I, Part II and Part III) were administered in the following order.

Part I

A rating scale designed by Cooper and Greenfield[4] to determine the absolute frequency with which Spanish and English words are encountered was used in connection with the domain of school and the domain of home. From the 45 English words to be rated on a seven-point scale in connection with how often they were heard or said, 16 were selected to be scored and analyzed for our purposes. Of these 16 words, 8 represented the home domain and 8 represented the school domain.[5] The same 45 words were subsequently presented for rating in Spanish translation and in a randomized order.

Part II

The 16 words which represented the home and school domains were presented as stimulus words to be rated on 12 bipolar semantic differential scales. For the purpose of our study we used the 6 highest loading scales on Osgood's evaluative dimension as well as the 3 top loading scales from his activity dimension. The 3 items from the power dimension and the 3 items from the activity dimension were combined (in accord with a suggestion from Osgood) into one factor labeled the dynamism dimension.

Each of the 16 stimulus words (8 representing the home domain and 8 representing the school domain) was presented at the top of a different page containing the 12 bipolar scales (6 from the evaluative dimension and 6 from the dynamism dimension). Each Subject (S) rated each word on each bipolar scale, thus performing 16×12 or 192 ratings in all. To control for possible boredom or fatigue in a task of this length, the 8 home domain words and the 8 school domain words were alternated with respect to order of presentation. To control for a possible position bias, the evaluative bipolar scales and the dynamism bipolar scales were also alternated on each page. Although separate Spanish and English versions of Part II were utilized with different groups of Ss, the instructions were not translated and were presented only in English to all subjects.

Part III

A 5-point rating scale was designed to determine relative frequency of use of the 16 words utilized in Part I and Part II. The En-

[4] Robert L. Cooper and Lawrence Greenfield, "Word Frequency Estimation as a Measrure of Degree of Bilingualism," in Joshua A. Fishman, Robert L. Cooper, Roxana Ma, et al, op. cit. and also in The Modern Language Journal, Vol. LIII, No. 3 (March, 1969), pp. 163–166.

[5] In a pilot study, nineteen members of an Aspira club in a New York City high school rated these sixteen words from a list of forty-five words as being the most unambiguous, both in Spanish and in English, with respect to the domains of school and home. The selected home words were: family, father, house, dish, salt, soup, room, parents and their respective Spanish translations. The selected school words were: school, chalk, lesson, teacher, student, blackboard, history, science and their respective Spanish translations.

glish and Spanish word-pairs were presented together and Ss were asked to determine whether or not they heard or used the English word more than the Spanish equivalent, whether or not they used the English word and the Spanish word equally often, or whether or not they used the Spanish word more than its English counterpart. The words were presented in the same order as in the semantic differential study (Part II), i.e., school words and home words alternately.

Subjects

The subjects were 46 Puerto Rican high school students from *Aspira* clubs in Brooklyn, New York.[6] Membership in these clubs was assumed to be indicative of average or better school performance, thus ruling out reading problems among our Ss.

Years spent in the United States ranged from 1 year to 19 years with the median years spent in the United States being 12. Of the 46 subjects in the study, 13 were male and 33 were female. However, of the 36 who completed the study, only 4 were male. Two males did Part II in Spanish while the other two did Part II in English.

RESULTS

Part I

Table 1 reveals the main effect of language (B) to be significant at the .01 level in accord

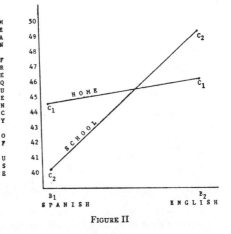

FIGURE II

with hypothesis 1. The English word list in the absolute measure of language use yielded a significantly higher mean frequency than did the translation list of Spanish words. Neither years in the United States per se nor domain per se were significant main effects. The interaction between years in the United States and absolute frequency of language use $(A \times B)$ was significant at the .01 level.

As Figure I indicates, those subjects who had been in the United States for 11 years or less claimed a mean frequency of use which is approximately the same for the English list and for the Spanish list of words. However, for those subjects who had been in the United States for 12 or more years, there was a significantly higher mean frequency of use in English than in Spanish.

The interaction between language and domain $(B \times C)$ was also significant at the .01 level. As Figure II indicates the home domain remained relatively stable on both the English and Spanish set of words with respect to frequency of use. However, in the school domain there was a significantly higher mean frequency of claimed use in English than in Spanish.

The interaction between years in the United States and domain $(A \times C)$ was also significant $(p < .05)$ but does not pertain to our current interest.

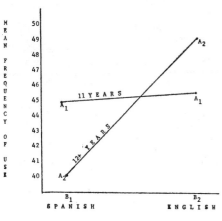

FIGURE I

[6] Because of lack of time, Part II was completed by only thirty-six Ss. Of these, twenty-two took Part II in English whlie fourteen took it in Spanish.

TABLE 2

ANALYSIS OF VARIANCE FOR RELATIVE FREQUENCY OF USE

Source	ss	df	mss	F
Total	4,454.990	91	—	—
Between subjects	2,987.490	45	66.388	—
Years in United States (A)	133.923	1	133.923	2.02
E_1	2,853.567	44	64.853	—
Within subjects	1,467.500	46	—	—
Domain (B)	740.466	1	740.446	45.73**
Years×Domain (A×B)	14.880	1	14.880	<1
E_2	712.340	44	16.189	

** p<.01

Part III

As Table 2 reveals the instrument designed to measure *relative* frequency of use yielded a significant domain (B) difference at the .01 level. This finding is also in accord with hypothesis 1 since a significant domain effect in a relative use measure is equivalent to a significant language×domain interaction in an absolute use measure.

The home domain words were claimed more in Spanish than in English ($\bar{x}=21.3$), while the school domain words were claimed more in English than in Spanish ($\bar{x}=15.6$).

Part II.

Hypothesis 2 posits a significant interaction between domain and language on the evaluative and dynamism dimension. Tables 3 and 4 indicate that this hypothesis was not confirmed.

However, the analysis of variance of the semantic differential ratings reveal that the main effect of domain (C) was significant on the evaluative dimension at the .05 level and significant at the .01 level in the dynamism dimension. On the evaluative dimension, the home domain words had a mean score of 124.2 (more positive) while the school domain had a mean score of 153.5 (less positive). On the dynamism dimension, the school domain had a mean score of 145.3 (more positive) while home domain had a mean score of 155.0 (less positive). Hypothesis 3 is, therefore, fully confirmed.

CONCLUSIONS

This study has confirmed 2 of its 3 initial hypotheses.

a) An absolute rating of frequency of lan-

TABLE 3

ANALYSIS OF VARIANCE: SEMANTIC DIFFERENTIAL
(EVALUATIVE DIMENSION)

Source	ss	df	mss	F
Total	72,327.653	71	—	
Between subjects	49,054.153	35	—	
Years in United States (A)	105.124	1	105.124	<1
Language (B)	1,144.545	1	1,144.545	<1
Years×Language (A×B)	1,056.183	1	1,056.183	<1
E_1	46,748.301	32	1,460.884	
Within subjects	23,723.500	36	—	
Domain (C)	13,695.124	1	1,369.124	5.13*
Domain×Years (A×C)	136.125	1	136.125	<1
Domain×Language (B×C)	910.716	1	910.716	3.41
Domain×Language×Years (A×B×C)	0.000	1	0.000	<1
E_2	8,531.537	32	266.610	

* p<.05

TABLE 4

ANALYSIS OF VARIANCE: SEMANTIC DIFFERENTIAL
(DYNAMISM DIMENSION)

Source	ss	df	mss	F
Total	58,026.445	71	—	
Between subjects	48,100.445	35	—	
Years in United States (A)	1,073.389	1	1,073.389	1
Language (B)	80.970	1	80.970	1
Years×Language (A×B)	114.056	1	114.056	1
E_1	46,832.030	32	1,463.500	
Within subjects	9,926.000	36	—	
Domain (C)	2,069.389	1	2,069.389	9.09**
Domain×Years (A×C)	256.888	1	256.888	1.12
Domain×Language (B×C)	49,525	1	49.525	1
Domain×Language×Years (A×B×C)	265.435	1	265.435	1.16
E_2	7,284.763	32	227.648	

** $p < .01$

guage use yielded a significant overall difference between English and Spanish (English words being claimed more frequently than Spanish words) as well as a significant language by domain interaction between home domain words and school domain words.

b) A relative rating of frequency of language use yielded a significant overall domain difference between home words and school words. Because of the nature of the instrument this was equivalent to a significant domain by language interaction. Thus, both rating scales agree that Spanish and English were reported as being differentially domain related.

c) Domain difference also appeared on two major semantic differential dimensions. Home words were rated more positive on the evaluative dimension and school words were rated more positive of the dynamism dimension. This confirms Fishman's hypothesis of congruence between domains of societal interaction and the major value clusters that subsume these domains.

d) We failed to find the hypothesized language by domain interaction on each of the semantic differential dimensions. Nor was there a significant language difference on either of these dimensions.

All in all, we have demonstrated that value clusters are differentially domain related and that the languages of bilinguals are differentially domain related. We have failed to link these two findings to each other (as would have been the case had we been able to show that language and domain both interacted significantly and oppositely in two different value dimensions) and, therefore, this task remains for future research.

A METHOD
FOR RECORDING AND ANALYZING
THE PROSODIC FEATURES OF LANGUAGE

Stuart H. Silverman

A Method for Recording and Analyzing the Prosodic Features of Language*

STUART H. SILVERMAN, *Yeshiva University*

ONE purpose of the work reported in this paper was the development and assessment of a method for transcribing and analyzing such paralinguistic features of speech as stress, juncture and intonation. The rationale for the study comes as a result of the ideas of Halliday, Bolinger, Pierce, and many other linguists.[1] These workers have argued strongly that intonation (pitch), juncture (pause) and stress (emphasis) are of prime importance in the communicative process. These features of speech are generally referred to as "prosodics."

Stress is employed for the purpose of indicating the importance of certain words and/or syllables and for indicating that a particular part of the utterance contains new information in terms of the speaker's intent. Juncture is used by the speaker to divide and organize the message into what he feels are "meaningful units." The functions of intonation are somewhat less clear than those of juncture and stress although pitch usually works in conjunction with stress. More often than not, a stressed syllable is accompanied by a rise in pitch. Intonation seems to be employed by the speaker in the expression of mood, and in part, to distinguish certain types of sentences (for example, interrogative) from others (like declaratives).

A new system for recording and analyzing the prosodic features of verbal communication was needed because of serious lacks in the two most commonly used systems which were available. The first of these methods attempts to draw an intonation contour for each utterance under examination.[2] Thus, for example, the sentence: "did you go yesterday?" might be represented as:

did you go : yesterday

indicating that the first three syllables have a low, unchanging pitch level. The first two syllables of "yesterday" are higher in pitch yet constant. The final syllable rises in pitch still further. This notation system is not subject to quantification except in a very gross manner. In other words, two identical utterances, coded in this manner, could be superimposed on one another so that gross differences could be examined.

The second system attempts to chart relative pitch levels.[3] It utilizes the numerals "one" (1) through "four" (4). It assumes that all speakers have four basic pitch levels, with "one" representing the lowest and "four" representing the highest. Under this schema, the sentence: "when are you going home?" might be analyzed as:

²when are you ³going home¹

indicating that the query begins on a "medium" pitch level and continues on that level for three syllables. The fourth and fifth syllables are slightly higher. The last syllable falls sharply. This method is unsatisfactory for analyzing the free conversation of speakers in that its measures are too gross. That is, they can only account for "major" intonation changes. It is also unsatisfactory because it assumes that any given speaker has only four pitch levels. Finally, both methods allow comparisons between relative, but not absolute, intonation contours.

* The research reported in this paper was supported by a grant from the U.S. Office of Education, Contract No. OEC–1–7–062817–0297, "The Measurement and Description of Language Dominance in Bilinguals," Joshua A. Fishman, Project Director. Data analysis was supported by a grant to the Project Director by the College Entrance Examination Board. The author is grateful for the assistance of Mr. Parrish Merriwether.

[1] M. K. Halliday, "The Prosodic Features of American English," unpublished lecture presented at Queens College, March, 1968, Dwight L. Bolinger, "A Theory of Pitch Accent in English," *Word*, Vol. XIV, No. 2–3 (August-December, 1958), pp. 109–149, and Joe E. Pierce, "The Supra-segmental Phonemes of English," *Linguistics: An International Review*, Vol. 21 (April, 1966), pp. 54–70.

[2] William A. Smalley, *Manual of Articulatory Phonetics*, Tarrytown, New York: Practical Anthropology, rev. ed., 1964.

[3] Andreas Koutsoudas, *Writing Transformational Grammars: An Introduction*, New York: McGraw-Hill, 1966.

One application of a more refined connection with the major purpose of this paper, namely, to determine whether research clearly indicates that when a person is talking, the grammatical structure of his speech, as well as the phonological and lexical structures, may shift to a great degree as a result of changes in the topic being discussed, the place where the discussion is being held and the people participating in the conversation.[4] An example of this "code switching" might be the contrast in speech between a youngster talking to his friends in the playground and the same youngster conversing with his teacher in the classroom. No evidence, however, has been gathered to show whether there is a shift in prosodics which accompanies lexical, grammatical and phonological shifts in code (or variety) switching. The second major purpose of the present research, then, was to see if this paralinguistic shift can be found to coincide with shifts in code.

PROCEDURE

Tapes of the speech of three native speakers of Puerto Rican Spanish were selected to serve as the sample upon which the method described below was applied. The tapes were chosen, on the basis of independent linguistic analyses, to represent three maximally different types of speaker. The basis of the selection was not made known to the prosodic recorder until after the method had been applied. For each of the speakers selected, there were two minutes of tape recording. The entire six minutes were in Spanish. Each subject's tapes contained one minute of paragraph reading (the same paragraph for each speaker) and one minute of free conversation. These two contexts were chosen as being maximally different in terms of formality, with paragraph reading designated as "formal" and free conversation designated as "informal." It had been demonstrated that the formal-informal dichotomy was associated with systematic phonological variation in Puerto Rican Spanish.[5] The system used was the conventional musical notation system with several modifications. First, the "bar" or measure was not defined in terms of number of beats. It was determined that any given measure would refer to all those notes which fell between any notation indi-

cating a rest or pause and the first rest notation which either follows or precedes it. Justification for this may be found in Halliday's notion that the analysis of conversation should be in terms of "intonation units" (those verbalizations which occur between pauses). He argues that in orthography the message is divided into meaningful segments via the sentence, while in verbal communication the speaker uses pauses to signal the end of a message or thought and the beginning of the next thought or message.[6] Each stretch of speech was also divided into ten-second intervals. Thus it became possible to compare the usefulness of time and intonation as sampling units. Stress was indicated by the use of accent marks (/) above each stressed syllable. Since this is a first effort at using a musical notation system for recording prosodics, steps were taken to somewhat simplify the process. Notes were recorded in terms of eighth and quarter notes. Rests were noted in terms of quarter, half and full notes. It was recognized that some degree of precision was lost due to the above self-imposed limitations.

Each tape was listened to several times so that a starting note could be chosen. One of the tapes began with a medium tone (as compared with the other five tapes) and this tone was arbitrarily assigned the value of "middle c." From that point on, each beat (syllable) was assigned a note value and length value relative to the preceding note. A piano was used to accurately judge the pitch distance between beats. In other words, the "tune" on the tape was con-

[4] Joshua A. Fishman, "Intellectuals from the Island," in Joshua A. Fishman, Robert L. Cooper, Roxana Ma, et al., Bilingualism in the Barrio, Final Report: Yeshiva University, Contract No. OEC-1-7-062817-0297, U.S. Department of Health, Education, and Welfare, 1968, pp. 99–123, and William Labov, "The Effects of Social Mobility on Linguistic Behavior," in Stanley Lieberson, ed., Explorations in Sociology, Publication 44 of the Indiana University Research Center in Anthropology, Folklore, and Linguistics, pp. 58–75, and also Part II of The International Journal of American Linguistics, Vol. XXXIII, No. 2 (1967).

[5] Roxana Ma and Eleanor Herasimchuk, "The Linguistic Dimensions of a Bilingual Neighborhood," in Joshua A. Fishman, Robert L. Cooper, Rosana Ma, et al., Bilingualism in the Barrio, Final Report: Yeshiva University, Contract No. OEC-1-7-062817-0297, U.S. Department of Health, Education, and Welfare, 1968, pp. 636–835.

[6] M. K. Halliday, op. cit.

verted into piano music. The length values of rests were timed on a stopwatch.

Seven analyses of variance were performed on the data. The first one was done to determine whether there were significant differences in the number of intonation units observed between the three speakers and two contexts. Also to be determined here was whether any speaker or context had more of a different length of rest than any other speaker or context. For example, did the formal context contain more longer (whole) rests and less shorter (one quarter) ones than the informal context? The second and third analyses were performed to test for the significance of differences in the number of eighth and quarter notes between the three speakers and two contexts. The first of these was done on the basis of intonation units and the second was done on the basis of the ten-second time units. Another purpose of the two analyses was to gain some idea of the speed of talking. It was assumed here, for example, that if the formal context contained fewer quarter notes and more eighth notes than the informal context, that the former could be said to be slower than the latter. The fourth and fifth analyses were to determine whether there were differences in the number of stresses between speakers and contexts (again, by time and intonation units). Finally the range of notes was divided into seven categories, each containing two notes. The note categories were: 1) low F, G; 2) A, B below middle C; 3) C, D below middle C; 4) E, F below middle C; 5) G below middle C and middle A; 6) middle B, C; 7) middle D, E. The last two analyses sought to determine whether there were differences between the speakers and contexts in terms of the seven categories for both time units and intonation units.

Results

All seven analyses of variance are summarized in Table 1. They indicate that the method of prosodic notation employed was precise enough to distinguish between different speakers, different contexts, and different categories within the criterion measures used. For example, the first analysis indicates that significantly more of one length of rest was produced than another. It also indicates that the number of different lengths produced varied significant-

ly as a function of context. That is, there were more of one type of rest in one context (e.g., full rests in the formal context) than in the other. In addition, it indicates that although the three speakers did not differ significantly with respect to the total number of pauses made, they did differ significantly with respect to the number of certain *types* of rest produced. That is, one speaker produced significantly more of a given length of rest than did another speaker.

For each of the significant effects found in the seven analyses, a Newman-Keuls test was performed so that the significance of differences between pairs of speakers, contexts, types of criterion measures, and between the interactions of these variables, could be determined. For example, in the Newman-Keuls test of the significance of differences between the average number of types of rests per time unit as observed for the three speakers, a significant difference was seen between the average number of quarter rests given by the third speaker in the formal and informal contexts. Of the differences between 62 pairs of means in this particular analysis, about 30% were significant. After all Newman-Keuls tests had been performed, it was found that 60% of all possible differences were significant.

While there appeared to be no objective advantage in using intonation units rather than time units many investigators may continue to prefer the former for the study of prosodics in view of the fact that such units stand closer to the natural organization of speech.

Conclusions

The present study reveals significant differences between the prosodic structures of the speech of three independently selected speakers, each speaking in two different contexts. The results obtained suggest that with some degree of refinement and modification, the recording and analysis of prosodics through a musical notation system appears to be both practical and valuable. The practicality of this method lies in the fact that anyone with a working knowledge of some musical instrument and/or some training in the theory of music can rapidly be trained to record pitch, pause and stress. Its value lies in the increased precision it makes possible in the

TABLE 1

ANALYSES OF VARIANCE FOR
SEVEN CRITERION SCORES

Source	df	ms	F
Rests by time units			
Between Subjects	16		
Group (C)	2	.57	.90
Error (b)	14	.63	
Within Subjects	85		
Context (A)	1	.80	.27
Rest type (B)	2	8.30	16.60**
AB	2	9.79	18.47**
AC	2	.12	.04
BC	4	1.75	35.00**
ABC	4	4.19	7.95**
Error (w)	70		
Error₁ (w)	14	2.92	
Error₂ (w)	28	.05	
Error₃ (w)	28	.53	
Total	101		

Notes by time units			
Between Subjects	53		
Group (C)	2	131.47	7.62**
Error (b)	51	17.26	
Within Subjects	270		
Context (A)	1	179.67	4.43**
Note type (B)	2	438.02	137.31**
AB	2	88.03	326.03**
AC	2	11.12	.27
BC	4	62.32	19.54**
ABC	4	20.53	76.04**
Error (w)	255		
Error₁ (w)	51	40.56	
Error₂ (w)	102	3.19	
Error₃ (w)	102	.27	
Total	324		

Notes by intonation units			
Between Subjects	16		
Group (C)	2	145.69	6.94**
Error (b)	14	20.99	
Within Subjects	85		
Context (A)	1	89.47	13.37**
Rest type (B)	2	1341.83	30.20**
AB	2	168.29	58.84**
AC	2	315.91	47.22**
BC	4	1.47	.03
ABC	4	5.74	2.01
Error (w)	70		
Error₁ (w)	14	6.69	
Error₂ (w)	28	44.43	
Error₃ (w)	28	2.86	
Total	101		

TABLE 1 (continued)

Stresses by time units			
Between Subjects	16		
Group (C)	2	37.63	9.46**
Error (b)	14	3.98	
Within Subjects	17		
Context (A)	1	11.01	2.01
AC	2	.09	.02
Error (w)	14	5.86	
Total	33		

Stresses by intonation units			
Between Subjects	53		
Group (C)	2	15.69	7.13**
Error (b)	51	2.20	
Within Subjects	54		
Context (A)	1	25.00	23.58**
AC	2	30.96	29.21**
Error (w)	51	1.06	
Total	101		

Pitch levels by time units			
Between Subjects	16		
Group (C)	2	40.06	6.80**
Error (b)	14	5.89	
Within subjects	221		
Context (A)	1	14.63	5.36*
Pitch (B)	6	795.86	53.39**
AB	6	54.54	5.46**
AC	2	.64	.23
BC	12	34.67	2.33*
ABC	12	46.48	4.66**
Error (w)	182		
Error₁ (w)	14	2.73	
Error₂ (w)	84	14.91	
Error₃ (w)	84	9.98	
Total	237		

Pitch levels by intonation units			
Between Subjects	53		
Group (C)	2	31.17	8.56**
Error (b)	51	3.64	
Within Subjects	702		
Context (A)	1	41.90	3.72
Pitch (B)	6	214.82	50.67**
AB	6	26.49	17.00**
AC	2	1.52	.13
BC	12	13.54	3.10**
ABC	12	12.62	8.04**
Error (w)	663		
Error₁ (w)	51	11.27	
Error₂ (w)	306	4.24	
Error₃ (w)	306	1.57	
Total	755		

* p<.05   ** p<.01

description of prosodics in comparison to previously recommended methods. The results certainly suggest that the method is useful in describing the prosodic variation accompanying other sociolinguistic variation, inasmuch as the method was able to distinguish not only between linguistically diverse speakers (as independently determined) but also between two different contexts. Finally, the results also suggest that prosodic variation, like phonological variation, is in part a function of the contexts in which speech is produced.

A NOTE
ON THE PERCEPTION AND PRODUCTION
OF PHONOLOGICAL VARIATION

Charles E. Terry
and
Robert L. Cooper

A Note on the Perception and Production of Phonological Variation*

CHARLES E. TERRY AND ROBERT L. COOPER, *Yeshiva University*

LABOV has demonstrated the relationship between phonological variation and both social stratification and the casualness of the speech elicited.[1] The present report describes the perception of phonological variation by members of the same speech community that produces such variation. The report also relates the ability to perceive this variation to several criterion variables.

METHOD

As part of an intensive study of bilingualism within a Puerto Rican urban neighborhood near New York City, the speech of 45 bilingual respondents elicited during extended interviews was subjected to a phonetic analysis.[2] This analysis was made in terms of the phonetic variation which was observed in the realization of several English and Spanish phonological "variables" over five elicitation contexts.[3] Selected English and Spanish phonological variables were also studied with respect to the respondents' ability to perceive differences between alternative phonetic realizations. Perception was assessed in the following manner. The respondent heard on tape three realizations of a word in which a variable was embedded. For example: interasado, interasao, interasado. He was then asked whether the third realization sounded more like the first or more like the second. Sixteen items were presented in all, the first half of which represented Spanish variables, and the second half, English variables. The perception test was given to 36 of the respondents.

The ability to perceive the distinction em-

bodied by each item was related to the relati frequencies with which the alternative realiz tions of that variable were produced in each the five elicitation contexts. In addition, pe formance on each perception item was relat to ratings on the following criterion scales, ma by the linguists who had performed the ph netic analysis.

1. English repertoire range: the number English speech styles observed and the fluen with which they were judged to be used.

2. Accentedness: the degree to which t phonological and syntactic structures of o language appeared to influence speech produc in the other. High ratings indicated Spanish i fluence on speech produced in English, lc ratings indicated English influence on spee produced in Spanish, and intermediate ratin indicated maximum language distance, wi

* The research reported herein was supported by DHE Contract No. OEC-1-7-062817-0297, "The Measureme and Description of Language Dominance in Bilinguals Joshua A. Fishman, Project Director. Data analysis w made possible by a grant to the Project Director by t College Entrance Examination Board.

[1] William A. Labov, *The Social Stratification of Engl in New York City*, Washington, D. C.: Center for Appli Linguistics, 1966.

[2] Joshua A. Fishman, Robert L. Cooper, Roxana M et al., *Bilingualism in the Barrio*, Final Report: Yeshi University, Contract No. OEC-1-7-062817-0297, U. Department of Health, Education, and Welfare, 1968

[3] Detailed descriptions of the phonological variabl studied as well as of the five elicitation contexts in whi they were observed may be found in Roxana Ma ar Eleanor Herasimchuk, "Linguistic Dimensions of Bilingual Neighborhood," in Joshua A. Fishman, Robe L. Cooper, Roxana Ma, *et al.*, *op. cit.*, pp. 636–835

each language exercising minimal influence upon speech produced in the other.

3. Reading: the degree to which the respondent was able to read in one language only. High ratings indicated that the respondent could read only in Spanish (or not at all), low ratings indicated that he could read only in English, and intermediate ratings indicated that he was able to read in both languages without difficulty. The ratings were based on the respondent's reading of two word lists and four paragraphs, presented during the interview. Half of these were in English and the other half in Spanish.

RESULTS

No differences were observed between the average difficulty of the English and Spanish items, both groups of items being passed on the average by two-thirds of the respondents. With only two exceptions, the percentage passing each item was relatively stable, varying between 50% to 75%.

The correlations obtained between the ability to perceive each of the 16 items and performance on the corresponding alternative variants in each of five contexts constituted 215 coefficients in all. Of these, only 24 were significant ($p < .05$). Inasmuch as one could expect that about 11 coefficients would be significant by chance, it can be said that in general perception and production were not particularly related.

Although performance on the perception test was not a good predictor of phonological variation as observed in speech, performance on three

TABLE 1

CORRELATIONS BETWEEN SELECTED PERCEPTION ITEMS AND THREE CRITERION VARIABLES ($N = 35$)

Perception item	Criterion variable		
	English repertoire range	Accented-ness	Reading
n≠V[pan/paŋ]	.23	− .44**	− .47**
sC[gusto/guhto]	.35*	− .34*	− .48**
I[hIt/hit]	.40*	− .46**	− .43**

* $p < .05$
** $p < .01$

perception items were significantly related to ratings on the criterion variables. Two of these tested perception of Spanish variables (n≠V, as in [pan/paŋ]; sC, as in [gusto/guhto]) and one tested perception of an English variable (I, as in [hIt/hit]). These coefficients, presented in Table 1, ranged from .23 to .48, with the median at .43.

SUMMARY

Puerto Rican bilinguals' perception of phonological variation in Spanish and English was in general not found to be related to the relative frequency of their production of these variables. Perception of some items, however, was related to performance on three criterion variables. The latter finding suggests that the use of selected perception items, which are relatively easy to administer, might be useful in language surveys where the validity of more direct questioning is in doubt.

SOME THINGS LEARNED;
SOME THINGS YET TO LEARN

Joshua A. Fishman

Some Things Learned; Some Things Yet to Learn

JOSHUA A. FISHMAN, *Yeshiva University*

1. SOME THINGS LEARNED

. The adequacy (and, frequently, the superior-
ty) of self-report measures of bilingual profi-
iency and bilingual usage—when rather global
r summary criteria like those that we have uti-

lized are acceptable—is well documented in this
report. Populations that lack any particular ideologized awareness of their proficiency and
usage are still *able* to reply to sociolinguistically
significant queries in substantially reliable and
valid ways. The purposes of self-report mea-

sures are normally quite apparent to such respondents. The validity of their responses probably depends as much on their *desire* to accurately describe their self-image as bilinguals as upon their self-monitoring *insight*. Somewhat less transparent self-report measures (e.g., word frequency estimation) are reasonable substitutes for more obvious survey instruments but are not as easily designed to yield both proficiency and usage scores.

b. Domain analysis is a fruitful middle range approach to the description of societal patterns of bilingual proficiency and bilingual usage. It is neither as abstract nor as removed from the contexts of verbal interaction as are value clusters nor is it as impossibly detailed and fleeting ("impossibly" from the point of view of research on human aggregates larger than the face-to-face group) as the situation. Domain analysis has proved to be useful and reliable in conjunction with self-report measures and performance measures, usage data and proficiency data, a priori scores and empirical scores, sociological data and psychological data. It has clarified the difference between social units that locate the immediate context of speech acts and speech samples per se and social units that are derivative from aggregate data on speech acts and speech samples. Domain analysis attempts to relate social structure to social process in sociolinguistics by deriving domains—which are themselves akin to societal institutions or structures—from obviously congruent social situations. Domains are constructs that should prove useful to future sociolinguistic research that is primarily concerned with large scale social change rather than with contextualized linguistic description for its own sake.

Domain of societal interaction seems to be no more an abstraction from reality than "language." It is an abstraction that many bilinguals handle easily and consistently. It corresponds closely to the way many bilinguals think of their language-choice regularities. Domains do not contradict the reality of metaphorical switching but rather provide the normal ground against which metaphor can be recognized as such.

c. On the basis of our experience, the promise of compositing methods of data analysis defi-

nitely seems to be great in connection with f ture sociolinguistic research. This is particular so in connection with sociologically orient data on the one hand and linguistically orient data on the other. In the former case the R fa tors provided sensible confirmations as well emic refinements of *a priori* domains, where the Q clusters provided eminently reasonab and meaningful groupings of behaviorally co sistent (and, simultaneously, behaviorally co trasted) individuals. However, in both of thes connections R and Q analysis merely confir their prior and documented functions in soci science research. In the realm of our linguist data their services were both novel as well more fundamental. Here they demonstrated th possibility of deriving sociolinguistic varietie and sociolinguistic networks in much more rig orous and in much more exhaustive ways tha had hitherto been attempted or thought to b possible.

The factor analytic demarcation of sociolir guistic *varieties* is based directly upon the notio of demonstrated co-occurrences across elicita tion or realization contexts. The factor analyti demarcation of sociolinguistic *networks* is base upon the maximization of within-cluster sim ilarities plus between-cluster differences. Thu whereas the demarcation of varieties is fully i accord with prior theoretical notions the demar cation of networks represents an improvemen over such prior notions and their concern wit density of communication rather than wit within-group similarity and between-group con trast as useful boundary-defining notions. Obvi ously, this departure is both more emic in th sense of being empirically consequential as wel as more parsimoniously applicable to data fror larger numbers of speakers not all of whom nee be in face-to-face interaction.

d. The feasibility of utilizing a mini-kit in fu ture sociolinguistic descriptions of large popula tions appears to be well documented on the ba sis of our experience. This is not at all to say that our particular mini-kit can be transferred in whole or in part, from our study context t any other. It is to say, however, that sufficien time per subject spent in studying a smalle population intensively can provide the informa tion needed so as to fruitfully spend less tim per subject in studying similar but much larger populations. This is a most promising lead since it implies that more time can be available in the future for work on other sociolinguistic parameters than those that we were able to emphasize in the present project. Nevertheless, it is instructive to note that even the most parsimonious mini-kit that we could devise for the range of criteria we considered essential did not turn out to be disciplinarily monistic. Genuinely *inter*disciplinary work is needed for sociolinguistic description. Without such work sociolinguistics becomes a disciplinary diversion rather than a realistically problem-centered pursuit.

2. SOME THINGS YET TO LEARN

a. Given the obvious utility of self-report measures such as those designed for the present study, in conjunction with the kinds of criteria here employed, how much further can both these instruments and these criteria be refined? This question deserves exploration at two levels: (1) at the level of structurally or institutionally relevant measurement which deals with quite global and structured behaviors, and (2) at the level of more process-oriented measurement which deals with more fleeting, more subtle, and more minute behaviors. Can most (or at least some) respondents reply accurately to questions concerning metaphorical and situational switching, concerning intra-language rather than merely inter-language switching, concerning personal and transactional interactions, concerning their open and closed network behaviors, concerning role repertoire and linguistic repertoire ranges? We have little experience with how such questions should be put and less with how reliable or valid the answers to them may be for particular population segments.

A further extension of this point deals with behavioral (role repertoire, role relationship, etc.) explorations and even with detailed linguistic inquiries concerning the realization of values of diverse variables. What are the limits of self-report for various kinds of speech networks?

b. Our methods for deriving and validating domains are still exceedingly rough. In this project they were primarily based upon hunches stemming from extensive participant observation

and from reviews of the literature. That these hunches were frequently rather good is illustrated by the number of times in which empirically composited (i.e., factor analytically based) scores proved to be domain scores. However, this was not always the case and we do not at this moment know why certain instruments *did* yield empirical domain scores whereas others did not. Domains do not seem to be too distant from the ways in which ordinary informants view their own behavior. Domain based questions seem meaningful to ordinary respondents and elicit reliable and seemingly valid responses from them. This may be why self-report and usage measures showed a somewhat greater tendency to yield domain-related empirical scores than did performance and proficiency measures.

Further efforts might usefully try to refine and revise domain specifications by constructing and cross-validating domain measures on the basis of prior data analysis rather than merely on the basis of sociological insight. Had our project had another year to run this is exactly what it would have attempted, selecting some self-report measures that seemed to benefit so much from domain analysis as well as some performance measures that did not seem to benefit as greatly from domain analysis for such further inquiry.

c. Given the substantial contributions of R and Q analysis, two less than fully satisfactory outcomes must be admitted for future clarification. The first, a sin of commission, deals with the relative meaninglessness of many of the R factors derived from psychologically oriented studies. It is not at all clear whether this was a by-product of our *particular* instruments and the data they yielded or whether there is a more *general* lesson to be learned here with respect to the potential contribution of empirical compositing methods for the analysis of psychologically oriented sociolinguistic measures.

Our second disappointing outcome is a sin of omission which might well have been avoided had not time run out on us, namely, the lack of a direct, quantitative indication of accentedness and of repertoire ranges for each subject. The precise linguistic realizations from which scores dealing with these matters should have been extracted were utilized in the R and Q analyses of our linguistic data. These very same realizations might have been further analyzed in purely quantitative terms in order to yield *for each individual* an accentedness score, a Spanish repertoire range score and an English repertoire range score. Such scores would have been superior to the judgments that were finally used in connection with these criteria, since they derived from more detailed and from more objective data, although the judgments had their fully justified role to play in our research design.

In an initial study it is good to show that hitherto unfamiliar quantitative and objective treatments of data add up to make good impressionistic and judgmental sense. However, once these initial feelings of uncertainty are assuaged it should prove possible to proceed directly with the most precise data available and this we did in every instance except in connection with the criterion scores themselves.

d. The four aspects of societally relevant sociolinguistic description that still seem to require most attention in the immediate future are: (1) role repertoire range measurement and description—to which we paid little attention in terms of instrument construction or general methodological-theoretical clarification, (2) perfection of field methods for inter-language performance measures paralleling in depth the intra-language measures developed in the current project, (3) direct application of sociolinguistic description to pedagogically relevant concerns—of which we were aware but to which we could not give explicit attention, and (4) encompassing description of a full range speech community rather than of a delimited range neighborhood. A *model* study of the latter kind is particularly needed now that sociolinguistic surveys of entire countries or regions are coming into fashion. While our project has much to contribute to such surveys even as it stands it was too focused on a lower-class population to be greatly instructive in connection with the sociolinguistic description of more fortunate, more literate and more linguistically conscious populations which also deserve and require careful study.

BILINGUAL-BICULTURAL EDUCATION IN THE UNITED STATES

An Arno Press Collection

Allen, Harold B. **A Survey of the Teaching of English to Non-English Speakers in the United States.** 1966

Allen, Virginia F. and Sidney Forman. **English As A Second Language.** [1967]

Aucamp, A.J. **Bilingual Education and Nationalism With Special Reference to South Africa.** 1926

Axelrod, Herman C. **Bilingual Background And Its Relation to Certain Aspects of Character and Personality of Elementary School Children** (Doctoral Dissertation, Yeshiva University, 1951). 1978

Bengelsdorf, Winnie. **Ethnic Studies in Higher Education.** 1972

Berrol, Selma Cantor. **Immigrants at School: New York City** (Doctoral Dissertation, City University of New York, 1967). 1978

Cordasco, Francesco, ed. **Bilingualism and the Bilingual Child.** 1978

Cordasco, Francesco, ed. **The Bilingual-Bicultural Child and the Question of Intelligence.** 1978

Cordasco, Francesco, ed. **Bilingual Education in New York City.** 1978

Dissemination Center for Bilingual Bicultural Education. **Guide to Title VII ESEA Bilingual Bicultural Projects, 1973-1974.** 1974

Dissemination Center for Bilingual Bicultural Education. **Proceedings, National Conference on Bilingual Education.** 1975

Fishman, Joshua A. **Language Loyalty in the United States.** 1966

Flores, Solomon Hernández. **The Nature and Effectiveness of Bilingual Education Programs for the Spanish-Speaking Child in the United States** (Doctoral Dissertation, Ohio State University, 1969). 1978

Galvan, Robert Rogers. **Bilingualism As It Relates to Intelligence Test Scores and School Achievement Among Culturally Deprived Spanish-American Children** (Doctoral Dissertation, East Texas State University, 1967). 1978

Illinois State Advisory Committee. **Bilingual/Bicultural Education.** 1974

Levy, Rosemary Salomone. **An Analysis of the Effects of Language Acquisition Context Upon the Dual Language Development of Non-English Dominant Students** (Doctoral Dissertation, Columbia University, 1976). 1978

Malherbe, Ernst G. **The Bilingual School.** 1946

Mandera, Franklin Richard. **An Inquiry into the Effects of Bilingualism on Native and Non-Native Americans** (Doctoral Dissertation, University of Illinois, 1971). 1978

Materials and Human Resources for Teaching Ethnic Studies. 1975

Medina, Amelia Cirilo. **A Comparative Analysis of Evaluative Theory and Practice for the Instructional Component of Bilingual Programs** Doctoral Dissertation, Texas A&M University, 1975). 1978

National Advisory Council on Bilingual Education. **Bilingual Education.** 1975

Peebles, Robert Whitney. **Leonard Covello: A Study of an Immigrant's Contribution to New York City** (Doctoral Dissertation, New York University, 1967). 1978

Reyes, Vinicio H. **Bicultural-Bilingual Education for Latino Students** (Doctoral Dissertation, University of Massachusetts, 1975). 1978

Rodriguez M[unguia], Juan C. **Supervision of Bilingual Programs** (Doctoral Dissertation, Loyola University of Chicago, 1974). 1978

Royal Commission on Bilingualism and Biculturalism. **Preliminary Report and Books I & II.** 3 vols. in 1. 1965/1967/1968

Streiff, Paul Robert. **Development of Guidelines for Conducting Research in Bilingual Education** (Doctoral Dissertation, University of California, Los Angeles, 1974). 1978

Streiff, Virginia. **Reading Comprehension and Language Proficiency Among Eskimo Children** (Doctoral Dissertation, Ohio University, 1977). 1978

Ulibarri, Horatio. **Interpretative Studies on Bilingual Education.** 1969

United Kingdom, Department of Education and Science, National Commission for Unesco. **Bilingualism in Education.** 1965

United Nations Educational Scientific and Cultural Organization. **The Use of Vernacular Languages in Education.** 1953

United States Bureau of Indian Affairs. **Bilingual Education for American Indians.** 1971

United States Commission on Civil Rights. **Mexican American Education Study.** 5 vols. in 1. 1971-1973

United States House of Representatives. **Bilingual Education Programs.** 1967

United States House of Representatives. **United States Ethnic Heritage Studies Centers.** 1970

United States Senate. **Bilingual Education, Health, and Manpower Programs.** 1973

United States. Senate. **Bilingual Education, Hearings.** 1967

Viereck, Louis. **German Instruction in American Schools.** 1902